Kevin
With the very

Kobus
97-3-7

CW01654779

HIDDINGH-CURRIE 5

UNISA

ALONG EDGES

Religion in South Africa:

BUSHMAN, CHRISTIAN, BUDDHIST

J S Krüger

University of South Africa
Pretoria

© 1995 University of South Africa
First edition, first impression

ISBN 0 86981 907 0

Typeset by
Pretoria Setters, Pretoria

House editor: Liz Stewart
Cover design and layout: Hetta Oosthuizen

Printed by
National Book Printers, Drukkery Street, Goodwood, Western Cape

Published by the
University of South Africa
PO Box 392, 0001 Pretoria

© All rights reserved. No part of this publication may be reproduced in any form or by any means – mechanical or electronic, including recordings or tape recording and photocopying – without the prior permission of the publisher, excluding fair quotations for purposes of research or review.

CONTENTS

PREFACE

This book took shape on the boundary between the old and the new in South Africa. It is a time of re-orientation, with profound religious implications. As the format and style of the various chapters will show, I strive to communicate clearly with a wide spectrum of my compatriots who, in this situation, may be interested in religious matters, even if not necessarily religious themselves, at least not in the conventional sense.

I sincerely wish to thank my family and a large number of friends, colleagues, specialists in various academic fields and students for their invaluable support and help in this effort by being available to discuss aspects of this book and to read and challenge portions of it, or for just listening and talking. For fear of unintentionally overlooking someone, I refrain from naming specific persons who gave so generously of their time. Without them the work would not have been possible.

The various chapters that have been added together here have a checkered history. Parts I and III bring together, in somewhat reworked format, material presented to my students over the last ten years, as well as a number of unpublished talks and papers presented at different times to different audiences (students, academics, members of the general public) over that same period. Part II is a drastic revision of an introduction to the study of religion that originally appeared in 1982.[1] Part IV contains the results of research into the religion of the South African aboriginal hunter-gatherers (or, more succinctly, aborigines, Bushmen, or San[2]) that was conducted in 1992. I levelled out the most serious bumps and removed the most obvious overlaps and repetitions in these twenty essays and welded them into a coherent argument. Stylistically, nevertheless, their diverse origins remain apparent. The book as a whole has grown and been pruned on and off over several seasons.

---

1 J S Krüger, *Studying religion. A methodological introduction to science of religion*, Pretoria: Unisa, 1982.

2 The terminological problem will be discussed in chapter 12. There seems little reason to be dogmatic about any of the terms (none of them really satisfactory) used for the aboriginal people of South Africa.

After an introductory chapter analysing the ambivalent situation in which these essays arose (chapter 1), four topics are treated in the four parts of the book:

Part I develops a theory of religion in terms of a naturalistic, conditionalist dual-edged perspective of the world and our being in it (chapters 2–4).

Part II proposes a comprehensive, multidimensional model of enquiry into religion (chapters 5–9).

Part III places religion in evolutionary perspective (chapter 10) and evolution in religious perspective (chapter 11).

Part IV reviews and interprets the history (chapters 12–15) and religion (chapters 17–20) of the Bushman hunter-gatherers in conditionalist perspective, and makes a short excursion into Christian theology (chapter 16).

Pretoria
1994–04–28

1 Intervals

Religiously South Africa is as effervescent and pluralist as the Hellenistic world was two thousand years ago, or as California is today. By way of introduction I will indicate the intertwinement of the exploration attempted in these essays in that wider socio-religious complex. This would be a never-ending task, since any such setting is really an inextricable, ever-changing network of factors, a series of ever-turning wheels within wheels implying past, present as well as future; economic, political as well as cultural dimensions; personal as well as collective forces; and so on. A 'context' cannot be arrested for a moment like a static thing. The world of this book by the time it was completed (April 1994) was not the same as the one in which it was begun; the one in which it will appear will be yet another world, and we don't know what it will be like by the time the reader puts it down. It is merely a small throb in a vast field of change. Aware that these meditations interlock with an inconstant context, we are yet unable to oversee that context fully. In this introductory chapter I will explore a number of thresholds in this world in which I exist, thresholds which divide, separate but also join, marking an awkward and dangerous nonposition between leaving and entering.

Between past and future, order and chaos, separateness and unity

The first threshold is the break *between past and future*, between what have come to be known as the *'old'* and the *'new'* South Africa, taken in a very wide sense. It is common knowledge that South Africa is in the painful throes of transition, not just from one century to another, but also from one sociopolitical epoch to a new one. The old is well known. It is the history of colonialism culminating in the system of apartheid, which now finally seems to have run its course. But the new has not yet manifested itself. Some see the present as the beginning of a dark age, others as a moment of birth. It is certainly an ambiguous time of epochal transition, a moment of crisis. Five years ago we lived in a rigid, semitotalitarian order. What will come in its place? A new order, equally totalitarian? Complete disintegration of society, perhaps chaos? Or a genuinely open pluralism? The argument of this book seeks to provide support for the latter.

Although the idea of putting this book together was born in 1989, for various reasons it was only completed in the same month as the inauguration, for the first time in the history of South Africa, of a government elected by the country as a whole. More than a change of government is at stake. An order is disintegrating – an order built on the ruins of various older orders on which it had imposed itself over more than three centuries. What is occurring at present is, however, not a restoration of those older orders. European expansion is irreversible, and is continuing in ways other than political conquest. Yet something new is in the making, with all the risks attendant on such a large-scale process of disintegration and transformation.

But I must be careful: the word 'process' implies meaningful coherence. Is there really such a thing present? How? And what would its status be? Does this series of events somehow constitute a drama, divided into various coherent acts? Again, the word 'series' suggests a pattern. Perhaps the drama should be conceived of as a tragedy. But even the notion of 'tragedy' implies an order of sorts, at least according to Aristotle's classic definition: it is a representation or imitation (*mimesis*) of *significant* and *complete* human actions. It is not just a clutter of incidents. It has meaning, and requires or posits a wider framework. Have all such 'frameworks' not become suspect, to the point that we are left with only utter confusion? On the other hand, even words such as 'confusion' and 'chaos' parasitise on our ingrained need for order. The question remains: can even the destruction of the Bushman culture somehow be viewed as part of a meaningful mandala, without being subjected to cheap rationalisation of a grim, often gruesome line of events? If such a mandala is not discoverable as an act of *mimesis* in the Aristotelian sense, can it be construed at all? Somehow we seem to be in need of a catharsis, a purification of sorts, coming to terms with the past, creating a future. Somehow we need an alignment of 'old' and 'new', of the very movements of integration and disintegration between order and chaos.

These are religious questions, I submit. Let it be added immediately that I do not take religion to be the equivalent of either belief in an afterlife, or belief in one or more supernatural beings, or myth, or ritual, or the sum of these. By 'religion' I understand in a general sense the dream and the effort found in all cultures to look at our ordinary world *sub specie aeternitatis*, in the widest horizon possible. The topics usually associated with religion (afterlife; God or gods; myth; ritual) make sense only in the light of that idea. My thesis is that the religious dimension of our present situation (taken in that wide sense) has not been thought through sufficiently. It is important, for religion is vital to the way we approach the enormous challenges facing this country – ranging from the distribution of wealth and power, labour relations, and education to the population explosion and ecology.

Once in a while the times call for a new beginning on a grand scale. This is true of South Africa at present – also as far as religious thought is concerned. The religious crisis, I submit, certainly springs from the work of thinkers such as Freud, Marx and Nietzsche. But concretely, as a national crisis, it is demonstrably bound up with the specific socioreligious history of the past 350 years in this country. When speaking about 'crisis' I am referring to the mainstream of 'white' Christian theology that has dominated religious discourse in South Africa: a crisis has arisen, in spite of powerful resources inherent in Christianity for developing an inclusive, nondiscriminatory religious philosophy.

It is true that over the past decades a considerable amount of thinking, focused on political issues, was done in established Christian religious institutions (to restrict myself to that religion for now) and academia. But virtually all of this, whether politically conservative or politically progressive, remained within the framework of conventional theology of an orthodox and mid-orthodox bent. Even the more angry white theological critiques of the South African society of the apartheid era were based on and in fact strengthened precisely those 'fundamental' premisses. Virtually all of the 'critical' Christian theology produced in South Africa over the last twenty years amounted to a mopping up operation of a political problem, but with few creative religious impulses.

Today those premisses must be relinquished. This book challenges that well-established religious paradigm. Religious *re*-storation is not enough. Religion in a new key is needed. This does not necessarily mean the rejection of (for example) the Christian faith, but it does mean a radical reinterpretation of it. Reflecting on our sociopolitical history, we are driven into less well-charted depths of religion. We need to explore the terrain lying beyond the apartheid barrier, including its religious dimension (what I would call *religious apartheid*). This concept stands for more than the specific sociopolitical system devised after 1948 or its antecedents under colonial rule. It stands for more than socioeconomico-politics altogether. It stands for a way of looking at everything – ironically, not necessarily from a point of view outside traditional Western religion (such as Nazism or Communism), but from within a commitment to traditional Western religion. I am not suggesting that religious apartheid is unique to South Africa, or to traditional Christianity. It is rather, I suggest, a strong, latent possibility in every institutionalisation of religion as such.

A point of departure of this book is that the notion of 'separateness' has religious roots and should not be restricted to the sociopolitical sphere. In fact, for the ideas of separateness as well as unity I shall substitute the ideas of togetherness, relativity and uniqueness as focal points of religious thought. Togetherness and relativity, involving the risk of being suspended between order and chaos, unity and separateness (not only in political matters but also in our religious thought) will be the overall aligning ideas. By religious apartheid I mean an attitude towards religious matters, even an actual religious attitude itself. At its core it is a religious phenomenon, with wide practical ramifications. It is a basic attitude of *fundamental division*: between human beings themselves (including their societies, cultures and religions); between human beings and nature; between human beings and what is commonly referred to as the divine or ultimate.

In the course of this study we shall return to these issues. Yet it may be useful to highlight some of them at this stage. As for the ecological concern, it is certainly one of the most pressing problems facing South Africa as we approach a situation in which the natural resources of the country will be exhausted in order to support an enormous population. Humanity has become a cancerous growth in the body of the world. It is quite true that voices are being raised to awaken the public conscience. Yet what is lacking is a religious philosophy capable of providing an adequate motivational framework.

The social dimension of the apartheid syndrome displays the following features: *conformism*, that is a subordination of individual experience to group thinking; *dogmatism*, that is a tendency towards fixed standpoints; *exclusivism*, that is an overwhelming emphasis on differences between groups; and *negativism* vis-à-vis other groups. It expresses itself in attitudes and practices of resentment, isolationism, exclusivism and domination, and not only in the sociopolitical field. It is an attempt at nonrelation – yet inescapably, within a de facto context of negative relation, such as indifference, rejection or control.

Yet in escaping from the separate little identities of the 'many' we should not be lured into the big identity of a monochrome 'One'. The idea of 'unity' must be exploded by dialectically relating it to the ideas of multidimensional exuberance and dynamic open-endedness. Both the ideas of 'separateness' and 'oneness' will in themselves lead to intellectual, and ultimately political and physical, violence. 'Unity' ('the One'), whether in religion or in politics, is an authoritarian concept. It tends to become simply the end of the road; the full stop. The point is precisely to get out of the dilemma of *either* unity *or* separateness, (closed) 'order' *or* (chaotic) 'disorder', 'identity' *or* 'confusion'. The uniqueness of each of the many little knots in the pluralist world is important, not in spite of, but precisely because of its togetherness with all the others.

The notion 'concrete' will be a recurring theme in these essays. It implies the following: firstly, that of a *plurality* of factors, not a 'one', a singularity; secondly, not a random scattering, but a *togetherness*: some factors in that plurality mutually imply one another, so that they indeed become related aspects of something bigger – plurality becomes pluralism, until in the end each is related to all; thirdly, *uniqueness*: not a grey mixture of all in all, but specific knots, each with its own character; fourthly, *reality*: the concrete moments here-and-now are real data of our experience, and they interact with others, making a difference.

For many, God the great Father is dead. But so are Hermes, and Aphrodite, Dionysus and the rest. And the African /Kaggen as well. Yet those old religious worlds may still be able to provide symbols capable of expressing our peculiar historical moment of ambivalence. It is the time of Janus, the guardian of gates, seated at the point at which two worlds hinge. We are caught up in the dance of Shiva, the two-edged force of life, destroyer of the old and herald of the new. Re-enter /Kaggen, the hero-trickster frolicking on both sides of all boundaries. The Death-and-Resurrection of Jesus Christ remains the most powerful religious symbol for the vast majority of South Africans. Old sacred canopies are caving in; can we hear a new fluttering of angels' wings?[1]

On a tightrope there is no standing, only walking or falling. All we can do on the knife edge between totalising order and scattered fragmentation is listen to the voices of the prophets and visionaries coming down to us in the history of religions, trust the depth within ourselves, and sound the context in which we find ourselves as we feel our way forward. In the decades to come we may expect dramatically new and creative developments in religious experience and thought. In fact, it has set in already, often observable outside the circles of official religion. To such new thinking I want to make a contribution.

To achieve that, we are driven back into a genealogy of religion. We have to re-evaluate the beginnings of Western Christianity in South Africa. Also, having lived through four decades of human engineering second only to that perpetrated in the Stalinist Soviet Republics, the oldest known religious tradition on this subcontinent (that of the Bushmen) takes on new meaning. To be healed, we need contact with the earliest inhabitants of this land. To find and give expression to an as yet nonexistent, new and unique experience, we need to return to the old. The quest for the roots of South African religion implies reflection on the origin of religion as such, including the reconstruction of its very basics, not only in a chronological but also in an ontological sense: how do the various historical religions relate to the human quest for meaning?

Between prophecy and academia, Euro-America and Africa, theory and practice

By profession I am an academic, a scholar of religion. Yet I find it irresponsible of scholars of religion simply to stand back and watch what is happening in society from the sidelines. The demand is not that everyone should involve themselves in social and political currents all the time, nor do I regard political correctness as necessarily equivalent to good scholarship or good religion.

The academic should not pose as a guru. But our situation today is in need of voices that in an earlier age might have been called 'prophetic': speaking from one's own experience as a human being, searching for new paths that will lead into a new future. If scholars of religion are debarred by their professional ethos from speaking to a situation in which they breathe and read and teach, then who will? What is the use of all their scholarship? Unless it has heart and soul, a primitive passion for what is real, scholarship degenerates into mere learnedness, and intellectual brilliance into mere cleverness.

So, without too many pretensions but aware of the tension *between prophet and academic*, I offer this tract for our times, readily admitting that it overflows the boundaries of the academic subject of religious studies. But in South Africa, at this time, the luxury of withdrawal from society and its needs is ill affordable, and the evasion of practical, philosophical and religious questions should be counted as positivism. To make headway in an academic subject may require blinkers that screen out what goes on on both sides. It is a way of dividing up a big job, trying to ensure that through many piecemeal efforts some progress is made. The dangers of such an approach, as far as the study of religion is concerned, are great. Instead of covering a field by cooperative teamwork between various disciplines, a theme may become completely fragmented, and each discipline may end up like one of the blind men in the old Indian tale: getting hold of tail or trunk, not knowing what it is or what the whole elephant looks like. Sadly, this is what our national universities are threatened with as far as the humanities (not only the study of religion) are concerned. Worse, inevitable subject-blinkeredness turns into metaphysical blinkeredness when the validity of certain questions is simply denied and academics become intellectual technicians. When faced with a mountain, we may be forgiven for digging a tunnel. But we needn't become moles.

The academic field of religious studies is not a timeless enterprise for free-floating intelligences. It operates in certain social environments, for example those of Europe and North America, that differ vastly from the circumstances prevailing elsewhere – for example in South Africa. Here this branch of the academic enterprise should be generated and done truly from within South Africa, with this country and continent as an original, creative source of meaning, the matrix, context, womb of the whole enterprise. Religious Studies should visibly and organically grow from South African soil.

Only then will it be a universal, dialogical, pluralistic adventure. But that basic condition has not been met yet. We are not out of the colonial phase yet. What exactly could a radical turning of our minds to Africa mean, if it is to be more than a superficial, romantic gesture without any real content? Where exactly would the African parameters of religious studies lie? That cannot be answered in the abstract. It can be done only through a piecemeal (re-)appropriation of Africa, which is what I am trying to do here. It would amount to turning the intellectual map of the world upside down. Then, suddenly, South Africa would no longer be an appendix to the world. The pluralist world is multicentred. Unfortunately, on a practical level, it must be conceded that in this country there are not sufficient numbers of scholars trained in this field to effect such a 'revolution' on a significant scale.

Tied up with this whole problem is the question of the 'neutrality' of science, specifically religious studies. 'Neutrality' is obviously used in a variety of senses. We may mean by it an attitude of impartiality and fairness, wanting to do justice to somebody else's worldview. This is good, without any qualification. In more practical terms, it may also refer to being nonaggressive and nonimperialist, no one religious ideology striving to lord it over others. Good again. We have had enough of that sort of thing for all lifetimes to come. It may, however, also refer to the illusion that the scholar is a mirror passively (neutrally) reflecting an object out there. Or it may indeed mask positivism – the denial, indefinite postponement, referral to other specialists of critical and constructive thought; the excommunication of philosophy; disregard of the problems of religious value, meaning and truth; deliberate refusal to reflect on the relevance of the academic enterprise. Or it may be an akward way of expressing the very opposite – not forgetting personal biases, but declaring them and thereby disciplining and using them positively in the process of understanding. The latter is the position adopted in this study.

I have a conviction that religious thought should be as concrete as possible. By that I quite literally mean that it should be 'grown together' with its environment and the raw stuff of life, as thorn tree and bushveld cohere, sustaining the tension between *thinking* and *being* (your breath, life and blood). The act of thinking carves up reality conceptually. Concepts (for example 'time', 'space', 'religion') as socially shared conventions are abstractions from the concrete flow of reality. Conversely, thinking imposes abstract categories on the sensory flux. In concrete thought an effort is made to realise that thought and experience, theory and practice, are involved in a process of osmosis, mutual support, grinding and honing – not as a matter of course and unconsciously, but consciously, deliberately and critically. In that case the stuff of life is not merely the field in which your theory is applied or illustrated.

Of course the world has become one vast network in which everything is related to everything else, and of course 'South Africa' shares in the wider debate of humanity. But this is a regional, sociohistorically very specific book: it is not about 'the universe', 'the world', 'humanity', 'civilisation', 'the West' or 'modernity' and its ills; it reflects, and reflects on, a very specific socioreligious situation. To be honest, I have not read much locally produced literature on religion celebrating the anguish and the joy of birth in this country today.

Obviously various elements from the wider world went into the syncretism presented here. Perhaps an exercise in distinguishing the various factors adding up ('eclectically') to this collage could be interesting. But the final test is simply whether the elements are aesthetically convincing and 'work', fitting in with one another and the lived environment, and making sense of it. My concern was to weave some of the manifold strands of thought drifting around our world, and our local raw experience, into a 'South African' patterned design.

What is needed today is sustained and even ruthless theory, thought, philosophy (in a wide sense), which is prepared to take very little for granted as it fulfils its responsibility towards tomorrow. I wish to make a contribution to that sort of concrete thinking: more 'thought' than the autobiographical confessions of sin, faith or fear that emerge readily in a situation such as ours at present, and more 'concrete' than the paraphrases of Euro-American philosophies that make up a considerable part of our local intellectual diet.

One looks at our social revolution and is reminded of how Augustine looked at the fall of the Roman empire in the north at the beginning of the fifth century CE in religious perspective. That the perspective in these essays diverges widely from that of the great church father and the great movement of thought he inspired will become clear enough. The view presented here shares his insistence on the vanity of history, but not his insistence on an eternally substantial kingdom beyond and separate from this world.

It will be apparent by now that the reflections offered here are intended to be (to use a much-favoured contemporary term) 'relevant' to our regional situation. I find it necessary to comment on the ideal of 'relevance'. The answer to the question, 'why be relevant?' is perhaps not as self-evident as it may seem. Relevance is not the absolute, self-explanatory virtue it is usually taken to be. So some qualification of this concept is in order.

On closer inspection it becomes apparent that relevance is multifaceted. The very etymology of the word (*relevare*, to lift out, and hence to emphasise) suggests that 'relevance' implies comparison with other things, being relative to them. Nothing is relevant in itself, in the abstract. Relevance implies an ever-widening system of relations and relevances. Now some important distinctions would have to be drawn, for example between direct/immediate relevance and indirect/mediate relevance; between short-term, medium-term and long-term relevance; between obvious relevance and hidden relevance; between surface relevance and depth relevance; and so on. Very few people know the names of five creative physicists in the world today – but surely that does not make them or their work 'irrelevant' to the rest of us. On the contrary, they are shaping the cosmology of tomorrow, laying the foundations of the science of tomorrow, and eventually their work, while abstruse to most of us, will have enormously important practical implications for better or for worse for everyone on an everyday level. Also, it is not fair to expect the results of academic and religious thought to be available immediately in tangible form, demonstrating immediate and patently obvious political relevance – although in the end it must most certainly be required that such talk make a difference to people's lives.

Relevance can be analysed in other ways as well. Obviously 'the relevance *of what?*' would be one such angle of enquiry. Another angle would be 'the relevance *of whom?*' For example, the relevance of leaders is different from the relevance of explorers and pioneers. The former may have large numbers following right on their heels and may be pushed onto pedestals; the latter may end up in unmarked graves in uncharted territory – but are they 'irrelevant'? The history of heretics proves the reverse. 'Relevant *to what?*' is another angle. There are differences between political relevance and academic relevance, however closely they may be intertwined. In one perspective, the lowly Bushmen may be 'irrelevant' in the South Africa of today. In the perspective of this book, they are highly relevant. And then there is the crucial question 'relevance *for whom?*'. Who will be the beneficiaries of whatever is said? And so on and so on. Even these cursory distinctions make it clear that whoever wishes to present something as relevant would be wise to do it with great circumspection. Relevance could be just another dimension added to the interminable game of cultural, academic and religious one-upmanship, 'more relevant than thou' being a slightly more fashionable pose than certain others.

In a verbose time such as ours it is understandable that some perceptive people of a mystical bent would emphasise the relevance of being irrelevant, of beginning to listen anew to the life-giving silence behind the all-important noise. The Hebrew Bible has something to say about this. Once, when Moses thought to make himself relevant to his fellow Hebrews he was told, 'Who set you up as an officer and judge over us?' Only after he had herded sheep in a desert for forty years and had tried to evade his calling ('O Lord, I have never been a man of ready speech ...; I am slow and hesitant of speech') did he become useful. True prophets and saviours are reluctant ones. Also, observe the scavenging human vulture, feeding on the carcasses of society, actually making a career out of the mistakes and weaknesses of others. Relevance cannot be claimed, and it cannot be consciously cultivated; it is a gift bestowed on a person. One can do much worse than simply going one's way, being neither prophet nor priest, neither preacher nor politician nor partisan; having no axe to grind and no score to settle, belonging to no party and no clique; simply doing what one believes in, speaking for oneself from a personal point of view, without bothering too much about relevance.

These essays submit that the deepest level of our crisis is religion, and that religious intellectuals are called to think as profoundly and as freshly as they are able, exploring the cracks that have become so abundantly apparent by this time, and opening up new possibilities.

Between religious studies and religion, and between academic disciplines

These essays add up to an intellectual prolegomenon to a South African spirituality – one concretely born of this reality and this history. In addition to the three expanding concentric academic functions (*research*, *teaching* and *direct community service*), I see the sphere of *spirituality*, of *religious intuition and thought*, as a fourth and innermost circle. It is indeed the hard, brilliant diamond at the heart of the entire enterprise, or the soft radiance surrounding it. These essays are academically informed, but they are not addressed to specialists in religion only. Moving *between religious studies and religion* they are addressed to the intellectually inclined and religiously interested (but not necessarily 'religious' in the conventional sense) wider audience of our society, which knows intuitively that something new is in the air.

As far as academia is concerned, the book certainly ties up with the discipline of religious studies. The adjective 'religious' as it is used in this academic convention does not indicate that the 'studies' themselves are religious – no more than the term 'human sciences' differentiates certain disciplines from others which are presumed to be sub- or superhuman, animal or divine in character, or than 'social sciences' implies that those 'sciences' are themselves social, whereas others are individual or perhaps antisocial; or than the term 'natural sciences' distinguishes them from unnatural or supernatural ones. Yet I candidly admit that this work does not fall within the boundaries of religious studies as generally defined, and that I venture into an area which is not considered to be part of it (or of science of religion, another name for the same academic enterprise). In a wide sense (wider than the academic discipline itself) it is indeed religious studies.

Neither is it theology – I insist against those who might claim that all value- and praxis-oriented thought must be theology (or crypto-theology). It does not proceed from some divine revelation, and it does not accept any religion as its axiom and norm. Nor is it philosophy in the technical, professional sense of the word. It explores the interfaces *between various academic disciplines*, touching on evolution theory, archaeology, cultural anthropology and history as well, as my reader will find. I prefer to call it simply *religious thought* or *religious philosophy*: 'philosophy' in the nontechnical sense of love of wisdom. It is made up of personal reflections, against a backdrop of scholarship, based in the science of religion, in the context of a changing society to which and for which I am (co-)responsible. I would present them as essays ('efforts'), personal experiments – not as established 'scientific' fact or conclusion. They are not built on those sciences, and I am certainly not writing as an amateur archaeologist or biologist. Moving in the interface with those sciences and presupposing dialogue with them, these essays do not stand or fall by their scientific correctness. Yet I did seriously consult the disciplines of archaeology, cultural anthropology and history in order to understand the Bushmen and what lies behind them. Those disciplines and their results are part of the set of conditions surrounding this effort at a basic reorientation. Where broad consensus in those disciplines at this stage of their ongoing development appears to have the status of provisional 'facts', I respected them. Yet I know very well that those 'facts' function in wider theoretical frameworks, and that they have theoretical and – in the long run – philosophical and religious implications. The latter are not always spelled out or even appreciated as interesting and important in those disciplines. Often they are dismissed as mere assertions or arbitrary speculations. Yet those frameworks and implications are the aspects which are particularly interesting for this attempt to establish whether those disciplines offer at least lateral support. So I do not offer these reflections as the result of a particularly serious 'interdisciplinary' dialogue in a strong sense. Such 'inter-'dialogue could in fact amount to a hardening of the walls between the very discrete and separate 'disciplines'. Rather, treading cautiously where I do not have any specialist knowledge, I was interested in finding out to what extent a broad 'conditionalist' religiotheoretical perspective would shed light on certain problems, and receive light from other areas, treating the inevitable and pragmatically useful boundaries between fields of study as soft and permeable, and believing that religious studies should not box itself in.

In a broad sense, these chapters are explorations, religious remembrances and visionings, not desiring to establish definite knowledge in any field – but to probe the open depth in whatever presents itself at any given time (which is what I understand 'religion' to be). Thus I move between the articulation of my own personal experience, listening to the mingling religious traditions and taking note of what the sciences have to say about the world – in a perspective that I call 'religious'.

Between religions

Religious thinking in South Africa needs to widen dramatically the horizon in which the traditional religious values of the West, the dominant set of values in this country, are overhauled in a trialogue that would embrace the East and the traditional values of Africa as well.

In our time we are witnessing an immense expansion of religious awareness. More than ever before people have access to religions in the plural. These chapters deliberately expose their readers to the strong, dangerous but exhilarating winds blowing outside the protected sanctuaries of the different institutionalised religions. They explore the spaces between religions: Christian, Buddhist, Bushman. 'In between' is the place for the adventurous spirits of our day to be. There religion in the sense of inherently original human search and discovery may be found. Opening the windows and doors of the organised religions to those winds carrying scents and sounds from afar and inviting the eye to scan the distance, saves the inhabitants from all manner of stuffiness. This is a study of interrelatedness and interpenetration in religious perspective. It means that we shall resolutely leave behind the idea that the three religions in question represent a mere aggregate of incomparable entities, each capable of being treated in isolation. In spite of some misgivings I settled for the term 'religion', but let it be added that in these essays the word does not necessarily imply (as convention probably dictates) adherence to any of the established religions of the world.

The book presupposes a life-long concern with Christianity. Yet it does not tap Christianity's resources for this kind of thinking. Neither have its implications for the understanding of Christianity in this region of the world been worked out. That is a debt that still has to be paid. Far from adding up to a rejection of Christianity, the tenor implies a rediscovery of that religion.

More obvious will be my effort to allow Buddhism (representing radical 'meta-' or 'post-religion') and Bushman experience (representing African 'original' religion) to speak to us. These two complexes are indeed far removed from present standard religious awareness in this country: on the one hand Bushman religion, representing the oldest known form of religion in South Africa, as indigenous as aloe and eland, on the other hand Buddhism, exotic to South Africa and universal; the former commonly and mistakenly considered as 'primitive' as can be found anywhere on earth, the latter philosophically as sophisticated as any system ever formulated; the former virtually extinct, the latter not yet fully arrived; the former despised in the official Christian view, the latter often feared as a threat. This study will trace some of the intricate lines of positive contact between these two that seem to stretch the religious continuum to the utmost.

I believe that the religions of the East, such as Buddhism and Taoism, add new dimensions to the dialogue between the 'West' and 'Africa' by expanding it into a multifaceted trialogue. The relationship between 'West' and 'East' (for our purposes, Christianity and Buddhism) has received as much attention as that between the West' and 'Africa'. But the third side of the triangle, linking Africa and Buddhism, has received very little, and the relation between Buddhism and Bushman religion none at all that I know of, apart from isolated references.

Buddhist philosophy in particular – extended beyond the realm of individual calm and insight into a religiohistorical, religiophilosophical, sociohistorical framework of understanding – permeates these essays. Buddhism, unfathomable in its historical diversity and philosophical richness, is a way of looking at the world. What the reader will find is a personal appropriation, relevant to this particular situation, of some key elements of Buddhist thought, seen through a South African lens. Against the popular local misconception that Buddhism amounts to a pessimistic escape from the world and a slightly eccentric flight into individual peace of mind, I wish to uncover some implications for thinking and action of the metaphysical intuitions of nonself and nonpermanence as an inclusive philosophical hermeneutic, related to the South African sociohistorical situation. In a sense I take up the challenge to proceed beyond the role of historical restorer, clinical anatomist and fair broker of religions, into the chemistry of religion itself, the dynamic movement underlying the religious institutions. Of course classical Asian Buddhism is changed by mixing in other ingredients, such as Bushman religion.

From this Buddhist-inspired point of view exciting possibilities of dialogue with Bushman religion open up. It means giving up the well-meaning, grimly serious Western missionary obsession with teaching, even the Western anthropological politeness of listening – and learning from the Bushmen.

The appropriation of African traditional religions in contemporary religious discourse is a sensitive issue. A clear distinction must be made between the religions of the *hunting-gathering*, Khoisan-speaking *Bushmen*, who can probably be traced back 30 000 years in South African history, and those of the Bantu-speaking *black pastoralists and agriculturalists* who entered the country about 2 000 years ago. As far as the Bushmen are concerned, I am not aware of any reception of their religion by contemporary black intellectuals. As will become clear later on, it has received a great deal of attention from whites. Yet the possibility of a positive relationship between Christianity and Bushman religion has never been treated seriously.

> As far as indigenous black religion is concerned – which, it must be pointed out, is not the theme of this book – there would certainly be great differences between:
>
> - □ the re-appropriation of that ancient wisdom in the black cultural context by those who have been stripped of it by a dominant foreign religion (Christianity), which has nevertheless been accepted and internalised by the majority of that culture;
> - □ the appropriation of it in the white (Western) cultural context where contempt of all things African (including and perhaps especially African religion) was axiomatic for so long and has become so deeply entrenched that abandoning it would amount to nothing less than a radical change of mind;
> - □ appropriation of it in an Eastern (for example Hindu, Taoist or Buddhist) religious context in which historical lines of contact were established between East and West but those between the East and Africa have yet to be explored. (Islam, by contrast, occupies a most interesting position in this field.)

In most discourse about religion a philosophy of identity is presupposed. There is, for example, one definite entity, a circumscribed world-view, a religion with definite contours (for example 'the West', or 'Christianity'). This you 'suspend' (*epoche*) if you are trained in phenomenology, and then enter an-Other one, with equally definite contours (for example 'Africa'). Probably, for the purpose of getting through life, we humans have to chop up the world into such discrete chunks. We need definitions and definite entities. But these are abstractions. The world is in dynamic flux – with most of us hovering somewhere *in between*, changing positions, identities and perspectives all the time. Who is the author of these essays? A Westerner? An African? Both? Neither? Sometimes one? Sometimes the other? In some respects one? In other respects the other? I am suggesting that this very ambivalent space *between* cultural and religious blocs is creative, and that intellectual enquiry into religion should focus on such interstices. I wish to stimulate this in-betweenness, the both-and, the nonabsolute, the relative, the dynamics of religion.

Such a nonexclusivist religiophilosophical framework would respect the integrity of the various religions, without claiming that they are or boil down to 'the same thing', or denying the very significant differences between them.

It is too early to enter into the difficult problem of how a comparative hermeneutic of religions may be reconciled with a commitment to one religion. The view taken here is that they are not necessarily irreconcilable. To use an example from family life: one's parents and one's children are certainly very special to people. But in a time of serious illness everyone is only too grateful for disinterested bodies of expertise such as gerontology and pediatrics which employ general, comparative frameworks, abstracting from this or that individual. My child is one of many; my parents belong to a multitude of aged people. Acknowledgment of the multitude of religions does not amount to a betrayal of one's commitment to one religion. The language of love should not be hardened into an exclusivist theoretical dogma.

As we have said, thresholds divide, but they also join. Lingering there, one is inevitably a nonconformist, not belonging to any camp. On the other hand, it creates the possibility of synopsis and synthesis. The liminal, occasional reflections offered here are experimental, exploratory and provisional, not proceeding from any dogmatic position and not arriving at any fixed, final standpoint. The basic operative presupposition, namely that the world is constituted by a never-ending process of relating, makes nonsense of any pretence at a final position. Inevitably they will reveal the hand and the personal (and contextual) viewpoint of their author. But such personal, nonconformist involvement in the chemistry of religion and the enquiry into religion is not necessarily tantamount to a whimsical selection, arbitrary lumping together and superficial mixing of irreconcilable elements from disparate sources. Of course such a syncretic view may turn out to be unsuccessful, in the sense that it may fairly be expected to represent an accountable view, persuasive in terms of intersubjective criteria. But such failure would not be inherent in a synoptic programme as such.

ENDNOTE

1 Cf the complementary books of P L Berger, *The sacred canopy: elements of a sociological theory of religion*, New York: Anchor, 1969; *A rumour of angels: modern society and the rediscovery of the supernatural*, Harmondsworth: Penguin, 1969.

1

RELIGION

2 Seeing the world from the inside

Ultimately any study of religion must clarify and give an account of its own depth dimensions. This entails critical thinking both about the actual process of enquiry and about its 'object' (religion). But religion cannot be merely the object of enquiry. In the end, any study of religion(s) itself has religious (in a broad sense) roots and fruits, antecedents and consequences.

We will now begin to present a broad framework for an integral and comprehensive enquiry into religion, and indeed for the drastic religious rethink that I consider necessary in the South African sociocultural situation. The core of this understanding can be stated forthwith: it consists in the recognition that the world as we feel it in our guts ('experience') is a dynamic interplay of interdependent, mutually conditioning forces and relations. It comprises not only a view of the world, but also a view of our viewing (that is our knowledge and feeling) of that world. As far as the fairly recent Western tradition of religious thought is concerned, 'conditionalism' (an alternative term could be 'radical relationality') links up with the work of people such as William James, C G Jung and A N Whitehead. It also seeks an alliance with Buddhist philosophy, which has developed a profound and subtle conditionalist philosophy of our being in the world. The advantage of the term 'conditionalism' is that it is relatively neutral, allowing for some free interplay among existing schools of thought.

But first it is necessary to say something about the status of this theoretical orientation, in order to counter the objection that the whole exercise amounts to a magician's trick: that what emerges from the hat, has been put there beforehand; that, logically, it must be a vicious circle. This I would deny. It is quite true that the leading ideas undoubtedly give form to the entire project, and that they contain in essence what will be developed cumulatively as we go along. Yet even if this book as a whole is a broad exploration of the argument from within, trying to understand and work out its ramifications, the basic ideas are open to correction, both from within and without.

There seems to be a widely felt need for an alternative vision of the world, other than the stark, unhappy ones of either rigid divisions or coerced unity. Instead of dogmatism and conformity it would adopt an attitude of free, open enquiry; instead of exclusivism and negativism it would opt for positive, inclusive relatedness. The principle of 'conditionality' implies a religious philosophy that would replace the psycho-socio-religious syndrome of separateness, substituting the notions of togetherness and relatedness for the notion of division at the very core of reality: togetherness of humans, of humans with nature, and of both humans and nature with God; more than that, humans, nature and God understood as *being constituted by* relatedness and the dynamic interplay of relations. 'Conditionalism' speaks of plurality and coherence in the same breath, the one qualifying the other. Plurality without coherence would leave us with a world chaotically shattered into fragments; coherence without pluralism would leave us with yet another closed monolithic world, only bigger than the many little worlds of apartheid. 'Conditionalism' seeks an alternative to both centrism and the mere scatter of fragmentation.

What would the epistemological implications of this view be in terms of religious understanding? What could religious 'meaning' mean here? I suggest that meaning becomes apparent, and that we understand, in the dynamic contexts constituted by the plurality of singular events – just as an individual word acquires its meaning from its relation to other words in the widening contexts of a sentence, a paragraph, a book, a literature, a language; and just as a language, a literature, a book and so on acquire their meaning from individual words in their interplay with others. In the same way, religious meaning emerges, or reveals itself concretely, in terms of the plurality of specific events, cohering in expanding circles and merging with wider fields of events. On the one hand 'South Africa' (on which our religious reflections are focused) is a unique entity, combining (with other similar entities) into more inclusive entities; and it is made up in turn of many smaller units, each composed of even smaller ones, and so on, all overlapping and mutually implicated. To understand religiously is to see and appreciate a single unit (for example a human person) in its unrepeatable uniqueness and originality, irreducible either to smaller units constituting it or larger units encompassing it; as interacting with other equally special units; and as part of larger units until eventually ('ultimately') it is comprehended in the widest context perceptible. No unit is isolated. Smaller and larger ones are interlinked through permeable membranes. All are synecdochically related, each relationally constituted, internally as well as externally.

'Meaning' refers to relationships in a context, and religious ('ultimate') meaning refers to relationships in the 'ultimate' context. Here some qualifications are necessary. Because of our human limitations, 'the Totality' cannot be overseen. In fact, because of the ever-changing nature of the pluralistic world, there is no fixed Totality – only a process in which we may surmise some trends. However, the need to see the particular as *related* ad infinitum is important, and it makes a difference.

The religious meaning that I am interested in would start from and strongly confirm very definite particular 'data' ('given') of experience, here-now. They are concretely real, presenting themselves to our attention. And in them other data are implied, in expanding connotations. They are unique – but only by comparison, highlighting contrasts and similarities within the wider networks. Like single sounds or colours, they only make sense in wider meaning-giving patterns. Given such a context, even a grunt could be revealing. The large (religious) horizon is anticipated and extrapolated intuitively from such experiences. And it in turn locates and ranks the particular experiences. As the small implies the large and encompassing, the large implies the small and constituent. Religion does not pertain to either the individual, existential moment or the big system. It is both, in their spiral interaction, which preserves the former from the threat of isolation and the latter from the threat of totalitarianism. All entities, from the subatomic to the universal, are open, relative 'wholes'. They are contingent: nonabsolute and fortuitous, always associated with others, dependent on them, determining them.

Religion is a matter of aesthetics, seeing proportions, hearing symphonically. To 'see' the entity 'South Africa' in religious perspective is to see through it, as transparent to entities smaller, larger and of similar size. It is to see it concretely, as caught up in processes of fusion and fission, both internal and external, as are all other things. To discover its relationality ad infinitum, we need both boldness of imagination in playing with open possibilities and meticulous establishment of fact; both dream and science, intuition and hard work.

This theory of religious knowing places all the emphasis on the real feeling of the world as a human world. For all practical purposes there is no other world. It is the only one we know, and can know. In current terminology this basic orientation that directs our understanding may be called *naturalism* or *empiricism*, or better still, *religious naturalism/empiricism*. I do not believe that there is an inexorable line leading from the empiricist insistence (at least in the limited sense that I use the word) that one cannot climb out of this world to the demise of religion and a closed, positivist secularism. On the contrary, I believe that this theoretical position in fact has a profound religious dimension. What has to be admitted right at the outset, of course, is that the metaphysical and religious statements expressing such an orientation must be part of and must follow from concrete, lived experience. They must not be deduced from a priori assumptions. By nature empiricism is low-key, inviting testing all the way, and the religious empiricism (or naturalism) advocated here is not dogma.

Why entertain this theory at all? Only because it seems to me to make better sense of our situation, and shows a better way out of the problems posed by our situation than other views. (Again, I take pains to understand 'situation' in a very specific, localised sense, as explained in chapter 1). It has no justification outside our concrete needs and practices. If all things hang together 'ultimately', we cannot know how they do so. But we can know and say how what we feel, feels like here-now, from where we are, aware not only of the mortality of our feeling, knowing and saying, but also of their morality: they pass away, but are important for a life of value. It is like 'seeing' a possible course down a turbulent rapid in a strong current. You have to see it, and act on the seeing, in a split second. You *negotiate* your way through the tumult of rocks and foam – and heaven help you if you don't. An order? Yes and no. Gazing up into the southern skies from here, we see the gestalt of the southern cross. Learning from science that it is really an optical illusion that disregards the real distances of the various stars merely shifts the perimeters of the basic fact that all our knowledge is a way of looking, but does not dissolve it. If the term 'metaphysics' could still be applied to such a centreless knowing and saying, well, then let's use it for the intellectual side of religion. The sort of programme suggested here might then perhaps be called a naturalistic religious metaphysics. It means assuming that one is not blind or hallucinating; looking as honestly and widely as one can; saying what one sees; and knowing that it is wholly contingent.

In modern Western academia the study of religion has increasingly adopted a naturalist stance, engaging in steady criticism of religion and with growing awareness of its social nature.[1] This has coincided with the discovery in the West of the vast world of religion outside Christianity. Progressively the study of religion became an aspect of the study of humankind. The whole development amounted to a conscious move away from the dominant theological paradigm, as well as from religious involvement. I fully agree that religious studies must necessarily be a naturalist undertaking, but in addition I believe that in the long run the scholarly study of religion, including historical and comparative studies of the kind attempted in these essays, inevitably issues in 'religious' (taken in a wide sense) questions and talk of some sort.

The academic study of religions has important, sometimes devastating, but also challenging religious *results* and *implications*, and must take full responsibility for these. Especially in a religiously pluralistic society such as South Africa it would be irresponsible to raise a hornet's nest and then simply stand back and refuse to take part in discussions about religious truth and value. The naturalistic study of religion must take full and explicit responsibility for the naturalistic implications of its understanding of religion. Certainly there are various levels of discourse about religion, as will be argued in following chapters, and certainly the matter of religious truth can only be raised meaningfully at its proper place and level, which is distinct from other levels such as description and phenomenological understanding.[2]

The academic study of religions also *depends upon* philosophical and worldview assumptions. Ultimately any and every scholarly enterprise rests upon such assumptions. Where such a basis or point of departure is implicit, the need to explicate it will sooner or later make itself felt. And where it may be absent, the need to develop it it will sooner or later arise. For example, whereas the modern physical sciences, which have made such impressive advances since the seventeenth century, depended upon a materialistic cosmology, the metaphysics of (for example) Whitehead may be understood as an effort to account metaphysically for the changes, brought about by scientific doctrines such as evolution and relativity, which have revolutionised science since the nineteenth century. We may debate the question whether such philosophical matters must be raised within the boundaries of religious studies itself (taken as a specialist academic discipline alongside others), or elsewhere, for example in philosophy. Exactly where we draw the line of demarcation between religious studies and philosophy of religion as institutionalised academic subjects is not important. The important point is to acknowledge that the empirical study of religion presupposes and leads to religiophilosophical and eventually in metaphysical and religious questions. I find it hard to imagine how religious studies can proceed without being consciously guided and challenged by such reflections.

I do not believe that 'religion' and 'naturalism' are mutually exclusive concepts. As indicated, the overall position adopted in this book could be described as 'religious/spiritual naturalism/empiricism' or 'naturalistic/empirical religion/spiritualism'; it does not accept the notion of two realities, an 'ordinary' one plus 'another', 'supernatural' one. 'Religion' and the 'divine' point to the radical depth dimension of *this* reality, not to a wholly other reality. In other words, it is not necessary to define religion in terms of a supranaturalistic, two-tier view of reality, of which the 'other' reality can either be accepted (as traditional theology demands of us) or rejected (as in the restrictive model of religious studies). If we do not define religion in supranaturalistic terms, it would not be necessary to sever the ties between religion and the study of religion and to insist that the study of religion should keep out of 'religion'. It seems that the restrictive model of religious studies, according to which the qualifier 'religious' signifies the object of study only and in no way qualifies the actual studies, shares with traditional theology the dichotomous view of religion and reality. The study of religion, I submit, naturally opens up into 'religious' dimensions of experience. Challenging the modern Western view that the world is one-dimensional and closed is not indicative of a retrogressive re-theologising of religious studies, but is a step forward.

Insisting that religious studies must necessarily be a naturalist, empirical undertaking, and seeing religious studies as distinct from theology, does not necessarily confine theology to a supranaturalist picture of the world. Nor does it deny theology the right to exist as an academic enterprise. This is not the place to argue about the relationship between religious studies/science of religion and theology, or about the merits of possible alternative models that have been developed by theologians to replace the supranaturalist one. As far as Christian theology is concerned, the names of Ernst Troeltsch, Paul Tillich and Wolfhart Pannenberg and their followers may be mentioned in passing, as well as process theologians such as John Cobb and David Tracy.

The most sensible distinction between theology and religious studies is not between a supranaturalist orientation on the one hand and a naturalist orientation on the other, but between an academic programme that theorises in terms of the historical tradition of *one specific* religion (for example Judaism or Christianity) that is accepted as axiomatic on the one hand, and an academic programme that does not do that on the other. The first would be the way of theology; the second, that of religious studies. In this way theology plays its role in the arena of intellectual pursuits, although it must be added that the traditional varieties of theology are certainly beset with grave difficulties. Religious studies explores the spaces between and around the various religions, without arguing from the belief-presuppositions of any particular religion as axiomatic points of departure in its theorising. Theology on the other hand is historically specific. It is by definition 'Jewish', 'Muslim', 'Christian' and so on. A theology may therefore be expected somehow to be in line with the original sources of that particular religion; to consciously articulate with such a tradition, and to reflect on and express that articulation. This does not mean that it must vindicate that religion in all respects and at all costs. It may well include a sharply critical element, in a spirit of loyal protest.

The argument developed in these essays is not a theological one. Yet I may mention in passing that I believe that a new-style theology is called for in our situation. Standing squarely and loyally in the historical continuum of one particular religion, such a theology would nevertheless deliberately explore the limits of that religion. It may constitute itself as an empirical discipline, not only in its 'practical' dimensions, but in its systematic and exegetical dimensions as well. The *other* religions would not be voices heard from afar, outside 'my' religion; they would resound inside 'my' religion. Such a theology would be thoroughly informed by religious studies. Religious plurality is the horizon of progressive theology today. It should see through its own historically handed down theological schemata into the homoversal experience of life, opening itself up to a disinterested universality and solidarity with all humankind, and with all religions. Theology has its own role in its own particularist religious context, which differs from the theoretical perspective that would make any particular religion intelligible as one of the plurality of the world's religions.[3] Between religious studies and supranaturalist theologies there are vast differences, especially inasmuch as these theologies tend to isolate themselves behind steep, closed bulwarks, defiantly or aggressively believing themselves to be the sole recipients of an exclusive revelation. They may also be associated with a less strident yet equally persistent, and equally intolerant, evangelical fervour. Social uncertainty seems to favour the rise of religious fundamentalism. As for South Africa, in the foreseeable future religious sentiments will probably remain divided between what I have called religious apartheid and a wider, more open orientation.

The term 'empiricism' covers a wide range of views.[4] Restricting ourselves to the modern application of this principle in Western philosophy, it becomes clear that since its launching by Hume in the eighteenth century, it has undergone a complex history of diverse developments. Hume's own classical empiricism – essentially a genetic thesis according to which all knowledge derives from individual sensory experience – was followed early in our century by logical empiricism, championed by Ayer, Hare and others,[5] which outlawed all metaphysics and reduced the status of religious language to that of purely subjective, emotive, noncognitive meaning. Related to this was the linguistic empiricism (analytic philosophy) of Wisdom and others, which (invoking Wittgenstein's theory of meaning as linguistic use) collapsed both experience and religion into its linguistic interpretations. Wisdom admits no appeal to any experiential data apart from linguistically expressed interpretations.[6] The question, 'linguistic interpretations of *what*?' cannot be answered. Picking up the older thread of American pragmatism, Rorty[7] also dismisses any lingering distinction between interpretive frameworks and extra-interpretive reality. Comparing language to some extralinguistic absolute is as impossible as stepping out of one's own skin. To this broad anti-representation current of thought Derrida gave the most radical twist of all: the best we can do is to gambol about within the texts, dispensing even with theorising about language, because that too is indicative of the illusion that we can deal with language from the outside.

In religious studies a similar position has been adopted by Katz and his collaborators in their studies of mysticism.[8] Whereas previous studies of mysticism tended to see conceptual and linguistic expressions as strictly secondary to prelinguistic experience, here the 'experience' is wholly prefabricated by the conceptual and linguistic moulds of the various historical religions.

This seems to be an unacceptable impasse. It is pointless to ask which comes first, language/concepts or 'mystical' experience. Posed as a genealogical question of origins, it should rather be left alone. Posed as a question about the functional relationships between language and experience, it seems wrong to want to give priority to either of the two or to reduce one to the other. Instead, the answer seems to lie in cyclic relationships of mutual involvement between language/concepts and 'mystical' 'experience' – and these in turn interrelate with a larger world that impinges on us, although experienced only from within our position in that world. Our linguistic texts are not absolute, but are woven into a larger textile of which we sense that we are part, but which we cannot oversee. We shall return to the possibility of understanding religion along such lines. But first we shall take a look at some other views of the nature of religious knowledge: the belief that knowledge of ultimate truth is obtained through supernatural revelation (the revelationism of theological orthodoxy); and the belief that there is no such thing as interreligiously communicable truth and that religion can be no more than a leap of faith into commitment (fideism). These approaches are not mutually exclusive and may be combined.

Revelationism entails that God, understood as a Wholly Other, supernatural person, has revealed truth. This truth may be understood in conceptual terms as truths about the world, the state of human beings, and so on; or it may be understood as the personal self-revelation of God. Revealed truth has to be accepted in faith and obedience. In South African Christian theology this is still the dominant position. From a conditionalist perspective it is impossible to leap out of the limitations of the human psyche and its capabilities. We can only experience the inside of the world, like intestinal bacteria. Hume already demonstrated that there is no way leading from human experience to the notion of a wholly other being or reality. A broad 'religiously empiricist' critique would not claim that there is nothing outside the realm of human cognitive categories, for that would be to overstep the empiricist criterion. It would be non-sense. The world may in fact have depths which we cannot reach linguistically and conceptually but which can be probed, or at least suspected, by highly sensitive ('mystical') outreaches of our sensorium. So empiricism would rest with the statement that whatever transcends the limits of human consciousness is unknowable or empirically indistinguishable from the latter. This was the point made by Jung: if it is only through the psyche that God acts upon us, then God and psyche are practically indistinguishable. The existence of any Other Entity outside the world of experience can only be postulated. Religious empiricism would see no need for it. Impulses from afar impinge on us. We sense that. Religion (not as dogma or social institution, but as mysticism) is receptiveness to those impulses. But we do not know their provenance, and certainly cannot describe it. Whitehead made essentially the same point as Jung, but with reference to cosmological proofs for the existence of God:

> *Any proof which commences with the consideration of the actual world cannot rise above the actuality of this world. It can only discover all the factors disclosed in the world as experienced. In other words, it may discover an immanent God, but not a God wholly transcendent.*[9]

The dilemma seems unavoidable: God is either transcendent or immanent, either remains unknown or occurs within the range of the normal human faculties. What is at stake here is certainly not the idea of revelation as such, or the idea of 'God', but the claim to supernatural revelation of and by supernatural entities of supernaturally guaranteed truth. The empiricist critique of these claims is that human beings can only know what is accessible to them within the perimeters of their physical and mental makeup. Extending Jung's psychological argument and Whitehead's epistemological argument, empiricism would argue that there is no fulcrum outside this world on which any human claim to absolute truth may rely for leverage.

The notion of 'revelation' may of course be retained in a conditionalist context, but it would then imply placing religious revelation on a par with other phenomena such as the quality of beauty in nature or art, or the quality of validity in science. Revelation becomes an aesthetic category, being drawn into the sphere of the experiential possibilities of human consciousness without loss of religious quality. At the same time the religious empiricist would be prepared to extend the range of normal experience beyond the rather limited one usually accepted in the West, to include the contemplative dimension. As in other respects, it would have to be admitted that not all people are equally gifted. Where one person merely hears a noise or sees a nondescript blot, another is able to discern subtle and exquisite patterns of sound, or of form or colour. The majority of humankind is admittedly rather unfamiliar with the type of experience in which the great mystic visionaries are at home. It is also true that psychology is starting afresh to seriously study parapsychological phenomena which may relate to deeper than usual states of awareness. Thus we must not assign too limited and shallow a meaning to the term 'experience'. A totally tone-deaf person cannot be taken as the norm to evaluate the music of Mozart. The same applies in the sphere of religion and mysticism: the fact that mystic experience transcends everyday reality does not mean that it is not true experience which, in principle, is open to everybody with a certain degree of ability, interest and discipline, and is therefore susceptible to experiential testing. A weakness of most of Western empiricism (classical empiricism, logical positivism as well as analytic philosophy) is its sensationalist theory of perception, restricting experience to the ordinary range of the five senses and their technological extensions.

If the above arguments apply to religious experience, they apply in even greater measure to the scholarly study of religion. Empirical studies of religion can obviously not rely on supernatural revelation to prove or provide a basis for its knowledge, or to lend it authority. It confines itself to experiential knowledge, accessible to every normal person via natural cognitive processes. A further implication of the empiricist approach for academic enquiries into religion is that none of the religions examined will be afforded any special, supernaturally sanctioned status. Nor will any of humanity's historical religions be denied the status of a legitimate and authentic expression of common human concerns. Stone Age Bushman religion and Buddhism are expressive of the same human psyche as Christianity. Nothing expressed by any one of the three is totally inconceivable in any of the other two.

Religion within the bounds of concrete experience would deny the relevance of any absolute foundation to its statements. It is nonfoundational. It does not enter the world of religion – or rather, of religions – armed with any a priori certainties. It undertakes an open-ended journey of discovery into relativity. It has no privileged absolute certainties or protected beliefs. It would not seek God anywhere except in the midst of this concretely experienced world.[10] Empiricist religion need not be anti-intellectualist; it may make full use of the discriminating possibilities of reason, admitting into its articulation of the experience of the world not only analytical reason to critically dissect our speech, but also constructive reason to postulate hypothetical models of understanding that necessarily exceed the immediately given.

The conditionalist view underlying the idea of religious enquiry developed here is distinct from *fideism*, that leap of commitment into subjective truth, combined with despair that any interpersonal, interreligiously valid criteria for distinguishing good from bad and better are to be found. Linguistic empiricism, focusing exclusively as it tends to do on the linguistic forms in which religion is experienced, strengthens the fideistic position.[11] Taken to its final conclusion fideism amounts to relativism of sorts – in spite of possible protestations that truth is absolute. For it simply latches onto a view, like a shellfish onto a rock in the wild ocean, without any possibility of interreligious communication or critique. One believes what one believes within the closed circle of one's belief, and that is that. And what is thus demanded for oneself may liberally and tolerantly be granted to others as well. Believe what you like, just don't confuse me. The only kind of criticism possible is intrareligious criticism. By contrast the kind of religious thought which should direct religious inquiry, while admitting that there is no such thing as absolute truth, also admits of the possibility of critical discussion between different views on (and within) a pluralistic world.

ENDNOTES

1 This historical development has been described by J S Preus, *Explaining religion: criticism and theory from Bodin to Freud*, New Haven: Yale University Press, 1987. Preus's historical reconstruction is complemented by Donald Wiebe's systematic arguments. In a series of articles and books he developed a naturalist position, demanding that the scholarly study of religion should keep aloof not only from theology, but also from any engagement in religion or metaphysics. For his statement that 'religious thought' and 'science' (including 'theology') are logically incompatible structures of thought, see D Wiebe, *The irony of theology and the nature of religious thought*, Montreal, Kingston: McGill-Queen's University Press, 1991.

2 That the truth question may not be divorced from the study of religion has been argued by D Wiebe in *Religion and truth: towards an alternative paradigm for the study of religion*, The Hague: Mouton, 1981.

3 A specimen of such a treatment of Christianity is A Fernando, *Christianity made intelligible (as ONE of the world's religions)*, Eldeniya, Sri Lanka: Inter-Cultural Book Promoters, 1990.

4 A critical overview of empiricism since Hume, with reference to its religious applications, may be found in N Frankenberry, *Religion and radical empiricism*, New York: State University of New York Press, 1987.

5 A few salient markers in this debate as far as religion is concerned: in his *Language, truth and logic*, Harmondsworth: Penguin, (1936) 1971, A J Ayer (applying to religion Wittgenstein's early ideas about meaningless and meaningful propositions)

suggested that metaphysical, religious and theological language makes no verifiable statements and are nonsensical – at most they express subjective, emotive, non-cognitive meaning. Similarly, R M Hare (Religion and morals, in B Mitchell [ed], *Faith and logic*, London: Allen & Unwin, 1957) regarded a religious statement as a 'blik', i e the expression of a particular angle on ordinary empirical reality. To A Flew (Theology and falsification, in *New essays in philosophical theology*, A Flew & A MacIntyre [eds], London: SCM, 1955, p 96ff) we owe the dictum that God, having been declared immune to any empirical test like the invisible, intangible and utterly undetectable gardener of John Wisdom, seems to have 'died the death of a thousand qualifications'.

6 See J Wisdom *Philosophy and psychoanalysis*, Berkeley: University of California Press, 1969, pp 149–168 for the famous essay in which he interpreted theism and atheism as two different ways of seeing – either you 'see' it (i e God, or the gardener) or you don't; there is no possible appeal to anything beyond the seeing itself.

7 Cf R Rorty *Philosophy and the mirror of nature*, Oxford: Blackwell, 1980; *Consequences of pragmatism*, Brighton, Sussex: Harvester Press, 1982.

8 Cf S Katz (ed) *Mysticism and philosophical analysis*, London: Sheldon Press, 1978; *Mysticism and religious traditions*, Oxford: Oxford University Press, 1983; *Mysticism and language*, Oxford: Oxford University Press, 1992.

9 A N Whitehead *Religion in the making*, Cambridge: Cambridge University Press, 1927, p 59.

10 Cf Whitehead, *Process and reality: an essay in cosmology*, New York: Free Press, (1929) 1978, p 256: 'You cannot know what is red by merely thinking of redness. You can only find red things by adventuring amid physical experiences in *this* world. This doctrine is the ultimate doctrine of empiricism.'

11 In this regard the writings of D Z Phillips are relevant. See his *Faith and philosophical enquiry*, London: Routledge, 1970; *Faith after foundationalism*, London: Routledge, 1988.

3 The conditionalist web

Out there is the great world with its cruelty and its peace, its catastrophes and its favours, in a sense existing independently of us yet at the same time intimately part of us, as we are part of it. Inside is the depth of one's own mind with its fears and hopes, its weaknesses and strengths, inseparable from the seething pool of shared human mentality which has evolved over millions of years as part of nature. Awe at the immensities and complexities of the world without and the world within is the genesis of religion, as it is of science and art.

There are three ways to come closer to discovering the religious meaning of things, revealed in the intertwined nature of the world: descent into the depths of one's individual existence; the investigation of nature, human and nonhuman; and attentive listening to the voices of humankind, past and present, which articulate the sum of human understandings of the world and its meaning. The first is the way of meditation, the second the way of science, and the third the way of hermeneutics. But, and this is the important point, the various avenues to orienting ourselves in the universe crisscross, although they do not merge into each other. There is no solitary meditation. The monk under the tree is pervaded by communal understandings of the world. Conversely, descent into the depths of the individual mind may broaden into a discovery of aspects of humanity and the nature of the world. The exploration of nature is at the same time an exploration of humanity and the nature of its knowing and being in the world. The natural sciences are hermeneutic exercises. Their history is one of successive interpretations of interpretations ... of nature. There is no Book of Nature, apart from the books of humans. Yet humanity is part of nature. Somehow the split in contemporary thought between 'science' offering representational truth of nature and 'rhetoric' merely manoeuvring on the social battlefield of human words is deeply unsatisfactory. But how to get rid of this cleft stick? On the other hand, can we ask for more than a multiperspectival, mutually translatable dialogue? The difficulty of achieving such a dialogue accounts for the enormous tensions pervading contacts between, for example, modern cosmology and theology.[1]

The third way is obviously the way of religious studies. It is the art of listening attentively to all religions, past and present. Yet it should not be insulated against the input of the natural sciences from which some of the most provocative challenges to contemporary religion have issued. Neither should it be cut off from personal experience and meditation.

For our present purpose we shall reduce the infinite field of interactions composing the world to the model of a triangle, whose three angles are 'person', 'nature' and 'society'.[2]

The notion of an 'individual' human being in the strict sense is an abstraction. A person comes into existence in a web of human social relationships, and never leaves it. Even the greatest and most daring spirits never escape from this conditioning. The way solitary individuals experience the world is necessarily mediated by the forms inherited from their predecessors and contemporaries. You may be continually present in my life as a major force even though I may not be consciously aware of your significance. You may also be one of the less significant individuals who act upon me and trigger off unreflective reactions. With increasing impersonality, you become a third person and confront me as he or she. You exert influence on me in the plural, as one of several groups of varying significance. You become they, those who act upon me in increasing degrees of anonymity and impersonality. Other people, whether living or members of past generations, form me through the processes of socialisation. Even though they may live in a distant part of the world, they nevertheless are here, co-present with me and with all the others shaping me and my world. Finally, there is the aggregate of all other people – society – which transcends and controls me through its institutions such as language, family, education and religion. Without society, the individual would not exist. I am part of a historically given world which is my social environment, my sociocultural milieu, and it is not of my own making. My behaviour is affected by psychological and sociohistorical pressures. To the domain of objective structures which antedate me, enter into me and lay claim to me by becoming part of me, belongs the objectified world of human culture, including the language through which I come to self-awareness, the system of morality prevalent in the group into which I am born, a centuries old ritual or myth, a holy book, an idea of God. Patterns of conduct, speaking, believing, thinking or feeling can hover over me (if they evoke reactions of fear) or embrace me (if they evoke reactions of glad submission) as mighty, unchallengeable entities without which I cannot imagine my being. They become part of my constitution to such an extent that I can hardly distinguish them from myself and cannot relinquish them except with great pain. Via many smaller and larger overlapping groups I am, in the end, a shoot from the rhizome of humanity.

It is true that the individual – its physical and mental makeup, its genes and its unconscious – is also part and product of forces that transcend collective social definitions of things. I am part of nonhuman nature, that large world of events and agencies that we moderns regard as subhuman. I am spatially and temporally linked to all other physical things. As far as my senses stretch, and much further, is a world of things with an enormous timespan behind and ahead of it, far exceeding my short life. I am inextricably part of this natural world. It surrounds me, and I bend to the physical forces of nature that operate within me and beyond me. My psyche is deeply rooted in the world of physical nature. In my conscious life I am only dimly aware, if at all, of the powers that bind me to animals, plants, rocks and water. Yet I am rooted in this deep, dark soil, and governed by physical and physiological regularities.

A conditionalist philosophy of religion would not accept that the individual is at the receiving end in its relations with society and nature, merely registering like a seismograph. I transcend society, and need to establish a distance in which 'I' become a relatively original source of life. Breach, alienation, individuation is an important component of the process of becoming a person. The fact that there is a socionatural world out there, beyond me yet constituting me, is counterpoised with the equally important fact that *I act*[3] upon the socionatural world. Apart from 'action', other terms such as 'freedom', 'responsibility'[4], 'praxis', 'projectivity' and 'existence', employed in various Marxian and phenomonological contexts, come to mind, all loaded but nevertheless pointing to this same quality of human life.

Action is not an absolutely original self-expression. I do not start from nothing, but from within an existing network of relations. Yet in my feeling, touching, seeing, listening, thinking, working, loving, believing and all my other self-expressions, I am – relatively speaking – the source of something new, with my own unique manner of being human, my very personal attitude which is not reducible to nature and society and not wholly explicable in terms of natural and social forces. The manner in which I am 'I' is permeated by an irreducible, personal quality imbued with my subjective meaning. The first field to which my actions are directed is nature. I can reach out and handle things, adapt myself to my physical environment, transform it to some extent and produce things, to mention just a few examples of this human capacity which in modern technological society has assumed such stupendous proportions. I also act upon the sociocultural world. Individuals encounter each other as persons, that is, as centres of action and meaning. The other to whom I express myself is not only an individual other I (you). It is also you in the plural. Interaction can occur indirectly, between me and him, her or them.

In this line of thinking even the anonymous, impersonal social forces which constrain people have their genesis in personal ways of being in the world, like fossils of once living beings. Although my present, individual character may seem fixed, it is the product of many previous decisions and actions and has its roots in a very basic, decisive attitude towards the world, which is uniquely mine. When we interact with one another, we jointly establish patterns of interaction, and to the extent that these become routine, they take on a transpersonal character. We do not have to start all over again every time, because a habit has been formed. But such patterns of typical expectations remain a by-product of our interaction.

However old and mighty, complex and wide-ranging such patterns of behaviour (institutions) may be and however strongly they may regulate our behaviour, they are nevertheless produced by persons' interaction. This view has highly significant implications for our interpretation and understanding of religious institutions. Seen thus, society is made up of acting persons and groups which subjectively intend meaning and respond to subjectively intended meaning. Culture (of which religion is a part)[5] is the objectified product or sediment of action. Thus the domain of objective structures confronting me (including language, a system of morality, a centuries-old ritual or myth, a holy book or an idea of God), which in one perspective determines and controls me, is in this second perspective person-made, appropriated by me in my own manner as a response-able person. Even if we cannot pinpoint the creation of a religious item in time, it remains a human creation, and it is always the individual who today attaches a certain meaning to the myth, who acts out the ritual in a distinctive way, who reads the holy book differently from other individuals, who responds to the depth dimension of reality and believes in God uniquely, differently from any collective institution. This is why religions, as collective-yet-individual systems of interaction with reality, *change*. There is nothing permanent, nothing eternally given in them.

So my acting-upon-and-being-acted-upon relationship with the world (the natural world and the world of objectified sociocultural products) reveals a triadic interactional structure. I am a condensation of many other persons and societies, a microcosm. Wittingly or unwittingly, I simultaneously deal with the world and with other persons, be they alive with me as contemporaries who share the same responsibility for the same world, my predecessors who acted in perhaps exemplary ways in a comparable world, or my successors who will one day respond to my present actions in their world, which will be the product of our actions today. Our human interaction meshes with nature, which is always present as a third partner.

Like the notion of the solitary individual, the notion of nature as such is an abstraction. Nature is nature-for-us, for humans, an appropriated and interpreted nature. For practical purposes there is no other nature. The act of observation alters the object of observation. There are no data detached from conceptual schemes. This is what modern empiricism from Hume onwards discovered: the world of nature is a thought, talked, conceptualised world. The strength of these forms of empiricism is their recognition that we only encounter a world that has already been thought. Their weakness is that they run the risk of isolating society from any input from that world.

Such a society would also be an abstraction. It amounts to a breach of the reciprocal links between nature and our thinking about nature. It ends up in a collective solipsism. Humankind thus stands alone with its thoughts, in touch only with itself, tragically isolated from nature, analysing only its own languages. The fact that culture is effectively impinged upon by the real world must be accommodated. Conversely, the fact that humankind transcends nature and needs to establish a distance between itself and the rest of nature must be recognised, as must the fact that culture is continually recreated by the innovations of charismatic individuals who intuitively penetrate to layers of experience of nature as yet unfathomed.

Somehow the person, society and nature (the universe) co-inhere and co-interact conditionalistically. Humanity is not the centre of the universe as pre-Copernican cosmology and theology assumed. We are drifting on a minuscule planet somewhere in a remote corner of the universe. And yet (as the 'anthropic principle' suggests)[6] our existence and our consciousness seem to be so finely attuned to very special sets of parameters in that universe that we can at least trust that we are 'in touch' with it. As we are adapted to the universe, so the universe is adapted to us. We can assume that our language games and conceptual constructs are not sealed off from the world but interlock with it.

And 'God'? In view of the substantialisation of this word in traditional Western theology, the widespread reluctance to use the concept at all is understandable (religious atheism). And yet there were others in that same tradition (Scotus Eriugena, Eckhart, Boehme, Cusanus, to mention a few) who used it in different, dynamic senses. The sort of religion hinted at in these essays would obviously refuse to identify 'him' as any one of the three angles mentioned, or to posit 'him' as a separate fourth pole. 'He' 'is' not less than a person, nor is he merely a Big Person, either present in the world (theism), or absent from it (deism); in fact, by being more than that, 'he' 'is' not: these words break down. Nor is 'God' the aggregate of nature (pantheism), or the mere scatter of the many (polytheism). Rather, 'God' as content of the religious dream would be the principle of conditionality, integrating the individual human person with a universal society of humans and nonhumans, yet simultaneously creating the open dynamism that prevents the whole, or any of its aspects, from becoming a closed thing (panentheism).

The manner in which this way of looking at religion emerged, and is being adopted and adapted and should be tested, illustrates the above argument. Of course it had no absolute beginning. One is born into it or one grows into it or steps into it. Yet the paradigm is not merely self-validating. Its thinking is not merely circular. It submits itself to external correction by competing interpretive schemes, and to challenge and inspiration from dimensions of reality not fully captured in existing networks of thought.

The point is not to get tied down to a binary opposition between the individual and the whole, but to understand the one in terms of the other, thereby changing both. I may say 'I', with full emphasis on my uniqueness. To see a person in terms of relations (internal and external) need not lead to devaluation of its dignity. On the contrary, my dignity derives precisely from my being a concrete node (an intersection, a component in a network, not a tightly tied knot) in the pluralistic world; a bud from which new growth sprouts in the beautiful jungle. For the same reason, I fully see, acknowledge and respect 'You' as my complementary counterpart. Which of the two we emphasise is a matter of relative focus. Even the most private, introverted mystic is an inner society, and even the most 'original' author quotes implicitly all the time. Even the most extroverted, explicitly quoting, name-dropping, self-contextualising, historicising author is a unique condensation point of all those influences, *and* is producing something new and 'original'. The one movement merges with the other. All the concrete growths are important, simply because they are there. This basic view has far-reaching implications: morally, it provides a criterion for distinguishing good from bad; politically, it points a way forward for our society; ecologically, it motivates a search for an alternative to the exploitation of nature. In fact, it may be called ecological religion.[7]

Conditionalism is compatible with the evolutionary perspective which presents itself to us, living on the oldest human continent. We are fortunate that archaeological remains found here point back far beyond the Bushmen, the oldest South Africans in historical memory, to a long line of human evolution, stretching back dimly to millions of years ago when the first hominids appeared, and far beyond, to the very beginnings of life. And what a pity that for so long the dominant religious thinking simply dismissed those reminders of the organic relatedness of us, *homo sapiens*, with animal life, insect life, vegetable life, inorganic nature – with the whole of nature as disclosed by modern science on both the infinitesimal scale of micro-events and the macroscale of cosmic events, dating back to the very origins of the universe. Tragic, because with this lack of insight and perspective went a lack of respect for life and nature. The point that concerns us in our present argument is that humankind emerges from the womb of nature itself, so that the human mentality should not be regarded as a strange intrusion into nature.[8] It evolved in intimate touch with the rest of nature, as an organ for adaptation in the sense not only of biological survival, but also of intuitive understanding of the world. Experiences that evolved in the world will somehow reflect the world. That is axiomatic for conditionalist empiricism.

This being-part-of-the-world in an intimate sense is where the genesis of religion is to be sought. The evolution of humankind may be seen as the process of its cumulative cosmic experience. Even as our forebears tens and hundreds of thousands of years ago tracked game across the veld, scanned the skies for rain and dug into the earth for food and water, they sought for more and found more. It is impossible to say when thought and religion started, but surely they can be said to be extensions of the process of mutual adaptation inherent in all of nature. One suspects that there must be very deep layers of primitive contact and interaction between human beings and their environment which would permit ongoing moulding and influence of nature on humanity. Humans respond to and interact with a world distinct from, yet organically intertwined with themselves and their experience in all its forms, whether sensory or intellectual. I believe that the essence and origin of religion must be sought in these deep layers of human participation in nature.

Groundwork for a science and philosophy of religion as interacting with the pluralistic network of the world has been laid by William James, C G Jung and A N Whitehead.

In James's essays in what he termed 'radical empiricism',[9] he defines that concept as containing two complementary aspects: it will not 'admit into its constructions any element that is not directly experienced'; nor will it 'exclude from them any element that is directly experienced'.[10]

The axis of his argument is the felt fact that there is a primordial, organic togetherness between human beings and their environment. 'Radical empiricism' articulates the epistemological implications of this fact. Knowledge, and experience generally, is nothing but a particular expression of this elemental relatedness of human beings and nature. The epistemology of radical empiricism is part and parcel of an ontology of dynamic relationality, of pluralistic flux, of transitions rather than fixed entities. It is vital to bear in mind that James interprets 'experience' very broadly. He does not make the usual contradistinction between 'knowledge' and 'experience'. Rather, thinking is merely a phase, a particular kind, of experience, that is, of felt relation. Conceptual knowledge, therefore, is simply one among many manifestations of experience such as volition and feeling.

A significant implication of radical empiricism is that it circumvents the dualism of subject versus object, of thinking and thing thought, which has plagued modern thought. James does this by means of the idea of 'pure experience' which is taken to precede the duality of consciousness and its contents. The one, same 'undivided portion of experience, taken in one context of associates, plays the part of a knower, of a state of mind, of "consciousness"; while in a different context the same undivided bit of experience plays the part of a thing known, of an objective "content"'.[11] James explains this by comparing it to an identical point lying on two different lines, which is possible at the point of intersection. Similarly an entity, for example a room, occurs twice or, as he phrases it, could be counted twice over: once as an element of the personal biography of the human being sitting in the room, and again as an element of the history of the house of which the room is a part. It is a matter of relations. Just as the same thing can be small or great, high or low, so it can be at once 'thought-of-an-object' and 'object-thought-of', depending on the context in which it appears. 'Pure experience' stands for the instant field of the present,[12] which is potentially either subject or object. That is why adjectives wander as if uncertain where to attach themselves – experiences of painful objects are painful experiences, and so on. According to James then, there are no radically heterogeneous, separate substances – subjective 'consciousness' on the one hand and objective 'things' on the other. They are merely aspects of the same stuff, namely what appears,[13] of 'pure experience'. 'Consciousness' is therefore not a metaphysical entity; it is the function of a relation. This does not mean that James makes no distinction between the real world out there and inner thought. He does so, using the notion of *acting* or *effectively making a difference* as his criterion. This is an application of his pragmatism. A real fire burns sticks. A mental fire does not.

For James, relations between things, conjunctive as well as disjunctive, are not merely imputed qualities; they are real, and are experienced or felt as real. This ties in with a fundamental aspect of his radical empiricism, namely that the world of pure experience is a flux of relationships without definite boundaries between things, diffusely merging, fringed by an indeterminate 'more'.[14] Our experience of the world is therefore vague and semichaotic rather than neat, clear and precise.

How does James's radical empiricism account for intersubjectivity, for shared and communicated experience between individuals? His answer is simple. If one and the same experience can figure twice, once in a mental and once in a physical context, it can figure many times over 'by running into as many different mental contexts, just as the same point, lying at their intersection, can be continued into many different lines.'[15] Experience is of a public nature.

James restores the organistic coherence of humans and nature, subject and object, thinking and feeling, in a pulsating flux of experience. The implications of this approach for a science and philosophy of religion are manifest. Clearly James's vision rests on a naturalistic metaphysic, which does not need to hypothesise a transempirical reality as a ground for experience. Certainly there is something 'more' (to use James's own terminology) to our everyday lives, but whatever it may be beyond our experiential capabilities, on this side it can only be felt in the field of experience, on the fringes and vague margins of our consciousness, as a result of the difference it makes in that field of experience. It does not presuppose any established certainties, but consists in radical sensitivity to the qualities of shifting relationships. Note that James did not claim that only things that are experienced in fact exist in reality. He merely insisted that such more-than-experienceable facts need not, should not and could not fruitfully be part of the material of philosophical debate. He takes care not to exceed empiricism's own criterion by making definite statements about more-than-experienceable reality. Clearly his is a consistent form of naturalism. The furthest he was willing to go was to declare that 'beyond each man and in a fashion continuous with him there exists a larger power ...'.[16] A monistic postulate, which James discovered at least latently in all philosophical theisms, exceeds the requirements of the facts. Neither did any kind of dualism satisfy him. He opted for a 'pluralistic hypothesis'. The world is a plurality of natural processes.[17] The divine is continuous with these.

Compared with the pluralistic tone of this phase of James's thought, Jung's psychology is 'holistic', tending towards a totalist view of the world and a monotheistic view of God. This was counterweighted by James Hillman's emphasis on the polycentric, polymorphic and by implication polytheistic nature of the human soul.[18] I shall argue that the point of subtle balance of the religious urge is to be found on the edge of chaos. In a conditionalist world where everything is in constant change together with everything else, chaos and order are permanently intertwined. We exist on that edge, with a foot on each side. In our present context the point is that in his writings on psychology and religion Jung adopted a consistent empiricist line,[19] accepting the indissoluble interaction between humankind and the world.

In this perspective the word 'God' is not allowed to stand for a metaphysical *ens absolutum*, but expresses a deep archetypal motif deriving from the collective unconscious:[20] the archetype of wholeness or what Jung calls 'the self', that is the totality of the person, the aggregate of conscious and unconscious contents.[21] The God-concept is 'the idea of an all-embracing totality'.[22] Although Jung takes care not to equate God with this archetype, there is no denying that for practical purposes this is what his position amounts to. Towards the end of his famous *Answer to Job*, he says:

> *It is only through the psyche that we can establish that God acts upon us, but we are unable to distinguish whether these actions emanate from God or from the unconscious. We cannot tell whether God and the unconscious are two different entities.*[23]

What can be established empirically, is that

> *... there is in the unconscious an archetype of wholeness which manifests itself spontaneously in dreams, etc, and a tendency, independent of the conscious will, to relate other archetypes to this centre. Consequently, it does not seem improbable that the archetype of wholeness occupies as such a central position which approximates it to the God-image'.*[24]

Empirically, God cannot be distinguished from the archetype of wholeness which rises up from the depths of the unconscious. As consciousness dims and the unconscious manifests itself, the forms of consciousness lose their distinctiveness and a sense of indefiniteness, oneness, wholeness emerges. In the unconscious nothing is distinct; things are vague and recede into a background of mutual contamination, to the extent that a feeling of the whole as one emerges.[25] In this context revelation finds its place as an unveiling of the depths of the human soul,[26] of its intimations of what lies on the edges of human experience which, Jung says, may arbitrarily be called the ultimate, the first, the last, the highest, or the lowest.[27] In sum, for Jung 'God' is the expression of the human search for wholeness, operative at the limits of his experience, surging up from the unconscious. Whatever else God may be, this is all we can know. As Dourley states,[28] 'the *deus absconditus*, the God hidden in man's unconsciousness, becomes incarnate through human consciousness and in so doing revitalizes, balances and enlarges life ...'.

By means of his distinction between the collective unconscious and the personal unconscious, the latter 'resting on'[29] the former, Jung accounts for the interaction between the individual and society as the collective entity, 'humanity'. For Jung the sense of God is a *consensus gentium,*[30] innate in the collective unconscious and in that sense 'objective'.

Between the human psyche and nature, which forms the third angle of our triad, he sees a subtle and insoluble interaction. In his *Psychological commentary on the Tibetan Book of the Great Liberation*, he argues that the act of apperception consists of two phases: first the perception of the object, second the assimilation of the perception to a preexisting pattern or concept by means of which the object is 'comprehended'. Every new representation arouses associations drawn from the storehouse of memory, that is from the preexisting system of the unconscious.[31] The psyche and its structure, that is the subjective factor in the cognitive process, transforms material objects into psychic images according to 'the eternal patterns of psychic functioning'.[32] The empiricist principle is: 'Existence is as we see and understand it.'[33] In this respect Jung sees a significant difference between the world-views and religions of the West and the East. The West emphasises externals, the East internal reality, and both are one-sided:[34] to Jung the two are intrinsically interwoven. Jung locates both religion and the study of religion squarely within the framework of human experience of the ultimate conditions of its existence, without recourse to extra-empirical realities. This does not mean that Jung's work has no metaphysical dimension, provided metaphysics is defined in empiricist terms as a doctrine pertaining to the essentials of the world, based on human experience only.

We now come to Whitehead. To appreciate the full relevance of his rethinking for religion, we have to go back beyond his theory of God to his basic metaphysical programme. This programme is a sustained effort to reintegrate human beings with nature, conceived of as an organism constituted by interaction. On the epistemological side, his philosophy certainly includes a rationalist element, demanding of metaphysical theory that it be coherent and logical;[35] but this is not incompatible with his empiricist insistence that experience is the final test to establish the applicability and adequacy of a metaphysical theory. His rationalism operates in an empiricist context.[36] Metaphysical theories must be rooted in experience and must pass the test of empirical fit, by which he understood, in a wide sense, that ideally all items of experience should be interpretable in terms of the metaphysical scheme. Where he differs from traditional empiricism is in his theory of perception. Traditional empiricism accorded vivid, conscious sense perception a status of ultimacy. Whitehead argues that the sensory mode of perception, which he calls 'perception in the mode of presentational immediacy', is of secondary importance, being a more superficial mode of apprehension. There is a deeper mode of apprehension, which is vague and dimly discerned. This he calls 'causal efficacy'.[37] It is an instance of causal interaction between humans and nature.

In its most basic form, the Whiteheadian metaphysic declares the world to consist of events constituted by a causally structured interaction with other events. The notion of 'substance', the predominant concept in traditional Western metaphysics, is thus replaced by the notion of 'events' (or 'actual entities') involving each other by virtue of their mutual 'prehensions' (that is interactions) to form *nexus* (that is facts of organismic togetherness) constituted in a dynamic process. Each event is itself a composite entity, and all entities in the universe are related, permitting Whitehead to declare that 'an actual entity cannot be a member of a "common world", except in the sense that the "common world" is a constituent of its own constitution. It follows that every item of the universe, including all the other actual entities, is a constituent in the constitution of any one actual entity.'[38] What this boils down to is that no individual event is a self-contained substance; it is a coming together of all the other events in the universe at that particular focal point, which in turn plays a part in the coming together of every other event and thus of the universe itself. The ultimate principle according to which the many enter into complex unities of new nexus (termed the process of 'concrescence') he calls 'creativity'. This is the principle of novelty in the universe. For our purpose it is not necessary to analyse his account of the process of creativity. That would involve his doctrine of the entities 'eternal objects' and 'God'. We shall restrict ourselves to his teaching of 'causal efficacy', alluded to above, and of 'prehensions'.

Whitehead presents his epistemology as an inversion of Kant's. For Kant 'the world emerges from the subject; for the philosophy of organism, the subject emerges from the world.'[39] Whereas *The critique of pure reason* describes a process through which the world is supposedly fitted into the categorial scheme of the subject, the philosophy of organism describes a process in which the world passes into subjective immediacy. The term used by Whitehead to indicate this primordial mode of the subject being affected by the world is 'perception in the mode of causal efficacy', as distinct from 'perception in the mode of presentational immediacy'. The latter refers to clear perception of a contemporaneous, spatially located area of the world by means of one of the senses, such as sight, or a combination of them. The former refers to the only vaguely discerned fact that the subject of perception is at a primordial physical level 'caused' by other things. So in contradistinction to Kant and the rationalists, who locate knowledge in the conceptual capabilities of the subject, and to the traditional empiricists who locate it in superficial sense awareness, Whitehead locates it in the subject being organically, on a physical level, imbedded in the causal network of the real world. Consciousness arises only in a late phase of complex integrations that constitute the world; it 'only dimly illuminates the prehensions in the mode of causal efficacy, because these prehensions are primitive elements in our experience'.[40]

This does not mean that Whitehead regresses to a framework of naive realism. He states clearly that he accepts 'the subjectivist bias of modern philosophy'.[41] According to his ontological principle[42] nothing is to be received into the philosophical scheme which is not discoverable as an element of subjective experience. This position, which he calls the 'reformed subjectivist principle', underlines the radically empiricist impetus of his philosophy. He speaks about an external world, but only as subjectively experienced.

All things are mutually immanent, not in the sense of passive static presence, but in the sense of dynamic interacting. From a thing, wherever its focal spatiotemporal region, its influence streams throughout the utmost recesses of space and time. For things 'are' what they do. The very meaning of existence is 'to make a difference'.[43] The most fundamental category in Whitehead's metaphysic is activity or, in his terminology, 'creativity'. All individual entities are individualisations of this primordial principle of creativity. For the present we abstract from the two derivative principles structuring the world, namely the principle of ideal entities ('eternal objects') and the principle of concretion ('God'[44]), and draw attention to his account of the mutual apprehension by entities of their mutual interacting. He explained this in terms of his theory of 'prehensions' (or feelings). 'Prehension' refers to the mutual involvement of actual entities. In keeping with his doctrine of causal efficacy, it is important to protect the theory of prehensions against subjectivist misinterpretation. It is not 'a quasi-mental 'grasping' of the antecedent data'[45] – any more than the being-acted upon may be construed as mere passive inertness. Acting on and being acted on are the two sides of interacting. Furthermore, Whitehead did not divorce physical interacting from mental interacting, but related them intimately. It adds up to a view of human experience as a particular manifestation of the cosmic fact of dynamic interacting, deeply rooted in the organic nature of reality. What humans apprehend, mentally and physically, is the stuff of reality itself. Humans have a direct experience of the world, which is a world of interrelatedness. Whitehead's contribution to a philosophy of religion lies not in his treatment of the special themes of 'religion' or 'God', but rather in his reconstruction of human existence in the world and human experience of the world, and his definition of the world.

Much older, and coming from a very different cultural setting, is the Buddhist religiophilosophical account of human experience. Without forcing any similarities with the Western scholars just discussed, it may be said without fear of contradiction that from its sober beginnings in the recorded teachings of Gautama to the speculative flights of Hua-Yen, Buddhism represented a consistent application of a conditionalist theory of the world and an empiricist theory of experience.

The most succinct ontological statement of early Buddhism recorded in the Pali canon is the formula:

> *When this is present, that comes to be; from the arising of this, that arises. When this is absent, that does not come to be; with the cessation of this, that ceases.*[46]

Kalupahana[47] draws attention to the 'objective' character of this all-encompassing and all-structuring causal principle called *idappaccayatā* ('conditionality'), *paṭiccasamuppāda* ('causality') and *kamma* ('action'), meaning that it was not just a mental construct. It refers not to a category of relations among ideas, but to a category of relations inherent in the actual world, human and nonhuman. Like Whitehead, early Buddhism accepted the causal relations themselves to be objects of experience.[48] The interdependent nature of reality is necessary and invariable, allowing no exceptions. Yet early Buddhism took care to steer clear of determinism and fatalism.

The interconnectedness was conceived of so that it also avoided the extreme of pure chance or indeterminism. Between determinism and haphazardness lies the universe of interrelatedness. This intuition was applied very much to the domain of the human psyche, especially to the spheres of morality and the perceptual process. Yet its relevance to the world of natural events and the interaction between human existence and the natural world was fully recognised.[49]

The teaching of interrelatedness expresses in positive terms what the teachings of *anatta* (nonsubstance), *anicca* (nonpermanence) and *dukkha* (nonsatisfactoriness) express in negative terms. The secret of human unhappiness is the persistent belief in self-contained entities. This belief is subverted. The world is a field of forces structured by interaction. The notion of 'action' (*kamma*) contains both elements: freedom, or creative novelty (to use Whiteheadian language), and the flow from action to causally produced results at all levels of reality. It would take us too far afield to explore all the varieties of Buddhist thinking used to articulate this vision philosophically throughout its history of two and a half millennia,[50] from the various doctrines of early Buddhism, such as Sarvastivada pluralistic realism, to the Mahayana vision of ontological emptiness (*sūnyatā*), reaching unequalled heights in the Hua-Yen philosophy of the unobstructed interpenetration of all things[51] and Dogen's philosophy of the absolute now: the dynamically unfolding reality that manifests itself in each and every particularity.[52] Buddhist philosophy in all its manifestations makes one point: the world is a flux of nonsubstantial factors. Everything else flows from this, the watershed between Buddhism and all forms of theism and monism. Yet it ties in remarkably well with nonsubstantialist forms of Western thinking.

Is there a basic flaw in the Buddhist thinking, in that the teaching of nonsubstantiality (*anicca-anattā*) must render meaningless such notions as friendliness, sympathy and devotion to others (traditionally expressed in the *Bodhisattva* ideal) in a world constituted by *paṭiccasamuppāda*? Is morality ultimately dispensable? No. Buddhism is not nihilism, teaching that nothing exists. It teaches that everything exists in relationships, and draws wide-ranging ethical implications from this.[53] A paradox? Perhaps. On the other hand, it is simply *religio perennis*: I am saved by losing myself. A comprehensive idea of universal interrelatedness is admittedly not limited to Buddhism. Yet the radicality with which this intuition has been worked out in Buddhism is unequalled.

How was this eternally existent pattern of things (the *dhammadhātu*) known, according to early Buddhism? The truth was empirically discoverable, not speculatively or by supernatural revelation, as some of its Vedic predecessors and Upanisadic contemporaries maintained. By that, early Buddhism meant that the limits of human knowledge were co-extensive with the limits of human experience. This included an amount of inductive reasoning. It would therefore be more correct to state that early Buddhism did imply a metaphysic (one based on actual experience, that is an empiricist metaphysic) than to insist that it was antimetaphysical in intent. What it did insist on was that any statement about the general character of the world should have a base in experience, that it should not exceed the limits of experience and that it should be relevant to the betterment of people's existence in the world. The empiricism of Buddhism is not a simplistic descriptivism, purporting to simply reflect a state of affairs immediately experienced in direct intuition. There is more to it. It contains an explanatory element as well. This becomes particularly apparent in the Yogacara philosophers of the third and fourth centuries CE. Their concept of *ālāyavijñāna*, for example, was no more a simple descriptive term than James's notion of pure consciousness, Jung's concept of the unconscious, or Whitehead's idea of a sub-sensory stream of causal efficacy.

The meditative way is a descent into the deep layers of human consciousness. The road to the inner depths passes through the levels of conceptual thinking, conations and emotions, into and beyond an equanimous state of mental purity, beyond the ordinary experiences of space and time and ordinary dichotomous (subject vs object) consciousness. At these levels a mode of experience far more subtle and sensitive than ordinary sense experience, although not radically discontinuous with it, becomes possible. These modes of depth experience are collectively known as 'higher knowledges' (*abhiññā*). Far from being tricks of the mind, these knowledges refer to an extraordinary degree of sensitivity and immediate contact with the pulse of fluid reality: the superficial patterns known through ordinary physical experience are transcended; perception of the hidden workings of human mind is greatly increased; and direct perception of the causal interdependence structuring all events in the non-substantialist universe becomes possible. Far beneath ordinary sense experience and thought, in the depths of the radically contingent matrix of reality itself, religious intuition discerns truth. The purpose of Buddhist meditation is enlightenment: an understanding, without intellectualisation and affective contamination, of reality as a web of relationships and an existence to match.

ENDNOTES

1 Cf V Brümmer (ed), *Interpreting the universe as creation*, Kampen: Kok Pharos, 1991 for various contributions highlighting the tensions of these interparadigmatic discussions.

2 H Plessner, in his major work *Die Stufen des Organischen und der Mensch: Einleitung in die philosophische Anthropologie*, Berlin: De Gruyter, 1928, identified the three life-worlds: the outside (natural) world, the inside (interior) world, and the social (intersubjective) world.

3 The term 'action' was given wide currency, following Max Weber (cf his *Wirtschaft und Gesellschaft*, Tübingen: Mohr [Paul Siebeck], 1972), and was developed by Alfred Schutz (*Collected papers*, Vol I: *The problem of social reality*, 1973), although neither of them defined it in a way that was fully adequate for a theory of religion. A further step was taken by phenomenological sociologists such as P L Berger & T Luckman, *The social construction of reality*, Harmondsworth: Penguin, 1966.

4 H R Niebuhr, *The responsible self: an essay in Christian moral philosophy*, New York: Harper & Row, 1963 developed this concept as a fruitful point of departure for a theory of religion.

5 Cf C Geertz, Religion as a cultural system, in M Banton (ed) *Anthropological approaches to the study of religion*, London: Tavistock, 1966, p 1ff.

6 Cf J D Barrow & F J Tipler, *The anthropic principle*, Oxford: Clarendon Press, 1986.

7 As H Mynarek does in his *Ökologische Religion: ein neues Verständnis der Natur*, München: Goldmann Verlag, 1986. Various implications and applications of such a religion of relationality have been spelled out by Griffin and his collaborators in D R Griffin (ed), *Sacred interconnections: postmodern spirituality, political economy, and art*, New York: State University of New York Press, 1990. A holistic motivation for an ecological religion has been put forward by J Fourie, S C J Joubert & J A Loader, Environmental education – an approach based on the concept of life, *Koedoe*, 1990, 33(1), pp 95–10; cf also J A Loader, Life, wonder and responsibility: some thoughts on ecology and Christian mission, in *Missionalia*, 1991, 19(1), pp 44–56.

8 Cf Whitehead's argument in *Nature and life*, Chicago: Chicago University Press, 1933, p 70ff against the scientific presupposition that mental functionings are not properly part of nature. On the contrary, he maintains, this 'sharp division between mentality and Nature has no ground in our fundamental observation' and that, in fact, 'we should conceive mental operations as among the factors which make up the constitution of Nature'.

9 W James, *Essays in radical empiricism: a pluralistic universe*, Gloucester, Mass: Smith, 1967. These essays, published separately between 1905 and 1907, were collected and published posthumously in 1912.

10 Ibid, p 42.

11 Ibid, pp 9ff.

12 The obvious links between James's thought and phenomenology has often caused him to be regarded as a pioneering phenomenologist – cf B Wiltshire, *William*

James and phenomenology, Bloomington: University of Indiana Press, 1968. Comparable to James's empiricism, Husserl's transcendental phenomenology eschews speculative world-hypotheses and restricts itself to the analysis and description of the 'data' of concrete experience. However, James is less open to Derrida's critique of the subjectivist substantialism lingering on in Husserl's thought (the transcendental ego).

13 James, *Essays ...*, pp 26ff.
14 Ibid, p 71. This concept appeared earlier in the postscript to his *The varieties of religious experience*, New York: Modern Library, 1902.
15 Ibid, p 80.
16 James, *The varieties of religious experience*, p 525.
17 Ibid, p 131.
18 For example in his *Re-visioning psychology*, New York: Harper & Row, 1975.
19 Cf his Psychology and religion (originally written in 1937) in *The collected works of C G Jung,* Vol 11, London: Routledge & Kegan Paul, 1958, pp 5ff; also his Foreword to White's 'God and the unconscious' in the same volume, pp 300ff. For a discussion of Jung and religion, see M Stein & R L Moore, *Jung's challenge to contemporary religion*, Wilmette, Ill: Chiron Press, 1987.
20 Archetypes are 'forms or images of a collective nature which occur practically all over the earth as constituents of myths and at the same time as autochtonous, individual products of unconscious origin. The archetypal motifs presumably derive from patterns of the human mind that are transmitted not only by tradition and migration but also by heredity. The latter hypothesis is indispensable, since even complicated archetypal images can be reproduced spontaneously without there being any possibility of direct tradition' (Jung, *Psychology and religion ...*, p 50).
21 Ibid, p 82.
22 Ibid, p 456.
23 Ibid, p 468.
24 Ibid, p 469.
25 Ibid, p 491.
26 Ibid, p 74.
27 Ibid, p 455.
28 J P Dourley, *C G Jung and Paul Tillich: the psyche as sacrament*, Toronto: Inner City, 1981, p 9.
29 Jung, *Collected works ...*, p 573.
30 A consensus of all nations – ibid, p 6.
31 Ibid, p 486.
32 Ibid, p 487.
33 Ibid, p 486.
34 Ibid, p 493.
35 A N Whitehead, *Process and reality: an essay in cosmology*, New York: Free Press, 1979 (1929 1), pp 3ff. Cf I Leclerc, *Whitehead's philosophy between rationalism and empiricism*, Leuven: Center for Metaphysics and Philosophy of God, 1984, pp 43ff.
36 The interplay between reason and observation is explained by comparing the true

method of discovery with the flight of an aeroplane: 'It starts from the ground of particularobservation; it makes a flight in the thin air of imaginative generalization; and it lands again for renewed observation rendered acute by rational interpretation' (Whitehead, *Process and reality ...*, p 5).

37 For this seminal distinction, cf his *Symbolism: its meaning and effect*, Cambridge: Cambridge University Press, 1958 (1927 1), and *Process and reality ...*, p 168ff.

38 *Process and reality*, p 148.

39 'Thus for Kant the process whereby there is experience is a process from subjectivity to apparent objectivity. The philosophy of organism inverts this analysis, and explains the process as proceeding from objectivity to subjectivity' (ibid, p 156).

40 Ibid, p 162.

41 Ibid, p 166.

42 Ibid, passim, eg pp 19, 24, 40.

43 Cf his *Adventures of ideas*, New York: Free Press, 1967 (1933 1), p 197.

44 For Whitehead, less radical than Buddhism, God as the principle of limitation and as such a nontemporal entity (not an actual occasion like the rest of the world) somehow remains outside the interdependence of all things (Whitehead, *Process and reality ...*, pp 342–351). Cf M Abe (edited by W R LaFleur), *Zen and Western thought*, London: Macmillan, 1985, pp 152–170.

45 Leclerc, *Whitehead's philosophy ...*, p 52.

46 The theme of *paṭicccasamuppāda* is dealt with often and variously in the Pali scriptures, for example in the *Mahanidana Sutta*; cf Bhikkhu Bodhi, *The great discourse on causation: the Mahanidana Sutta and its commentarial exegesis*, Kandy: Buddhist Publication Society, 1984. Among Western interpretations, see J Macy, *Mutual causality in Buddhism and general systems theory: the dharma of natural systems*, New York: State University of New York Press, 1991.

47 D J Kalupahana, *Causality: the central philosophy of Buddhism*, Honolulu: University Press of Hawaii, 1975.

48 Ibid, p 96.

49 Ibid, pp 110ff.

50 For what may constitute the essential thread of continuity in Buddhist thought, cf the contributions by M Pye (Comparative hermeneutics in religion), D Bastow (Continuity and diversity in early Buddhism) and K Werner (Authenticity in the interpretation of Buddhism), in M Pye & R Morgan (eds), *The cardinal meaning: essays in comparative hermeneutics: Buddhism and Christianity*, The Hague: Mouton, 1973.

51 Excellent treatises on the brilliant Hua-Yen religious thought are readily available today. Cf F H Cook's book *Hua-yen Buddhism: the Jewel Net of Indra*, London: Pennsylvania State University Press, 1977, as well as his various articles, e g The dialogue between Hua-yen and process thought, *Eastern Buddhist*, 17, 1984, pp 12–29; The Jewel Net of Indra, in J B Callicott & R T Ames *Nature in Asian traditions of thought: essays in environmental philosophy*, New York: State University of New York Press, 1989, pp 213–229; Garma C C Chang, *The Buddhist teaching of totality: the philosophy of Hwa Yen Buddhism*, London: Pennsylvania State University Press, 1977. For another fine comparison of Whiteheadian and Hua-Yen thought, cf S Odin, *Process metaphysics and Hua-yen Buddhism*, Albany: State University of New York Press, 1982.

52 Seven centuries after his death, the Japanese Zen teacher Dogen (1200–1253 CE) is finally coming into his own. Cf H-J Kim, *Dogen Kigen: mystical realist*, Tucson: University of Arizona Press, 1987. Cf also S Heine, *Existential and ontological dimensions of time in Heidegger and Dogen*, New York: State University of New York Press, 1985.

53 Cf R L F Habito, *Total liberation: Zen spirituality and the social dimension*, Maryknoll, NY: Orbis, 1989; K Jones, *The social face of Buddhism: an approach to political and social activism*, London: Wisdom, 1989; A H Badiner (ed), *Dharma Gaia: a harvest of essays in Buddhism and ecology*, Berkeley: Parallax, 1990.

4 The spiral movement

Integrating and transcending

There are times when people sense the world around them as an inviting and protective home, challenging them to explore, rewarding them for their efforts, and allowing for their mistakes. However, human beings also, and certainly more often, sense a threat of disjointedness in the ever-changing interplay that is reality. People have always sensed disjointedness in various well-known experiences. On the physical level, there are sickness and death; killing seems to be inherent in the nature of things; catastrophes such as droughts and earthquakes are part and parcel of reality. Conflict and war for domination are endemic in human society. Psychologically, most individuals are racked by anxiety and suffering. The problem of evil cannot be thought away.

There is an urgent universal human need to make sense of the world, to see the threatening chaos transformed into a meaningful cosmos. This is an empirical statement, saying how things are for humans – not a prescriptive one, saying how things ought to be. A basic orientation in the world would enable them to live happily and act responsibly, responding to reality in such a manner that their thoughts, words and deeds fit into a larger scheme, and thus are meaningful, 'good' and 'right'. That is the dream, and I would assign half the meaning of the word 'religion' to this *cosmic orientation* – no, cosmic *orienting*, with the emphasis on the ongoing *act* rather than on a supposed steady *state* of being oriented.

'Religion' as *comprehensive and radical integrating* therefore (partly) refers to humanity's effort to constitute a cosmos and to live in harmony with it. At certain times or in some respects it becomes a reality for some people and they joyously celebrate the way things are; for other people, at other times or in other respects, it remains a dream. But dreams are real. There remains the deep-seated need to experience the eternally shifting world as a coherent whole in which all things great and small, human and nonhuman, past and present, physical and mental, hang together, and thus to find peace. It is the insatiable longing to move beyond banality, evil, suffering, injustice, ugliness, un-truth and half-truth towards an ultimately integrating horizon. Humankind needs to relate meaningfully to the interrelatedness of the many. The historical religions are answers which have been evolved in an attempt to tame the confusing, threatening aspects of life by incorporating them into coherent patterns. Chaos becomes cosmos.

The integrating function has an 'objective' as well as a 'subjective' pole. The first refers to the world that is experienced, the second to the experiencing subject. The first provides a sense of integration; the second a sense of integrity. The latter pole has a social as well as an individual side: 'Who are we as a group?', and 'Who am I as an individual?'. These two questions cannot be divorced from 'What is the world?'. The search for personal and group identity[1] is closely interwoven with the search for the 'identity' of the cosmos. Societies, whether they be families or nations, churches or political parties, long for integrity, that is, inner completeness. Individuals long for this same sense of integrity. They want to know, feel and act in a coherent way, without inner conflict, and without conflict with fellow human beings and with the natural environment. One does not wish to think confusedly, feel lost or act aimlessly. To the extent that religion helps people to experience all things, and themselves in the midst of all things, as whole, it gives salvation. It reconciles one to oneself and to the world. One feels certain, has deep insight and acts correctly, one believes. Suffering becomes tolerable if one is liberated from the torment of senselessness. The confidence thus generated imbues individuals and groups with enormous strength and endurance.

However, what has been said so far must be severely qualified. It draws a picture of one of the two aspects of human life that I wish to highlight. There is a second aspect that must be emphasised equally strongly, in conjunction with the first: *transcending*. The human spirit is constantly seeking further, deeper, higher, beyond. It has a strange fascination with heights and depths of any sort, an enormous capacity for wonderment. 'Religion' is the most radical form of 'boundary experience', with the boundaries forever receding. The human mind needs to move towards an ultimately integrating horizon – and through and beyond every such horizon. It must and will go beyond the limits. This is not only an inherent drive of the human spirit. It is also forced on us by the changing external factors conditioning us. This is the second principle of religion, dialectically tied to the first: the need to penetrate and dis-integrate any received and achieved synthesis. Neither of the two principles or movements is reducible to the other.

Putting the two aspects together, religion can be described as a spiral movement towards ultimate width and depth, ultimate openness and coherence, consisting in the alternating, complementary, even mutually inherent experiences of integration and transcendence/penetration, the one shading into the other. It is a transcending with a view to integrating, and a transcending of every achieved totality. Both aspects are of equal importance in the urge defined here as 'religion'. Religion is the plumbing of every depth, the crossing of every boundary. It is the ultimate frontier experience, forever reaching out to the furthest, deepest, highest, widest limits of experience, inevitably defining it and then – prodded on by the everchanging sets of circumstances and by the inherent nature of this drive – wanting to leave the achieved experience of completeness behind as a conditioned thing, and the definition as a limitation. Religion is both rest and unrest, both settling and unsettling, both ordering and opening, both centring and exploding, both perching and flying, both reason and the dark side of reason when logic goes awry.

What we called *transcending* involves two movements. It moves outward, as described above, expansion making possible the progressive comprehension of limited closures of meaning into ever-widening complexities of interrelationships. It also moves inward into every completed act of comprehension, breaking open every closed system in which the exuberant play of factors has been encapsulated, freeing the inherent dynamic of relationships from fixation. It is more than just leaving things behind, leaving them as they are. It has a much more dramatic impact, allowing the celebration of pluralistic coherence. Religion is as much the breaking of all moulds as it is the creation of moulds. It is the definition of contexts, and it is also the unravelling of every definition so as to permit a never-ending redefinition of contexts. I believe that it is vitally important to recognise both the centripetal and centrifugal forces of religion. In the ongoing process of finding meaning, times of search are followed by times of maintaining what has been found, and invariably these are followed by times of destruction of what has been maintained. It would be truer to see these not as neatly serial stages, but as overlapping forces in a precarious effort to hang on between the disappearing old and the not-yet-arrived new. As a result of temperament, time and circumstances, some individuals in every society are pioneers, bold or reluctant, seeking out the new; some are consolidators, fanatic or merely cautious, of what has been found; and some the destroyers, brutal or pitiful, of what has been consolidated. In our own time South Africa is witnessing the disappearance from under our feet of an old order. We are moving into the field of gravity of a new horizon. Some things will be carried forward, and some left behind.

Viewed thus, religion is not a separate sphere with a separate object of experience, but is interconnected with various provinces of experience. It is the widest expansion, the deepest penetration of consciousness. Religion is the demand to follow this trend to the utmost. It is an extension and intensification of ordinary life, science and art, the predisposition for truth, beauty and goodness taken to the limits of comprehensiveness and radicality. I as an individual am constantly transcending the here and now in which I find myself[2] and constructing a world. We experience love, in which 'I' am transcended by and bound to 'you'; humour, which removes the sting from misery and relativises it; and hope, in which the present is transcended by the future. A flower dropping from a plant in the street that you walk every day on your way to work may awaken you to the mystery of genesis and decay. A thunderstorm confronts us with the awesome power of nature. Neither is religion fundamentally different from what humankind does in its science, art and philosophy. To the extent that science, art and philosophy proceed beyond technicalities and are taken up in the process of radically breaking open the given and fundamentally ordering the new, they are religious. Religion is not a separate province of experience. It is just exceptionally deep experience. The new science of our day is of enormous religious importance. The dominant set of modern scientific ideas (relativity, quantum theory, evolution, etc) have abrogated the old restricted vision of the world. Similarly, the great art of an epoch – its music, architecture, literature – reveals its perspective on the world. Religion is not to be found only in holy places such as churches and temples, in sacred ceremonies such as initiation rites, or in holy books. It is the experience of the boundary where the ordinary and the banal are contrasted with the deeply mysterious. It is an extension and exceptional intensification of a natural propensity of humankind, a normal function of the human spirit.

This is a dynamic view of religion, in that it is not restricted to the specific historic religions that have become institutionalised in the course of time. That is why I prefer to use the expressions 'transcending' and 'orienting', in order to emphasise the idea of an ongoing, dynamic process, an action capable of manifestation in innumerable different ways, rather than focus on the various institutionalised forms. The historical religions are the concretised forms of these frontier experiences; the landmarks, through many millennia, of human beings' intuitions of ultimate reality, truth, beauty and goodness. There is therefore every reason to treat such forms with great respect.

Westerners are inclined to think of religion in terms of the particular forms it has assumed in the West, in Judaism and in Christianity, where the concept of 'religion as faith in a personal God' is prevalent. But in a broad, inclusive sense religion is more than 'gods-diens' ('service to god[s]') – unless we take 'god' to mean whatever is at the heart of a person's world, and 'service' to mean a deep sense of awe. Our concept of religion must accommodate the symbols of depth in prehistoric cultures, as well as the intuitions of depth among (post-)modern people who have never seen the inside of a church. I certainly do not make a maximalist claim that the view of religion presented here is the only one, or that it is the 'true' definition of religion. Yet I would posit the minimum claim that it is a useful perspective in which to make sense of what has been up to this point in history, according to all available evidence, a characteristic aspect of humankind's existence in the world. In that sense, we may speak of *homo religiosus*.

From this point of view the concrete historical religions are not static, homogeneous entities. They are multiform, changing organisms,[3] each one of them caught up in vast historical processes. New religions are born as mutations of their predecessors – as Bushman religion evolved in ways unknown from unknown forms of prehistorical African religion, as Buddhism emerged from Hinduism, as Christianity emerged from Judaism. For millennia religions may adapt to fluctuating circumstances and eventually – although not necessarily – die. And dying is relative. The veneration of fire and water in contemporary Zoroastrianism goes back to prehistoric Stone Age nomads on the steppes of Inner Asia. Indeed, Zoroastrianism illustrates the argument developed here excellently. Itself rooted in unreachable Indo-European times and beyond, it has exerted immense influence on Judaism, Christianity and Islam, and even on Mahayana Buddhism. And each one of these religions is in its turn involved in the large-scale processes of religious giving and receiving; developing and changing; integration, disintegration and reintegration; decay and rebirth.

Add to this the internal pluralism of each religion, the factions and schools grinding against one another through centuries, the varieties and conflicts within each, and we discover that no religion has a stable identity. At most there is changing, developing continuity.[4]

There is a further sense in which religion should be conceived of in dynamic, conditionalist terms. It is not localised in any one isolated function of the human personality. It is widely acknowledged among scholars of religion that it is multidimensional,[5] a total response of the total person. Yet a number of interrelated aspects may be distinguished.

Thus religion has a cognitive dimension, finding expression in myths and dogmas. This relates it to metaphysical systems, even to science. It also has an affective dimension, which may range from joy to dread, from emotional attachment to morbid fear, from childlike trust to suspicion of the powers that run the world. In addition, it has a volitional dimension, motivating attitudes such as commitment and surrender. People are prepared to die for a religious conviction. This distinguishes it from a scientific theory. And then it has a behavioural dimension, inspiring action: the performance of set acts at set times in set ways (ritual) to express and invoke the mystery; and codes of morality which may extend to the most mundane aspects of life.

All of these dimensions have both an internal and an external side. They are private and individual; and they are institutionalised and social, perhaps even organised. Together, they may be regarded as a pattern of 'symptoms', allowing us to identify the manner and degree of religiousness displayed by phenomena – even quantitatively (if we wanted to). They may be condensed and combined in various ways to formulate definitions, types and so on – in short, to devise criteria for identifying religion.

As said above, from a diachronic point of view, religions are changing organisms developing through time. Should we analyse them synchronically, instead of looking at them as a given phase in a historical process, it appears that 'a' religion is indeed an enormous complex of interacting forces. Practices (for example rituals), teachings and social forms condition one another.

And each of the subsystems such as doctrine, practice and organisation is a constellation of mutually conditioning factors, caught up in processes of transformation. New patterns constantly emerge, and simultaneously make way for others.

The broad view of religion adopted here does not mean that all people are religious, or that all societies express the drive for ultimacy equally strongly. There are many types and degrees of the twin needs to heal and to break. Of course there are people who have no use for the experiences of transcending and totalising, or who have got stuck at some stage in the process. When we call religion a continuation of all sorts of experiences, it implies that not all those experiences are religion in the full sense of the word. Where we locate the cut-off point between not-yet-religion and full religion, where we allow 'comprehensive' integrating and 'radical' transcending to begin, and where 'absolute' truth, beauty and goodness appear are largely matters of stipulation. They are relative, not exact. These may be points of debate and difference of opinion, dictated largely by the demands of a particular context.

Phenomena which fall outside religion may be classified in two types: phenomena that are open to religious deepening, and phenomena that obstruct the process of radical transcending and totalising. To the first type belong experiences of the grandeur of nature, of love, humour, death, or hope; on another level, science and art; some manifestations of modern atheism. Obstruction is antireligion. A case in point would be nihilism, as the consistent denial of meaning. Of course, there are also less systematic and less integral forms of nihilism. Some people are simply not interested. Nihilism may also arbitrarily elevate to the status of quasi-absolute values things which manifestly cannot have any ultimate meaning. Textbook examples from our era are those ideologies in which race or nation was elevated to the status of ultimate values. Or power, wealth, learning or technology may acquire pseudo-ultimate meaning. Needless to say, in terms of comprehensive, radical orienting, such fixations are not very advanced.

The perspective suggested here moves between integration and transcendence, rather than depicting a homeostatic, stable middle position between two extremes. Equally important, I wish to avoid entrapment in either of the two in a binary opposition. In a sense, of course, it is a movement of integration. But I qualify that immediately by insisting that it is an open-ended perspective, useful in our cultural context, I trust, and with greater power of penetration than theories of religion that would walk on just one leg. Besides, even a radical theory of disorder could lose sight of its own sociohistorical contextuality and become a new integral position, a new establishment with a tyrannical streak. Let me add that although the perspective developed in these essays is highly critical of substantialist thinking, it is also historical: it accepts that there are certain pan-human continuities persisting throughout the course of human history. I do not see how intercultural debate can be conducted without some acceptance of diachronic and synchronic cross-cultural continuities.

Individuals and societies oscillate in the dialectic pull and push of opposing forces, between the frightful whirlpools of chaos on the one hand and the perilous cliffs of closed order on the other. At both ends the sweet songs of sirens lure into anarchy or tyranny. We are also pushed and pulled forward into those rapids, and do not pass through unscathed. To change the metaphor, the ideal (the religious ideal, shall we say) would be to move outwards in a continuous spiral from small identity/integration through transcendence to wider identity/transcendence, from small transcendence through intermediate consolidation to larger transcendence, on to infinite largeness. Or, conversely, to spiral inwards into infinite depth.[6]

But it is not simple progress. Such a smooth continuity is a utopian dream. The reality is one of crises and catastrophes. Within each *pax* the seeds of its overthrow are germinating, and within each revolution something of the old order is carried on and the next status quo is eager to settle. Restorations of past orders and impositions of final solutions do not solve this ambivalence. At best a permanent revolution of sorts may be achieved. Play, and jokes, are ways of shaking the cage. But that act of breaking out can be extremely painful – psychological dismemberment, philosophical destruction, iconoclasm, heresy. Yet it is inevitable and necessary, like darkness and death, the corollaries of light and life. Transgression of the boundaries may unleash the demons lurking in the soul. All this is not evil. The good is the movement, whether with ease or with great difficulty, into deeper and larger complexities. Evil is the reversal or obstruction of that process in either of its alternate episodes. It is irrelation, rejection of the co-inter-acting with the multitude of others.

The complementarity and mutual involvement of opposites set out above are merely a rather cerebral restatement of the ancient mystical intuition that has been expressed in symbols such as the serene Taoist *yin-yang*, the sexual Tibetan *yab-yum*,[7] the perennial contrasts of female-male, night-day, death-life, winter-summer. It has been told dramatically in the Babylonian myth of Marduk, the creator of the cosmos and hero of the struggle against chaos, doing mortal battle with Tiamat, the dragon of the unbounded, chaotic sea. In India it appears in the myths of Vishnu, the benevolent preserver of settled society and principle of conservation, who is opposed to yet inseparable from Shiva, the principle of fertile explosion, the patron of outcasts and outlaws. This same ambivalence appears in the Greek mythical figures of Apollo and his orgiastic brother and contrasting counterpart, Dionysus, the night prowler.[8]

A new era is emerging after the demise of modern mechanistic science (the automatised world) and the decline of supranaturalistic religion (the external God)[9] in the West. In this era, after classical science and classical theology, that ancient intuition may be assuming the role of a master paradigm, in science as well as in the new religion.[10] The cutting-edge today is the search for a new integration, but beyond neat rationalistic schemes. For example, in psychology (biogenetic structuralism) it emerges as the tuning between the complementary ergotropic and trophotropic neural systems, the first ensuring bursts of creative, moment-to-moment adaptation of the organism to its environment (roughly what we called 'transcending'), the second effecting the longer periods of rest and recuperation (roughly what we called 'integrating').[11] In quantum physics (for example as extended in the thought of David Bohm) the world, instead of being an explicate order of separate entities, becomes a flux of events and processes in the movement of becoming, a multidimensional implicate order in which everything is enfolded into everything and in which subtotalities are simply relatively independent abstractions from the ongoing process.[12] In this century for the first time Western cosmology conceived of an (at present still) expanding and (eventually) contracting universe, pulsating in an eternal rhythm without absolute beginning or absolute end, and with the implication that an external God is excluded.[13] In all branches of physics, Prigogine and Stengers conclude, moving as these disciplines are towards multiplicity, temporality, instability, fluctuation, complexity and radical uncertainty, 'nonequilibrium brings "order out of chaos'."[14] Searching for a Christian natural theology, John Polkinghorne portrays 'a world with ragged edges, where order and disorder interlace each other and where the exploration of possibility by chance will lead not only to the evolution of systems of increasing complexity, endowed with new possibilities, but also to the evolution of systems imperfectly formed and malfunctioning'.[15] The evolution of the universe is characterised by 'the fruitful interrelation of randomness and orderliness ... the interplay of chance and necessity'.[16]

For a theory of education, the complementarity of integration and transcendence means that child and adult in all spheres of life move from stage to stage, station to station. Forward leaps of discovery alternate with periods of consolidation. The yeast of growth must constantly be kneaded into life as a whole. In terms of religious education it means that the young child's as well as the adolescent's need for security must be counterbalanced by the contrasting need to explore the wide world with all the risks this entails. The child needs acceptance as well as challenge. The wise educator knows how to administer the right mix – but has no guarantee that the process of growth will continue.

For a theory of social institutionalisation, it sheds light on (among other things) the careers of religious organisations and the distinction between 'church' and 'sect'. Church finds itself close to the gravitational centre of societal forces in a given society; it is the area of synods, popes and dogmas. Sect finds itself on the periphery of the larger field, in the process of out-swing from the centre, or in the reverse process of in-swing towards the centre; it is the area of persecuted heretics, marginal minorities and creative nonconformists. In themselves, churches and sects may find themselves in the process of disintegration or, conversely, condensation to become centres of power, large or small. Equally, it sheds light on the continual syncretising and schismatising processes between various religions. Never a stable moment. Interplaying with hosts of broad social forces, religion is in a phase of greater inclusiveness on a world scale.

For a theory of knowledge, it means that knowing is to shape and organise the sensed in a process of orientation to and osmotic exchange with the world, from which the knower is not separate. Knowledge is clarity of recognition within a structured context (order); ignorance is the unclarity of not-(yet-)order, or no-longer-order, a lack of comprehension – that is, of a comprehended context. Knowledge is an act of perception of meaningful patterns (sets of coherent relationships). 'Truth' is not correspondence or even reference to extracontextual ('brute') reality; it expresses ordered experience and intracontextually produced ('made') facts. It cannot be absolute, only optimally context-related. Since the process of knowing turned into uncertainty, and vice versa, is continuous, knowledge, uncertainty and ignorance are not stark alternatives, but shade into each other and merge like light, shadow and darkness. At the radical and comprehensive level of mystical religion, Cusanus expressed the dialectic and mutuality of order-disorder paradoxically as learned ignorance (*docta ignorantia*), the coincidence of opposites (*coincidentia oppositorum*).

For a theory of science, it means that periods of consolidation in fixed disciplines, in definite bodies of knowledge and in powerful groups of experts are always threatened (and sooner or later followed) by periods of disintegration. Heretics challenge and sooner or later overthrow the established order. Why? Because, failing to provide answers to new questions in a changing environment, the established order loses its inner drive and becomes boring. Inner and outer integration break down. A new round starts.

Symbolic connections

How are the dizzy multitude of items in and around us integrated into coherent networks of meaningful relationships? By symbols (etymologically derived from 'putting together'). Symbols focus and order the motley impressions crowding in on my sensorium, aligning me with my fellows and nature, constituting the world. They establish networks of association among what would otherwise have remained an utter confusion of sensory stimuli. They are the frames creating order out of chaos, constructing a world out of an undifferentiated energy field. Without them we grope in the dark.

In its widest and simplest sense, symbolism means that some components of our experience are associated with and evoke other components of that experience. It is the basic mechanism by means of which people communicate with the world and with each other in the world about aspects of it, ranging from everyday life to art, science and religion. In chapter 3 the mental picture of a triangle, and in this chapter of a spiral, operated as symbols. An obvious example of symbolism is language. A certain sound that we hear or a certain combination of letters that we see evokes the mental picture of a dog; indeed, it evokes the dog itself, with all the emotional and other associations, such as affection or fear, of this picture. A symbol glides polysemically into an enormously complex field of expanding mutual references between items in our experience. The item that refers is the 'symbol'; the items referred to (that is implied) by the symbol in the association are its 'meaning'.

The word 'evoke' was used above to indicate the relationship between two items in human experience. What this means needs some further clarification. It certainly entails much more than mere comparison, which would only imply that A is like B. There are various degrees of intensity in the linkage of A with B. A may just neutrally remind one of B. It may carry strong emotional overtones, so that emotions associated with A are also associated with B. Emotions concerning B may be intensified considerably by linking it with A and thus with the emotions associated with A. Emotions about certain things in life are then aroused *via* the emotions that we already have about certain other things in life. Things are not linked at an emotional level only. The linking may include belief, understanding, even ways of acting. A traffic sign – for example a red-edged blue triangle framing a picture of a sheep – represents a set of things that we *know*: there are sheep around; it also evokes an appropriate *attitude* or *emotion*: extreme care; and it ensures a course of *action*: slow down. Symbols do the same at a deeper level.

Symbolism is the establishment of relations between things. It is an act of synthesis, that is, of connecting things, so that they become more than bits of flotsam and jetsam slung around in chaos. Through these synthetic acts of connection we humans establish meaning. Religion expresses the need to achieve comprehensive, radical meaning, through the establishment of comprehensive, radical coherence. It is an act of ultimate synthesis, attempting (even if not succeeding) to include even suffering, even evil. The act of integrating proceeds symbolically, as does the act of transcending: sparks of new meaning jump across the gaps between previously insignificant, isolated items of experience as the net of relationships is cast wider and wider.

Let us return to the triad described in the previous chapter. It is of great importance to the individual to achieve internal harmony; it is also of great importance to human society to achieve harmony, while allowing for some individual diversity, just as it is important that nature be seen as a coherent continuity from the past, through the present, to the future. If each of these harmonies is seen as an angle of a triangle, then religion is the circle, or better, the globe embracing and integrating all three – yet, given the pluralistic nature of the world, a globe that cannot be located, whose centre and circumference is nowhere and everywhere. A globe is of course a religious symbol par excellence; it evokes associations of perfect wholeness. 'Depth' is another symbol, eliciting all the emotions that go with discovery of the unfathomableness of reality. In the monotheistic religions 'Father' and 'King' present the unsayable ultimate in familiar images of power and trust. In Buddhism 'path' is a symbol for the gradual discovery of the ultimate, whereas the discovery itself is expressed as 'en-light-enment'. As Eliade described it,[17] everything in human experience – from sky, sun, moon and water to stones, earth, woman and plants – can become and in fact probably was at some time a vehicle for the ingression of the 'sacred' into 'profane' reality. Eliade's view of the religious role of symbolism may be illustrated by his observation about rocks:[18]

> *The hardness, ruggedness, and permanence of matter was in itself a hierophany in the religious consciousness of the primitive. And nothing was more direct and autonomous in the completeness of its strength, nothing more noble or more awe-inspiring, than a majestic rock, or a boldly-standing block of granite ... In its grandeur, its hardness, its shape and colour, man is faced with a reality and a force that belong to some world other than the profane of which he is himself a part. We can hardly say that men have always adored stones simply as stones. The devotion of the primitive was in every case fastened on something beyond itself which the stone incorporated and expressed.*

Where we should fault Eliade is in his restriction of this kind of experience to 'primitive' people. The suppression of religious symbolism in the modern time since the sixteenth century in the West (especially in Protestantism) was an unfortunate impoverishment of human spirituality. In our day such symbolism is starting to reassert itself. The world is being rediscovered by many as immensely rich with vast treasures of meaning, concealed just under the surface of the familiar. The ordinary world is no longer sterile. It is pregnant with religious meaning. That realisation was not unique to 'primitive' people.

Symbolism plays a role at all levels of religious experience. Symbols are replete with their religious referents. In dogma, words and abstract concepts stand for hidden dimensions of reality. In ritual, certain actions (for example dancing) efficaciously cause the presence of the sacred. But nowhere is symbolism more powerfully present than in religious art. Painting, sculpture and music bring forth the emotions and attitudes related to the Depth. Elementary colours and geometrical forms reveal the nature of reality and the structure of the human psyche in which universal reality is reflected – for example, the sphere represents perfection as well as fullness of potential, completeness as well as dynamism. Blue may symbolise metaphysical potentiality, green the harmony of nature, and so forth.[19]

The power of individual symbols does not last forever. They can wither away and die, losing their integrative and penetrating power in the experience of people.[20] As old symbols die, new ones may arise to express the intuition of the ultimate meaning of the world. As said above, 'meaning' is a function of relationships between items in our experience.

The dynamics of the lighting up and paling of symbols may be explained in terms of the inextricable nexus of person, society and nature. Homo sapiens is deeply embedded in nature, having arisen from it in the long course of the mutual adaptation of the elements of nature, which is the process of evolution. The power of sun and moon, rocks and mountains, fire and water, plants and animals, man, woman and child have been bred into mentality from the beginning, through the long chain of evolution. In Jungian terms, the collective unconscious is a storehouse of potential symbols, stocked from the dawn of time through the interaction of developing mentality with the developing world.

The person is deeply embedded in humankind, having arisen from it. It therefore shares the common symbols not only of humanity as such, but also of the particular society of which it is a member. The collective symbols of society bind the individual members to the meanings important to that society. The individual is integrated with society, and through society with nature, via the communal symbols of society. This places into context Geertz's emphasis on the social nature of symbolism when,[21] in his famous definition, religion is called

> *a system of symbols which acts to establish powerful, pervasive, and long-lasting moods and motivations in men by formulating conceptions of a general order of existence and clothing these conceptions with such an aura of factuality that the moods and motivations seem uniquely realistic.*

In other words, by means of symbols society prescribes to the individual what the world is and how to respond to it. But apart from historically particular group symbols, the individual, by virtue of the relationship between the ego and its own depths in collective humanity, has access to a vast reservoir of symbols. This was stressed by Jung, who grounded symbol formation in the primordial images (archetypes) of the collective unconscious.

Through humankind, the individual person is deeply embedded in nature, and has at its disposal in its unconscious a vast array of symbols connecting it with nature. So the great religious symbols are not arbitrary and trivial signs that may be invented or discarded at will. They are imbedded in the human mind as so many potential bridges for the transmission of meaning between humans and the vast universe.

Symbols are part of a shifting world in which nothing remains constant. Changes in social structure or in the interrelations between humanity and nature can therefore have far-reaching effects on the symbolism of a society. This explains why sometimes, for some societies structured along certain sociopolitical and economic lines, 'king' or 'father' may be *fitting* symbols for 'God'; these images may establish a satisfactory and successful link between familiar things and the mysterious meaning of reality as a whole. At other times, for other societies, structured along different sociopolitical and economic lines, 'mother' played the same role, as the history of religion proves.

New symbols are not made; they are found – or rather, we are found by them as much as we find them. The startlingly new energising of a familiar element of our experience to suddenly start glowing, illuminating the dark background of the world, is what 'revelation' means. The process may also be described from the other end: revelation is the powerful ingression of the hidden into the field of the manifest through association with familiar things.

In his theory of symbolism, on which this discussion is largely based, Whitehead[22] explains symbolism in terms of his distinction between 'presentational immediacy' and 'causal efficacy'. 'Presentational immediacy' refers to our perception of the world through our senses. It perceives and presents the world contemporaneously in its immediacy. This kind of perception is clear. It is also superficial, being a recent acquisition in the process of evolution. Therefore only advanced organisms have this ability. 'Causal efficacy', on the other hand, refers to a much more primitive mode of perception of the world. The other things are experienced vaguely, yet are inescapably forceful as things that take hold of us. It is a 'heavy, primitive experience', and discloses a very deep fact of actual, causal encounter: the vague, deep perception living things have of being affected, changed, caused by other things through time. This is not unique to humans; plants, for example, respond to light under the same heavy influence. But symbolism is unique to humans. It occurs when the readily available, handy, definite and manageable sense data illuminate the unmanageable, amorphous, ill-defined depth of experience. The familiar items of experience evoke very important yet only vaguely perceived items of experience. Although he does not speak of religion here, Whitehead's description of these depths strongly suggests religion. In his words:

> *But for all their vagueness, for all their lack of definition, these controlling presences, these sources of power, these things with an inner life, with their richness of content, these beings, with the destiny of the world hidden in their natures, are what we want to know about.*[23]

We must not be misled by his use of the word 'primitive' for these depth experiences. Symbolism does not bring about a primitivisation of human mentality, back to the amoeba; rather, it brings about heightened awareness of the hidden forces that operate inexorably in and on the human being.

Symbolism, as understood here, serves to correct the view currently dominant in studies of mysticism, namely that mysticism (that is experience of the depth dimensions of reality) is completely encapsulated in linguistic interpretations: in other words, that mystics are trapped in the particular doctrinal frameworks of their respective religions. This point was raised in chapter 2, in connection with the implications of linguistic empiricism. In our present context, we are entitled to argue that linguistic frameworks themselves are part and parcel of the symbolic process. While they point to the mystery and effectively cause it to be present, they are historically relative. They come and go, and are replaced by other symbolisms. The mystery forges its own new pathways.

The cycle of symbolic integration and reintegration of experience proceeds beneath the level of analytical, conceptual thought. These potent gestalts are discovered at the level of intuitive, instinctual 'feel'. They are polysemic, indefinite, half-known. Signs, on the other hand, being accepted conventions, are fixed, unambiguous, fully known. Signs float on the surface, symbols closely follow the contours of the deep. The clear conceptual categories of rational thought lose their firm outlines, and are replaced by the dark shadowy figures of symbols, suggestive of primal forces of the soul and the world. Arguments marching in file are ousted by spirits, animals and forces of nature as symbols combine to form symbolic clusters, recounted in myths. Symbols and myths create the world in terms of verbs and processes; analytical thought recreates it in terms of nouns and fixed entities. Go deeper than the symbols, and nonarticulate consciousness passes into nonarticulate stream of reality.

Whereas Whitehead stresses the derivation of symbols from the impact of the external world, Jung stresses the emanation of symbols from the deepest layers of the structure of the human psyche itself. It is also significant that as far as the relationship between the individual and the universally human unconscious is concerned, Jung emphasises individual symbol formation, although not at the expense of collective symbol formation.[24] In times of crisis, when a collective symbol system breaks down on a vast scale or when some individuals get hopelessly estranged from an existing one, those individuals may fall back on their own, very personal contact with the unconscious. One may develop one's own symbols. As was argued throughout, these three possibilities may be combined in a triadic structure of the individual, the collective and nature. A theory of religious symbolism must incorporate all three.

All of this has a direct bearing on the religious situation in South Africa at the moment. Our fragmented society needs to rediscover our *organic involvedness in nature*, to escape from the one-dimensionality brought about by modern technocracy – the more so since technology is spuriously being presented to us, as to all nonindustrialised countries of the world, as holding the promise for a new future. It needs to rediscover the vast resources for universal religious awareness that are present in our *common human mentality*. And it needs to rediscover the creative possibilities of being a *person* in the true sense of word – free not to conform, but to be original.

For us as a human community, reality does not exist outside the web of words in which we and the world seem to be suspended; and yet we know that the world is more than our words. When using the word 'religion', one is confronted with the dilemma that even if it is defined as ambivalent, the act of defining isolates and fixes it. In a way, by attaching a meaning to the word, what has been said above about 'religion' probably amounts to a definition of sorts. But not in the strict sense of delimiting it unambiguously. Instead, I try to follow it as one would follow a theme woven into a musical composition, interested to observe how it blends and eventually disappears into wider complexities. The above description of religion is shipwrecked on the beach of undifferentiated reality. Perhaps 'shipwrecked' is too strong a term. Perhaps our ship could simply be beached on that coast, enabling us to return from the realm of the undifferentiated to the differentiated world of conceptual thought – and to visit it again.

ENDNOTES

1 H Mol made the concept of identity the focal point of his theory of religion. See his *Identity and the sacred: a sketch for a new social-scientific theory of religion*, Oxford: Blackwell, 1976. Closely related is the systems-theoretical view of J S Cumpsty, *Religion as belonging: a general theory of religion*, New York: University Press of America, 1991. Proceeding from the assumption that the two basic human drives are the drive for physical survival and the drive for identity (ibid, p 161), religion 'is concerned with belonging, affectively and cognitively, individually and probably corporately, to that which emerges within the whole transitory parade of experience as the ultimately-real' (ibid, p 159).

2 For the relevance of this quality of transcendence to religion, see T Luckmann, *Das Problem der Religion in der modernen Gesellschaft*, Freiburg: Verlag Rombach, 1963; also T Luckmann, Religion in der modernen Gesellschaft, in J Wössner (Hg), *Religion in Umbruch: soziologische Beiträge zur Situation von Religion und Kirche in der gegenwärtigen Gesellschaft*, Stuttgart: Enke Verlag, 1972.

3 See N Smart, *Beyond ideology: religion and the future of Western civilization*, London: Collins, 1981, pp 49ff on the organic nature of religious systems.

4 Ibid, p 50 on 'Christianity' as a 'pigeonhole rather than a name tag', and also the chapter by P Moore, Christianity and the study of religion, in *Buddhist studies ancient and modern* (eds P Denwood & A Piatigorski), London: Curzon Press, 1983, pp 71–91.

5 For the dimensions of religion, see N Smart, *The phenomenon of religion*, London: Macmillan, 1973; and his *The religious experience of mankind*, New York: Scribner's, 1976; also M B King & R A Hunt, *Measuring religious dimensions: studies of congregational involvement*, Dallas: Southern Methodist University, 1972.

6 For the spiral as a mystic symbol, see J & M Argüelles, *Mandala,* Boulder, London: Shambhala, 1972; J Purce, *The mystic spiral: journey of the soul*, London: Thames & Hudson, 1974.

7 Cf C D Laughlin, J McManus & E d'Aquili, *Brain, symbol and experience: toward a neurophenomenology of human consciousness*, Boston: Shambhala, 1990, pp 208ff.

8 Cf A Daniélou, *Gods of love and ecstasy: the traditions of Shiva and Dionysus*, Rochester, Vt: Inner Traditions, 1992 (1979 1); W Burkert, *Greek religion, archaic and classical*, Oxford: Blackwell, 1985 (1985 1), pp 223ff.

9 For the likely resonance (mutual amplification) between these two discourses, see I Prigogine & I Stengers, *Order out of chaos: man's new dialogue with nature*, London: Heinemann, 1984, pp 44ff.

10 A substantial body of literature has grown over the last few decades to forge a synthesis in the West between new, postclassical science and new, postclassical religion. One example of such a merger, from a Jungian perspective, is J Hitchcock, *The web of the universe: Jung, the 'new physics' and human spirituality*, New York: Paulist Press, 1991.

11 Laughlin, McManus & d'Aquili, *Brain, symbol and experience* ..., pp 313ff.

12 D Bohm, *Wholeness and the implicate order*, London: Routledge & Kegan Paul, 1980.

13 S W Hawking, *A brief history of time from the big bang to black holes*, London: Bantam, 1988.

14 Prigogine & Stengers, *Order out of chaos* ..., p 287.

15 J Polkinghorne, *Science and creation: the search for understanding*, Boston: Shambhala, 1989, p 49.

16 Ibid, p 47.

17 M Eliade, *Patterns of comparative religion*, New York: New American Library, 1958.

18 Ibid, p 216.

19 Cf Lama A Govinda, *Creative meditation and multi-dimensional consciousness*, London: Allen & Unwin, 1977.

20 Eliade speaks of the degradation and infantilisation of symbols as they come to be interpreted on lower and lower planes. Cf Eliade, *Patterns* ..., pp 440ff.

21 C Geertz, Religion as a cultural system, in M Banton (ed) *Anthroplogical approaches to the study of religion*, London: Tavistock, 1966, pp 1–46.

22 A N Whitehead, *Symbolism: its meaning and effect*, Cambridge: Cambridge University Press, 1958 (1927 1); *Process and reality* ..., pp 168ff.

23 Whitehead, *Symbolism* ..., p 57.

24 For a comparison of symbolism according to Jung and Paul Tillich, see J P Dourley, *The psyche as sacrament*, Toronto: Inner City, 1981, pp 31ff. Tillich gave a clear summary of his theory of symbolism in his *Symbol und Wirklichkeit*, Göttingen: Vandenhoeck & Ruprecht, 1962.

II

DIMENSIONS OF ENQUIRY INTO RELIGION

In Part II various dimensions of enquiry into religion will be discussed. In one (rather mechanical) sense these dimensions could be presented as distinct steps:

(1) getting the external data
(2) introspection
(3) understanding the intended meaning
(4) theory formation
(5) evaluation
(6) religious thought
(7) mysticism
(8) morality

Dimensions (1) and (2) will be discussed in chapter 5; (3) in chapter 6; (4) in chapter 7; (5) in chapter 8; and (6), (7) and (8) in chapter 9. Shifting from one to the other will be similar to changing the gears of a heavy vehicle: smoothly and without grinding them, starting with first gear and moving up or down, as required. Making clear when one is doing what would obviate a lot of misunderstanding.

In another (more organic and more satisfactory) sense, they are mutually implied, a galaxy in which any one dimension could be at the centre at any time, involving all the others. Not good enough are philosophy of religion not steeped in history of religions, fieldwork without theoretical and philosophical sensitivity, theory ignoring its own moral dimension, and so on. The dimensions analysed here are not claimed to be exhaustive. For example, the requirement of definitional clarity and consistency certainly has its place.[1]

Whereas only (1) and (4) of these dimensions would fit a narrow nonnormative model of religious studies/religion studies/science of religion,[2] (2) and (3) would tie in with a phenomenological model. Between them (1) to (4) jointly make up the core of the discipline of religious studies as generally defined. Number (5) would count as philosophy of religion, but (6) less readily so. The last three dimensions (6), (7) and (8) of what I call comprehensive *enquiry into religion*[3] would fall altogether outside most of the currently accepted models of religious studies/religion studies/science of religion. Yet I believe that such an inclusive methodological paradigm, allowing for specialisation but at the same time coordinating such specialisation, is what is needed in the end. Only then a field of study (demarcated by academic convention; let's call it 'religion') would be 'studied' (that is researched, taught, investigated) comprehensively. At the same time such a paradigm should remain open-ended and adaptable, merging with disciplines that focus on related areas of human life such as society, the psyche, history, and so on. Of course none of this is absolute and final. Absolutised disciplinary boundaries stifle rather than promote focused research. The model proposed here would encourage cross-fertilisation between religious studies and adjacent disciplines and the integration of their approaches and findings with its own frame of reference.[4]

As for theology: to the extent that the study of any one religion (its classical texts, history, forms of organisation, beliefs and so on) moves decisively away from a monoreligious horizon to a pluralistic horizon, both in principle and in practice; and is done empirically, not claiming privileged access to a supernatural realm, it would be part of such a comprehensive programme of enquiry into religion/religious studies – but it would not be theology as usually understood. To the extent that a study of any one religion is absorbed in the self-vindication of that religion, proclaiming *the* truth, it will not be part of such a comprehensive, homoversal programme.

5 Looking outwards and inwards

A starting point for enquiry into religion is lively curiosity about the concrete world surrounding us. Southern Africa offers a wide open invitation to observe and describe the fascinating religious aspects of a society in rapid change. To the young at heart and open-minded for whom life is a voyage of discovery full of surprises, sympathetic curiosity about religious matters comes naturally. One of the most depressing aspects of our society is to observe how many people still believe that they can be loyal to their own convictions only by looking down their noses, with pursed lips and empty if not hostile eyes, at others' efforts at making sense of life. Normal healthy people are fascinated by birds, reptiles, dinosaurs, stars, music and what not; why not, then, by all the different ways, some sublime, some admittedly bizarre, in which people have tried to move beyond the banalities and threats of life and to achieve an all-embracing understanding of the world? We live in a polyreligious world, and our region is a gold mine in this respect. Fortunately there seems to be an upsurge of interest in the plurality of religions among the general public. Increasingly people want to become acquainted with the 'facts' of the religions around them. When did Mohammed live? What is the Bhagavadgita? What are the teachings of the Greek Orthodox Church? These questions lie on the fairly superficial (but nevertheless important) level of simple *factual, descriptive* understanding – the level of who? what? where? when?.

Religious studies as an academically established enterprise does this fact-finding in a methodical, disciplined manner, using the same research procedures and techniques as other social sciences. These range from *quantitative* ways (counting, sampling, using questionnaires, scales of measurement, graphic representation of results in tables and diagrams, and statistical manipulation of findings) to *qualitative* ways (concentrating on the quality of interaction between the researcher and the people researched). Either of the two basic procedures may be useful, and decisions regarding research procedures are made on pragmatic grounds.

The dimension of commitment to observing the real world out there, establishing the 'facts', is an implication of the empiricism discussed earlier. Extrospection saves us from abstract theorising that is not organically tied to reality 'out there'. It is equally important to emphasise that *data* are 'given' and that *facts* are 'made'/'produced' by the wider contexts in which they occur and from which they emerge, including the context of interaction between the seen and the seer. The mark of good enquiry (research) is that it is specific and does not deal with vague generalities. It has a passion and a sharp eye for detail. It is focused – yet, in relating the uniquely concrete to wider patterns, it is not a mere piling up of trivialities.

The relationship between a single datum and the plurality of factors from which it derives its meaning can be illustrated by the complex concept 'religion'. To speakers of Western languages the word 'religion' may seem to refer very straightforwardly to a thing out there. However, this concept and the words expressing it are not universally found in other languages. There is no direct and immediate correspondence between this Western word/concept and a simple, observable datum or entity (a 'thing') in the world out there. 'Religion' is a complex idea, by means of which we link a wide range of other data. Most of what we ordinarily call 'facts', meaning that they are perfectly obvious, there for everyone to see, are not really simple data of experience at all. The 'facts' of everyday life are the products of standardised, generally agreed upon ways of organising the world. Scientific 'facts' are the same, this time agreed upon by a community of scholars. Even seemingly simple concepts such as 'altar', 'holy book' or 'prayer' are complex compounds. We see a certain facial expression, a certain bodily posture, hands folded in a certain way; we hear certain sounds, uttered in a certain way, and after a number of exposures to these and in communication with fellow human beings, we add them all up and conclude that that particular group of data that we are observing is 'prayer'. To 'see' prayer, religion and so on is therefore not to pounce on entities with definite contours. It is more like the diagnostic work of a doctor: the recognition of a set (pattern, class) of symptoms, thanks to previous experience, one's own and that of one's fellows, which has grown into an interpretive framework.

It presupposes wide background knowledge. The more we know beforehand, the more we see. The concept 'religion' is particularly saturated with theoretical meaning. The content one attaches to it will be determined by one's overall theoretical position. In this sense, 'religion' is the sediment of theory. The concept is abstract, but by linking together aspects of experience it 'gives' a *datum*. The womb of the context produces the *fact*.

To use the picture of the triangle again: interacting with you (making an us) and interacting with the world, I see and name 'facts'. No less than the facts out there, 'I' am a shifting, conditioned knot where various lines of action in the dynamic network of the world intersect. 'I' too, the person, am a *datum*, a *fact*, made up of a multiplicity of aspects – yet not a mere product, but a source of effective energy, keeping the wheels of change turning. It is that 'I' that looks out with curiosity, and whose looking is an interaction with what it sees. It is therefore necessary to develop a reflexive awareness of the personal factors that make up my 'individual' observing of the world.[5] Such reflexive awareness is a form of meditation, entering the internal constitution of the knowing subject.

An important question is: is it possible for one to establish even the external facts of religion, and to describe these, 'objectively', 'neutrally'? It is generally accepted that the researcher should acquire sound knowledge which is true to what is known. Usually, this ideal is expressed with the word 'objectivity'. On the other hand, the objection is regularly raised that when it comes to religion that ideal is unattainable and should perhaps not even be the ideal anyway. Are religion and enquiries into religion not completely 'subjective'? Everything, of course, depends on what we understand by terms such as 'objective' and 'subjective'. Insofar as these two terms do *not* articulate the idea of essential reciprocity between knower and known, they are completely unacceptable. The point I want to make is that the ideal of valid, reliable and adequate knowledge, even at the level of establishing and describing facts, is reached not by trying to eliminate our being persons, but by taking it seriously. 'Objectivity' is established at the heart of 'subjectivity'.[6] That ideal is an aspect of human response-ability, that is, of persons responding to other persons and to the world. 'Objectivity' is a virtue. The alleged value-freeness of science is itself a valuational postulate, referring to the professional ethics of the scholar. It implies a moral attitude towards oneself and the 'objects' of one's investigation which permeates the whole process of investigation, from the problems selected to the results obtained. Humility before the facts, integrity and honesty, courage of one's convictions, caution and conscientiousness are virtues to which the student of religion must be committed. This is indeed a far cry from the myth of science as the work of a disembodied, unfeeling intellect.[7]

An attitude of disinterestedness is not anaemic intellectualism. On the contrary, it is carried by a high regard for the dignity of human beings. Zijderveld once summed up this attitude in the phrase 'intellectual asceticism'. To illustrate the meaning of the phrase he tells the story[8] of the Spanish poet and scholar Luis de Leon (1527–1591) who returned to Salamanca, after being held prisoner by the Inquisition for five years, to resume his lecturing. His audience expected an emotional outpouring, denouncing the Inquisition. Instead, he started by saying: 'As we said yesterday ...', picking up the thread of his lecture where it had been interrupted five years before. However, this iron discipline is not irreconcilable with reflexive awareness of personal factors influencing observation. Rather, they hang together. What is required is not a personal striptease, but awareness on the part of the investigator of his or her personal input into the 'seeing' of the facts.

In giving an account of the process of enquiring into religion, it is therefore not sufficient to refer to the publicly accepted procedures. Hidden from sight, yet influencing the research, is an array of personal factors of which I may not even be consciously aware. It is not enough to admit that such personal factors 'of course play a role' in the investigations – and yet to believe that they are negligible, irrelevant or innocuous, since they are presumably automatically cancelled out by the public discussion; or that it is in any case impossible to investigate them; or that they can be neutralised by a mere decision; or that blunt admission of one's prejudices is enough to exorcise them; or that deliberate flaunting of bias, which would obviate any open encounter with the other, is equivalent to honesty.

My point here is that an important element of objectivity is to recognise these hidden facets, and by doing so to discipline them. Once we get to know them, their status and role change. It is better to declare them than to allow them to be smuggled surreptitiously, as if through customs, into the process of enquiry. The demand that the enquirer should simply (neutrally) black out his or her own input into the observation, description and understanding of a phenomenon is unrealistic. The claim to be ideologically neutral is itself an ideological position. Only by becoming conscious, as far as possible, of my hidden points of departure, my perspective and my dogmatic presuppositions can they be sorted out and prevented from running amuck. I then begin to take responsibility for them. This may not be easy. It may be disquieting, and perhaps it is not possible for everyone to pursue it very far. But recognising the inevitability of being conditioned by a variety of factors is a first step towards overcoming their possibly deterministic character.

In this respect, criticism from others is necessary. Through suspicious, even viciously debunking confrontation of enemies and the cooperation of friends I discover myself. A reflexive spiral is part of the movement into religion: in discovering others, I discover myself; and discovering myself creates the possibility of moving beyond the boundaries of my present situation and of making creative use of my own background in order to discover others. Self-knowledge and knowledge of the other hang together. The Bushmen fascinate us because in them we discover ourselves.

To what extent such a declaration of my background assumptions should be made publicly or privately is a matter of decorum, time and circumstances. It seems that at least enough should be stated that others might understand one's peculiar perspective, as I hope to give my reader sufficient information regarding the biographical perspective in which these essays were written. For the moment I shall simply discuss some of the features of any such perspective on a general level.

First, there is one's *general cultural and religious background*, the typical assumptions one has as a representative of a particular culture. We hold certain things to be obvious and normal. This taken-for-granted milieu forms a background to all our religious investigations. Moving into a strange new world we carry these familiar truths with us. They pattern our observing. Without them we would not be able to gain new knowledge. They are indispensable; but they have to be transcended. I become aware of them as mine in the confrontation with unfamiliar forms of human life. They are ambivalent: they are the wall between me and those other people beyond my everyday world; but I can haul myself up them in order to look over them.

The religious milieu (for example 'Christian' in the wide sense of the word, as the assumed majority orientation in this country) into which one was born has the same ambivalent character. Belonging to a religion in that sense obviously has enormous advantages for studying it, since one can draw on a vast store of inside knowledge. This level of belonging should be distinguished from that of existential commitment (being personally religious). The religious milieu is obviously extremely valuable, since it enables one not to merely look at a religion from without, but to explore it from within. Yet nothing calls for greater circumspection than the overly familiar.

People enquire into religion with different motives and purposes, compelled by different needs (the common word nowadays is *interests*). One might be attracted by the possibility of obtaining power – for or against religion; another might be drawn by the hope of prestige; a third might view it as a means towards some religious end, for example to reach a deeper level of religious experience; or to find confirmation of the belief that all religion is an opium of and for the people; a fourth might be driven by the urge to widen the arc of cultural experience; a fifth might envisage a possibility of improving the lot of humankind; a sixth might hope to escape from the technocratic mentality, or to become more adept at it; and so on. There are probably as many nuances of interest as there are people interested in religion. Consciously or unconsciously, and very subtly, they influence the way in which investigations are conducted, in which conclusions are drawn, and in which results are reported and used.

A related concept, often bandied about as a term of abuse by opposing parties, is *ideology*. For present purposes, it refers to a set of ideas and values which reflect the interests of a society or a section of a society, and which tends to be justificatory and apologetic, thereby mobilising the society with a view to the attainment of some (often economic and political) goal. Ideologies are based on interests, but they go further in that they clothe the naked interests in elaborately contrived intellectual garments. Parading as pictures of reality (even as scientific, objective pictures), they tend to obfuscate their true character as intellectual constructions, reflecting interests, rooted in social contexts, mobilising groups. Ideologies close themselves to critical questioning. They conceal the presence of the speakers in the speech and the contingent nature of that speech. They decontextualise themselves. Inevitable as they are in society, the danger lurking in them is that they tend to become absolute systems of legitimation – without needing legitimation themselves. The result is that they easily – all too easily, as we have had opportunity to witness in this country – insinuate themselves into the individual's mind and insidiously become an uncritically accepted frame of reference. The enquirer into religion is by no means immune to this possibility. Necessary precautions are self-critical suspicion of one's own masked ideological position, searching scrutiny of one's own mind and social position and role, and reflexive challenging not merely of one's own untruthfulness, but of one's own sureness and purity.

One's *personal world-orientation* (whatever that may be, conventional or unconventional, clearly articulated or unconscious) or lack of it will influence one's probing of religion. Everybody starts somewhere. The richer one's own experience in the search for cosmic orienting, the richer will be the yield of understanding of novel forms. Note that I am not saying that one must proceed from and return to some unchallenged dogmatic position or established religious convention, but merely that one's own religious situation is inevitably one's point of departure, even when moving far away from it. Where it leads to may be left open. And must it lead to some specific position?

The converse is equally true. An investigation of religion will affect one's personal world-orientation. According to some it will open the floodgates of relativism and scepticism. The position adopted here is that it will have liberating, therapeutic value. Reflexive, self-critical enquiry sets people free from reified, absolutised religion, that is, religion that has become hardened into thing-like solidity, forgetting that what we know as religions are the deposits of experiences lying beyond the institutionalised religions themselves. Faith is discovered as a human response to the world. By uncovering the human, all too human quality of the various responses, enquiries into religion can reawaken people's receptivity to mystery. It could make one conscious of one's own response (or lack of it), its strengths and weaknesses. In a religiously pluriform society it has the value of helping people relate in a relaxed manner to strange religions.

Taking one's own subjectivity seriously – or reflexiveness, radical introspection – calls for rigorous discipline of the mind. Increased self-awareness means penetrating the closed shell of my world; it also means expanding the scope of my encounter with humanity at large – with Bushmen, Buddhists, Christians, and many others – and with nature. It is part of the way of meditation: a progressive descent into deeper levels of the individual consciousness, penetrating and peeling off layer upon layer of sedimented experience, revealing the individual as a throbbing node in an ever widening network. This process of breaking out of 'self' as determined at any given stage is healthy, both psychologically and religiously. Insistence on a heavy, irrevocable 'commitment' to any position once taken up as the demand of religious integrity is mistaken. Entering into the logic of religion means willingness to enter reflexively into the structure of one's commitment: to what extent is it unconscious residual historical legacy, involuntary emotional attachment, conscious choice and identification? To what extent absolute final obligation, or provisional, hypothetical stance?

Whoever wishes to investigate religion undertakes the task of digging for the religious facts out there and stirring up the murky depths of one's own soul. We have to move beyond this into theorising, stringent criticism and bold constructive religious thought.

ENDNOTES

1 See R D Baird, *Category formation and the history of religions*, The Hague: Mouton, 1971; R Machalek, Definitional strategies in the study of religion, *Journal for the Scientific Study of Religion*, 1977 16, pp 395–401; J S Krüger, *Studying religion: a methodological introduction to science of religion*, Pretoria: Unisa, 1982, pp 56–77.

2 Such as implied by J G Platvoet, The definers defined: traditions in the definition of religion, *Method and Theory in the Study of Religion*, 1990 2(2), pp 180–212. In his Normative and non-normative positions in the study of religions (unpublished lecture), 1991 he distinguishes four paradigms: the traditional orthodox Christian position (theological reductionism); the positivist reductionist position (viewing religion as illusion, etc); the religionist position of liberal Christian theology and phenomenology; and the upcoming nonnormative position, claiming to be 'metaphysically, cosmologically and ideologically neutral' (p 11). As indicated earlier, I do not believe in either the feasibility or the desirability of such an attempt at 'neutrality' in *the long run* and in the *broader context* of religious studies. It is neither realistic nor good. However, Platvoet might merely be demanding neutrality in a somewhat artificially restricted sense as the stipulation of the boundaries of an academic discipline, without denying the legitimacy of the other aspects of enquiry. But to my mind even that is too restrictive. The paradigm I am advocating in these essays does not fall within any one of his four categories, certainly not under 'religionism' (for his very wide application of that term, see his Programmatic statements from Africa, 1982–1992, *Numen*, 1993 40, pp 322–342).

3 D F Berg's proposal of an *integral science of religion* seems to be pointing in the same direction. However, given the style in which most Christian theology, whether conservative or revisionist, is done in South Africa, I see such a 'comprehensive enquiry into religion' as markedly different from theology. Cf D F Berg, Toward an integral science of religion: theology, philosophy, science and religion in a pluralistic context, in K K Klostermaier & L W Hurtado, *Religious studies:*

issues, prospects and proposals, Atlanta, Ga: Scholars Press, 1991, pp 292–308.

4 Cf Krüger, *Studying religion...*, pp 5ff. That book, however, did not include dimensions (5) to (8) in the ambit of this intellectual enterprise.

5 *Reflexivity* may approximate what is called *epoche* in phenomenological religious studies. However, the latter is often naively understood to imply a simple suspension of all the scholar's presuppositions, likes and dislikes, preferences and beliefs by an act of will, simply excising them from one's mind. It would be closer to Husserl's probable intention with his notion of phenomenological reduction, described in several works (for example *The crisis of European sciences and transcendental phenomenology*, Evanston, Ill: Northwestern University Press, 1970) to understand it as a kind of spiritual discipline, a therapeutic process of sorts.

6 As H Spiegelberg, *Doing phenomenology: essays on and in phenomenology*, The Hague: Nijhoff, 1975, p 78, said: 'There is then no escape from subjectivity. The only cure for subjectivistic subjectivity is more and better subjectivity, more discriminating subjectivity, and more selfcritical subjectivity, which will show the very limits of subjectivity.'

7 In a very different setting this scientific ethos was formulated admirably 30 years ago by A Kaplan, *The conduct of inquiry: methodology for behavioral sciences*, New York: Crowell, 1964, p 380.

8 A A Zijderveld, *De relativiteit van kennis en werkelijkheid: inleiding tot de kennissociologie*, Meppel: Boom, 1974, p 222.

6 Understanding you

I, the individual person, proceed from my own self and my understanding of humanity and the world. I become aware of my side of the wall between me and other people. But my purpose is to scale it, to get to know the other side, your side, of it. I need to discover you, the Other, the Other as the you who transcends me. The challenge is not only to see you from my point of view, but to discover how you, from your point of view, see yourself and the world, your world. In an important sense understanding religion is a function of the relationship between 'you' and 'me'.[1]

Like me, 'you' are not an absolute entity, but a continuous process – also continuous and merging with a context that is a pluralistic, conditionalist flux of many aspects, social and natural. You are an aspect of various human societies, according to whose rules you put on a face and play a role. Ultimately you are one short-lived manifestation of humanity. Humanity creates its own unique world of signs, but that world rests on and springs from the subhuman bed of nature, like a jungle island rising from the ocean. At any moment you are merely a snapshot, taken from one angle, in a vast moving field. Yet you are not reducible either to society and its conventions or to nature. You are a concrete node in the pluralistic world, a fruit of that growth, a point of convergence of many forces and of the dissemination of many seeds. Therefore you are significant and your world of interior experience deserves attention and respect. All of this applies to you not only in the singular, but also in the plural, as a group – for example a religious one. This chapter is meant to highlight the imperative to understand other interiorities: yours. By that is meant not merely your deliberate, conscious, chosen, express intentions, but also your involuntary, unconscious, inherited, repressed propensities. It includes attitudes, thoughts, feelings, motives and intentions.

Discovering somebody else's religious world from within, however, is easier said than done. Daunted by the practical difficulties involved, positivist human science has backed away from it, satisfying itself with the externally observable aspects of human life: what cannot be quantitatively measured and formalised is left out of account. Human beings are reduced to their external behaviour, which is seen as determined by external stimuli. 'Neutral' scholars, ignoring their own human contribution to the production of knowledge, easily eliminate the inner life of freedom of their objects as well. Seventy years ago Joachim Wach said that the cardinal methodological problem in religious studies was whether or not one has to participate in another's religion before one could claim to understand it.[2] Indeed, it is necessary to remind ourselves of the gap between the one who understands and those who are to be understood, even when they share the same general cultural and religious milieu. What superficially could appear to be mere nuances within the same religious milieu may turn out to be vastly different things when one uses a finer sieve to capture the subtler shades of experience. This problem is of course enormously compounded when contact is sought across the barriers of different cultural worlds.

This line of argument reflects awareness that concepts and theories about religion have to keep in close touch with the human reality they deal with. It seeks to honour the integrity of the phenomena we study by trying to meet religious people on their own ground and on their own terms, and by not forcing phenomena into the moulds of our own conceptual schemes. It is senseless to argue that since it is impossible to reach the deepest recesses of others' inner lives, we might as well give up the entire effort to see their religion as if through their eyes. In our everyday lives we simply assume that, however imperfectly, our points of view can coincide or converge, and that I can put myself in your place as you can put yourself in mine. At least we assume that through mutual effort our viewpoints can be brought sufficiently close to make communication possible. This assumption is developed in the kind of approach suggested by the phenomenological[3] and hermeneutic[4] styles in religious studies, and the 'emic' style in cultural anthropology.[5]

What is the basis of this possibility of understanding other religions from within? As said above, it is our common humanity, the fact that religious and, indeed, nonreligious people are, before anything else, members of the species *homo sapiens* and share the same nature. We do not need as a basis the idea of some hypothetical universal religion, assuming that deep down all religions are the same. Neither does it presuppose sympathy in the full sense of hearts beating together in warm fellowship. But it does presuppose that all human beings share the same human continuity, that they have similar fears and longings, and that their religions, as humanly constituted systems of meaning, often show remarkable parallels and similarities, making it possible for members of one religion (or no formal religion) to sound the depths of other religions in some measure. This is why people of the industrial age can be moved by a rock painting of a Stone Age Bushman artist. One discovers oneself, in one's own search for meaning, in those strange figures depicted in faded colours. In this respect religious studies entails the living of an ethic of *Mitmenschlichkeit*, beyond positivist-neutral description. It respects the human dignity of the other, however different from me, and crosses that bridge of difference. It does not have an attitude of aggression, debunking or condemnation, hitting out at the wrongs of any religion. Neither is it a sentimental plea for understanding. Its service in our pluralistic world is to introduce people to one another under the aspect of religion, and this implies that each individual or group be allowed to present itself. Surely this society of ours needs such respect for other religions and for others' understanding of their religion. It is quite incredible that what should be a self-evident axiom in civilised society must in this country be defended and substantiated as if it were an extremely dangerous novelty.

Defining Buddhism as part and parcel of one common human world of which Christianity is another part is difficult enough in our troubled society. It gets even worse when we seek a relationship with Bushman religion. Anthropology[6] and theology share a ghastly record of discrimination against the 'primitives' – not through physical violence, but simply by relegating them to an age of 'barbarism', where 'they' may condescendingly be kept at arm's length, at best as examples of stages that 'we', thank God, have long left behind.

Interpreting religions is a social responsibility. It is part of the debate between the many, often conflicting factions of *homo sapiens*, and between the present generation and the many past generations of that species. The kind of interpretation I have in mind is neither directly 'prophetic' (reforming), nor 'priestly' (protective). It does not strive to debunk any religion or to propagate any religion, to convert anyone or to encourage apostasy. It may cause shock, or the sober peeling away of layers of religion may uncover a gem of rare value. It may lead to a deeper understanding of itself by a group studied, and it may evoke that religion for outsiders. The attitude that I have presented here seeks to combine humaneness with unsentimental insight into human realities, realising that religion has often masked extreme arrogance, extreme folly, and extreme injustice. Things are not always what they appear to be. In this irenic-ironic spirit religious studies has a role to play in our society, opening people's eyes to themselves and to others.

Three kinds of pretheoretical understanding may be distinguished: existential understanding, insider (participant) understanding, and outsider understanding, using as a criterion the degree of sympathy and intimacy between the person who understands and the person(s) understood.

We may speak of *existential understanding* when the relationship is close. The interpreter shares the existential commitment that inspires a group. This could happen either because of birth and the ensuing process of socialisation, or through conversion. Explanation here means making clear what 'we' intend in 'our' religion. Here too there are degrees of understanding. The purest case is of course the individual's self-understanding. Existential understanding shades off into lesser degrees of being affected by or joining in a religion, until it merges with insider understanding.

Insider (participant) understanding occurs when the interpreter has sufficient knowledge of the general setup of a group to get around quite easily. One may have been born into the group or one may have joined it (conversion would be too strong a word); one may be able to play the role of a member successfully or one may have been accepted by the group as an interested and sympathetic outsider, one who may be trusted.

Outsider understanding occurs when the interpreter does not in any meaningful way share 'their' commitments or 'their' world. This sort of understanding is not difficult to achieve. In fact, it is the kind of stereotyped knowledge most people are satisfied to have of most other people most of the time, but its degree of adequacy is low.

In the next chapter we shall discuss the level of *theoretical* understanding and explanation. It is claimed that in fact all theoretical understanding of religion must rely on participant and even existential understanding of some sort. In the previous section I said that investigators' experience of their own personal religion or lack of it, and of their own world (their existential self-understanding and participant understanding of their own general cultural background and religious milieu), inevitably plays an enormous role in their reconstruction of the religion of others. Here we add the further requirement that sound existential, or at least participant understanding of the *other's* religion is necessary for a reasonable degree of adequacy. It is imperative to find out, respectfully, how the persons one is studying experience themselves and their world.

Adequate understanding is therefore not a unilateral achievement by the student of an-Other religion. It is the result of, at the very least, *encounter* and *dialogue* between the investigator and the persons being investigated. Then comes self-immersion into the setting one is trying to understand by *becoming a participant*, living with the people, learning (if possible) their language and their history and appreciating their religious heritage. This is followed by *imaginative re-enactment of the existential understanding* of the other persons, entering into their skins and minds, admittedly only by way of make-believe, but still very useful; the adoption, as far as possible, of the frame of mind of the other. This 'as if' existential understanding, this 'imaginative re-experiencing'[7] or 'imaginative participation'[8] is at best precarious and in need of stringent empirical checks. An extreme possibility is actual *conversion* to that religious commitment. However, this term has the connotation of leaving a previous religion, turning your back on it and choosing an alternative one in a harsh either-or option.

ENDNOTES

1 This maxim has been adopted variously in phenomenological religious studies, which (rather loosely) go back to the philosophical impulse of Edmund Husserl. According to W C Smith, Comparative religion: whither – and why? in M Eliade & J M Kitagawa, *The history of religions: essays in methodology*, Chicago: University of Chicago Press, 1959, p 42 'no statement about a religion is valid unless it can be acknowledged by that religion's believers'. W B Kristensen, The phenomenology of religion, in J Bettis (ed), *The phenomenology of religion*, London: SCM, 1969, pp 41, 48ff believed that '[e]very religion ought to be understood from its own standpoint, for that is how it is understood by its own adherents ... They [ie historians and phenomenologists of religion] must investigate what religious value the believers (Greeks, Babylonians, Egyptians, etc) attached to their faith, what religion meant to them ... For the historian only one evaluation is possible: 'the believers were completely right'.' In a sense this is true, but it is not the whole truth. In phenomenological religious studies this is referred to as *intentionality*. Exponents of this approach are

G van der Leeuw, *Religion in essence and manifestation*, London: Allen & Unwin, 1964; N Smart in his many publications, e g *The phenomenon of religion*, London: Macmillan, 1973; J Waardenburg, *Reflections on the study of religion*, The Hague: Mouton, 1973; and D A Crosby, *Interpretive theories of religion*, The Hague: Mouton, 1981.

2 J Wach, Zur Methodologie der allgemeinen Religionswissenschaft (originally published in 1923), in G Lanczkowski, *Selbstverständnis und Wesen der Religionswissenschaft*, Darmstadt: Wissenschaftliche Buchgesellschaft, 1974, p 35.

3 In religious studies the term 'phenomenology' is used in two distinct senses. Firstly, it is used to denote that branch of religious studies which systematises and classifies religious phenomena. Some researchers, especially in Scandinavia, Italy, Holland and Germany, have insisted that 'phenomenology of religion' should be organised as an independent subdiscipline of religious studies, alongside history of religions. Secondly, it is used in a wider sense to denote a method, broadly associated with the philosophy initiated by Edmund Husserl. Examples of this latter style of religious phenomenology are found in J Waardenburg, *Reflections on the study of religion ...*; N Smart, *Concept and empathy: essays in the study of religion*, London: Macmillan, 1986; D Allen, *Structure and creativity in religion: hermeneutics in Mircea Eliade's phenomenology and new directions*, The Hague: Mouton, 1978; and others. This style found an ally in sociological phenomenology which started to make inroads on the methodology of the social sciences in the sixties and seventies, mainly as a result of the work of A Schutz, *Collected papers I. The problem of social reality*, The Hague: Nijhoff, 1973; P L Berger & T Luckmann, *The social construction of reality: a treatise in the sociology of religion*, Harmondsworth: Penguin, 1975, and others. In phenomenological studies of religion every effort is made to understand the 'intentionality' of the religious actors. The phenomenological perspective has recently been restated clearly by J Cox, Methodological considerations relevant to the truth of African traditional religions: a phenomenological perspective, unpublished paper read at the Regional Conference on the Study of Religions in Africa, held under the auspices of the International Association for the History of Religions, at the University of Zimbabwe, 15–19 September 1992, pp 48–57.

4 Cf H G Gadamer, *Wahrheit und Methode: Grundzüge einer philosophischen Hermeneutik*. Tübingen: Mohr (Paul Siebeck), 1972; P Ricoeur, *The symbolism of evil*, Boston: Beacon Press, 1969; J Wach, *Understanding and believing*, Westport, Conn: Greenwood Press, 1975.

5 Cf M Harris, *The rise of anthropological theory: a history of culture*, London: Routledge & Kegan Paul, 1968, p 571: emic statements relate to what is regarded as 'significant, meaningful, real, accurate, or in some other fashion ... as appropriate by the actors themselves'. 'The natives's point of view' is a criterion of adequacy. Also see M Bourdillon, Anthropological approaches to the study of African religions, unpublished paper read at the Regional Conference on the Study of Religions in Africa, held under the auspices of the International Association for the History of Religions, at the University of Zimbabwe, 15–19 September 1992, pp 34–47.

6 Cf J Fabian, *Time and the other: how anthropology makes its object*, New York: Columbia University Press, 1983.

7 Kristensen, The phenomenology of religion ..., p 42.

8 Allen, *Structure and creativity ...*, p 90.

7 Seeing patterns

To theorise is to see provisional patterns. Patterns are coherent pictures. That is why they bestow meaning and have explanatory force.

Theorising is implied in each of the dimensions of enquiry into religion previously mentioned.

Firstly, the *concept* 'religion' involves a certain degree of theorising (chapter 4).

Secondly, the *facts* of religion are only intelligible within a theoretical framework of some sort (chapter 5). Without an orienting frame of reference, empirical research will produce only a jumble of unintegrated data, just as theory uninformed by reality will be mere speculation or analysis of empty concepts. In fact, without theory of one kind or another the concept of research becomes meaningless. Research is directed, systematic search. Theories are not merely formed at the end of research. They function at every stage, anticipating the discovery of facts. Theoretical changes or advances, reorganising the existing stock of knowledge and 'seeing' new *gestalts*, are the major breakthroughs in any field of scholarship. Good theory reveals connections.

Thirdly, inasmuch as discovering and stating a coherent personal worldview requires some distance and abstraction on the part of the observer, it tends to establish an interpretive pattern (chapter 6). There is more to religion than meets the eye of the *adherent*. However important the verdict of the believers may be, it cannot be taken as the only or final word about their religion. Human beings are often unconscious of their own motivations. Religion merges with ideology, and reality is covered with rationalisations. Even fully conscious intentions are part of much wider patterns – of which the actors may be completely unaware. The quest for *meaning* requires more than consciously intended personal motivations. It also entails multicausal impersonal interconnections of a wide variety of social factors. People's thoughts and actions are woven into wider webs. So in order to *understand* and *explain* a religion, theories are needed that inevitably exceed the self-expression and self-understanding of its adherents. In addition to emic ('insider') explanations conforming closely to the views of the adherents, etic ('outsider') explanations are necessary.[1]

To 'understand' is to have satisfactory knowledge, not only in the small sense of personal feelings of delight. Such knowledge must be convincing to a forum of researchers by meeting certain explicit criteria. The words 'understanding' and 'explanation' are deliberately juxtaposed but not contrasted. Where a heavy contrast is made,[2] 'explanation' implies subsuming the particular thing that you wish to explain under a general law. This deductive nomological model of explanation, and probably also the less stringent form (inductive nomological explanation) would rule out the possibility that religious studies could ever really explain anything. To that school of thought, 'understanding' (*Verstehen*) is mere intuition: a soft, vague and nonrigorous feeling of sympathetic acquaintance, perhaps useful in the early stages of an investigation, but not yet 'scientific', and not yet 'explanation'. Some advocates of *Verstehen* accept this dichotomy and even support the notion of understanding as being only a vague, unarticulated intuition. In keeping with the more everyday usage of these terms, we should rather see understanding and explanation as presenting two stages of the same process. When our understanding of something is deficient or shaky, we are in need of explanation as a means of making it plain, making sense of the puzzle – that is, of understanding.[3] A successful explanation is one that allows us to understand; a sound understanding is one that, for the present, is not in need of explanation. Explanation gives understanding; understanding gives explanation. This applies as much to the problem of why the car would not start this morning or what has happened to the pair of pliers that has disappeared from its usual place, as it does to the question of whether Bushman religion and Zen have anything in common.

Enquiry into religion needs vigorous, rigorous theorising.[4] Such theoretical understanding is not religious confession, but is characterised by an attitude of intellectual discipline, suspending (not turning a blind eye to, but reflexively taking into account) the natural and (non-/anti-)religious commitments of life far more rigorously than is required for ordinary understanding. It engages in the ongoing public debate about religion and is not a purely private statement of opinion.

In seeking to envision coherent patterns, theorising is a 'systematising' process. This by no means implies that enquirers into religion should be devotees of the formally exact types of theorising used in the natural sciences. Excessive emphasis on formalisation would be inhibiting and harmful rather than helpful. The other extreme would be the very personal expression of insight found in art. Whereas formalisation can be sterile, poetry remains pregnant with many hidden meanings. Perhaps the style best suited to meet our present needs in the investigation into religion lies somewhere between these two. It would include consistent use of terminology in coherent arguments; clear, definite pictures, presented in a style not too far removed from that normally encountered in literary works such as novels. Theoretical work links various phenomena in a network of relationships.[5] In terms of this approach a fact is explained if we are able to indicate how it fits into a coherent pattern. Explanation has to do with the discovery or determination of relations between factors. These need not be of a one-to-one causal nature, they need not be expressed in terms of 'laws', or of mathematical or formal logical symbols. As far as religion is concerned, we want to see how previously unrelated odds and ends hang together. Then we understand.

Although systematic, theories of religion should be open, dynamic, anti-authoritarian, antidogmatic, relative, cultivating the germ that will lead to their own demise. Developing their own potential and possibilities, they should also critically explore their own limits,[6] realising that sooner or later their inner energy will be exhausted; that they will be overtaken by new developments in thought, either from within themselves, or from the side of other perspectives, or both; that they will fail to account fully for altered circumstances. At best, a theory will for its own time, in a given society at a given juncture, understand and explain the religious dimension of things; as for the future, it is hoped that it may make a change for the better. In keeping with Socratic thinking theory formation regarding religion is part of the never finally answered question: 'How shall we live?'[7] Theories of religion do not uncover and express timeless, essential truths. They need to be conceptually clear and rigorous in order to be part of the ongoing, never ending dynamics of our balancing in the world.

Intrareligious patterns reflect the inner composition of the syndrome of religion,[8] for example the relationship between ritual and myth. How do the telling of stories of origin and the acting out of sacred drama hang together? Or such patterns explain the internal constitution of specific historical religions, such as the three considered in this study. How was the trance dance of precolonial Bushmen connected with their rock art? How do practices, teachings and social forms condition one another in Buddhism and Christianity? That they do is beyond doubt. In Christianity, theological teachings concerning God cannot be isolated from the practice of worship and from the structures of the organised Christian churches; the theological texture of a one-month-old charismatic church differs from that of a routinised, long-established mainline church. Hua-yen Buddhist views on the interpenetration of all things are not independent of the socially institutionalised practice of meditation. And each of these (doctrine, cult, organisation) is in turn a constellation of mutually conditioning factors, caught up in processes of transformation.

Religions may also be seen as *embedded in wider sociocultural contexts*. A conditionalist approach would want to discover how they interact with these contexts in mutual dependence and stimulation. For it assumes that religion is formed by the multitude of economic, geographic, climatic and other factors with which it is interwoven, and that in turn it forms some of them. Religions exist symbiotically with such contexts. A widely recognised example: the ancient Semitic patriarchal concept of God and patriarchal society coexisted in a relationship of elective affinity (*Wahlverwandschaft*, to use Max Weber's phrase); they found and reinforced one another. Modern industrialised society followed and led cultural developments in the formation of a unique sociocultural climate in which the traditional patriarchal concept of God seems to be losing power – and vice versa: the widespread questioning of the traditional concept of God in the modern West has weakened the grip of this millennia-old legitimation of those old social patterns. Another example: in modern Japan the relationship between Buddhism and Christianity was intimately connected with the political, diplomatic and social upheavals in that country following Western incursions into Japan since the sixteenth and seventeenth centuries.[9] In a society such as that of the Bushmen, it is even less possible to isolate religion from the seamless fabric of communal life. Religion was not a separate institution at all. Thus neither an idealistic determinism assuming that religious ideas determine society and culture, nor an economic determinism emphasising one-sidedly the influence of economics on religious thought, nor any other kind of determinism provides an adequate principle of explanation – not in primal societies, and not in modern societies.[10]

Interreligious patterns have to do with the dynamics of the relationships between various religions. As in the previous two cases, the spiral of understanding would cut deeper, through the level of adequate description of the historical facts of interaction to an insider understanding of these processes, to a theory of the wider forces operative in such encounters.

Traditionally, the various religions have usually been observed as if they were completely separate entities, like towns spread over a wide area, each isolated and remote from the others. Here is Christianity, there is Judaism, over there the foreign Islam, yonder on the horizon lies Hinduism, and out of sight somewhere are African traditional religions, Buddhism, and the rest – with *nothing in between but empty barrenness* that only the hardiest of missionaries ever cross. I propose a drastic shift of focus to precisely those spaces between religions. Suddenly the picture changes. We see connecting roads, often well worn with the traffic of ages, stretching from China to Ireland, from America to Australia, from Europe to Africa. If we go back far enough into history, we would even pick up a faint trail starting in ancient Africa and leading elsewhere. I direct the attention of my reader to the spaces between religions as the territory where religious discoveries may be made in our time. The spaces between towns are much more than empty stretches to negotiate. Rich with possibilities for religious experience, they are covered with the footprints of many ages. Religions interrelate and interpenetrate dynamically and syncretistically.

In this respect theories on a variety of levels are possible, ranging from small-scale, localised, 'case study' comparisons, through middle-range theories, to wide-ranging, general comparative theories. All are necessary. Let us for the moment restrict ourselves to the latter type. Speaking ideal-typically, what are possible options when constructing a comparative theory of religions and interreligious relations? Without entering into a detailed discussion of the vast literature on this terrain,[11] let us focus on the cognitive dimension of religion and delineate some abstract possibilities in order to indicate the position taken here.

At one end of the spectrum is the view that all religions teach essentially the same thing. This would be the position of *general identity*. All may be true (or false, according to Marxists of the old school). The problem with this view is that it underestimates the real and often stark differences between religions. It also easily loses sight of the fact that the various religions, in the course of their long historical development, gave rise to a plurality of internal accents, leading to stresses and strains, and creating enormous difficulties when trying to establish the 'essence' of any religion. What, indeed, could be the 'essence' of Buddhism, Christianity and Bushman religion? It also ignores the fact (to which I drew attention above) that one factor, such as doctrine (in a wide sense that includes the cognitive aspect of Bushman religion as well), is integrally connected with other factors such as rituals, having its full meaning only in that nexus. Decontextualisation can have fatal results for the item isolated in this way. Insofar as it postulates that all religious truth claims are equally valid, it promotes an unacceptable relativism of the 'anything goes' variety.

At the other extreme would lie the view that their teachings differ essentially and are wholly incompatible. This would be the view of *general incongruence*. All religions cannot be true, but all can be false. This view does not take the real similarities – sometimes close, sometimes vague – between historical religions seriously. Like the view of general identity, it overgeneralises and oversimplifies. After all, 'religion' as a generic concept is not a completely fanciful idea. In at least some cases there are indeed remarkable similarities, or at least comparabilities, between *very different* religions as regards the problems tackled, ideals set, precepts given, doctrines taught, and social forms and cults evolved. The interfaces between Buddhism, Christianity and Bushman religion are alive with potential for creative dialogue.

One position between these two extremes might propose that all of them bar one are grouped together as essentially of a kind, and that that one differs essentially from all the others. This may be called *exclusivism*. In exclusivist schools the one is usually regarded as true – the rest as false. Apart from the criticism of oversimplification, this theory is exposed to the reproach that it can at best find expression in friendly tolerance; at worst in arrogance, defensiveness, discrimination, aggression, proselytising and even coercion, forcing one brand of religion down people's throats whether they want it or not. This kind of religious zealotry is not unknown in the religious history of South Africa.

Other intermediate positions are possible, and are in fact held. One is that of *limited identity*. At least two or three religions (for example Judaism, Christianity and Islam) may be seen as essentially identical or partly the same, at least as regards a core of their teachings (for example their theism). The criticism levelled against the theory of general identity also applies to this more moderate version.

Another possibility often followed in various religions is to order religions hierarchically (*inclusivism*). One religion stands at the top as the truest or even the only true one, the others are graded with reference to that one, from partly true to completely false; or they may be assimilated to the true one as preparations or stages or anonymous forms of the highest one. This view comes closer to a conditionalist approach. It represents an understandable stage in the development of interreligious dynamics, since it is only natural that people who are convinced of the truth of their own religion, on discovering beauty and truth in others, would interpret those others as variants of their own.[12] The problem here is the arrogance and lack of understanding that may lurk in this evaluation or that may be perceived by the adherents of the 'other' religions. In addition the various facts of interreligious dynamics may not be taken seriously enough – the normative religion may be presupposed to be a closed truth, as if dropped from heaven in some original purity, uncontaminated by other religions. Any sober historical approach to religions shows that this is completely untrue. In this sense, there is no 'pure' religion.

Yet another possibility is to accept that religions differ, even fundamentally, but that at least some of them may be interpreted in such a manner that they at least point in the same direction (*convergence*). This programme would leave room for a dynamic process in which the various parties in the interplay may reinterpret themselves and undergo changes – but it may still be hypnotised by the ideal of a stabilised, final synthesis. Nevertheless, this ideal must not be slated. On the microscale of individual life histories, many individuals in situations of religious pluralism are today engaged in such highly personal efforts to harmonise divergent systems that they are involved with. Quaker Buddhists and African Initiated Churches are evidence of this. On the macroscale of great intellectual movements influencing entire civilisations, the examples of Christianity (doctrinally, a syncretism of Hebrew and Hellenistic elements) and Ch'an Buddhism (a synthesis of Taoism and Indian Mahayana Buddhism) are well known. In various black South African societies general protection by those stronger neighbours was often traded for Bushman rain-making powers.

In the theoretical framework proposed here, the various historical religions appear as relative focuses of the religious ideal to see panoramically. They cannot be conceptualised and formulated finally in any dogma, institutionalised finally in any social form, expressed finally in any set of emotional sentiments. The attitude arising from this discovery is not inevitably 'relativism', in the form of a despairing levelling of all teachings, or a frenetic, arbitrary absolutising of some of these teachings. John Dunne once wrote: 'The holy man of our time, it seems, is a man who passes over by sympathetic understanding from his own religion to other religions and comes back again with new insight to his own. Passing over and coming back, it seems, is the spiritual adventure of our time.'[13] This is certainly true of many people today. But for many others this picture is too stark. When coming back, the 'other' religion(s) may not be left behind at all. Some who venture forth do not come back at all. There are those with a dual allegiance, and those with no formal allegiance at all. These may also be the 'holy women' and 'holy men' of our time.

When relating two or more religions, it is certainly important to do justice to the historical uniqueness of each as a growing organism. Due appreciation must be shown for the integrity of *that* very particular phenomenon at *that* very specific time. The next step, that is the explicit comparative relating of religions with one another, is enormously difficult. Any meeting with a strange religious universe is implicitly comparative in any event, in the sense that the strange is inevitably understood in terms of the known. But this is not sufficient, for religions could still, like parallel lines, never meet. A dialogical meeting between religions marks another and most important step. But even this step could still imply a fixation of both, as if they were timeless entities. So religious encounter should be enclosed in a wider strategy in which full rein is given to a creative, mutually transforming process of reinterpretation and reconstruction.[14] 'That one' and 'they' become 'you', become 'us'; together we seek ways to fulfil our human responsibility for our common world. As I mentioned before, in this process harmonisations and syntheses may develop, and they need not necessarily be rash, superficial syncretisms. Conditionalism emphasises the interwovenness of the various religions in the past; as for the future, it emphasises open dialectic, creative difference, challenging questioning, mutual opening up of as yet unrealised possibilities in each, stimulating each to greater self-awareness as a changing network caught up in bigger ones, more translucent to the openness beyond itself and more comprehensive.

Interreligious dialogue with its risk of reification of the separate substantialised religions must be widened into transreligious multilogue. The various religions are arrows into the darkness of the world, beams sweeping across the night sky, varying in the width of their arc and the depth of their probing power. In such a theory of religions an extended horizontal axis analysing the differences, the unique and specific, would intersect a vertical axis synthesising the similar, the homoversal and general, in order to understand the full range of religion.

Conditionalism acknowledges the *phenomenological* emphasis on intentionality, but it (dis-)integrates the subject with wider social and natural forces (and, as will be argued in subsequent chapters) it forges ahead into critical and constructive religious thought.

It can applaud the *hermeneutics* of Gadamer[15] with its emphasis on the fusion of horizons, but it radicalises Gadamer's programme. What need to be fused are not just the past and present of a single religiocultural tradition, but multiple religiocultural horizons. Although 'fusion' suggests that the various elements are not 'welded' into one undifferentiated mass, it does not express strongly enough the pluralistic, explosive, mutually transformative (Cobb) quality of such encounters.

Conditionalism can endorse the underlying assumptions of *critical theory*[16] that human action is steered by the twin interests of relating to the environment and to fellow humans, both unified by the interest in becoming truly free. It can also sympathise with the ideal of domination-free communication, and can agree with the critique of modern technocratic mass society where work (technical manipulation) is inexorably expanding at the expense of free communication between human beings; where traditional systems of legitimation are eroded and supplanted by the technocratic ideology which justifies mass society and thus succeeds in keeping the individual captive in it; where humans become manipulated parts of a social system from which escape to freedom is hardly possible; and where cultural values shrivel as everything is subsumed under an instrumentalist and rationalist means-end schema. Although it operates within a Marxian framework, critical theory is aware of the value of religions as traditional systems of legitimation which strive to keep alive the ideals of human meaning, human communication and human freedom. Yet it reveals a serious limitation as far as religion is concerned. It sticks to society and does not move on to a wider religious framework.[17] Applied uncritically to theology and religious studies, Marxian approaches can be quite misleading. They could – and in fact I believe they did and still do in much of South African religious talk – stop short at the social problematic, not continuing into the problematic of religious metaphysics. Such talk remains at most angry social comment, easily married to an unreflected if not fundamentalist theology, without pushing on critically and constructively into the 'metaphysical' context from which human society derives meaning. Unless it takes account of that dimension, religious thought will run out of intellectual steam.

A pluralist, conditionalist approach objects to what in studies of religion is generally known as *reductionism*, with its close focus on causal relationships, such as the physical, economic or social conditions that are assumed to produce certain religious results. The application of such a selective interpretive criterion is not wrong in itself. The problem arises when it is abstracted from the wide field of forces to the extent that its inevitable methodological one-sidedness becomes hardened into a closed, deterministic worldview. This was the problem with old-style Marxist and old-style Freudian analyses of religion: religion was taken to be completely determined by economic or repressed sexual forces, 'nothing but' an epiphenomenon of other aspects of life. The opposite kind of determinism, equally simplistic, is an idealism of sorts, according to which religious beliefs and attitudes completely determine society. Naturally any methodological approach is selective and therefore 'reductionist'. This is inevitable. Causal determinism, however, charging down one lane of the road without noticing the traffic coming from the opposite direction, tends to lose sight of the multirelational reciprocity and the involvement of factors. Such one-lane approaches, from sociologism, psychologism and materialism to religious idealism, isolate and elevate one factor (whatever it may be) to the status of the absolute determinant of everything else. This is quite unacceptable in a pluralist perspective.

The much-debated theoretical position of *functionalism* (less popular these days than ten or twenty years ago)[18] does to some extent approximate a conditionalist explanatory style. Its basic premise is the idea of a system, consisting of a number of interdependent parts. A second assumption is that such a system aspires to a condition of equilibrium. Inasmuch as the parts contribute to the equilibrium of the system, they are functional. However, they can also, according to some functionalists, be dysfunctional in that they can disturb the equilibrium of the system. 'Function' refers to the effect of a part on the whole (system). In studying religion, this approach can be applied in various ways. For example, religion can be viewed as part of the social system, its function being the furtherance of social equilibrium. At an individual level, one can look at religion as functional for the equilibrium of the personality. Religion can also be regarded as a system in itself, in which the various elements function as a harmonious complex. The usefulness of functionalism is that it reminds us that religious elements do not exist in isolation. Also, it breaks out of the nomological model of explanation. It does not offer 'causal' explanations of either religion or society. Instead, it tries to make religious phenomena comprehensible by fitting them into coherent patterns.[19] So far, so good. However, it is also beset by grave weaknesses, as has often been pointed out. It overemphasises the supportive, subordinate or contributory role of religion and does not give due recognition to its relative autonomy or to its creative and *de*stabilising role. It tends to be reductionist in the sense that religion is assimilated to its psychological or social functions. It tends to ignore religion as experienced by its adherents which, as has become clear, must be allowed for in an overall strategy of enquiry. It shields itself from the effects of extraneous factors on the assumedly smooth-running society. Functionalism is unaware of the pluralistic interplay of forces right across the integrated societal structure, and of the religious dimension of transcendence/penetration. It tends to sanction whatever is conducive to a harmonious system, and to underplay the elements of tension, strife and the urge to explode any system that is felt to be oppressive, which according to our understanding are inherent in religion. Functionalism is conservative, allowing for smooth progression along established lines. It does not recognise the principle of radical disintegration or the explosive quality of many forms of interaction.[20] If we were to stick to functionalism, we would end up with the various religions of the world in neat, discrete, separate and impenetrable compartments, all of them greasing the wheels of society. As an academic construct, functionalism's ideological function is to promote social integration.

Structuralism[21] insists on an unconscious mental structure underlying, unbeknown to religious actors, the directly describable manifestations. But its idea of the atemporal, essential self-identity of the human mind condemns it to remaining an abstract scheme of interpretation, aloof from the real actors. At the same time it uncritically imports Western suppositions, such as the prevalence of stark binary oppositions, into what is presented as an atemporal structure of the human mind. In the conditionalist perspective proposed here humanity is seen as embedded in and emerging from nature through a long evolutionary process. Humanity came into being some time ago, is in a process of change, and will pass away in due course. Temporality is its hallmark. This, however, does not rule out the idea of *continuity* through time, implying the existence of certain typical features of the mind of *homo sapiens*. In certain ways all humans are alike. The human mind collectively shows diachronically evolved similarities and synchronically present regularities. But this must not be emphasised at the expense of the creative input that individuals make. The overall frame must account for individualism and pluralism. In structuralism religion becomes a system ignoring the understanding of its individual participants, imposing its rules on them.

ENDNOTES

1 Cf M Harris, *The rise of anthropological theory: a history of theories of culture*, London: Routledge & Kegan Paul, 1968, pp 568ff.
2 By, for example, C G Hempel, *Philosophy of natural science*, Englewood Cliffs, NJ: Prentice-Hall, 1966.
3 According to W Pannenberg, *Theology and the philosophy of science*, London: Darton, Longman & Todd, 1976, pp 135ff.
4 As has rightfully been demanded by J Platvoet in his various publications, e g Drie stromingen in de godsdienstwetenschap: een korte geschiedenis van dit vak, in D J Hoens et al, *Inleiding tot de studie van de godsdiensten*, Kampen: Kok, 1985, pp 45–60; Normative and non-normative positions in the study of religions, unpublished lecture, 1991. The danger of his overall position (demanding 'neutrality' and 'objectivity', and severing all links between religious studies and philosophical reflection) is that it verges perilously on positivism (by which I understand the rejection or avoidance of all reflexive 'meta'-questioning).
5 For this kind of theory A Kaplan (*The conduct of inquiry: methodology for behavioral sciences*, New York: Crowell, 1964) coined the suggestive term 'concatenated theory'.
6 Cf the critical rationalist idea of falsification, i e the deliberate search for errors, and its scientific, moral and political implications, as developed by K Popper (*Objective knowledge: an evolutionary approach*, Oxford: Clarendon Press, 1972; *The open society and its enemies*, London: Routledge & Kegan Paul, 1973; *Conjectures and refutations: the growth of scientific knowledge*, London: Routledge & Kegan Paul, 1974), H Albert (*Traktat über kritische Vernunft*, Tübingen: Mohr [Paul Siebeck],

1968), W W Bartley (*The retreat to commitment*, New York, London: Chatto & Windus, 1964), W Pannenberg (*Theology and the philosophy of science ...*) and others.

7 See R C Scharff, A Socratic approach to time, space and knowledge, in R H Moon & S Randall (eds), *Dimensions of thought: current explorations in time, space, and knowledge,* Vol I, Berkeley, Calif: Dharma, 1980, pp 59–93.

8 See N Smart, *Concept and empathy: essays in the study of religion*, London: Macmillan, 1986, p 75.

9 The developments from the forced opening of Japan in 1854 to the last decade of the nineteenth century have been described by N R Thelle, *Buddhism and Christianity in Japan: from conflict to dialogue, 1854–1899*, Honolulu: University of Hawaii Press, 1987.

10 J Platvoet correctly points out that this is an important intermediate level of explanation, and that in spite of the complexities of these correlations the establishment of instructive regularities is attainable (De eigenheid van godsdiensten van volken zonder schrift, in T Chowdhury, W Claesens & W Logister (eds), *Het kosmisch patroon: het vele en het ene in de godsdiensten*, Tilburg: Tilburg University Press, 1989, pp 26ff).

11 Valuable contributions to this developing field include P Moore, Buddhism, Christianity and the study of religion, in P Denwood & A Piatigorsky (eds), *Buddhist studies ancient and modern* London: Curzon Press, 1983, pp 74–91; D Tracy & J B Cobb, *Talking about God: doing theology in the context of modern pluralism*, New York: Harper, 1984; H Coward, *Pluralism: challenge to world religions*, Maryknoll, NY: Orbis, 1985; J Hick, *Problems of religious pluralism*, London: Macmillan, 1985; J Hick & H Askari (eds), *The experience of religious diversity*, Aldershot: Gower, 1985.

12 Coward (*Pluralism ...*, p 97) called this 'the superimposition of validating criteria'.

13 J Dunne, *The way of all the earth: an encounter with Eastern religions*, London: Sheldon Press, 1973, p vii.

14 Examples of this sort of approach are J B Cobb, *Beyond dialogue: toward a mutual transformation of Christianity and Buddhism*, Philadelphia: Fortress Press, 1982; A Fernando, (with L Swidler), *Buddhism made plain: an introduction for Christians and Jews*, Maryknoll, NY: Orbis, 1985; and C G Hospital, *Breakthrough: insights of the great religious discoverers*, Maryknoll, NY: Orbis, 1985.

15 H-G Gadamer, *Wahrheit und Methode*, Tübingen: Mohr (Paul Siebeck), 1960.

16 Powerfully represented by J Habermas in his *Zur Logik der Sozialwissenschaften*, Frankfurt: Suhrkamp, 1978, and *Technik und Wissenschaft als Ideologie*, Frankfurt: Suhrkamp, 1978.

17 This is the important point raised by Pannenberg (*Theology and the Philosophy of Science ...*, pp 185ff) in his discussion of Habermas.

18 Clearly stated in the pioneering works of E Durkheim (*The elementary forms of the religious life*, London: Allen & Unwin, 1957), A R Radcliffe-Brown (*Structure and function in primitive societies: essays and addresses*, London: Cohen & West, 1952), B Malinowski (*Magic, science and religion and other essays*, London: Souvenir Press, 1974), T Parsons (*The structure of social action*, New York: Free Press, 1968;

The social system, London: Routledge & Kegan Paul, 1970); and others such as N Luhmann (*Funktion der Religion*, Frankfurt am Main: Suhrkamp, 1977). Durkheim's classic definition of religion presents it as a unified system of beliefs and practices, with a unifying function in society, forging its adherents into a unity. It creates, confirms and preserves social solidarity. At the other end of this spectrum Luhmann advances the idea that religion need not be system-integrating, but can also be disruptive.

19 The thrusts and parries in the debate about the explanatory value of functionalism vis-à-vis causal explanation by H H Penner (The poverty of functionalism, *History of Religions*, 1971 [2], pp 91–97) and P Achinstein (Function statements, *Philosophy of Science*, 1977 [44], pp 341–367) reflect the gist of the various arguments.

20 Neither does general systems theory (as set out by L von Bertalanffy, *General systems theory*, New York: Braziller, 1968).

21 As exemplified in the thinking of C Lévi-Strauss (cf his *The savage mind*, London: Weidenfeld & Nicolson, 1966; *The raw and the cooked*, London: Cape, 1968). For an example of its application to the study of religion, see H H Penner, Creating a Brahman: a structural approach to religion, in R D Baird, *Methodological issues in religious studies*, Chicago: New Horizons Press, 1974, pp 111–125.

8 Better or worse

Radical religious enquiry issues in critical investigation, sifting better from worse, convincing from unconvincing, not only in theories about religion, but also in religion itself.[1] In a sense Kristensen had a point when he said that the believer is always right. In another sense this is patently not so. Believers are sometimes very wrong, even (I would say, particularly) when they are very sure that they are very right.[2] Throughout history religion has inspired individuals as well as groups to display nobility and compassion. It may have been the greatest civilising force overall in the history of humanity. But both individual and collective religion were at times grossly mistaken, ignorant, superficial, hypocritical and party to evil. Religion may have been the greatest inhibiting force overall in the history of humanity.

The question is: on what basis, according to which criteria, can we discriminate between better and worse? Are there any norms we may use to evaluate what we find – not stopping short at descriptions and explanations of external facts and internal intentions, not coming up with private new brews of religion, not promulgating truth and untruth by decree, not allowing any one religion to lay down the rule from on high? How can we *talk together* about religion, *argue* about it (even vigorously if necessary – that would be quite healthy), and get somewhere? How can one be true to one's personal taste of the world, bold in one's thinking, loyal to one's fellow human beings and humble before the facts, all at the same time? Somehow all these ingredients and more make up the notion of religious validity.

Space does not permit discussion of the various ways in which the establishment of religious validity and invalidity has been viewed. It would take us into philosophy, both Western and Eastern.[3] Instead, I shall attempt to outline briefly a criteriology that ties in with the overall conditionalist perspective and the circumscription of religion developed here.

The first thing that needs to be said is that the leading idea of universal relativity does not entail an epistemological relativism in the sense that anything goes. Neither does the leading idea of empiricism entail that all phenomena are on the same plane. I believe that our empirical view of religion permits us to distinguish between major and minor religious phenomena, even while operating on a purely experiential basis. So I maintain that the circumscription of religion as radical orienting, comprising totalising and transcending, both describes the universal human phenomenon and allows us to distinguish between stronger and weaker, more and less developed. To give an example: a mystic, steeped in overwhelming realisation of the coherence of all things, surely represents a more advanced level of religious insight than an ideologue who manipulates a holy book to further factional interests. But how do we 'know' and 'justify' that?

After having done full justice to the human meaning of religion, critical investigation may proceed. Criticism may be both positive and negative. It may highlight strengths and weaknesses. To repeat, relevant criticism presumes thorough knowledge. It is remarkable how freely people condemn religions (especially 'other' religions) while knowing little or nothing about them. It is the bane of our society. We have yet to cross the bridge leading to pluralism. Before a medical doctor takes up the scalpel or prescribes pills, she must be able to diagnose a disease correctly, having first made a study of the human body. Before a mechanic can repair a fault, he must surely first know how the car is put together and how it works. We have very definite opinions about quacks and tinkerers. Why should we be less critical when it comes to religion? One can express a view on the rightness or wrongness of a foreign religion only after a careful and sympathetic study of it, not beforehand. Evaluation must follow investigation, not precede it or proceed without it. Empiricism subverts the complacency of those, theologians and nontheologians alike, who declare any religion inferior.

In a broad sense the criteria that will be deployed here apply to religion as well as to academic theories about religion, since there is no absolute division between religion, metaphysics and science. Science seeks patterns on a limited scale; religion and metaphysics on a universal scale. Religion and metaphysics focus on the background to experience, receding into infinity; science focuses on definite objects, somewhat arbitrarily fixed (disciplined, that is, trained to order, brought under control) in the foreground.

Basically, the two general criteria for evaluation proposed here have to do with clarity and comprehensiveness (the first criterion), and with radicality and incompleteness (the second one). We need to apply both at the same time.[4]

The first general criterion is the integrative power of religion[5] and theories about religion. According to it, theories should establish relationships between things (thereby constituting facts) in a limited area under investigation. Religion may be required to restore to the individual a sense of inner integrity and solidarity with humanity and with nature.

The second general criterion, not separate from but in association with the first, is the transcending/penetrative power of religion and theories about religion. Theories should pioneer new, more satisfactory ways of understanding the relationships between things. Religion may be expected to fulfil its role of radically opening up new orientational possibilities and creating freedom.

Each of these master criteria can be broken down into a number of aspects. First, we discuss four which derive from the master criterion of integrative power, and then four which derive from the master criterion of penetrative power.

Firstly, a theory may be required to be *coherent*, that is, the main ideas should hang together and imply one another, each deriving meaning from the whole which they jointly constitute. The requirement that a theory of religion should be logical ensures coherence by eliminating contradictions. The various parts of a theoretical argument should hang together consistently.[6] The present study is at least partly to be judged by its success or failure at combining the various angles it chose to highlight in a coherent argument.

A religion itself may be tested for inner coherence too.[7] That is largely what the long histories of doctrinal (metaphysical) refinement of Christianity and Buddhism are about. A religious system can tolerate paradox but not flat contradictions that destroy its tenuous balance. Both Christianity and Buddhism have developed notions which are of a paradoxical nature. The notion of religious paradox points beyond reason, and in doing so it makes it possible to tolerate quite harsh contrasts in the religious system. For example, somehow religions have to come to terms with both good and evil simultaneously – neither allowing them to slip so far apart that the whole religious universe disintegrates, nor cheaply harmonising them. Paradoxes and contrasts do not necessarily affect the integrative power of a religion. On the contrary, they enhance that power. But a flat contradiction like 'God did not create evil and he did create evil' does. Logic, giving rules for rooting out contradictions and principles of correct inference, is a formal instrument necessary to ensure this quality of religious coherence. Not only Western thought, but also Buddhism and Indian religions generally have developed extremely sophisticated traditions of logic, in India mainly in the context of religious philosophy.[8]

Logical consistency functions in conjunction with other criteria. If it were allowed to function in isolation, anyone would be free to dream up the most far-fetched religious system and pass it off as 'true' as long as it is internally consistent. Logic requires only that propositions correlate well with other propositions. That, however, does not imply that they also correlate well with the world.

Why be logical in religious discourse? Because this urge relates to one half of the 'logic' of religion itself, namely to seek coherence and integration. Socially, it facilitates intersubjective communication. It enables people with diverse religious views to join in meaningful dialogue. This is far better than religious violence and persecution. Chaotic thinking is just as disturbing as a chaotic reality, a chaotic personality and a chaotic society. So it may be said that logic plays an essential constructive and critical role in religions. Sooner or later religions which had had the opportunity to sharpen their intellectual tools strove to develop a comprehensive body of coherent teachings. This was how the great theologies and metaphysical systems developed.

Secondly, the requirement of *simplicity* in a theory is implicit in the requirement of integrative ability. It insists that the ideal of comprehensiveness should be attained as economically as possible. A good theory is streamlined, a thing of intellectual beauty and elegance.

The appraisal of religion itself is largely an aesthetic judgement. Religions appeal to us in their wholeness, their completeness, their balance, their harmonisation of contrasts and discords. That is one side of it. They establish relationships between the very diverse elements of experience. They are compositions. Religious experience is the intuition of a beauty that passes understanding. This is a far cry from prettiness. It may be fearful. A religious vision embracing all things may work with shocking contrasts. And even when religions fall short of such inclusiveness, they strike a chord which reminds us of that dream. The aesthetic appreciation of religion is linked with the nature of religion as a growing awareness of increasing complexity: seemingly unrelated or discordant things are woven together to form new, bolder, wider, finer textures.

Religion finds a natural ally in art. This does not apply to religion, or art, as a frivolous statement of the obvious, an affirmation of our complacent order. That would be religious, and artistic, kitsch. Art shocks and provokes, penetrating to another less obvious dimension of reality. So does religion. There is an aesthetic not only of symmetry and harmony, but also of asymmetry and disharmony. The latter may be taken to the absurd, the incoherent and the chaotic, as contemporary drama and painting show. All I am saying is that the two aesthetics are two sides of the same coin. Which side is up depends on the needs of the times and the circumstances. The other's turn will come. In our present context, the accent is on the harmonising, symphonising function of religion. In Bushman painting, for example, the beauty resides not only in the graceful forms, but above all in the vision of a world of harmony in which eland and shaman are conjoined, and in which death is harmonised with life. In Christianity a gruesome death on a cross is redeemed by assimilating it to all-embracing love. In Buddhism the ideal of perfect harmony of all living beings reaches an unsurpassed pinnacle. In religion, beauty is a fundamental category. Its inherent quality appeals and convinces directly. This direct apprehension of religious beauty is not the same as an arbitrary preference for this or that, any more than it is in art. It is an appreciation of harmony which is given with human nature, and which may be cultivated like any other taste.

Thirdly, the requirement that a theory should *link up with existing thinking* about a subject ties in with the ideal of integration. For optimal power, individual efforts are combined, sometimes over many generations. It could take centuries, even millennia, of effort to fathom and exhaust the possibilities of a frame of thinking. Only by stepping into the history of research in a given area can we make sure that all the facts are indeed accounted for adequately. There is progress. The wheel has been invented. Today it would be as anachronistic to use the nineteenth-century concepts of mana or taboo to interpret Bushman religion as it would be to view Bushman painting through colonialist eyes as the result of importations by whites from the north. Normal science is conducted in normative paradigms (Kuhn). Taking seriously the overall, recognised state of thinking in what is called, with good reason, a discipline is a part of the drive to see comprehensively. The mass of idiosyncratic views and private theories is called to order and placed under the discipline of the paradigm. This requirement obviously functions conservatively. Investigation into religion, like all other branches of scholarship, runs in channels dug by great creative pioneers.[9] At this stage of its development religious studies does not have a generally accepted paradigm. What will emerge from the present process of fermentation is uncertain, but that schools, clusters and trends with certain shared academic values and norms will keep on forming is certain.

Coming to religion itself, this criterion may be applied to establish its value, for example to establish whether rituals, teachings and so on are in fact in line with the religious tradition in which they purport to stand (that is, if they stand in such traditions at all, for, as I argued earlier, religion is wider than the various religions). Religions are vast models of the world, prescribing how their adherents should think about it and act in it. Whether they have a known beginning in the past (like Buddhism and Christianity) or not (like Bushman religion), these models have developed over long periods of time. Whatever the present generation does must somehow articulate with that tradition, and is good and true to the extent that it accords with the established norm of the religion. This is obviously an intrareligious criterion. Nevertheless, even from the point of view of studies that are not formally confined to any specific religion, it is still important to evaluate whether a certain thought is 'good' Christianity or Buddhism, in other words, whether it falls within the ambit of acceptability of that particular religious pattern as a whole. Religions are historically grown complexes, like rivers meandering through time, accumulating much as they move through different territories, losing some things, forming stagnant pools and paltry streamlets alongside the main stream. This historicist view differs vastly from a dogmatic view. The former would see Christianity or Buddhism as the sum of its historical development. Yet even so, that view would allow for some measure of evaluation.

This criterion derives from the fact that a religion is a sociocultural, historical, linguistic convention, integrating individuals into a symbol-sharing community. That allows us to develop a *type* of, say, 'Buddhism' or 'Christianity'. Such a type would consist of a core, a margin of tolerance and outside limits. Using that as an empirical benchmark, one can make useful distinctions between 'good' and 'bad', 'better' and 'worse' Christianity or Buddhism. 'Good' would refer to thoughts, words and actions that fall well within the parameters of that empirical norm, 'bad' to what falls outside it. Monotheism would make 'bad' Buddhism, as the idea that Satan is part of the Trinity would make 'bad' Christianity, clearly falling outside its historical tolerance span. Obviously this criterion would have to be refined. The criteria of establishing such historical types would have to be spelt out. Would the *norm* be the historically earliest, or the historically most recent, or some or other incisive moment during that history, or the sum total of the process as a whole?[10] Would it be the differences from other complexes, or its similarities with others? Would it be a collection of features, or one decisive feature? Would it reside in the social, the doctrinal, the moral or the ritual sphere, or in a combination of these? And so forth. Constructing the measuring instrument would be a matter of agreement and clear stipulation, not an absolutist either-or decision. Generally it seems to me to be a very useful empirical tool, at least making possible intersubjectively debatable conclusions.

My argument is not that this is a sufficient or a necessary criterion to establish religious validity. We cannot say that a statement is valid because religious convention X dictates so. The question whether a statement conforms with religious convention X (however important it may be in its own limited context) is not the only question to ask. Another equally important one is whether it meshes with the world. We cannot insist that *because* it conforms with a holy scripture, tradition or person, a pronouncement meshes with the world, for such books, traditions and persons themselves have derived authority. They purport to reveal the world. Ultimately, the religious founder does not claim 'this is true because I say so', but 'I say so because it is true'. This criterion follows from the nature of religious social endeavour, as developed in chapter 3. A religious book, tradition or person essentially points beyond itself. It seeks alignment with the world.

We have now moved onto the fourth subcriterion: the implication of the requirement of integration that explanations of religion should apply adequately to the array of items they wish to explain. They should *cover the facts*. This may be done in two ways: by extension and by intension. Extension, like a jigsaw puzzle, incorporates new pieces (for example more religions) into the growing pattern. Intension, like the progressive lighting of a dark room or the focusing of a telescope (Abraham Kaplan), shows up the details (for example of the dimensions of the Buddhist concept of emptiness) better. Therefore, the more new facts it covers (the greater the range, the wider its comprehensive power), or the more hidden aspects of known facts it encompasses (the subtler its comprehensive power), the better the theory. This is not requiring that the explanation should depict reality. A theory is a map, helping us to survey a new territory, not a photograph of it. It is an invented instrument, not a photocopy. This does not mean that the theorist simply fabricates it. In the sixteenth century Francis Bacon compared the scientist to a bee collecting nectar, processing it and then producing honey, rather than a spider spinning her web purely from within herself, or an ant collecting data to pile in a heap. In our mechanised century Kurt Lewin compared a theory to a network of freeways, designed to cover an area as efficiently as possible and therefore naturally adapted to the topography of the land. A metaphor in a poem is the creation of the poet, yet there is a difference between a good metaphor, which reveals a profound meaning, and a bad one, which is merely contrived. A theory is not a blueprint of the world, only a profile of it. A theory must proceed from and be sensitive to the world, but it is not a direct reflection of it. What is needed in religious studies is therefore not the one and only 'true' understanding of religion. There may be many understandings, more adequate or less so, of the set comprising Bushman religion, Buddhism and Christianity. A good understanding would disclose a pattern never spotted before, discover connections where none existed before, and produce a flash of fresh insight.

In religion itself, validity is more than just the coherence of propositions, or coherence with the established tradition. It is a matter of coherence with the world. Religions claim to give their members reliable maps of the cosmos. It may therefore be asked whether these religious maps are indeed congruent with the topography of their terrain. A map's failure to show a sheer cliff where there is one could be lethal. Unless religions stay in touch with the changing external environments around them, they lose their power in the long run. I wish to understand this criterion in terms of the conditionalist empiricist assumption that religious societies and the world at large, including nature, are attuned to each other (chapter 2). 'Experience' is an ambivalent concept. It has a 'subjective' side: it is *my* experience. It also has an 'objective' side: I experience not myself, but *the world*. The two sides mesh, so that the one cannot be separated from the other. The blueness of the flower is part of the flower as much as of my looking. This follows from the assumption that our consciousness of the world emerged in the evolutionary development of humankind as a part of nature. This unfortunately does not imply that 'my' experience is always correct. The link between my impression and reality may be skewed. The way it appears to me may not be the way it is. The world is deep and wide, and my apparatus for observation is small. The field of my apprehension of things is not very large, although symbolism helps a lot by creating the possibility of leapfrogging over the known into the relatively unknown. The point here is that validity has to do with the question of whether my experience articulates with the world; in Whitehead's terms, whether Appearance and Reality are conformal.[11] This has a direct bearing on religion. Through direct intuitive apprehension, as well as through symbolism, people attempt to reach out as far as possible. Religion aims to be attuned to the real world.

How would we 'know' religious validity? 'Proofs' (rational arguments, based on logic and/or empirical evidence) *for* the 'truth' of any comprehensive vision are futile. Validity here, if it is evident, needs no proofs; and if it is not evident, no proofs will induce it. Either you see it, or you don't. Religious insight is an aesthetic category: it is a seeing (which does not exclude the possibility that it may be wrong). It is not mere subjective expressiveness, but not hard objective fact either. On the other hand, I suggest that rational arguments (based on logic and/or empirical evidence) can *disprove* religious views. The criteria that we have discussed so far, and the ones we shall still be talking about, serve not so much to prove truth as to unmask untruth. A disjointed, contradictory, ugly, depressing religion does not have very good credentials to make us trust that it might fit reality well.

Religious insight into the network of reality operates at a deeper level than can be formulated intellectually and expressed linguistically. Ask the mystics. Nevertheless, *if* a religion does make intellectual statements about reality, the congruence with reality of such propositions may be tested. *Insofar* as it makes such statements, it cannot claim special privileged status but has to compete on the open market of ideas – with electricity, so to speak (Bultmann). Then the view that the world was created in six days must compete on equal terms with the theory of the Big Bang. As our politicians keep repeating: the playing fields must be levelled. Whether or not such questions are difficult or easy to answer, or will perhaps never be answered, is beside the point.

What matters is that they relate to the general field of experience accessible to normal, waking, everyday awareness and to science (which is, after all, an extension and refinement of everyday experience), and that they are in principle examinable.

A believer may of course say: 'In terms of my religion I make no conceptual statements about reality at all', and thereby withdraw from this test. The modern history of Christianity demonstrates that under the impact of modern science cognitive propositions that were once unproblematic tenets of the Christian credo (for example creation in six days) have largely ceased to be that. Instead of definite factual propositions about a historical state of affairs, the accounts of creation have been reinterpreted by some as mere expressive, emotional utterances of a feeling and an attitude of dependence. What I am saying, is merely that *if*, and *to the extent that* a religion lays claim to factual, conceptual, objective agreement with how things are, it can and must be tested critically.[12]

We now come to four applications of the requirement that theories of religion and religion should demonstrate a transcending/penetrative power.

Firstly, the fact that religions are systems of orientation inextricably enmeshed in the conditional network which is reality implies that religious truth is *perspectival, relative, historical*[13]. One only knows in terms of a specific here and now, a limited relative position in the wide field of relationships. That relative position is by no means fixed. It is shifting, relative to all the other changing and shifting points in the changing developing contexts with which it is intertwined. The acts of religious orientation are determined, furthermore, by a host of physical, psychological, social, economical, historical and other factors (emotions, desires, interests, etc), uncovered by psychology, sociology and other human sciences. Emphasising this flux does not exclude the possibility that perspectives may be *more* or *less* adequate. Like all forms of knowledge, religion is a relation of mutual conditioning of the known and the knower. The known affects the knower, and at the same time its constitution in the perception of the knower is coloured, in a variety of ways, by the knower. Yet it is a real relation. People can imagine things, and deliberately distort the perspective. Certainly no perspective can lay claim to absolute accuracy. And certainly the fact of multiperspectivism should be appreciated. It could be used as a means of comparing and cross-checking, a kind of extended triangulation. You over there and I here see different sides of the same tree; we can start talking, and thus form a better picture of the whole tree. The problem is that neither you, nor I, nor the tree is static, simple, fixed. All three of us are in flux, and without definite contours. This perspective of perspectivism by no means implies a contradiction. That would only be the case if it claimed a privileged position of absoluteness, which it does not. It makes no absolute claim to relativity, only a relative claim. It does not reject absolutism on absolute grounds, only on relative, provisional ones. It fails to be convinced by absolutism on empirical grounds, and does not argue on a priori grounds at all. I submit that this relational approach obviates the apparent dilemma of both relativism (in the sense of arbitrary subjectivism) and absolutism.

Religion is orientation. Given the nature of reality, religion is a never-ending series of balancing acts, a receptive creative interplay with reality. To allow the flow to coagulate into a solid, unchanging state would run contrary to the logic of the religious impulse. Therefore conceptual closure in absolute dogmas and dogmatic systems is an attempt to escape from the dynamic of creative adaptation from moment to moment. Religious forms are landmarks left from other people's journeys. They are indispensable pointers for others. But sooner or later they are left behind. None of them is absolute. So in the end there is no absolute, final truth. People move. The world forever changes, partly because of our interaction with it. All we can aspire to is a slightly more inclusive perspective, here and now, on our never-ending journey. On this journey truth is a matter of unlearning rather than learning, stripping rather than adding, eliminating rather than establishing certainties. We may even play between the rules of logic. Unless religion, like art, exists on the dangerous threshold of the unknown, it becomes shallow. The general conditionalist strategy is not to launch a frontal attack on the enemy, forcing an immediate clear win or lose. Rather, it is analogous to the luring of Napoleon and Hitler into the boundless hinterland of Russia, where aggressive self-assurance eventually dissipates.

The historicity of religious truth means that what was right in the seventeenth century may no longer be right today, and that what is right for a group of us (constituted of individuals, each with its own angle) here and now, in this real world of today, will have lost much or most, if not all, of its relevance fifty years hence, if not sooner. The history of even the greatest religious visions proves that no single insight remains unaffected by time. Even if they give general direction to people's lives for millennia, they are reinterpreted and adapted from generation to generation, and they vary from individual to individual. It is impossible, even if we wanted to (as fundamentalists do), to hold the world still, or to go back to the conditions of days long past. This principle of change and perspectivism holds for theories of religion as well.

Does the unequivocal acceptance of radical conditionalism inevitably result in flabby, noncommittal lack of character and definition? No. On the contrary, it realises (understands clearly; achieves fully) the unrepeatable uniqueness of this momentary flash of meaning and insight, fragmentary and limited as it is, warranting (as Dogen passionately insisted[14]) total exertion.

Secondly, it is vital to draw a clear distinction between *authority* and *force* in religious matters. For present purposes, I situate *power* ambivalently between them, and relate *violence* closely to force. The distinction between authority and force applies to theorising about religion as much as to any other sphere of life. A thug with a gun may wield force over people, but he has no authority; a Beethoven symphony performed by a great orchestra keeps people spellbound purely by the authority of genius – you can get up and walk out any time you want to. Wielding a stick – or a book – is an act of force and violence. A clear criterion for distinguishing between good and bad religion at a given time is the degree to which it relies on either authority (*auctoritas*) or force (*potestas*). The torturing and burning of witches and heretics was perpetrated officially and with the blessing of church leaders in Christian Europe not so long ago. This is a chilling reminder of a constant possibility in religion. The smoke from the stake at which Servetus was incinerated, allegedly for a deviant view of the Trinity, hangs over Calvinism. The history of religions, no less than the political field, teems with tyrants, big and little. In the historical religions violence is as real as authority.

The essential difference between authority and force is that whereas authority pursues the principle of transcendence, achieves a balance between integration and transcendence and is legitimised by referring to what lies beyond itself, force resists that principle. Power corrupts – when it becomes 'absolute', that is when it loosens itself from the dynamic complexities of life. In idealised terms: authority avoids centrism as well as chaos, the encapsulation of possibilities in a closed, realised state as well as the confusion of non-relation. Authority creates and constantly recreates an open order. Authority is crucial to religion as a process of growth; force and chaos are alien to it. Authority invites, lures, challenges and pushes you forward into freedom; force threatens, stifles, represses and pushes you back into submission. Authority convinces you by its own inner strength; force overpowers you by physical violence, verbal abuse, academic browbeating and financial manipulation – the list is very long, and force is very ingenious, as the history of religion shows. Authority allows itself to be challenged, in fact, it can afford to invite challenge, confident of its own strength yet aware of its own provisionality; force inflates itself as far as possible and tries to safeguard itself against any challenge, sensing its own lack of inner strength. Authority may slap you to wake you up; force slaps you to keep you quiet. Authority lays itself open; force entrenches its own position. Authority encourages individual autonomy; force imposes conformism. Authority encourages free enquiry; force blocks it. Authority seeks to make itself superfluous; force can only be overcome by resistance.

Thirdly, the progressive principle in theorising is that it should be *fruitful* and *stimulating*. Standstill is equivalent to regress. The value of a theory lies in the questions it raises as much as in the answers it provides. Like dynamite, it breaks rock, allowing the search for new treasures. No explanation of religion should ever be regarded or passed off as final. The correlational network can always be extended and intensified. What Max Weber said about scholars working in the sure knowledge that their painstaking labour is destined to be superseded, and what Karl Popper said about the scientific process being a constant striving for falsification, apply also to enquiry into religion. Explanation has a heuristic function: it encourages fresh thought and invites renewed searching. Or rather, it should. This principle does not mean that once an explanation has been superseded by another, it becomes valueless. It has served its purpose in that it has stimulated a better one. In religious investigation no explanation must be blindly accepted or rejected the moment it shows weaknesses. Any explanation can be improved on, and even a poor explanation may contain valuable elements.

Enough has been said on the preceding pages to make clear that this criterion also holds for religions. Certainly there are differences. Religions cover a much wider area of life than partial theories. For that reason most people would make greater emotional investments in religion than in science. Religions have had a stronger hold on cultures and civilisations over much longer periods of time than scientific theories. The experiment that seeks to exhaust the meaning of a great religious vision needs a much longer timespan than scientific experiments. Religious systems are not organised scepticism, as science is. The idea is not to get rid of them as soon as possible. Religions have a stronger conservative instinct. But the basic principle of conditionalism remains that the value of all human systems of meaning lies in their ability to keep alive and to stimulate the ongoing search for meaning, necessitated by the ongoing dynamics of reality.

Fourthly, it may be asked what the effects of intellectual work are on the individual, society and the world at large (including nature). The *difference it makes for the better* is a most important criterion of its value. As argued earlier, the academic study of religion cannot wash its hands of its effects on society.

Regarding religion, it must be asked: *Does it have transformative power?*[15] Does it make people freer and happier? Does it liberate? Partly, this is a critique of religious ideas. Are they trustworthy lodestars? Where do their respective inherent logics lead to in real life? *What do they do*? What are their consequences and ripple effects? Resist in the beginnings, as the Romans said. Example: once it has been accepted that heresy is punishable by death, a culture of violence follows. Another example: from this point of view, triumphant academic Christian theology in this country, whether in conservative, liberal or radical garb, is vulnerable to the criticism that it did not contribute in the past to the widening of religious discourse. Even when it criticised social apartheid, it did little to break down religious apartheid and to create an open religious space. The criterion of *real consequences* applies not only to ideas, but to religious behavioural patterns, ethics and ritual as well. It also implies a critique of religious people. Are they *authentic* in their following and appropriation of the inherited ideas? What matters, according to the norm of authenticity, is not the significance of religious ideas in the abstract, but whether they are recreated in freedom. *What is done with them*?

How does one know what is good in this regard? In the case of coherence we have the rules of logic, and in the case of faithfulness to reality we have reality itself as a touchstone. But here? Is 'good' not whatever religion proclaims to be good? I maintain that if we take the empirical datum of 'religion' itself as our premise, and we clarify what is entailed by transcending and integration, we have a basis for discussion. The usefulness of religion as a process of transcending and integrating is that it aims at liberating individuals from the desperate effort to protect themselves and their position. Its purpose is to enable one to live openly and freely, with joy and confidence, and with the strength to endure hardship. It aims to release one from the compulsion to possess all sorts of things – from material goods and other people ('love') to error-free dogmas. It aims to get people to the point where they are able to live together in peace and justice in open universal fellowship, in which group egoism is transcended just as surely as individual egoism. It seeks to integrate humanity with a world in which it is linked to animal, vegetable and inanimate nature in cosmic solidarity and responsibility, with reverence for the mystery of all these things. This also permits negative criticism. Where religions legitimise the exploitation of nature or fellow humans, they must be criticised ruthlessly for deviating from the religious intention. The arguments that religion is the universal obsessive neurosis of humankind (Freud), that it is an opiate of the oppressed (Marx), that it is the self-deification of society (Durkheim) are legitimate exposés of some forms of religion. The list of restrictive abuses is longer. Not least among these is the phenomenon of a religion closing in on itself, becoming introverted, setting up its dogmas and forms as inviolable, acting as jailer rather than liberator. The justification for such criticisms becomes evident when we see them against the background of the urge to open up occlusions.

ENDNOTES

1 In its general drift this chapter concurs with the contributions of M Prozesky, Is there a place in religious studies for the criticism and reformulation of religion?, *Religion in South Africa*, 6(1), 1985, pp 71–81; and Judging religion, in J K. Roth & F Sontag (eds), *The defence of God*, New York: Paragon, 1985, pp 102–119. Also see the pertinent remarks by N Smart, *Concept and empathy: essays in the study of religion*, London: Macmillan, 1986, pp 72ff. M Pye (Religious studies in Europe: structures and desiderata, in K K Klostermaier & L W Hurtado, *Religious studies: issues, prospects and proposals*, Atlanta, Ga: Scholars Press, 1991, p 51), while presupposing the generally accepted core of the discipline of religious studies, states: '... where else but in the university context can advanced consideration be given to the truth claims inherent in (if not explicitly advanced by) various religions? This implies the cultivation of a critical philosophy component in religious studies, broadly conceived, which takes account of the diversity of religion and is not restricted to the theistic traditions.'

2 This has been pointed out by M Bourdillon, Anthropological approaches to the

study of African religions, unpublished paper read at the Regional Conference on the Study of Religions in Africa, held at the University of Zimbabwe, 15–19 September 1992, pp 43ff, using the following example: 'When members of a millenarian movement destroy their means of livelihood in the belief that such action will bring in a new age of prosperity, while we may understand their frustrations, we know that their perspective is wrong and will lead to hunger rather than to prosperity.'

3 The concepts of truth in Western philosophy, Hinduism, Buddhism, Judaism, Christianity and Islam have been thoroughly surveyed by H M Vroom, *Religions and the truth: philosophical reflections and perspectives*, Grand Rapids, Mich: Eerdmans, 1989.

4 The range of these criteria could possibly be extended to make them applicable to the reasons that religious groups succeed or fail in the arena of history, and that people join or leave groups.

5 Cf Vroom, *Religions and the truth ...*, pp 362ff.

6 H G Hubbeling (Theology, philosophy and science of religion and their logical and empirical presuppositions, in Th P van Baaren & H J W Drijvers (eds), *Religion, culture and methodology*, The Hague: Mouton, 1973, pp 9–33) insists on the importance of logic in religious studies.

7 Cf M Prozesky, *A new guide to the debate about God*, Pietermaritzburg: University of Natal Press, 1989, pp 11ff.

8 As pointed out by D Daor, Modes of argument, in B-A Scharfstein et al, *Philosophy East/philosophy West: a critical comparison of Indian, Chinese, Islamic, and European philosophy*, Oxford: Blackwell, 1987, pp 162–195. This does not imply that the so-called 'primitive' mind is innocent of this same kind of logic. See E D Prinsloo's conclusion (Logic and culture, *South African Journal of Philosophy* 8(2), 1989, pp 94–99) that the principle of noncontradiction or consistency applies to 'primitive' as well as to Western cultures, and that 'three-valued logic' (regardless of its logical acceptability) appears in both Western and 'primitive' thinking.

9 The history of this field of study has been reconstructed by (among others) E J Sharpe, *Comparative religion: a history*, London: Duckworth, 1975; F Whaling, *Contemporary approaches to the study of religion*, Berlin: De Gruyter, 1983 (Vol I), 1985 (Vol II).

10 These criteria are discussed in M Pye & R Morgan (eds), *The cardinal meaning. Essays in comparative hermeneutics: Buddhism and Christianity*, The Hague: Mouton, 1973.

11 A N Whitehead, *Adventures of ideas*, New York: Free Press, 1933, pp 241–272.

12 Although the word 'truth' is problematical here, and the relevance of the idea of conceptual, propositional tallying with reality in religion is suspect, D Wiebe's overall conclusion (*Religion and truth: towards an alternative paradigm for the study of religion*, The Hague: Mouton, 1981, p 228) goes a long way: '... even though 'religious truth' is something more than mere propositional truth and so, in a limited sense beyond the observation and critical analysis of the 'objective' observer, it is nevertheless intimately (necessarily) connected with propositional truth, thereby making it subject to objective discussion, analysis, and criticism'.

13 For the relativity of belief in a Whiteheadian framework, see J Cobb's comments in D R Griffin & T J J Altizer (eds), *John Cobb's theology in process*, Philadelphia: Westminster Press, 1977, pp 165ff.

14 See H-J Kim, *Dogen Kigen: mystical realist*, Tucson: University of Arizona Press, 1987, passim, on the notion of *gujin*.

15 Cf Vroom, *Religions and the truth* ..., pp 366ff; Prozesky, *A new guide* ..., p 13.

9 Thinking(-speaking), silencing, doing

To round off Part II, this chapter will summarise and extract some presuppositions and implications of the conditionalist perspective that were already explicitly or implicitly present in the previous chapters. The enquiry into religion will proceed to the three dimensions of *religious thinking (-speaking)*, *silencing*, and *doing*. Concerning the four 'm's' that will be discussed (metaphysics, myth, mysticism, morality), I believe that myth remains the strong undercurrent of religion; that metaphysics is inevitable and could be useful; that when passing into mysticism, metaphysics is silenced; and that enquiry into religion has a moral dimension.

In this study the cognitive dimension of religion is the centre of interest. Ritual, social form, art and so on are looked at indirectly, as they relate to cognition. I shall presuppose the triangular model put forward in chapter 3, where it was postulated that human life has three points of reference: you (society), it (the world), and I (the individual). None of these is isolated. Each is connected with and implied in the others. There are also three basic types of cognition, again mutually implied in many ways, correlating (but not coinciding) with the three points of reference: *mythic* cognition, *conceptual* cognition, and *mystic* cognition. About these last three I need to say more.

I am not suggesting that the three kinds of cognition are in any way graded hierarchically from low to high in the history of humanity. On the contrary, I postulate that all three are part of the pan-human field of cognition. Neither is an evolutionary scheme 'from Bushman to Buddhist' constructed. Rather, it is suggested that in the ongoing spiral of religious discovery all three have their roles to play. Furthermore, I am not suggesting that they are separate. On the contrary, they are continuous. Yet it seems irrefutable that in certain epochs certain emphases and combinations occur more frequently than in others. In some individuals, in some societies, in some periods, one of the three – the *you*-mode (mythical cognition), the *it*-mode (conceptual cognition) or the *I*-mode (mystical cognition) – may all but absorb the others.

More boldly (but still not an extravagant statement) it may be suggested that in the *overall* history of humankind (as far as it is known) one can discern a shift away from an overwhelming emphasis of mythic cognition to an overwhelming emphasis of conceptual cognition, and that mystic cognition rose to relative prominence later (fairly recently, a mere few thousand years ago), responding to conceptual cognition. Not to digress into a lengthy reconstruction of history, a few examples will make the point: in traditional Bushman culture the overwhelming emphasis was on mythic cognition. Since the development of the sociocultural complex marked by urbanisation, metal-smelting and agriculture a meagre few thousand years ago, conceptual cognition has grown in significance. Mysticism can be seen as a reaction to that development.[1] Modern European culture (from the sixteenth century onwards) places an overwhelming emphasis on conceptual cognition. Part of what is going on in contemporary Western culture is to seek to redress that imbalance, hence a keen interest in mythic and mystic cognition is observable.

Myth

In *mythic* cognition the human being participates in a universal fellowship of living things. The knower is not separated from but near and intimately involved with other living beings as so many 'yous'. The world itself is conceived of as a community of life peopled by manifold beings, a community of 'yous', itself a 'you'. It remains a constant feature even of contemporary societies, more noticeable on its unofficial fringes. It has been the underlying passion of the protesting (post-)modern forms of art and religion.

Mythic cognition derives from the unconscious dimension of human existence. Because human life is rooted in nature, the elements of nature can project themselves into the human psyche as powerful anthropomorphic symbols, illuminating the world. Myths are the elaboration and combination of such symbols into comprehensive explanatory paradigms, often in the form of dramatic stories enacted by mythic personae (animals, spirits, gods, therianthropic beings, etc). They are true in the sense that they compellingly reveal the intuitions of the human mind concerning the structures of reality and express a social group's understanding of the world, spread out around its now-here. Where does it all come from, and where is it heading? Why is it the way it is, and what must be done to maintain this delicate balance, threatened as it is by disruptive forces?

Since myths are the dreams of humankind, revealing the 'true' world, they are also powerful motivating forces that may set loose tremendous revolutionary energies for changing states of affairs that are perceived to be at odds with the 'real, true' world. A myth can be 'true' in the sense that it refracts (reflects, like a drop of water trembling on a moving leaf) a passing scene from the world, but not in the sense that it isomorphically presents or represents reality like a snapshot. Myths move with time. As the now-here changes, the whole pattern surrounding it changes. The refracting stories too. Myths die when their inner force is spent, and they are replaced by others more capable of serving the religious needs of a new epoch. Whenever myths stagnate, they inhibit religious development and sooner or later are removed. Such interim periods – times without myths that link humanity with the roots of its existence – are times of emptiness and suffering. The rhythm of meaning-giving myths arising from the unconscious and passing into oblivion is the rhythm of religion. The religious history of the world illustrates that movement over and over again. It also manifests itself in South Africa. The ancient mythology of the Bushmen has been destroyed. The modern mythology of European supremacy has been destroyed. In most of our regional Christianity the magnificent biblical myths of creation, incarnation and resurrection are presented as quasi facts.

Metaphysics

In *conceptual* cognition a 'third world' of ideas (Popper)[2] is created. Conceptual cognition creates a split between the knowing subject and the known object. It observes and analyses from a distance, and abstracts from the warm stuff of life. If this orientation loses its intertwinement with the other two altogether, then 'yous' tend to be seen as lifeless 'its', and life becomes a manifold of controlled, manipulated 'things', a dissected cadaver.

I now return to the first point made at the outset of this chapter: religious metaphysics (a conceptual, systematic account of the most general features of the phenomenal, cognised world) cannot be 'objectively' 'true', but it remains inevitable, and could be useful as a world-orientation. Even if it were to try to avoid the dimension of religious thinking fraught with dangers ranging from presumptuousness to word-mongering, a radical enquiry into religion is inescapably drawn into it.

In the conditionalist perspective drawing on Buddhist and Whiteheadian thought, the many individual things making up the universe appear as an inexhaustible multitude of ever-changing constellations, momentarily poised in ever-shifting now-heres. 'I' – and that goes for everything else – am a shortlived constellation of factors in a series of shifting intersections in a throbbing field of relations; conditioned, at every moment from whatever distance, by every other vibrant intersection, indirectly and directly, mediately and immediately, as well as conditioning every other intersection; conditioned at every moment by its own past, that is by all the preceding intersections in its own immediate series, and by its future, that is by the anticipated intersections in its own unique, relatively open series advancing into the future; conditioning (reconstituting) at every moment its own past and conditioning (constituting, creating) its own future; receiving at every moment the cumulative effect of the universe, and contributing at every moment to all other intersections making up the unbounded universe. Every action of every individual thing at every moment is like a pebble striking water – causing not merely ripples on a flat horizontal surface, but reverberating multidimensionally through the numberless vastnesses of now-heres, through the indeterminate infinity of all the other intersections and their actions until it eventually peters out (but not absolutely) in the immensity of the world, its effects conditioned from moment to moment by the myriad other inputs in that pulsating field. The world is not a uni-verse ('turned-into-oneness') in the strict sense of the word: it never solidifies in a fixed unity, however vast, and it has no one fixed, stable centre; every fleeting intersection is a centre, a *now-here* – and a *no-where* in the sense that it does not take up any fixed space for any fixed time.

It is not a static but a pulsating world. The reciprocities between the incalculable number of relative constellations, large or small, clustered around intersections never let up. Religion has always latched onto the symbolic value of rather small clusters (numbers): twos (male-female, day-night, creator-creation), threes (the trinities of various religions), fours (the four quarters of the world), and so on. Furthermore, each constellation changes perpetually, having come into being in the relatively near past and being due to pass away in the future. Birth and death – of small constellations such as cells as well as larger ones such as civilisations and even larger ones such as stellar galaxies – are inherent in the pattern of the world. Coming into being and passing away are relative. The now-here contains the past as the fullness of what has been, as well as the relative openness of the future. In mutual conditioning, the past will be present in the future as a set of limitations and invitations arising from completed possibilities, just as the future was present in the past as a set of limitations and invitations arising from new possibilities.

In this world the human being has a strangely ambivalent character. It is the being who may attain to full awareness of the relative nature of the universe; it is also the being in whom the open dynamic of the universe tends to close down – the being who refuses to die, in this world or in a next one; it is also the being in whom discovery of the full implications of its own death is the discovery of the nature of the world itself. The human being tends to close down both the past and the future – the past by repression of it and by historical determinism ('it could not have happened differently'); and the future, by teleological determinism ('the predetermined future bears down on us like a train from a tunnel'). Both the past and the future may be opened up – the past, by reinterpretation and reintegration with the ongoing process of life; and the future, by picking up the signals of new possibilities, being open to surprises, and assuming responsibility for the ongoing process of life.

What is required is to maintain the mutual implication of the two movements of thought (integrating and transcending). The great danger besetting religious thinking is closed thought (totalism, centrism). To avert this danger, two strategies could be followed: firstly, to abstain completely from any systematic thinking about the world, human beings, the nature of knowledge, and so on; or, secondly, engaging in it as if one were not engaging in it – that is, dis-integrating it at the very moment of integration. The second, with its permanent reflexive self-subversion, is the better strategy. The problem with the first strategy is that it is not really possible to stick to it indefinitely, and that it could inadvertently turn into a fixed position itself.

The problem with any god-concept, whether monotheism, polytheism, pantheism, panentheism or whatever, is that it chokes the dynamics by forcing it into narrow confines. The only tolerable idea of God would be one that has implanted in itself the germ of its own explosion, its own radical relativising. Then the idea of God would not impose a limitation on the conditionalist universe, and would not be an exception to it[3] – but would be symbolic of its depth and mystery. It would be the most comprehensive and the most explosive symbol of radical conditionalism and contingency. It implies the death of God as absolute basis and support, whether immanent or transcendent, as well as the death of humanity as God's substitute in the scheme of things. In the words of Panikkar, paraphrasing the teaching of the Buddha, 'ultimately there is 'nothing' to be said about God because God 'is' precisely this 'nothing'.[4]

Seeing all things large and small, simple and complex, beautiful and ugly, good and bad as moments in this vast unfinished interplay, conditionalism would stop short of a theodicy, that is, of any fixed and final theoretical explanation of things, and not only of evil. Reality as an essentially open interplay is not primarily an object of contemplation, but the field of active, creative response-ability. Evil cannot be thought away. It can only be overcome. The evil of the past cannot be obliterated miraculously and instantaneously by confessing it – then lo! it has disappeared, and may now be forgotten. On the contrary, it must not be forgotten. The point is not to keep alive a morbid sense of guilt, but to push ahead soberly and practically, uprooting that evil. For it insinuates itself into the texture of things, almost ineradicably, like a cancer, carrying on even in the reactions it provokes. Violence breeds violence breeds violence breeds violence. An admission of guilt can at most be the beginning of a process of cleansing. Unless it is followed by a long, determined practical and intellectual cleaning out of all its subtle causes and effects, it remains just an emotional discharge. Evil can only be overcome progressively by weaving a wholly new fabric in which the evil of the past will gradually fade into the background of a larger pattern, as a reminder of what is never to be repeated.

As an academic pursuit, religious studies (including the philosophy of religion) has its limits. Aware as it must be of the limits of our everyday experience and of our intellect, it cannot exceed those limits. Yet by clearly acknowledging its own limits and limitations, it may remind of silence. Religious metaphysics is conceptual cognition, and exposed to the dangers attending that, mentioned above. The ultimate aim of a radical enquiry into religion cannot be to defend any definitive position, or to head towards one. Its function can only be to provoke people to start moving from wherever they may be in their personal or collective biographies. To embark on this journey is to be religious in the terms that 'religion' is used in these essays. By extending the circle of the known, improving communication and achieving greater understanding, it integrates. By criticising, it jogs people out of their complacency. Like lye, it strips off preliminary and superficial fixations in the religious process. As the spiral thread of a drill bit grips in order to bore deeper, integrating and transcending constantly alternate in the movement into the depth. It is natural that an individual or a group, having advanced to a point, will consolidate that new experience into a standpoint, a position, a totality, an identity – until the intrinsic dynamics of the process, perhaps as a result of external factors, comes into play once more and triggers a new round of movement. One can never say: 'Now I have it!'

Conceptual cognition, utilising unambiguous definitions and the rules of logic, has a demythologising function. This is not to say that its function is wholly negative. It may fulfil the very important function of showing up the limitations of any mythology. Looking at the Greek Enlightenment from the sixth century BCE onwards, as well as at the European Enlightenment of modern times, it is not self-evident that the emergence of rationality in itself caused the demise of the old myths; in both cases, rationality arose partly because the old myths were losing their powers of religious legitimation. Reason may play both a revolutionary and a conservative role. It is a critical as well as a constructive instrument. In the language of this book, it may serve the integrating and the transcending functions of religion, and it may serve both functions badly or well. Reason may be misused in a totalitarian sense to construct or uphold total systems, impervious to criticism, as is well known from the history of religions. It is well used in debunking such absolutes.

Yet it can become totalitarian in its criticism as well. Hypertrophied reason leaves no place for the vital mythic dimension. In modern Western Christian theology there has been a strong tendency to rationalise the Christian myths. For example, the myth of creation often became a pseudo-scientific proposition about how the world came into being, leaving it to the artists to salvage the essential mythic qualities of religion.

Mysticism

In *mysticism* the subject-object split inherent in conceptual cognition is sensed, and an effort is made to overcome it. The interior life is explored. However, the term 'mysticism' as it is widely used allows for the acknowledgment, to greater or lesser extent, of all three of the focal points of human orientation: the individual, society and the world. On the basis of a very similar model Minnema[5] distinguishes three forms of mysticism: *cosmic mysticism* (with relative emphasis on the external world); *person mysticism* (with relative emphasis on the social world); and *identity mysticism* (with relative emphasis emphasis on individual subjectivity). In all three, however, the 'I' is strongly maintained, he claims.[6] In view of the testimonies of mystics (mainly in Buddhism), as well as the approach to religion followed here, this view must be qualified strongly. In the more far-reaching forms of mysticism (as radical 'transcendence'), thinking and thoughts are silenced, and the 'I' (the small one) as a separate pole of orientation is left behind.

Mysticism wafts on the edges of thinking-speaking. Religion becomes truly penetrating when we have talked ourselves to a standstill and are weary of thinking. Wordless, conceptless silence (meditation) lies further along the religious path than rational thought. That there is something (or nothing) is an assumption or an intuitive shot in the dark, perhaps an experience for some, and cannot be proved. However, it is claimed by some great mystics themselves. In its ongoing quest, the religious drive uses conceptual logic, then lays it aside. So neither a boundless confidence in reason nor a despairing mistrust of it is called for. The conventional entities of 'ego' and 'objects', the totality of the conceptually dissected world, are transcended without being denied their relative role. An academic programme of religious investigation can only study the outside of such (non-)cognition. At its very best, it can perhaps point to the experience of what has previously been called the depth of conditionalism.

Mystical cognition refers to a quality of trans-cognition. As various religious traditions know, mysticism is graded. At its ultimate, the symbols, the socially constructed sacred stories (myths), concepts and theories, the very act of thinking are often reported to have been left behind. Trance is transcendence. The estrangement of a human being from its source, the great context, has been overcome in the discovery of its relatedness with everything that is. Is it possible for the very unique, solitary individual, entering the great depth, to leave behind every limiting schema?[7] In the end only those who have been there will know, and will not be able to communicate their vision except in terms of the culture-bound elements of the available symbols, myths and concepts. The claim of many mystics is that such a transcendence of conceptual thought is possible. In the traditional scheme of the Theravada, for example, the mystical descent progressively leaves behind analytical, discursive thought and, in the deeper stages, the entire realm of perception, until eventually consciousness ceases. On what grounds should that claim, backed by reported experience, be doubted? An assumption of this study is that the great contemplative can indeed go beyond the linguistically and culturally constructed views of self and the world, and escape from the captivity of conventional human signs.

It seems that within the domain of mysticism a fundamental distinction must be made between mysticisms of substance, of fullness; and mysticisms of nothingness, emptiness, silence. Of the latter type Buddhism is the prime example. In a conditionalist perspective the claim would not be made that mystical experience is somehow exempt from conceptual, linguistic, cultural, institutional, historical, traditional, disciplinary and other contexts. The point made brilliantly by Katz and his collaborators cannot be ignored. Neither would a consistent conditionalism endorse an attempted escape *back* into prelinguistic substance. Yet it would endorse a move *forward* into postlinguistic 'emptiness '. That is what the 'silence' of the Buddha may mean. The 'post-' does not indicate *less* conditioning, getting out of the webs, but an awareness of *more* and *wider* conditioning, in which human language loses its absolute character. What is intended, is not breaking free from conditioning, but radicalising it. In that sense, speaking with James, 'pure experience'[8] is taken to be possible. In a Buddhist perspective of meditative experience, the contextualism of, for example, Don Cupitt[9] would appear too limited, homocentric and restrictive: language seems to become the all, an absolute from which there is no escape – there is nothing but words and more words. Yet the web of words is just another web, not the absolute web, and it merges into wider and deeper ones. Admittedly this insight itself is mediated by all sorts of cultural conditioning – which leads to an impasse where no absolute position is achievable and silence seems to be the only reply.

Words and concepts came late in the evolutionary process. However, that is itself a statement, a linguistically articulated thought. *We think* and *say* that that is the case. It seems that we are trapped in a dilemma: speaking-thinking is a part and a result of the conditionalist process of the world; it also constitutes that process. Yet we sense that that process is not simply co-extensive with and does not collapse in our human speaking-thinking. We sense that our words and thoughts have edges where they break down. We cannot climb out of them onto another plane. They implode into silence.

Morality

So far, we have discussed some cognitive implications of an investigation into religion. Now a further step must be taken – into the *moral* dimension. Here we repeat some general trends of an ethic of conditionality.

Four formal characteristics of this ethic are the following:

Firstly, it has a religious but not a supranaturalistic justification. It is a *naturalistic* ethic.

Secondly, it has no abstract, absolute norms, but is *situational* and *historical*. Moral wisdom consists in having breadth and depth of insight into the set of historical conditions in which one must act. It also knows that the various moral norms adhered to in various cultures and religions (which it respects highly) evolved historically. And it accepts that, given the historical evolution of the human species, there are indeed certain relatively constant homoversal convictions of good and bad.

Thirdly, given its constitutive principles, it can distinguish right from wrong and can give moral guidance. It does not amount to relativism in the sense that any behaviour is as good or bad as any other.

Fourthly, it is *not dualistic*. It does not assume in the abstract that there is an absolute right, absolutely distinct from its opposite, absolute wrong. The world is an intricate process, in the face of which humans, in times of severe stress, can be forgiven for tending to oversimplify things and longing for simple justice. Yet this ethic would be critical of any absolute light-versus-darkness view of the world.

Three characteristics of its content are the following (I maintain that these three are equally important, that none of them operates in isolation from the others, and that each one merges into the others):

Firstly, the principle of *respect for the given concrete*. This ethic values the multitude of concrete manifestations of the world process, and treasures the individual as unique and unrepeatable. The concrete 'I', 'you', 'it', 'we', born of an unfathomable network, are worthy of respect – simply because they are there. Each given *this* moment, leaping out in its singularity, is precious. This extends to the many historically grown products of various cultures, such as religions and moral systems. This ethic is opposed to violence, that is to the violation of the right of existing things to exist. This fleeting precious moment is loved but not substantialised, for in its existence, and its passing into nonexistence (death), it is part of the ocean of being. If this principle is isolated from the others and absolutised, apartheid in any of its many forms is the result.

Secondly, the principle of *integration with widening contexts*. This ethic encourages individuals, social groups and humanity to involve themselves in widening ecological contexts comprising human societies, nonhuman life, and nonlife as well. Not homocentric, it seeks a relaxed fitting into the multiform changing universe, a letting go of self-centredness. If this principle is isolated and absolutised, centristic totalism and totalitarianism is the result. It is an ethic of *universal solidarity*, *response-ability* and *compassion*.

Thirdly, the principle of *freedom on the creative edge*. Not being an ethic of indifference to the real world and of withdrawal into fine webs of thoughts and words, it emphasises *freedom* and *creative action* on the edges of the existing. If this principle is isolated, escapism instead of permanent transformation is the result. Concrete deeds are important. Thoughts and words are deeds. They make a difference here and now, and for the future. A conditionalist ethic knows about the need for struggle, and the effort it takes to keep the permanent transformation from stagnating. Operating close to reality, it is wary of abstract utopias, aware that evil (like good) is part of the texture of human society and its institutions, carried and transmitted through the myriad threads of interaction, and removable from individual and collective life only with patience, wisdom and courage.

Thinking(-speaking) and silencing are themselves part of concrete life, and serve it. Ethics itself is still rational reflection. Morality is never divorced from it. Yet in the end, in our being, speaking, doing, it is a matter of simple respect, community, openness, whether we are dealing with humans or with the nonhuman and nonliving dimensions of the world.

ENDNOTES

1 I follow F Sierksma's distinction of mysticism and shamanism (*De religieuse projectie: een anthropologische en psychologische studie over de projectie-verschijnselen in de godsdiensten*, Delft: Gaarde, 1957, pp 163f): shamanism occurs in societies where the subject-object split has not yet occurred. Mysticism presupposes that split, and hence only occurs in so-called 'high' cultures. 'The Eskimo shaman is not unified with the Goddess of the Deep, but speaks to her and if necessary fights her' (transl, JSK). Sierksma's distinction was brought to my attention by L Minnema, *Bespiegelingen aan het venster: anthropologische bouwstenen voor een vergelijkend-godsdienstwetenschappelijke verheldering van interreligieuze dialoog. Naar aanleiding van K Nishitani's boeddhistische en K Rahner's christelijke godsdienstwijsbegeerte*, Kampen: Mondiss, 1990, p 220.

2 Cf K R Popper, *Objective knowledge: an evolutionary approach*, Oxford: Clarendon Press, 1972, pp 107–152.

3 'God is not to be treated as an exception to all metaphysical principles, invoked to save their collapse. He is their chief exemplification' (A N Whitehead, *Process and reality: an essay in cosmology*, New York: Free Press, 1978 [1929], p 343).

4 R Panikkar, *The silence of God: the answer of the Buddha*, Maryknoll, NY: Orbis, 1989 (1st Italian edition, 1970), pp 167ff).

5 Minnema, *Bespiegelingen ...*, pp 241ff.

6 Ibid, p 241: 'Should the 'I' be released, the mystic becomes disoriented, desperate' (transl, JSK).

7 Starting with the classic of W James (*The varieties of religious experience*, New York: Modern Library, 1902), this century has produced a vast literature on mysticism. Other classic studies include R Otto's two works *The idea of the holy: an inquiry into the non-rational factor in the idea of the divine and its relation to the rational*, London: Oxford University Press, 1950 (1917), and *Mysticism East and West: a comparative analysis of the nature of mysticism*, New York: Meridian, 1957 (1932), and E Underhill's *Mysticism: a study in the nature and development of man's spiritual consciousness*, New York: Dutton, 1961 (1911). A resurgence of interest some time after World War II resulted in R C Zaehner's *Mysticism sacred and profane*, Oxford: Oxford University Press, 1961 (1957) and W T Stace, *Mysticism and philosophy*, London: Macmillan, 1961. The last twenty years have witnessed a particularly marked increase of interest in this field. Some of the important studies are the volumes edited by S Katz, *Mysticism and philosophical analysis*, London: Sheldon, 1978; *Mysticism and religious traditions*, Oxford: Oxford University Press, 1983; and *Mysticism and language*, Oxford: Oxford University Press. Excellent surveys of issues and positions in the field are to be found in P G Moore, *Problems in*

the analysis of mystical experience with special reference to the work of R C Zaehner, W T Stace and M Laski, PhD thesis, University of Lancaster, 1977; D Green, *A study of mysticism and its forms of expression*, PhD thesis, University of Stirling, 1983; and C E T Kourie, Elizabeth Catez of the Trinity, 1880–1906: an interpretation of her mysticism, unpublished DTh thesis, University of South Africa, 1990.

8 Cf R E Carter, Paradox, language and reality, in R E Carter (ed), *God, the self and nothingness: reflections Eastern and Western*, New York: Paragon, 1990, pp 245–264 on this concept in thought of William James and Nishida Kitaro. To Nishida, applying Zen philosophy, 'pure experience' is 'an actual and direct experience', the 'instant field of the present, the immediate flux of life before categorization' (ibid, p 250).

9 In his *The time being*, London: SCM, 1992. For various views of whether the deconstruction of Derrida (as opposed to the thought of Nagarjuna) also remains dualistically (difference versus identity) within the entrapments of language, cf D Loy, *Nonduality: a study in comparative philosophy*, New Haven: Yale University Press, 1988, and H Coward, *Derrida and Indian philosophy*, New York: State University of New York Press, 1990, pp 125ff.

III

AFRICAN ROOTS OF RELIGION

This Part consists of two chapters which tie the religious thought of conditionalism to the evolutionary history of humankind.

In chapter 10 I shall reconstruct the evolutionary emergence of human beings and their religion in southern Africa, drawing on the available palaeoanthropological and archaeological evidence. These specialised aspects have been checked by experts in the relevant fields. The chapter makes no claim to contribute empirically to these disciplines. Neither is the basic theoretical argument dependent on those disciplines. The aims are: to provide an overview of the main findings of science insofar as they may have a bearing on 'religion' as circumscribed earlier; to speculate, in terms of that view of religion, on the origin of religion in the evolutionary process; and to evaluate the available empirical evidence in the light of that theory.

At this stage I have to repeat that for the purposes of this book 'religion' is not understood substantively to be either the belief in life after death, or the acknowledgment of a supernatural power (or powers), or myth-making, or ritual, or any combination of these. Of course, working with a more substantive definition of religion might have yielded testable chronological hypotheses as to when religion appeared for the first time. By 'origin', however, I do not mean a definite chronological beginning that could be pinpointed throught excavation or other means. This chapter does not contain any new scientific data. I have something else in mind, taking 'origin' to refer to the multiconditioned co-arising of 'religion' (the most comprehensive and most radical orienting of the human being) contemporaneously with the general evolution of humankind, as far as the latter has been provisionally established by science.

In chapter 11 we explore some dimensions of religion in the light of evolutionary theory. The question is whether, working from within the logic of evolution itself, openings of a religious nature might occur. The religious view, however, does not follow or emerge from evolutionary science. The fact is that there is no single generally accepted scientific theory of evolution. Furthermore, as they stand, such theories are interwoven with wider worldview ideas from the outset. The chapter is basically a meditation on some presuppositions and implications of being *human* in our part of the world from a religious point of view, and in evolutionary perspective. However, it is not an esoteric religious extension of science. Rather, its inner dynamism derives from religion itself, as unfolded in previous chapters.

10 The evolution of 'Homo religiosus africanus'

I believe that any effort to rethink our African heritage, as we are called to do in the present southern African situation of drastic reorientation, has to begin at the beginning, as far as that can be established.

SubSaharan Africa has turned out to be the area where, according to the majority of scholars, several important developments in the evolution of human beings occurred. Africa, and southern Africa in particular, was thrust into the limelight with the discovery of the first *Australopithecus* at Taung in the northern Cape in 1924, much to the surprise of the scientific world at the time. Yet more than 50 years before that momentous discovery Charles Darwin, in *The descent of man*,[1] had speculated – uselessly, as he himself believed – that 'it is somewhat more probable that our early progenitors lived on the African continent than elsewhere', on the grounds that 'in each great region of the world the living mammals are closely related to the extinct species of the same region'. The opinion ventured in 1978 by Beaumont, De Villiers and Vogel that 'the physical and cultural evolution of our own species ... took place largely or entirely on the stretching game-rich savanna landscapes of sub-Saharan Africa'[2] seems to have gained ground among palaeoanthropologists and to be accepted as a strong probability. On the whole, however, the jigsaw puzzle of the emergence of anatomically modern human beings from early hominid stock is by no means completed.

The playfully coined term *Homo religiosus africanus* in the title of this chapter is not an addition to the somewhat bewildering existing nomenclature of early humans and their ancestors. It merely wishes to focus attention on the central thesis, namely that any serious study of religious history (and southern

African religious history in particular) would gain depth by being situated on the large map of human evolution.

Certainly, one reason for the hesitancy in religious studies to deal with the origin of religion from an evolutionary point of view is an understandable reaction against discredited nineteenth century theories such as those of Edward B Tylor, Herbert Spencer and James G Frazer – shot through as these were with unwarranted extrapolations from their limited observations of a small number of contemporary so-called 'primitive' societies, with the ideology of progress and European supremacy as the supposed culmination and destiny of the evolutionary process.[3] Today views such as these have been discarded. Let me add that the concept 'evolution' will here be applied only to the history of humankind prior to the emergence of anatomically modern humans, not to its subsequent history.

A second reason is that a cease-fire between 'science' and 'religion' still obtains in many quarters – certainly in this country. To most religious thinkers (particularly theologians) evolution is still a bogey, better left alone.[4] And scientists, whether open towards religion or biased against it, seem equally eager to preserve the brittle peace by steering clear of religion. In the vast majority of publications on human evolution the topic of religion is ignored.

Of course, a third important reason for the relative silence on the evolutionary emergence of religion is the sheer difficulty of the task. The evolution of religion is even more difficult to trace than that of some other cultural features such as language. The reconstruction of the emergence of language can rely on anatomical peculiarities found in the fossil evidence such as the development of speech areas in the brain and of vocal organs, as well as on nonhuman linguistic analogues. Not till quite late in the evolutionary process, with the lithic and skeletal remains of cultural innovations such as art and burial, does possible evidence of the religious factor come to the fore, and then only indirectly. For the period prior to these phenomena, all we can do is fall back on the general picture of human cultural development as drawn by archaeology, and on analogues with aspects of animal behaviour that may be interpreted as ritual, play, and so on.

Evolution has become part and parcel of contemporary scientific thinking. *That* evolution occurred is regarded by scholars in the field to be as close to certain as science can get. In this sense, it is 'fact'. Yet the explication and explanation of this 'fact', the theorising about the *why?* and the *how?*, is subject to much, sometimes heated debate. Theoretical and worldview assumptions inevitably enter into scholarly accounts of the facts.

A condensed outline will now be given of those aspects of human evolution on which there is some measure of agreement among scholars in the field.[5] Speculation which has no, or perhaps only a tenuous link with current informed academic opinion in the sciences dealing with human evolution will be avoided. We shall therefore confine ourselves to the largely (but by no means unanimously) accepted body of information on the questions of *what, when* and *where*. Obviously the current state of opinion (inasmuch as it exists) is not final. The story of human evolution cannot be written definitively. The gaps in the factual information are too many and too large, the possible reconstructions of the course of events too numerous. On almost every issue there is disagreement. However, I shall give a tentative reconstruction of these developments, drawing on expert opinion – realising that as new techniques develop, new finds are made and new hypotheses open up new angles, the current body of opinion is bound to grow and change.[6] In a few years' time there may well be dramatic discoveries that will change the picture of human evolution. Yet these will confirm that the human mammal and its religion emerged in an evolutionary process. Informed religious thought must reflect the reality of evolution.

Before the hominoids

Homo sapiens was born from the womb of an incomprehensibly vast and complex universe which, according to prevailing opinion in contemporary physics, started twenty to ten thousand million years ago from a single event, infinitesimally small, which ever since has continued to expand.[7] It follows that in the final analysis everything existing in this universe, being the continuation of that single event, is of a kind. Everything is related to everything else – both in the sense of being connected with and of being akin to. This, of course, has always been the intuition of mystics, and it seems to be borne out by contemporary physicists pursuing the mystical implications of their science. Religion in its mystical depth is awe before this intricate vastness of which we humans are a small yet significant part; it is the aspiration to realise our relatedness to all things – both by sensing it clearly, and by actualising it in our thoughts, attitudes, words and deeds.

It is widely accepted that natural processes led to the formation, five thousand million years ago, of an ordinary star – just one of a hundred thousand million stars in an average galaxy, which in turn is just one of a hundred thousand million galaxies in an expanding, changing universe. Around this particular star a body of stellar debris collected four thousand five hundred million years ago to form an average-sized planet, one of several orbiting its sun. On this planet, Earth, emerged the only life in the universe that we know of so far. As the earth cooled, formed a crust and acquired an atmosphere, primitive forms of life originated in the oceans, at or before three thousand five hundred million years ago. Such organisms, more than three thousand million years old, have been found preserved in the Barberton mountains. Near Pretoria, where I am writing, in the Transvaal Sequence of the Magaliesberg, algal stromatolites over two thousand million years old are visible in the dolomite deposits. At that stage (pre-Cambrian) Africa was not yet a separate continent but the central part of the large landmass of Gondwanaland. These first primitive forms of life, evolving over billions of years, released oxygen into the air, gradually changing the atmosphere and allowing the evolution of more complex forms of life. The first multicellular organisms emerged before the Cambrian period (600–500 myr ['million years ago']) of the Palaeozoic Era (600–230 myr); primitive fish emerged 500–450 myr; land plants emerged 425–405 myr; reptiles emerged 345–280 myr; dinosaurs emerged 230–181 myr; birds and mammals emerged 181–135 myr. Prior to 25 myr, protomonkeys and protoapes evolved from more primitive prosimian forms. From these Miocene apes, hominids eventually evolved during the Pliocene (5–2 myr). *Homo*, in whom consciousness of this immeasurably vast, immeasurably multifarious, expanding yet coherent, evolving universe eventually reached an extraordinary level, appeared only towards the end of the Pliocene, 2 myr.

In an evolutionary perspective, religion appears as continuous with the most elementary forms of creative adaptation to the vast world around us. Of course, humans reveal novel dimensions of this creative adaptation, because of their exceptionally high intelligence. The human being is moved by the same forces as all inorganic and organic beings, from the amoeba to its nearest cousins in the mammal world – and by more, since the human world is constituted by a subtler sensorium than theirs. The cumulative residues of all past experience of the universe are deposited in its body-mind. In addition, conscious rational thought has reached a peak unequalled among living beings. And mystics claim that it has the ability, by cleansing its cognitive faculties, to penetrate to the heart of reality intuitively (supraconsciously). From an evolutionary point of view, precursors of 'religion' in the more specific sense (that is as found among humans) are evident in other forms of life, however primitive, when they respond to the cosmic rhythms surrounding them and interacting with them.

It follows, as Robert Ellwood[8] suggests, that instinctual animal behaviour such as territoriality, ritualisation, play and an unmistakable incipient capacity for feelings of meaning and loss (death) may be seen as precursors of the human sense of sacred place and time, of ritual and myth, ecstasy and mysticism. Darwin himself made this same point 120 years ago when he viewed animal and human emotions and behaviour as a continuum, even the highest human expressions being extensions of instinctive responses of a related physical, neurological structure: 'there is no fundamental difference between man and the higher mammals in their mental faculties', including not only play, courage and timidity, love and jealousy, wonder and curiosity, memory and imagination, but also language, sense of beauty and religion:

> *The feeling of religious devotion is a highly complex one, consisting of love, complete submission to an exalted and mysterious superior, a strong sense of dependence, fear, reverence, gratitude, hope for the future, and perhaps other elements. No being could experience so complex an emotion until advanced in his intellectual and moral faculties to at least a moderately high level. Nevertheless, we see some distant approach to this state of mind in the deep love of a dog for his master, associated with complete submission, some fear, and perhaps other feelings.*[9]

There is no reason to fault Darwin in this respect from a religious point of view.[10].

Hominoids

Although *Homo* carries within itself the seeds of all earlier life forms, from single celled amoebae onwards, its immediate ancestry in the animal kingdom appears in the Early Miocene, round about 20 myr. This is probably when the primate superfamily *Hominoidea*[11] evolved in Afro-Arabia.[12]

The Miocene saw several families of primitive hominoids, all probably arboreal omnivores (perhaps mostly forest-adapted herbivores). Among the more important from the point of view of human evolution are *Proconsul* (20 myr, several species of which once lived in East Africa) and *Sivapithecus*. Related to the latter was *Ramapithecus*, once considered the first hominid but has fallen out of favour since the eighties.

Following Pilbeam, it may be surmised that during the Middle Miocene, between 18–12 myr, hominoids spread from Africa to Eurasia across dry land. This was made possible by the closing of the Tethys Sea (of which the present Black and Caspian seas are remnants) which previously had separated Africa and Eurasia. It was a time of various climatic, geographic and habitat changes. Climates cooled and became more seasonal, and in some areas forests were replaced by savannah and woodlands. This period marked the initial split of the large hominoids into two branches: a mainly Asian one, which ultimately produced *Pongo*, and a mainly African one, which contained the last common ancestor of *Pan*, *Gorilla* and *Homo*.

A combination of the meagre fossil data available at this stage and the results of comparative molecular studies of the DNA of these species suggests that the hominid line arose when it diverged from *Pan-Gorilla* in tropical Africa fairly recently, around 5 myr or, to play it safe, between 7 and 4 myr. This is much more recent than the traditional dating of roughly 10 myr for the beginning of this development. In any event, clearly humans and the large African apes, particularly chimpanzees, are very close relatives. This is borne out by close genealogical, morphological and behavioural similarities. *Gorilla* and *Pan* continued to evolve, and protohominids very dramatically. It has to be added that there have been some rapid new developments and changes in learned opinion on this score.

Hominids

Hominids lived in Southern Africa from at least 3 million years ago, which is quite recent compared to their fellow inhabitants of the veld. Kudu, eland, baboon and elephant were already browsing and grazing on the southern African veld, along with a host of other mammals which have since disappeared.

The earliest hominids evolved from existing higher primates in the tropical and subtropical parts of Africa, and appear in the fossil record for the first time around 4 myr. Since there is no consensus about the emergence of this revolutionary new genus of ape, we shall simply sketch what is arguably the majority opinion. Many points are unresolved and will probably remain so for a long time to come. Although our interest is primarily southern Africa (South Africa, Namibia, Botswana, Swaziland, Lesotho, Angola, Zimbabwe, Mozambique, Zambia, Malawi, and parts of Zaire and Tanzania), developments elsewhere (ie for practical purposes, East Africa) are obviously highly relevant.

The first hominid find ever, the fossilised skull of a small child, was made near Taung, a Tswana village in the northern Cape, during mining operations in 1924 and was described and named by Raymond Dart in 1925. This specimen revolutionised scientific thinking about the origin of humankind, primarily because it was much older than any human-related remains uncovered up to then (Dubois' finds of *Homo erectus* in Java). In addition, instead of Asia (as was the scientific bias at the time), Africa was now thrust forward as the place of human origins. Thirdly, the new evidence did not conform to the dogma of the time that human development started with a disproportionate enlargement of the ape-size brain. This creature certainly walked upright and had small human-like canine teeth – but its brain was no larger than that of apes. This completely upset the hypothesis that human development had started with the enlargement of the brain. Dart took the bold step of assigning this remarkable creature hominid status. Curiously, this seems to be belied by the name he gave his find - 'southern ape of Africa'. Only decades later did the academic establishment fully vindicate his identification of *Australopithecus africanus* as hominid. The particular specimen discovered near Taung is thought to be about 2,5 myr.[13]

A small, incomplete fossil skeleton of an adult female belonging to a very early hominid species was found at Hadar in northeastern Ethiopia in 1974. Its discoverers, D C Johanson and his colleagues, named this remarkable individual 'Lucy', and allocated it to a new species which they called *Australopithecus afarensis* (after the region of Ethiopia where it was found). At this stage of the fossil-hunt it is widely regarded as probably the earliest hominid. Lucy herself is taken to be at least 3 million years old. Earlier specimens of East African *A afarensis*, such as the ones found by Mary Leaky at Laetoli in Tanzania, are assumed to have lived at least 3,5 million years ago. However, the taxonomy of *Australopithecus* is still very much debated. Since 1974 further discoveries of *A afarensis* have been made, and recently (1994) a well-preserved skull was discovered at Hadar in Ethiopia.[14]

All the australopithecine species that have been identified so far share a number of distinctly human characteristics. As said, they were small-brained compared with modern humans. Yet significant changes in brain *organisation* may have started to take place even at that early stage. The brain's enlargement came with *Homo habilis*,[15] no less than two million years after the start of upright walking, indicating that these two developments should not be associated too closely. Clearly the process of becoming bipedal (using only two extremities for walking, thus freeing the others for new functions) would have involved a significant restructuring of the brain,[16] which in turn would have involved significant behavioural changes. What tips the scale in favour of these specimens being hominids is not brain size, but the fact that they were in all probability capable and perhaps even obligate bipeds. Humans emerged when hominids began to walk upright.[17] Although bipedalism would have freed their hands to carry and manipulate objects, they must still have been skilled arborealists, utilising trees for some of their food and shelter. Bipedalism is more than a means of locomotion. It involves behaviour such as feeding strategy, which in turn relates to factors such as social organisation, sexual behaviour, and technology.[18] None of these developments occurred in isolation from major climatic, geological and ecological events, such as the shrinkage of forest during the late Miocene. These factors were interdependent.

The reorganisation of the brain at that stage of evolution (which must be distinguished from both brain size and the growth of the neocortex) would have created at least the *condition*[19] for the development of higher cognitive functions such as language – and religion. The evolution of the brain involved not only the development of intellect (supposing for the moment that 'intellect' is one), but other functions as well, such as emotions and attitudes which are rooted in the limbic system of the brain, not in the much more recent neocortex. The period of the australopithecines witnessed a dramatic and crucial expansion of consciousness involving a host of interrelated factors – biological, technological as well as behavioural.

In addition to being small-brained, the australopithecines with their relatively heavy lower jaws, powerful chewing muscles and large, hominised teeth were probably generalised omnivores, although predominantly vegetarian and probably mainly frugivores. That meat played a role in their diet is generally accepted, but its importance has not been established. Neither is it clear what their hunting capabilities were at that stage. Probably they relied heavily on scavenging and opportunistic killing rather than on systematic hunting for their meat. At this stage there simply is no direct evidence to ascertain the role of hunting as opposed to scavenging; current thinking seems to be sceptical about pre-*Homo* hunting.

Neither is there sufficient evidence to say anything definite about their social organisation and behavioural patterns. Perhaps, given the available facts of bipedalism and its implications (free hands to carry and make things), one could speculate that these pre-habiline beings would at least have been organised in small bands, sharing food consisting of vegetable material and at least some meat.[20]

The answers to questions such as whether or not the prehabiline hominid females were continuously sexually receptive, whether these creatures were monogamous or polygamous, what the division of labour between females and males might have been, to what extent females were dependent on the provisioning males, whether males and/or females left from home bases to forage and returned to these, and whether they already possessed language (or at least the capacity to develop language) are largely dependent on theoretical models of evolution.[21]

In previous chapters I suggested that religion should be seen as the dialectic between the synthesising faculty of the human mind operating at its most inclusive level and the urge to radically transcend the given. In the sense that humans are driven by their very nature, by their very being in the world to experience the world as a meaningful *gestalt*, I would speak of a religious imperative. To be human (that is to have arisen from the deep, vast network of the evolutionary process) is to be religious (that is to search for cosmic orientation). That is not to deny that some individuals and some cultures in some epochs of their history are religiously 'unmusical' (Max Weber), just as some individuals and societies have or do not have a penchant for the visual arts. In spite of variations in interest and endowment, religion, like art, is a homoversal phenomenon. Taken in that wide sense, religion would have been part and parcel of the whole emergent reticulum consisting of the dramatic development of consciousness, new forms of social institutions, new ways of locomotion, new ways of interacting with the natural environment (diet, carrying, using and making tools, etc). Religion was the extension of instinctual drives within the human being, continuous with animal behaviour.

This evolutionary approach to religion finds support in the work of D'Aquili, Laughlin, McManus and their co-workers, conducted from a biogenetic structuralist point of view.[22] According to them religious ritual has phylogenetic origins. The power of religious ritual, for example, derives from the effects of repetitive auditory and visual stimuli on the limbic system of the brain: it leads to pleasurable, ineffable experiences, and to experiences of unity and harmony between individuals, eventually – at the level of human religion – between the human being and the universe as a whole. In many animal species ritual behaviour permits cooperation and bonding between individual members. Ritual courtship behaviour, which makes copulation possible by overcoming the social distance between individual animals, is a prime example. Religious ritual is an extension and development of such repetitive, rhythmic patterns of behaviour, and it has similar effects, albeit at a higher level.[23] As far as the australopithecines are concerned, they believe[24] that although the minimal neural requirements for myth structures and religious ritual existed a million years ago or more, it is unlikely that any elaborate myths and rituals would have developed in the absence of spoken language.

Homo habilis

Accepting the widely held unilineal model of human evolution (from the australopithecines via *H habilis* and *H erectus* to *H sapiens*), the first evidence of the emergence of *Homo* as a distinct genus appears at least 2 myr.[25] The formation of the Arctic ice sheet had important floral and faunal repercussions, including the emergence of *Homo habilis*. Especially in East Africa (Olduvai Gorge in Tanzania, the Omo Valley in Ethiopia, Lake Turkana) the fifties and sixties saw substantial discoveries of a human type filling the gap between *A africanus* and *Homo erectus*, leading Louis Leakey, Tobias and Napier in 1964 to postulate an early, incipient stage in the evolution of *Homo*. The youngest specimens found so far are dated at 1,6 myr. Fossil remains grouped with this new genus by Tobias in 1965 had been discovered at Swartkrans and Sterkfontein even before the discoveries in East Africa.

Anatomical peculiarities such as a dramatic increase in brain volume (almost 50 per cent larger than that of *A africanus*) and a further reduction in tooth size mark the new stage in hominid evolution. In fact, it is generally accepted that significant enlargement of the brain occurred only with the arrival of *Homo habilis*. Increased brain size in itself would not account for increased intelligence. It has to be viewed together with the overall organisation of the brain and with the emergence of special features that would facilitate special abilities.[26] Among the latter, speech ability is of special importance. Since 1980 Tobias[27] has argued that the brain enlargement coincided with the manifestation of those cerebral areas that govern spoken language and that articulated language, albeit rudimentary, was within the capacity of *H habilis*.

Concurrent with this inferred ability were indications, substantiated in the archaeological record, of cultural activity such as deliberate toolmaking. This technological advance was first associated with this genus by Mary Leakey. The relationships between anatomical changes and behavioural changes such as speech and toolmaking are far from resolved at the present stage of the debate.

Intentional stone toolmaking almost certainly began relatively suddenly between 2,5 and 2,0 myr, contemporaneously with the emergence of the first larger-brained hominid.[28] The technological attainments of this new stage are reflected well in its name *Homo habilis* ('handyman'). The Stone Age had taken off. Of course, it was not an absolute beginning but the continuation and development of a proficiency already present among earlier hominids, which began with the use of opportunistic tools.[29]

Development of the toolmaking ability was probably concomitant with an increased role of meat in the diet. Although there is as yet no consensus regarding the hunting abilities and diet of *H habilis*, broken bones, some displaying cutmarks and found with artefacts, indicate that by then meat had become an important item of the diet.[30] It does not, however, prove that *H habilis* was an efficient hunter; on the available evidence it is possible, even probable, that this species still, at least in the early stages, depended on scavenging to a greater degree than on hunting. Only later was organised hunting of large animals added to scavenging and collecting plant foods. However, it is widely (though not universally) accepted by scholars in the field that systematic hunting started with *H habilis*.

If it is true that for over 99 per cent of its time *Homo* was a hunter-gatherer, that over 90 per cent of all humans who ever lived were hunter-gatherers[31] and that *Homo* in fact probably evolved as a hunter-gatherer, then surely this mode of existence would have been ingrained in its psyche. Compared with other hominoids who did not really hunt in a systematic way, hunting seems to have been added to the behavioural repertoire of humans at an early stage, which obviously must have had important social and psychological ramifications in the subsequent stages of their evolution. As Washburn and Lancaster said, hunting is 'far more than a technique or even a variety of techniques. It is a way of life, and the success of this adaptation (in its total social, technical, and psychological dimensions) has dominated the course of human evolution for hundreds of thousands of years. In a very real sense our intellect, interests, emotions, and basic social life – all are evolutionary products of the success of the hunting adaptation.'[32] The biology, sociology and psychology of our species were formed during the hunter-gatherer period, a relatively long one in terms of human development. We, living in the technological age, are still rooted in the agricultural way of life with its accompanying emotional and psychological makeup, which in turn has evolved (but by no means escaped) from the earlier hunter-gatherer outlook. This casts light on the incisive psychological implications of, for example, a religious choice for vegetarianism.

The relationship between changes in inherent mental capacity, behavioural and social changes, and technical innovations is a major unresolved issue in the present debate.[33] This has an important bearing on the question of when and how human cognitive, symbolic, logical faculties arose, including expressions such as language, art and religion. Given the very high probability of habiline toolmaking and probably even incipient speech, it is tantalising to speculate that religion, for which the conditions had been created as much as two million years earlier with *Australopithecus*, started to articulate itself in inchoate speech, symbolic acts (ritual) and world construction (myth).

What forms early religion would have adopted we have no way of knowing. Nineteenth- and early twentieth-century speculations about original *animism* (Edward B Tylor); the *personification of natural objects* such as the sun, moon and thunder (Max Müller and E Siecke); *fetishism* (August Comte and J Lubbock); *manism/spiritism* (Herbert Spencer); *totemism* (William Robertson Smith, Emile Durkheim and Sigmund Freud); *magic* (Sir James

G Frazer); preanimist *animatism/mana* (R R Marett); *monotheist belief in a high God* (A Lang and Wilhelm Schmidt), in the perspective of today's knowledge, are all just that – speculative and in some cases fanciful constructions without any archaeological base. This is not to deny that such accounts may have a heuristic value for understanding the role of religion in human society. The more modest theoretical postulate that religion coemerged in intimate mutuality with the host of other factors touched on above rests on far more solid ground empirically.

Homo erectus

Approximately 1,5 myr there was a dramatic sophistication in the manufacture of stone tools. It is associated with a distinct early human species, *Homo erectus*, which might have arisen well before 2 myr (1,8 – 1,7 myr). The line of their descent, via *Homo habilis*, has not yet been clarified. By 1 myr it was the only surviving hominid species in Africa. Perhaps the other hominids were wiped out because of unsuccessful competition with the cleverer technology of *Homo erectus*. After all, its cranial capacity, although quite modest by modern standards (the brain size of *H erectus* was about two thirds that of modern humans), greatly exceeded that of its fellow hominids. Only with *H erectus* did the neocortex rapidly expand. Anatomically they differed from modern humans in certain respects.[34] Whereas at one time it was commonly accepted that they practised cannibalism (which could be interpreted as having been a ritual and hence as religious practice), this interpretation of the nature of the skull and facial remains associated with *H erectus* finds has become suspect.[35]

By that time hominids had acquired the ability to survive in widely differing habitats. They were no longer restricted to Africa.[36] Specimens of *H erectus* are known from Indonesia, China, North and East Africa, and probably parts of Europe (although their presence in Europe has not been firmly established).[37] Except for very few fossils found at Swartkrans, remains of this species have thus far not been discovered in South Africa. The oldest African specimens (1,7 myr) were found in East Africa. These are probably the oldest in the world, which points to (but does not prove) an African origin of *H erectus*.

By approximately 1 myr *H erectus* may have spread throughout Africa except for the rain forest, and started to migrate from the continent, first to the Middle East and the Asian tropics.[38] Probably *H erectus* was the first wave of human migration from Africa, another being *Homo sapiens sapiens* which could have interacted with *H erectus* and/or existing archaic forms of *Homo sapiens* that by then would have been indigenised in various places of the Old World. For close to 2 million years *H erectus* flourished in Africa and elsewhere, undoubtedly changing over this period, eventually disappearing in Asia around 200 000–100 000 years ago. What eventually happened to the *H erectus* populations in Asia is unknown. It is possible that they, like the Neanderthals, became extinct at an unknown date and for unknown reasons, although the influx of modern humans could have been a factor in their demise.

They may have been hunters, probably roaming semi-nomadically in small hunter-gatherer bands and using semi-permanent home bases; the chances are that they were at least opportunistic fire users.[39] It may be assumed with reasonable safety that the regular use of fire was established by at least 1 myr. They were probably opportunistic omnivores, with meat perhaps even a significant part of their diet. As for the nonmaterial aspects of their protoculture, such as mating patterns, sex roles and social organisation, nothing is known. Fortunately, a much clearer picture of their material achievements can be drawn.

It is widely surmised that with *H erectus* culture (that is the package of things such as language, toolmaking, social organisation, art and religion) started to emerge as a major factor in the evolution of humanity itself. Up till then culture would have been rudimentary. With them culture also started to exert a strong influence on the evolutionary process – the various cultural items interacting with one another, with anatomical changes taking place in the human body (especially brain development) and with changes in the human environment, qualitatively influencing evolution to such a degree that special terms ('social evolution', 'biocultural evolution') have been coined to describe this new phase. Human evolution shifted into a new gear, with sociocultural factors playing an increasing role in its course. To mention one important consequence, the change was certainly accelerated. As a result of the newly acquired communication skills (especially speech) new patterns of behaviour could be transmitted to a new generation much more quickly. They no longer required the slow way of genetic transfer to a new generation.[40] Without straying too far from established fact we may conclude that religion, as symbolic integrating of expanding experience, would by now have reached a fair level of articulation, compared with the preceding phase.

Homo sapiens

When, where and how *Homo erectus* (which would have comprised a variety of subspecies) gave rise to *Homo sapiens*, has not been agreed by the scholarly community.[41] Most specialists accept that early *Homo sapiens* emerged in Africa from basic *H erectus* stock, but consensus about the time of this emergence has not been reached. Estimated datings of the variety of archaic *Homo sapiens* forms lying between *Homo erectus* and anatomically modern humans range from a relatively early 700 000 BP to a relatively late 125 000 BP.[42]

To what extent the *anatomical* changes marking this new development were accompanied by significant *behavioural* and *cultural* changes has not yet been determined. Towards the end of the eighties Mellars and Stringer[43] mentioned this as one of the burning problems of evolutionary theory at this stage.

In southern Africa very few skeletal remains of early *Homo sapiens* have been found, perhaps because, unlike the Neanderthals of Europe, they did not bury their dead. In any event, no very complete skeletons have been recovered. Noteworthy are finds at Broken Hill near Kabwe in Zambia (estimated to be at least 125 000 years old), on the farm Elandsfontein in the Hopefield district, and at the Cave of Hearths in the Transvaal (more than 50 000 years BP[44]). These remains are taken to represent a distinct southern African subspecies of *Homo sapiens*, called *Homo sapiens rhodesiensis*, differing from the subspecies *Homo sapiens neanderthalensis* which occurred in Eurasia and Mediterranean Africa, but not in southern Africa.[45]

Although *Homo sapiens neanderthalensis* is not our central concern here, a quick glimpse at this subspecies is appropriate. Neanderthals can be traced from about 100 000 years ago to about 35 000 years ago, when they became extinct quite rapidly. Interbreeding between Neanderthal and modern humans is regarded by some scholars as highly unlikely, or at most on a very limited scale. The emergence of *H s neanderthalensis* is shrouded in as much mystery as its demise. Although it is generally assumed that they did evolve from *Homo erectus*, the locality (Europe or migrants from Africa?) and manner of their first appearance is unknown. The overwhelming view at this stage is that modern humans did not evolve from the Neanderthal people, but replaced them in some way which has not been clarified yet.[46]

The Neanderthals certainly demonstrated a level of material and cultural achievement far more complex than that associated with *Homo erectus.*[47] There is certainly enough evidence to ascribe to them a highly developed awareness of death (burials) which could be taken to imply awareness of transience and continuity – and thus of religion in the sense that we have circumscribed it. Whether they had the power of speech, and if so, to what degree, is debated. Art in the form of body-painting is accepted to have been part of their cultural repertoire. They probably clothed themselves and used fire to survive the cold climate of the time and to prepare food. The acquisition of meat (large game) probably necessitated a sophisticated level of social organisation.

Apart from *H s rhodesiensis*, a second early southern African subspecies has been distinguished, *Homo sapiens afer*. It is thought possible that it included the common stock ancestral to the modern Khoisan and Negro populations, although there is not sufficient hard evidence to postulate such direct evolutionary continuity with the archaic people of South or East Africa.[48] At this stage the tempting idea that the recent Bushmen evolved locally, in subsaharan Africa, from such archaic populations, cannot be propounded definitely. It remains possible that they moved into southern Africa from other regions.[49] In any event, the early Middle Stone Age populations of southern Africa resemble recent people much more closely than do the Neanderthals. The overall conclusion could be that modern human beings, linked with living African groups, emerged in Africa more than 100 000 years ago – 40 000 years before modern populations occurred in Europe.

Homo sapiens sapiens

As to where anatomically modern humans (*Homo sapiens sapiens*) emerged, there is a widely held opinion that Africa, eastern or sub-Saharan, is the most likely locality, and that that early population radiated from Africa to the rest of the Old World. This could have been a third major wave of radiation from Africa, the first being the dispersal of *H erectus* perhaps 1,0 million years earlier, and the second that of early forms of *H sapiens*. However, as with the transition from *H erectus* to archaic *H sapiens*, the question whether *Homo sapiens sapiens* emerged gradually in a single locality or parallelly in several localities has not been decided.[50] On the whole, however, the 'out of Africa' hypothesis seems to be carrying the day.

Recently linguists produced evidence supporting the thesis that modern humans had their origin in Africa. Continuing the long series of efforts (pioneered at the end of the eighteenth and early nineteenth centuries by William Jones, Franz Bopp, Jacob Grimm and others) to reconstruct a genealogy of languages by means of comparative linguistics, Vitaly Shevoroshkin and John Woodward hypothesise that the first common human language ('the mother tongue of humankind', or 'proto-World') can be traced back to 100 000 years ago.[51] Their findings seem to support the results of genetics that humankind in its modern form is a fairly young species, originating in Africa. From the point of view of our interest in the Bushmen in these essays it is worth noting Shevoroshkin's conclusion that 'the Khoisan languages of the Hottentots, the Bushmen and other tribes of southern Africa constitute the oldest phylum of them all',[52] implying that they appear to have been the first group to split off from the original population of *H sapiens*.[53]

What happened after these early moderns had left their African homeland? How did they interact with the existing populations of earlier, archaic humans elsewhere? Did they interbreed with them, and if so, to what extent? Or did they replace them by violent or nonviolent means? When and how did the contemporary races come into being? These issues are currently being debated, and no consensus seems to be emerging right now.

The notion of a common underlying linguistic stock would lend support to the idea that all human thinking, including mythology and religion, must share very similar basic cognitive patterns which condition and limit human responses to the environment. This would allow us to assume that the religious expressions of Upper Palaeolithic Europeans, of Stone Age Bushmen, of the classical religions of India and the Levant and of us moderns stem from the same panhuman consciousness. Here too the researcher in comparative religion is confronted with a complex set of problems in view of the demonstrable differences between religions. In the perspective of evolution it seems obvious that a middle road must be found between a type of relativism that sees no possibility of interreligious translation of meaning between linguistic communities and cultures, and a type of universalism that reduces all religions to one and the same set of attitudes, actions or beliefs. Given the common origin of humankind as one species not too long ago, the term 'homoversals', coined by Henry Rosemont and meaning 'for all human beings, physiologically and mentally constituted as they are', seems very appropriate.[54]

To come to more specific data concerning the presence of modern humans in southern Africa: these are asssociated with MSA (Middle Stone Age) lithic industries which first appear at 2,0 myr, and persist, in places, to after 30 000 yrs ago. These assemblages indicate that marine sources were exploited, and that haematite was mined and ground, probably for use as a body paint. Perhaps important from the point of view of ritual are bone fragments scored with multiple incised lines that resemble ethnographic specimens produced by shamans as part of acts of participation or invocation. By that time, and perhaps much earlier, human control of fire was widespread in southern Africa. At Klasies River Mouth continuous MSA human settlement can be traced for a period of more than 50 000 years, from ± 130 000 to ± 60 000 years ago.

Putatively the earliest remains of an anatomically modern human being in the world, older than 100 000 years, have been found at Klasies River, in the southern Cape Province.[55] Deacon's conclusion is that the Klasies River finds 'could represent a southern African endemic type ancestral to the modern San'.[56] In subsistence behaviour as well as economic and social organisation, Deacon believes that there are no essential differences between Later Stone Age (LSA) people (Bushmen) and those MSA people of 80 000 years and more ago. Southern Africa is regarded as a distinctive region, evincing high levels of similarity in material culture throughout the last 100 000 years, containment (if not isolation) of populations, and genetic and behavioural continuity between the Middle and Later Stone Ages. People in the southern Cape were not only anatomically modern some 100 000 years ago, but also behaviourally. Klein, on the other hand, hypothesises that MSA people differed significantly from later groups as far as behaviour is concerned.[57] In other words, the appearance of modern physical form preceded the appearance of fully modern behaviour.

Border Cave at Ingwavuma in northern Natal also revealed a long record of

MSA occupation. The human remains from this cave are all modern in their anatomy. One of these, an adult cranium, may be close to 100 000 years old and appears to fit best with Khoi or San males.[58] Rightmire's conclusion is that 'Border Cave approaches several modern populations and in fact lies closest to Hottentot (Khoi) and Bushman (San) groups.'[59] These early finds prove the great antiquity of modern humans in southern Africa, perhaps even of direct antecedents of recent Africans, but it does not prove conclusively that modern humans evolved first, or only, in southern Africa.

Seemingly the earliest evidence of deliberate burial discovered so far in South Africa, that of a small child buried in a shallow grave with a perforated *Conus* shell, was found at Border Cave, and has been dated at ± 100 000 years ago.[60] Surprisingly, in view of the numerous burials of Neanderthals, this is apparently the only southern African burial definitely associated with MSA. Relics such as these indicate significant advances not only in economic and social systems, but also in aesthetic, ethical and religious ways of thinking and acting.

Fragments from Klasies River and Border Cave permit the tentative conclusion that there was an anatomically and also behaviourally modern human population in South Africa, with very definite Khoisan-Negro affinities, at least 100 000 years ago. It cannot be stated categorically when the Bushmen, as known from the LSA context, emerged. The date of 25 000–15 000 years ago, proposed by Tobias for the splitting of the Khoisan and Negroes, both going back to a common stock, may be too late.[61] Speaking of the Bushmen, it would be a serious mistake to impute cultural forms known from present day Bushman hunter-gatherers to prehistoric hunter-gatherers, even assuming that they were Bushman or proto-Bushman. The Bushman culture is extremely old, and underwent many innovations and changes through time. The Bushmen, or rather the many fluid Bushman groups, adapted and responded to a great variety of environmental conditions over a long period, and in the process developed a wide range of cultural forms.

The later stone age

Although the time of the transition from the MSA to the LSA is very elusive, the LSA may have begun approximately 40 000 years ago. According to Clark, 'certainly by 30 000 years ago, Modern Man with a regionally variable

Later Stone Age technology was present throughout the continent'.[62] In South Africa the shift from MSA to LSA is fairly abrupt, with the main factor distinguishing these technocomplexes being the technique of stone tool manufacture. However, there are also other, nonlithic material relics characteristically present in the LSA, and strongly indicative of the symbolism associated with modern religion: works of art (paintings, petroglyphs, decorated ostrich eggshell water containers, tortoiseshell bowls, decorated bone tools, beads, pendants and amulets), and indications of formal burial in graves marked by painted stones. These features of the LSA made their appearance in southern Africa from 40 000 years ago onwards, but only became common at most archaeological sites over the last 10 000 years.[63] There is no evidence that the LSA was initiated by a new subspecies of *Homo sapiens*.[64]

The oldest piece of rock art from southern Africa, dated 27 000 years ago and associated with a terminal MSA industry, is a painted slab recovered from the Apollo 11 Cave in Namibia.[65] The shift from full MSA to full LSA seems to have taken place over a fairly extended period of time, between 40 000 and 30 000 years ago. In Europe most paintings are in the 20–10 kyr range, with the earliest at c 27 kyr and only carved art ranging back to c 35 kyr.

The earliest evidence of deliberate burial in an LSA context is dated at 11 500–10 500 years ago.[66] Objects of art became numerous only during the last 10 000 years. The latter is the date assigned to rock engravings found in Wonderwerk Cave in the northern Cape.[67] These engravings indicate that the content and the technique used in art remained essentially the same for 8 000 years, until 2 000 years ago. As indicated by Thackeray et al, this art may be interpreted as (in the terminology of this chapter) essentially religious.

According to burial remains, people very similar to if not identical with contemporary Bushmen were most certainly present in southern Africa 12 000 years ago. It seems that by then the Bushmen had carved themselves a niche as highly successful specialists in southern Africa. Their basic life-style remained unchanged until ± 2 000 years ago, when it was challenged by alternative socioeconomic systems originating in the Near East, where significant changes had set in about 10 000 years ago: people began to domesticate plants and animals, use metals and make pottery. For a few thousand years, however, the Bushmen were preserved from this dramatic set of innovations that were to change the course of human history so profoundly.

The Holocene, starting ± 10 000 years ago, witnessed many subtle shifts in the subsistence of southern African people. As far as diet was concerned, the emphasis now fell on small solitary antelope rather than on large grazers, and on intensive plant food collection.[68] Wide distribution and the large number of sites suggest smaller groups of people occupying smaller territories, moving around seasonally and depending on plant food staples.

A new microlithic tool industry appeared over a long timespan, ± 7 000–3 000 years ago.[69] This type of industry coincided with a dramatic increase in burial sites (utilising ochre and painted gravestones), rock paintings and engravings. Works of art from this period were discovered at Boomplaas (± 6 400 BP), Wonderwerk (± 6 400 BP), Matjies River (5 400 BP) and Klasies River (4100 BP).

Conclusion

Drawing on and extrapolating within reasonable bounds from the available palaeoanthropological and archaeological evidence of the hominisation process in terms of the wide definition of religion employed here, it may be concluded that religion co-emerged with humanity itself.[70] For the origin of religion we should look to the evolutionary process of hominisation as such: beyond the first rock art discovered in southern Africa, probably Bushman, 25 000–27 000 years ago; beyond the first deliberate burial recorded in southern Africa, very likely proto-Khoisan-Negro, 100 000 years ago; beyond the emergence of modern human beings, perhaps 200 000 years ago; beyond archaic *Homo sapiens*; even beyond those precursors who probably started 2 million years ago to speak, act out rituals and construct myths in addition to making stone tools and elevating hunting to a way of life. For its beginnings, as distinct from the stirrings in our non-human forebears, we may look to the beginnings of humanity when australopithecines started to walk upright 4 million or more years ago.

In this chapter we have adopted an inclusive view of religion: the symbolic expression of the constant and urgent need to adjust comprehensively to the ever-changing conditions of life. Such a view permits one to recognise when integrating symbolic phenomena such as art, myth, burial (integrating life and death) and ritual (integrating various states of mind and various states of life) occur or can be deduced from empirical data. It includes but is not restricted to such specifics. In terms of this approach the occurrence of religion cannot be ascertained directly from hard evidence. Of course, that would be one way of defining religion and finding it. Understandably and correctly, the specialist fields dealing with the early history of humanity restrict themselves vigorously to the finding, analysis and explanation of hard empirical data. However, the route I choose is a combination of empirical findings and more wide-ranging and inclusive theoretical reflection. I do not believe that such situating of the empiricial evidence in a wider setting skews that evidence or amounts to vacuous speculation. On the contrary, it is very necessary work. After all (whether this is acknowledged or not), the empirical sciences are part of the ongoing cultural process of humankind, trying to orient itself vis-à-vis the natural world, its own history and its own self-understanding through time. It seems to me that much of the theoretical work done in the sciences dealing with the beginnings of humanity indeed provides support for an overall conditionalist view of things.

ENDNOTES

1 C Darwin, *The descent of man, and selection in relation to sex*, London: Wickering, 1989 (1871), pp 155–156.

2 P B Beaumont, H de Villiers & J C Vogel, Modern man in sub-Saharan Africa prior to 49 000 years BP: a review and evaluation with particular reference to Border Cave, *South African Journal of Science*, 1978, 74, p 417.

3 This sentiment was expressed brutally by E B Tylor (*Primitive culture: researches into the development of mythology, philosophy, religion, art and custom*, New York: Brentano, 1924 [1871], p 26) when he said: 'The educated world of Europe and America practically settles a standard by simply placing its own notions at one end of the social series and savage tribes at the other, arranging the rest of mankind between these limits according as they correspond more clearly to savage or to cultured life.' This same sentiment was expresssed by other theorists on the evolution of religion, such as Herbert Spencer and James George Frazer. An example is Frazer's treatment of the relationship between magic (practised by 'the savage') and religion (*The magic art and the evolution of kings*, 2 vols, London: Macmillan, 1932 [1890]), and the origin of the belief in immortality (*The belief in immortality and the worship of the dead*, 3 vols, London: Macmillan, 1913).

4 In the South African context, however, a promising constructive attempt at synthesising evolution and theology has been made by J Fourie, S C J Joubert & J A Loader, Environmental education – an approach based on the concept of life, *Koedoe*, 1990, 33(1), pp 95–109. The general lack of interest in the subject is probably

attributable to the hegemony of fundamentalist and neo-orthodox theology in South Africa, and to the fact that over the last half century theological energies have been channelled virtually exclusively into the sociopolitical battlefield. As will become clear, the debate on evolution has significant social implications.

5 For wide-ranging synoptic treatments of past and present studies of human evolution, see inter alia G Richards, *Human evolution: an introduction for the behavioural sciences*, London & New York: Routledge & Kegan Paul, 1987; P Mellars & C Stringer (eds), *The human revolution: behavioural and biological perspectives on the origins of modern humans*, Edinburgh: University Press, 1989; P Mellars (ed), *The emergence of modern humans: an archaeological perspective*, Edinburgh: University Press, 1990.

6 For example, recently B Wood (Origin and evolution of the genus Homo, *Nature*, 1992, 355, pp 783–790) criticised the generally accepted unilineal model of human evolution according to which *Homo habilis* succeeded the australopithecines and then evolved via *Homo erectus* to *Homo sapiens*. In its place he proposed a multiple-species model involving five species (*H rudolfensis*, *H habilis*, *H ergaster*, *H erectus* and *H sapiens*).

7 For various discussions of the relationship between physics, cosmology, evolutionary theory, etc and religious thought, cf R J Russell, W R Stoeger & G V Coyne, *Physics, philosophy and theology: a common quest for understanding*, Vatican City State: Vatican Observatory, 1988.

8 R Ellwood, *Introducing religion from inside and outside*, Englewood Cliffs, NJ: Prentice-Hall, 1983, p 42.

9 Darwin, *The descent of man ...*, pp 65/6–95/6.

10 Recent efforts to reconstruct the origin of religion from a biological point of view include: Edward O Wilson, *On human nature*, Cambridge, Mass: Harvard University Press, 1978, in a sociobiological framework; and in a biogenetic structuralist framework, the work of Laughlin, D'Aquili and co-workers – cf E G d'Aquili & C Laughlin Jr, The biopsychological determinants of religious ritual behavior, *Zygon* 1975 10(1), pp 32–58; E d'Aquili, C D Laughlin Jr & J McManus, *The spectrum of ritual: a biogenetic structural analysis*, New York: Columbia University Press, 1979; C D Laughlin, J McManus & E d'Aquili, *Brain, symbol and experience: toward a neurophenomenology of human consciousness*, Boston: Shambhala, 1990.

11 *HOMO AS PRIMATE* (adapted from V Grant, *The evolutionary process: a critical review of evolutionary theory*, New York: Columbia University Press, 1985, p 408)

Suborder: 1 *Lemuroidae*
- 2 *Tarsioidea*
- 3 *Platyrrhini*
- 4 *Catarrhini*
  - Superfamily 1 *Cercopithecoidea*
  - 2 *Hominoidea*
    - Family 1 *Pongidae* (apes)
      - Genus 1 *Hylobatidae*
      - 2 *Symphalangus*
      - 3 *Pongo* (orangutan)

4 *Pan* (chimpanzee)
5 *Gorilla* (gorilla)
Family 2 *Hominidae* (hominids)
Genus 1 *Australopithecus* (proto-humans)
Species 1 *afarensis* (4–3 myr)
2 *africanus* (3–2 myr)
3 *robustus* (2 myr –)
4 *boisei* (2–1,3 myr)
Genus 2 *Homo* (humans)
Species 1 *H habilis* (2,2–1,7 myr)
2 *H erectus* (1,8–0,2 myr)
3 *H sapiens* (0,7 myr – present)
Subspecies 1 *Hs rhodesiensis* (0,7 myr –)
2 *Hs sapiens/afer* (0,1 myr – present)
3 *Hs neanderthalensis* (0,1 myr-34 000 yr)

12 Cf D Pilbeam, Patterns of hominoid evolution, in E Delson (ed), *Ancestors: the hard evidence*, New York: Liss, 1985.

13 For the history of this famous discovery, see the contributions in P Tobias (ed), *Hominid evolution: past, present and future*, New York: Liss, 1985. In South Africa two species have been distinguished: *australopithecus africanus* and *Australopithecus robustus*. The first of these to emerge is thought to have been the gracile *A africanus*, specimens of which have been found at Makapansgat (estimated roughly 3 myr) and Sterkfontein (roughly 2,5 myr) in the Transvaal, as well as at Taung in the northern Cape. Specimens of *A robustus* have been found at Swartkrans and Kromdraai (roughly 1,5 myr) near Krugersdorp. The first find was made by Robert Broom, Dart's staunch supporter, in 1938. *A robustus* had larger teeth and a sturdier and larger body than *A africanus*, with an average mass of about 60 kg, compared to *A africanus*'s approximately 35 kg. It also had a flatter facial skeleton and a greater cranial volume. Its cranium was not rounded like that of *A africanus*, but had a characteristic sagittal crest on the braincase to which jaw muscles were attached, which suggests greater specialisation in crushing and grinding food. Because of these specialised features, most scholars do not regard it as ancestral to *Homo*. Its large molars and small incisors and canines indicate that fruit must have been an important dietary item, although the problem of Australopithecine diet remains unresolved. It seems probable that *A robustus* was mainly, if not exclusively, vegetarian, whereas *A africanus* could have been omnivorous. *A robustus* emerged around 2 myr, existed alongside *Homo habilis* and *Homo erectus* for a considerable period, and disappeared about 1 myr. These South African hominid fossils were all found in dolomitic limestone caves. Apart from Taung, the caves were not used as shelters (cf C K Brain, Some principles in the interpretation of bone accumulations associated with man, in G L Isaac & E R McCown (eds), *Human origins: Louis Leakey and the East African evidence*, Menlo Park, Ca: Benjamin, 1976, pp 97–116). Bones of hominids and other prey were probably left near the vertical entrances to the deep subterranean caves by large cats and hyenas, and were then washed into the caves during flooding. It may also indicate that these hominids sought shelter near the openings of the caves.

Extremely promising for filling in the gaps in our knowledge of human origins is the recently discovered South African cave site Gladysvale, also near Krugersdorp.

14 Apart from *A afarensis*, East Africa yielded fossils of another supposed species, *Australopithecus boisei*, which was even more robust than *A robustus*. It was first discovered by Mary Leakey in Olduvai Gorge, northern Tanzania, in 1959. Other discoveries of it were made elsewhere in Tanzania (Peninj), Kenya (Koobi Fora) and Ethiopia (Omo Valley). It is thought possible that *A boisei* may have emerged contemporaneously with *A robustus* roughly 2,5 myr, that is at about the same time that *Homo*, as *Homo habilis*, developed as a distinct genus. For a long time, at least 1,3 million years, these species and *Homo habilis* must have existed side by side. They may all have become extinct as a result of unsuccessful competition with *Homo erectus*, which arose approximately 1,7 myr.

15 The name given by L S B Leaky, P V Tobias & J R Napier, A new species of the genus *Homo* from Olduvai Gorge, *Nature* 1964 202, pp 7–9.

16 Cf R L Holloway, Human brain evolution: a search for units, models and synthesis, *Canadian Journal of Anthropology*, 1983 3(2), pp 215–230.

17 In 1977, in solidified volcanic ashes at Laetoli in Tanzania, Mary Leakey's team discovered more than 50 early protohominid footprints covering a distance of about 25 metres. These footprints are agreed to be 3,8–3,6 million years old, and are generally taken to have been made by *Australopithecus afarensis*. The question of the degree of similarity between the *Australopithecus* gait, as gauged from these footprints, and that of modern humans is still hotly debated, yet bipedal they undoubtedly were.

18 Whether the australopithecines made primitive stone artefacts remains an open question at this stage (J D Clark, Leaving no stone unturned: archaeological advances and behavioural adaptation, in Tobias, *Hominid evolution* ..., pp 65–88). Probably they used simple opportunistic tools such as sticks which would not have left any traces in the archaeological record. The first unequivocally accepted proof of stone artefacts, dated 2,9–2,7 myr, was found in the Hadar region of Ethiopia.

19 Richards, *Human evolution* ..., pp 136–152.

20 G L Isaac, Aspects of human evolution, in D S Bendall, *Evolution from molecules to men*, Cambridge: Cambridge University Press, 1983, pp 509–545.

21 As to the vexing question of the possible phylogenetic relationship between these hominids and the next stage of hominid evolution (*Homo habilis* and other early forms of *Homo* leading from there), learned opinion is at present much divided. Given the empirical evidence, a number of logical possibilities arise and are represented in scholarly opinion. (a) One possibility is, of course, to deny such a continuity altogether, and to argue that no *Australopithecus* (neither *A africanus*, nor *A robustus*, nor *A afarensis*) is ancestral to *Homo habilis*. In that case *Homo habilis* would have split off from some unknown ancestor that it had in common with the australopithecines. (b) Another reconstruction is that *habilis* did emerge from the *A afarensis* line, but split off prior to and independently of the other known australopithecines. (c) *Habilis* might have evolved from *A afarensis*, with the other australopithecines splitting off from this main lineage. (d) *A afarensis* could have split into the other two australopithecines (*A africanus* or *A robustus*), with

habilis emerging from one of the latter two. (e) Yet another model pictures *afarensis* developing into one of the other two australopithecines (probably *A africanus*, since its fossils are undoubtedly older), with the other one (probably *A robustus*) and *habilis* forking off from it, the latter split leading to reduced tooth size and increased cranial volume (cf G P Rightmire, The fossil evidence for hominid evolution in southern Africa, in R Klein [ed], *southern African prehistory and paleoenvironments*, Boston: Balkema, 1984, pp 155ff). This would mean that human ancestry can be traced back to *A afarensis*. At this stage, however, there is no certainty or even unanimity. Given the present state of the fossil record, position (a) is noncommittal with respect to the place of origin of *Homo habilis*. The implication of positions (b) and (c) is that *Homo habilis* most probably migrated to southern Africa from East Africa, where it had originated. The implication of (d) and (e) is that *habilis* was probably indigenous to southern Africa.

22 See note 10.

23 '... when ritual works (and it by no means works all the time), it powerfully relieves man's existential anxiety, and, at its most powerful, it relieves him of the fear of death and places him in harmony with the universe' (D'Aquili & Laughlin, The biopsychological determinants ..., p 54).

24 Ibid, pp 44ff.

25 Cf P V Tobias, From Linn to Leakey: six signposts in human evolution. Proceedings of a Nobel Symposium organised by the Royal Swedish Academy of Science and held at Karlskoga, Sweden on 21–27 May 1978. Reprinted in *The Leech* 1991 60, pp 16–25.

26 Richards, *Human evolution ...*, pp 136ff.

27 P V Tobias, The brain of *Homo habilis*: a new level of organization in cerebral evolution, *The Leech* 1991 60, pp 31–48.

28 Cf Clark, Leaving no stone unturned ..., pp 65–88.

29 The Stone Age lasted more than 2 million years. Stone tool technology was associated with the hunter-gatherer subsistence strategy which, with many variations over time and place, remained the basic mode of life of *Homo* for 99 per cent of its history.

As far as southern Africa is concerned, assemblages of the ESA were probably produced 200 000 years ago at the latest (Volman, Early prehistory of southern Africa, in Klein, *southern African prehistory ...*, p 184). Whereas at the beginning of this period early humans probably lived mainly by scavenging, hunting small animals and collecting insects, eggs and plant foods during brief stopovers, towards the end they lived by organised hunting of large animals, scavenging and planned collection of plant foods (Clark, Leaving no stone unturned ..., p 80).

The southern African MSA started more than 150 000 years ago, and continued until after 40 000 years ago. By the time of its inception hafting had already begun, and humans covered large areas in large bands, reoccupying specific camps in their seasonal transhumance (Clark, Leaving no stone unturned ..., p 80). Compared to the LSA, art objects, ornaments and graves, which could be counted as strong material indicators of religion, are still very rare.

The LSA started about 40 000 years ago. By then many regional traditions and functionally specific composite tool sets had developed. In southern Africa the period is marked by material items of the kind used by hunter-gatherers such as the Bushmen until very recently (Volman, Early prehistory ..., pp 170ff). The population had expanded significantly, and people lived in small bands, exploiting the seasonal resources in smaller areas intensively.

30 Clark, Leaving no stone unturned ..., p 73.

31 R B Lee & I de Vore, *Man the hunter*, Chicago: Aldine, 1968, pp 3ff.

32 S L Washburn & C S Lancaster, The evolution of hunting, in Lee & De Vore, *Man the hunter*, p 293.

33 Cf Mellars & Stringer, *The human revolution* ..., pp 2ff.

34 Possibly there were differences in gait. If the very meagre skeletal finds are extrapolated, they may have been surprisingly tall, in some cases approaching 2 metres. However, owing to the scarcity of fossils and the very wide spread of their occurrence from East Africa and Europe to China and Java, one has to be extremely cautious in extrapolating their physical appearance and way of life. In this area too, new discoveries and interpretations are to be expected in future.

35 Cf L R Binford & C K Ho, Taphonomy at a distance: Zhoukoudian – the cave home of Beijing Man? *Current Anthropology* 1985 26(4), pp 413–442.

36 Assuming that they had originated in Africa – a probability, but thus far not proved conclusively. In fact, the first specimen of *H erectus* was discovered in 1891–1892 in central Java by a Dutch army surgeon, Eugene Dubois. He called it *Pithecanthropus erectus*. His discovery reinforced the notion prevalent at the time that Asia had been the cradle of humankind. This bias continued up to Dart's discovery of *A africanus* in 1925, and partly explains the indifference with which the Taung child was greeted by the academic establishment of the time.

37 Recent reappraisals (cf for example *Antiquity*, 1994, pp 489–503) suggest that the occupation of Europe began in the south by 0,7 myr.

38 Clark, Leaving no stone unturned ..., p 76.

39 Ibid, pp 77ff; C K Brain & A Sillen, Evidence from Swartkrans cave for the earliest use of fire, *Nature* 1988 336, pp 464–466.

40 Richards, *Human evolution* ..., pp 205ff.

41 The two main schools of thought, namely that sapienisation took place at one time and locality (the two important contestants for this honour being eastern Asia on the one hand, and Africa and/or western Asia on the other), or that a variety of forms emerged at different times and localities still vie for support (Richards, *Human evolution* ..., pp 281ff). The basic problem is how to reconcile the east Asian with the Afro-west Asian and even the relatively prominent European material. Palaeontologically, the nature of this transitional material is still unclear, and the links between *H erectus* and the first anatomically modern human beings, the oldest fossil remains of which were discovered in sub-Saharan Africa, are at this stage still very obscure.

42 According to Clark, Leaving no stone unturned ..., p 76 characteristics of archaic *sapiens* and a variety of transitional forms between *erectus* and *sapiens* are widely recognised in African fossils from about 300 000 or more years ago.

43 Mellars & Stringer, *The human revolution ...*, pp 2ff.

44 See R Mason, *Prehistory of the Transvaal: a record of human activity*, Johannesburg: Witwatersrand University Press, 1969.

45 Rightmire, The fossil evidence ..., p 162. *Homo sapiens rhodesiensis* may have lived between 250 000 and 50 000 BP (P V Tobias, The last million years in southern Africa, in T Cameron, *A new illustrated history of South Africa*, Johannesburg: Southern, p 24).

46 It seems that for a period of at least several centuries late Neanderthal and early modern populations must have existed side by side in certain areas of Europe and western Asia. There is growing consensus that existing populations of *Homo sapiens neanderthalensis* were eventually replaced by the intrusive populations of *Homo sapiens sapiens*, with few if any indications of interbreeding (E Zubrow, The demographic modelling of Neanderthal extinction, in Mellars & Stringer, *The human revolution ...*, p 212). Zubrow (ibid, pp 212, 229ff) postulates that even a small demographic advantage such as a 1 per cent difference in mortality may have led to the extinction of the Neanderthals in 30 generations, or approximately 1 millennium. These matters are far from resolved at the present stage of thinking.

47 Cf A Marshack, Early hominid symbol and evolution of the human capacity, in Mellars, *The emergence of modern humans ...*, pp 457–498.

48 Cf Rightmire, The fossil evidence ..., p 163; also Rightmire, Middle Stone Age humans from eastern and southern Africa, in Mellars & Stringer, *The human revolution ...*, p 117.

49 Rightmire, Middle Stone Age humans ..., p 120.

50 Progress in dating is likely in the near future with the development of new dating techniques. This would solve some of the problems, although differences of opinion are bound to persist for some time to come. Apart from the view that modern humans arose in Africa and radiated from there, two other possibilities are submitted. One maintains that this new species came into being in East Asia. Evidence adduced for this view is based on anatomical characteristics shared by specimens found there and modern populations from that area as well as with *H erectus*. Another view is that hominisation took place in various areas more or less simultaneously (M H Wolpoff, Multiregional evolution: the fossil alternative to Eden, in Mellars & Stringer, *The human revolution ...*, pp 62–108.

Recently various geneticists developed a procedure to calculate the age of modern humans by working backwards from the mitochondrial DNA found in the placentas of babies born of a sample of women drawn from various modern human 'races'. Taking into account the probable rate of random mutations that would have occurred in the mitochondrial DNA of humans (estimated at 2–4 per cent over a million years for a wide variety of vertebrates), M Stoneking & R Cann (African origin of human mitochondrial DNA, in Mellars & Stringer, *The human revolution ...*, pp 17–30) came up with the suggestion that modern humans are a young species, having arisen only approximately 200 000 years ago (certainly, they argue, at least 50 000 and no more than 500 000 years ago). Arguing that the more mtDNA variability a population possesses, the older it is, African populations appear to be the oldest human group on earth (Stoneking & Cann, ibid, p 22). According to them the evidence points to subsaharan Africa as the most likely place of human origin

(South China is a less favoured locality among geneticists) – 'the common mtDNA ancestor lived some 200 000 years ago and was a member of an archaic African population of humans whose descendants underwent a transformation to anatomically-modern humans by 100 000 years ago. Some members of the anatomically-modern population dispersed out of Africa to other parts of the world, while others remained in Africa' (ibid, p 26; also cf J S Wainscote et al, Geographic distribution of alpha- and beta-globin gene cluster polymorphisms, in Mellars & Stringer, *The human revolution ...*, pp 31–38). This hypothesis implies that the *Homo erectus* forms in Europe and Asia did not contribute anything to the gene pool of modern humans. This view of a single locality of origin stands over against the hypothesis, based on an interpretation of fossil evidence, that modern humans developed independently, and much earlier, in various regions (Wolpoff, Multiregional evolution ..., pp 62–108). However, Wolpoff's position should not be taken to represent archaeological consensus. The palaeoanthropologist G Bruer (The evolution of modern humans: a comparison of the African and non-African evidence, in Mellars & Stringer, *The human revolution ...*, p 148) supports a global 'out of Africa' model for modern humans. This divergence of opinion obviously has implications for the relative homogeneity of modern humans, also for the degree of continuity between modern populations in Africa, Australasia, Asia and Europe, and the archaic populations whose fossil remains have been found in those parts of the world. Wolpoff (ibid, p 95) argues that a 2–4 per cent mutation rate of mtDNA, leading to the very recent one-locality ('garden of Eden') hypothesis, is implausible. Instead, he claims that *Homo erectus* was the first human species to be widely distributed around the world, and that the various modern populations have arisen independently from this same stock in various localities.

Clearly, the debate as to whether anatomically modern humans arose at one point or at several has implications for the vexing problem of the origin of contemporary human 'races'. If the emergence of modern humans was a series of parallel events in several places, then the contemporary 'races' must be regarded as much older than would be the case if modern humankind had one common recent origin. It is a fact that the entry of modern humans in remote areas of the globe such as Australia and the New World is of fairly recent date. In both cases, it occurred in phases during the last ice age, 50 000–40 000 years ago in the case of the former, and 30 000–10 000 years ago in the case of the latter. Even the most far-flung tribal societies reached their territories fairly recently, when seen on the larger timescale of evolution. This radiation seems to favour the localised rather than the dispersed origin of anatomically modern humans. But at this stage the genetic evidence does not justify any specific theory unequivocally in the eyes of all specialists.

The fact that differences between individuals far exceed national and racial differences in any event seems to be consistent with the notion that modern humans developed very rapidly in evolutionary terms and that contemporary differences are very recent (cf Rouhani, Molecular genetics ..., in Mellars & Stringer, *The human revolution ...*, p 58). On the other hand, Wolpoff is careful to exonerate his multiregional hypothesis from any racist overtones, arguing that the evolution of modern humans is a story of contacts and interaction over a long period of time, rather than a sudden and probably violent displacement of archaic populations by one, very recent group of humans. Bruer agrees that the fossil record does not favour a radical replacement process, but rather a multicausal process of archaic-modern replacement which was quite variable in the various regions. At this stage, this particular set of problems is far from being resolved.

51 V Shevoroshkin, The mother tongue: how linguists have reconstructed the ancestor of all living languages, *The Sciences* 1990 30(3), pp 20–27.

52 Ibid, p 26.

53 Ibid, p 27.

54 Cf his article Against relativism, in G J Larson & E Deutsch (eds), *Interpreting across boundaries: new essays in comparative philosophy*, Princeton: University Press, 1989, pp 36–70.

55 H J Deacon, Late Pleistocene palaeoecology and archaeology in the southern Cape, in Mellars & Stringer, *The human revolution* ..., pp 547ff.

56 Ibid, p 557.

57 R G Klein, Biological and behavioural perspectives on modern human origins in southern Africa, in Mellars & Stringer, ibid, pp 529ff.

58 Rightmire, Middle Stone Age humans ..., p 115.

59 Rightmire, The fossil evidence ..., p 165. This corresponds with the view of Beaumont et al, Modern man in sub-Saharan Africa ...

60 Beaumont et al, Modern man in sub-Saharan Africa ...

61 P V Tobias (ed), *The Bushmen: San hunters and herders of Southern Africa*, Cape Town: Human & Rousseau, 1978; cf Rightmire, The fossil evidence ..., pp 167–168.

62 Clark, Leaving no stone unturned ..., p 79.

63 J Deacon, Later Stone Age people and their descendants in southern Africa, in Klein, *Southern African prehistory* ..., p 222.

64 Ibid, p 320.

65 For the dating of rock art, cf A I Thackeray, Dating the rock art of southern Africa, *South African Archaeological Society, Goodwin Series*, 1983 4, pp 21–26.

66 J Deacon, Later Stone Age people ..., p 299.

67 By A I Thackeray et al, Dated rock engravings from Wonderwerk cave, South Africa, *Science* 1981 214, pp 64–67.

68 Deacon, Later Stone Age people ..., p 322.

69 This is Deacon's third period, the *Holocene microlithic assemblages* (8 000 – few hundred years BP in some areas).

70 This concurs with the overall conclusion of P Beaumont (The time-depth of aesthetic and symbolic behaviour in southern Africa, *Southern African Association of Archaeologists, Biennial Conference*, Book of Abstracts, 1–4 July 1992, University of Cape Town, p 39) that 'the capacity for symbolic behaviour is unlikely to have appeared in fully-fledged form at some specific point in time, but rather by way of protracted evolutionary accretions, of which an aesthetic sense, with its implicit concept of 'beauty', may be regarded as a primal manifestation'.

11 The new 'Homo religiosus africanus'

This chapter reflects on a number of features of a religious orientation prompted by the fact that human beings evolved in Africa.

Pilgrimage

As my research into the roots of religion in southern Africa progressed, I found that the compelling need to discover this place, in the long perspective of evolutionary time and in the context of the emergence of humanity as a species, was a pilgrimage (in the beautiful Afrikaans word, a *bedevaart*).

This struck me vividly one day while I was studying some exquisite Bushman engravings in the Upper Karroo. There they were, strange animal-like phantasmagoria on large black dolomite boulders strewn over a brown koppie on a vast, flat, hot, barren, to the casual visitor forbidding landscape. This had obviously been a 'place', in the full religious sense of the word, for its inhabitants or for those who sought physical and spiritual refuge on its bare slopes; not a mere locality, but a source and centre of meaning and power. Standing there in the hot sun, I could not resist the urge to go down on all fours and press my forehead to the dry soil in an act of homage and communion with those who had frequented that place and then been driven out. It was a deeply humbling and at the same time an illuminating experience to stand in a seemingly empty landscape and realise that in fact it is filled with a human presence thousands of years old. They were here, and in a sense still are. I was standing on 'holy' ground. Was my need to establish solidarity with the Bushmen and this land 'nostalgia for paradise', arising from the fact that we 'cannot live except in this sort of sacred space'?[1] I believe it was, and that it is not to be confused with sentimentality.

The long perspective of evolution gives one a sense of belonging to this vast continent where *Homo* arose, and from where it spread over the entire earth, discovering sacred places as far as it went. Today that dispersal is counterbalanced by the convergence of humankind. In the space age our small planet, virtually disappearing in the unimaginable vastness of outer space, has itself become our 'sacred place' – the place where we experience the depth. Ultimately place makes room for space. The ultimate religious *orientatio* leaves specific sacred places behind. In the end neither Europe, nor Africa, nor the earth is the centre of the universe. Yet the continent of Africa, the cradle of *Homo* and of religion, has a truly autochthonous (sprung from the earth!) religious dignity of its own. This is obviously not meant in an exclusive sense, as if to strip all other places of religious significance, and declaring only *this* one to be 'holy' in some supranaturalist sense. On the contrary, any place, if probed and plumbed, would open up the depth for anybody to experience. The most ordinary experience could yield this feeling of the mystery of things, paradoxically remaining simultaneously ordinary and most extraordinary. Southern Africa is an ordinary locality and in an ultimate sense, like all other places, it merges into the vastness of inner and outer space. Yet in a vigorous commitment to *this* experience *here* and *now* of those who look at it intently, meditating on it, it becomes a revelation, a focus of the religious limit experience. If it is true, as science postulates with considerable certainty, that Africa was the cradle of *Homo*, then the African soil takes on the characteristics of a 'holy' place. This is not to renege on the radical implications hinted at by evolutionary theory (which will be developed below), an insistence that certain things, places or times are exempt from the rule of change. All it maintains is that in certain concrete things and places and at certain times the truth of the world is felt acutely.

To most South Africans of non-African extraction (and to many indigenous South Africans too) the centre of religious and cultural gravity lies elsewhere – in Rome, Canterbury or Heidelberg, in Jerusalem, Benares or Mecca. Africa often happens to be the locality where prostrations are made in those other directions from which the various religions and cultures have been imported. Yet Africa claims her own. In varying degrees, deliberately or involuntarily, with difficulty or with ease, she is received into the soul of all her inhabitants.

The long road of change

As our society hurtles forward into an uncertain future a need arises to look back over the vast stretch of time leading up to the present. Not least, a survey of the human journey fills one with wonder at the tenacity of our predecessors here. The Bushmen were the first South Africans to appear in the clear light of history, and they had been here for a long, long time prior to that. It is time that, in an act of *anamnesis* by us, the generation of today, they enter – as honoured pioneers and founding figures – the collective remembrance of this society. Instead of relegating them to an inferior status as belonging to another 'primitive' time[2] by making the West and the period of its domination the yardstick as both anthropology and theology have done for so long, it is time to conceive of southern African history as one whole, all its moments co-present in a remembrance shared and valued by all its people. Only within such an inclusive framework could one speak, with some justification and great caution, of development.

Placing the dramatic and traumatic events of this century in our part of Africa into such a long temporal perspective relativises them. It is salutary to reflect that even the turmoil wrought by three and a half centuries of colonialism is but a short chapter in the long history of human presence here. It was preceded by the shock waves caused by the arrival of herders and Iron Age farmers 2 000 years ago. Beyond that, traceable to about 15 000 years ago, stretches the relative continuity of Bushman culture. Beyond that, even relatively certain points of reference are few and far between. A 100 000 years ago one picks up glimpses of common ancestors of the Khoisan and Negro in southern Africa. Beyond that the process of human evolution stretches back: modern humans emerging in Africa from archaic humans, emerging from protohumans, emerging from hominoids, emerging from the web of life like all creatures in a wonderful process of coming into being and passing away.

In this long perspective the human presence during two to four million years out of 3 500 million years of life on earth is very short, only about 0,1 per cent. If the scale is extended to encompass the origin of the earth and of our universe, we humans are reduced to a minuscule speck, present for perhaps 0,05 per cent of that time. To be religious in our time is to realise the implications of this discovery clearly. It amounts to an explosion of the smallness of the religious world-view of yesteryear, and a fundamental reorientation.

Evolution and religion

The relationship between evolutionary science and religion is intricate. It is vital for religious thought today to be in touch with the idea of evolution as suggested by the empirical sciences, and fatal to confront that idea as though it were an enemy. Without denying that the Genesis accounts of creation and other venerable cosmologies contain profound religious insights, it must be realised that the cosmologies of the classical religions are mythical, not scientific accounts of how the world came into being. The question of how (for example) the biblical myths may be interpreted lies outside the scope of this chapter. Suffice it to say that attempts such as the conflation of the six days of creation according to Genesis with the evolutionary time-scale strike me as contrived and unconvincing.

There can be no immediate, direct continuity from the 'facts' of evolution to a religious worldview. As Bowler[3] has indicated, throughout the nineteenth and twentieth centuries religious and political biases played a major role in shaping the various theories of evolution. Not even the materialists in the evolutionary debate escaped religion – only a particular type of religion, namely Judaeo-Christian orthodoxy. Stones, bones and blood in themselves do not proclaim any particular theory, philosophy or religion, and none can be found through pure induction. That much is generally accepted in scholarly circles today. The bones and other indicators have to be interpreted creatively in terms of meaning-constituting frameworks, suggesting a two-way process of influence and support, even of interpenetration, between science and religion. Science is never isolated from wider religious, worldview, philosophical and ideological values, and religion will always include elements of the store of knowledge accepted in a given culture. In the meeting of science and religion today the holistic modes of religious thought now emerging at the dusk of the modern period and drawing on existing resources in the major spiritual traditions have the edge over the dualistic modes of religious thought which were predominant in Western modernity. Evolution is a wide-ranging explanatory strategy, seemingly compatible with a religious vision in which the notions of change and relationality are central. Neither a simple derivation of worldview from scientific biology, nor of biological evolution from worldview is acceptable. Rather, a relationship of mutual discovery and support obtains. It is along these lines that I would defend not only the compatibility but also the inner affinity between evolutionism and the religious perspective suggested here.

A key element of the fundamental reorientation necessary in this country is the expansion of the boundaries of human society into unknown and untried dimensions. Related to that is the dual necessity of moving with the drastic expansion of time and space, and simultaneously effecting some measure of worldview integration. Religious thought here has yet to come to terms with the enormous vistas of time revealed by the Darwinian revolution, as it has to come to terms with the vistas of space that started to emerge with the Copernican revolution of the sixteenth century and with the other, more recent revolutions of relativity theory and quantum physics, which have finally exploded the old notions of time and space.

The glosses given here are not based on any specific scientific theory of evolution. As any survey of the literature will show, there are a number of such theories. Not only Lamarckism, but also 'neutralism', 'mutationism' and others[4] compete for the allegiance of biologists and palaeoanthropologists. As far as human evolution is concerned, many problems remained unresolved.[5] Not being a palaeoanthropologist, I am not competent to take part in debates on *how* (by means of which mechanisms) species evolved. Nor do I feel any need to resort to pop biology or pop physics to prop up my argument. It is sufficient to acknowledge that by and large evolution – as the broad notion *that* all existing forms of life go back to a common origin, from which they developed – has been accepted in contemporary biology, to reflect on the religious implications of that, and to approach it in a perspective that derives from an old mysticism. In general terms, then, in some respects it seems to me that the world-view of neo-Darwinism is more convincing (for example in its nonteleology), in others Lamarckism had something important to say (for example in its refusal to reduce nature to matter).

But all of that may be old hat in the light of the biochemical 'science of complexity' recently put forward by Stuart A Kauffman, who situates the origin of life precisely on the razor edge between order and chaos.[6] In fact all complex adaptive systems operate right there. The exciting religiophilosophical implications of this approach may be compatible with the basic idea developed in these essays.

Opponents of the kind of religious reflection advocated here often point out that evolution has not been 'proven', presumably meaning that it is not a perfect, final, cast-iron explanation; that there are a number of competing theories within the overall paradigm; that there are many gaps in the data; that many theoretical problems are unresolved; and that new hypotheses emerge and shifts and differences of opinion occur all the time. They then conclude that therefore it is null and void, or on a par with any opinion that anybody, however unschooled in the field, may care to express. It is hardly necessary to point out that that particular view of what constitutes science and scientific 'fact' has been discarded in the philosophy of science. Good science is its own severest critic. From a religious point of view, the importance of the broad evolutionary explanatory strategy lies in its wide-ranging integrative power, compatible not only with the findings of empirical research but also with ancient mysticisms.

Openness of being

Evolution is the expression of a thoroughly dynamic worldview, implying that there are no eternally fixed entities, whether individuals or species, and that from one million years to the next, from one moment to the next, everything is changing. Since its emergence in the second half of the eighteenth century, principally with Georges de Buffon's *Histoire naturelle* (1749–1767), it has played a major role in transforming the previously dominant Western worldview that reality is essentially static, ahistorical and atemporal into the modern dominant Western view that reality is dynamic, historical and temporally structured.[7] The old Western idea, going back to Greek antiquity, of a static chain of being in which all things are related (yet essentially *not* in the sense of temporal continuity and emergence) has been overthrown. The classical biblical myths (in the book of Genesis) of the origin of the world do, in fact, contain a historical element in that creation is said to have taken place over a period of six successive days. Yet, when turned into a pseudo-scientific account, its timescale is puny: it started a few thousand years ago (to be precise, said Archbishop Ussher in the seventeenth century, in 4004 BC), and it was all over in six days. Even when modern creationists no longer take the six days literally, the basic picture usually remains that of a short period of time. (Of course the Judaeo-Christian vision is not necessarily tied up with that particular cosmological myth or with its pseudo-scientific turn.) This conventional view is marked not only by a short timespan, but also by the notion of essentially distinct forms of life. Central to an evolutionary worldview is the realisation that existing forms of life have emerged from other forms of life, and that they may change drastically to become very different from what they are at present – that is, if they do not become extinct.

However, evolution is obviously much more than mere change. A whole library of publications striving to describe its quality and character has been produced over the last two centuries. To clarify this process in a religious perspective I propose that we apply the dialectic of integration and transcendence to look at the evolutionary process.[8] Religion as understood in these essays is not a dispensable quirk of the human mind. The historical religions are expressions of an ambivalent, paradoxical urge inherent in human nature to limit and to unlimit, to define and to explore, to find and maintain order and to give it up, to have a set of established facts and to live in the open process of discovery. This is not a strange, unaccountable urge. It is a necessity, a need, rooted in humankind's very bio-psychological constitution as beings in the world – a world which is overwhelmingly threatening and at the same time wonderfully beautiful, exciting and inviting. This double orientation is found among all animals, in fact all living beings on earth, although not in as complex a form. In animals the need for territorial integrity may be read as one aspect of the need for established order – to be balanced with the constant need and pressure to change in order to adapt to ever-changing sets of factors conditioning their existence. So religion follows from the logic of reality itself. Let us look at evolution in these terms. Life proliferates exuberantly, expanding its boundaries, and it forms temporarily stable identities (such as species).

Living beings appear as temporary manifestations of the dynamic process of life, which is a manifestation of the creative depth, freely spawning myriad forms. The world appears as a continuous *creatio ex nihilo* (to borrow a phrase from theistic creationism), as the sum of emergences from the depth from which they are not separable at all. Hence they are not separable from one another either.

The scientific idea of evolution can therefore be assimilated quite readily into the kind of religious worldview proposed here, articulated by Tarthang Tulku[9] as the dance of Great Space and Great Time. *Great Space* is not an external, extensive container, however large, but infinite, inexhaustible, unbounded openness, the all-transcending yet all-pervading and all-accommodating depth dimension of reality, its centreless 'centre' and groundless 'ground'; not a separate Entity somewhere – neither 'here', 'there' nor 'elsewhere' in the conventional spatial sense (for example in the world above of traditional religion). It is immediately and transparently present in all 'entities' everywhere, yet not even in the subtlest sense as a distinct Being or Entity, for all is Great Space and Great Space is all. *Great Time*, the inseparable partner of Great Space, is not a restrictive tube, stretching from a fixed beginning to an end, however distant, segmented into past, present and future, in which a linear series of events occur (that is conventional, egocentrically structured time) but the unimpeded and undistributed (non-distributive) dynamic dimension of reality, resounding 'in' Great Space, concretising its infinite possibilities. Not being linear, sequential or punctuated, Great Time does not 'pass'. It is inspiration, freedom, spontaneity, creativity, potentiated by Great Space and expressing Great Space in an infinity of manifestations.[10]

In such a view discontinuities between entities that may seem very fundamental in ordinary life or in science are deeply relativised. A case in point is the status assigned to the biological idea of *species*. This has of course always been a bone of contention in evolutionary thought. In all the major modern evolutionary theories the weight attached to species reflects deep-seated worldview assumptions.[11] In creationism, species have metaphysical status. The reason for the insistence that species are real, immutable and separate entities is the belief that the world was created according to an orderly, fixed and definite design. Each species was created perfect in itself, separately and miraculously; it could not interbreed successfully with other species (sterility was the result of such attempted miscegeny); and it would not become extinct. Although Linnaeus (1707–1778), the creator of the modern system of biological classification, did allow for some multiplication of species within certain bounds as a result of hybridisation, he believed that originally God had created only single species. On the other hand, another eighteenth-century thinker, Diderot (1713–1784), known not altogether correctly as a 'materialist', broke with the orthodox religious teaching of the time and saw the production of forms of life as an open-ended, immanently natural process, without a predetermined plan and without fixed species. Believing in the fixity of species until after his fiftieth year, Lamarck (1774–1829) – really the first person to produce a scientific account of evolution – then changed his mind radically and demolished the very idea of different species; forms shade imperceptibly into one another and species are delineated simply for convenience. To him the evolutionary process was essentially continuous, without any sharp breaks.

For Darwin (1809–1882) – even after completing his break with the religious convention of his time by accepting the transmutation of species – species, although not fixed, had real and objective existence. Neither were they (as the nineteenth-century Idealist school taught, following Plato) the manifestations of timeless, transcendental, ideal forms or archetypal essences. In his rigorously empirical and historical perspective Darwin believed that species are simply populations of individuals capable of breeding.[12]

However important classification schemes might be (and without them neither everyday life nor science would be possible), they are semi-arbitrary freezings of the stream of reality with the status of useful and necessary conventions. To live and to communicate we need categorisations, but the specific categorisations in which we box reality are not absolute. They are our ways of looking, grouping, framing, establishing order so as to know and to communicate. We cannot avoid chopping up the world, but it can be chopped up in many ways, as the social sciences demonstrate happens in diverse cultures – and, in an ultimate sense, it cannot be chopped up at all. As the modern debate between evolutionism and cladism illustrates,[13] the Linnaean classification is by no means absolute and final. Our categories do not correspond with an eternally fixed system of boxes. The various species of life are not ontologically fixed absolutes. It is we who freeze the flow of reality in all sorts of cubicles, such as types of living creatures. In this respect a conditionalist perspective is at odds with creationism and far more at ease with evolutionary thought, regardless of precisely how the changes of species are accounted for in biological theory.

A survey of recent theories of human evolution shows that a monocausal explanation for this process is simply not on.[14] The tendency is to realise that even if one item is seen as the critical factor, a host of other factors (such as bipedalism, brain organisation, provisioning, meat eating, sexual patterns, gestation period and toolmaking) have to be taken into account, all interacting, operating in feedback loops. It is a matter of many reciprocal relationships.[15] This way of looking at human origins applies to the evolutionary world process as such. From a religious point of view, it ties in with the notion of the world as an open, conditionalistically operating field in which nothing is isolated and everything is constituted throught its involvement with all other factors in the overall field.

God

The centre of the storm unleashed by Darwin was not the notion of species transformation as such, but rather that his theory seemed to render the traditional view of God to account for the world's existence redundant.

During the nineteenth century the growing influence of evolutionary thought gradually pushed the traditional theistic view into a defensive position. At the beginning of that century William Paley (his *Natural theology* appeared in 1802) could still state the optimistic view of natural theology: just as an intricate watch implies a designer and watchmaker, so the wonderfully complex world implies the existence of a powerful and benevolent Creator who saw to it that all things fit beautifully together. Even the problem of cruelty could be solved in that way. Carnivores remove the old and sickly who stand in the way of optimal harmony. Predator and prey collaborate to ensure the best world. After all, each species has been created perfect in the original series of creative acts. A few decades later the idea of evolution had taken firm root. Robert Chambers (*Vestiges of the natural history of creation*, 1844) illustrated the new thought. He accepted evolution, seeing it as the immanent unfolding of a divine plan programmed by God and built into the fabric of nature itself. God did not create through a series of supernatural miracles, but through the processes of nature. By the time that Darwin's *Origin of species* appeared in 1859, the idea of evolutionary development had already found wide acceptance in progressive thinking circles. Darwin's revolutionary idea was not evolution as such, but severing evolution from the assumption that the world is the flawless working out of a creator's purpose. For the will of a supernatural power, he substituted natural law; for a benevolent creator, relentless population pressure; for divine supervision, natural selection in a blind, brutish struggle for existence in which it is a matter of survival at all costs or extinction; for a nice balance of nature, ruthless competition.

There is no consensus on exactly how and when Darwin outgrew his initial allegiance to natural theology, or even to what extent he did so. By the time his *Origins* was published, he had already adopted his atheistic or at least agnostic position. (Incidentally, the word 'agnosticism' was coined by Darwin's champion, T H Huxley.) Probably Darwin shifted from an initial purely methodological restriction of biology to the investigation of nature to a full-blown metaphysical position – that is, from the limited perspective that science should restrict itself to natural explanations without venturing outside its brief into the 'supernatural' realm of God, to the bolder perspective that there is no supernatural God – in fact, no God at all. That at least seems to be the implication of his developing thought, and this is what Darwinism became: hard-nosed atheism.

Apart from creationism, which covered the spectrum from fundamentalist theology to theistic evolution, the great adversary of Darwinism, at a worldview level, was Lamarckism. In his own time Lamarck, who died when Darwin was twenty years old, was a neglected and soon forgotten figure. Yet towards the end of the nineteenth century, Darwinism, which had made such a strong impact in the decades after its debut, met with increasing resistance and many religious thinkers turned to Lamarck once again. Lamarck explained evolution as a process of slow adaptation by living things to their environment; the characteristics acquired during this process become hereditary. This allowed far greater room for the self-directing initiative of living beings. Life chose its own direction and development, responding creatively to environmental challenges. Evolution was not a blind mechanistic process, but had a creative dimension. Lamarckism replaced theistic evolution with an evolutionary approach that was compatible with, and indeed seemed to require, the acceptance of some divine element in the process. This trend was developed in the twentieth-century by thinkers such as Henri Bergson, Samuel Alexander, C Lloyd Morgan, A N Whitehead and Teilhard de Chardin. God was no longer a separate entity intervening in nature from the outside. Evolution itself, as a creative process, was divine. It is important to note that even some eighteenth-century 'materialists' (as they were known), notably Diderot, believed that matter was spontaneously active and that it could generate higher levels of being (life and awareness) by itself. In a sense Lamarck perpetuated views such as these. Darwin's approach, on the other hand, was far more reductionist and his views more inimical to religion. They were developed into a full-scale worldview in the revitalised form that Darwinism assumed in the twentieth-century after achieving a synthesis with genetics.[16] In these neo-Darwinist efforts (for example those of Julian Huxley[17]) the mechanistic and ruthless side of original Darwinism was softened to accomodate an ethic of human creativity and responsibility for the world.

Clearly there is a great difference between the traditional view of creation and evolutionism. The key metaphor of the first is planned making of the world by a designer from outside; that of the second cumulative change from within. From an experiential, radically empirical point of view the traditional concept of a supernatural God, ontologically distinct from and outside the creation which he produced in a series of separate miraculous acts, is problematical. But reducing the world and life to a blind mechanistic process (as in classical Darwinism) is not an adequate or necessary religious view either. Neither classic/traditional creationism nor materialism, neither supernaturalism nor one-dimensional naturalism has the requisite inclusive, comprehensive integrating power.

The cultural situation in which we find ourselves today calls for a new religiosity which integrates the concepts of mind and matter, spirituality and empiricism, God and the world – that is, if we dare to use the word 'G-o-d' at all. For we may opt for the way of apophatic theology, the way of silence, not knowing or saying anything about 'G-o-d'. Yet it may be possible to speak, haltingly and searchingly, new words that would not violate the silence, or perhaps even to utter the old symbol 'G-o-d'. In such a new spirituality, matter and spirit would not be two separate substances, but two aspects of the same process, and 'God' would be the depth of the dynamic universe, not a separate entity.[18] The empirically felt, dynamic universe peters out into unfathomable depth; it merges deep within itself with an open horizon, beckoning but not reachable by us. For the dialectically related dimensions of experience (the comprehensively Integral and the radically Explosive, corresponding to the dialectically related religious needs for integration and transcendence) I would use the word 'God', submitting that key Christian concepts such as *creation* and the *Trinity* could be interpreted in these terms, and also that this view may accord with the twin Buddhist doctrines of *kamma* (order) and *anicca/anattā* (radical openness). For example, in Christian terms 'Father' is God as the principle of integration, 'Spirit' God as the principle of transcendence, and 'Son' God as the principle of concretisation. Such a dynamic idea of divinity may be reconcilable with evolution as a biological paradigm, an idea propagated by process theology for some decades already. Lamarckism at least pointed in this direction.

In their own way the ideas expounded above suggest a *panentheistic* concept of God. Here, the concept of God is equivalent to the interrelatedness and combination of the twin concepts of the Integral and the Open. The divine is the di-une experiences of integration and transcendence at their widest and deepest, and pointing beyond our faculties of perception and comprehension. God is the given, total universe, plus the openness (the incompleteness, potentiality, negation) permeating and surrounding (transcending) it – in which the given, total universe is actualised and by which it is de-actualised.

This concept of God says that the universe is not self-contained and self-sufficient, or a substance, but radically contingent. In other words, it is not pantheism: the existing all is not closed. However, it does not postulate another extraneous Absolute Substance as creator and guarantor of the contingent universe. In other words, it is not theism. The problem with theism in this context is that it does not take the idea of transcendence (negation) seriously enough. For example, it cannot be maintained that God is a designer and maker, but operating in a totally different realm of being. Designers and makers are part of *this* realm of ours; about a totally different one we cannot know or say anything. One has to make a choice. Analogy does not solve the problem. Analogy can only illuminate the (partially) already known, not the radically unknown. It can only operate immanently.

In saying that the universe is not closed, the conditionalist view merges with agnosticism. It is a simple, minimalist concept of God, merely postulating that there is always an edge, a horizon. It suspects an unbounded openness with which the universe is intertwined, on the threshold of which it emerges, exists, subsides, disintegrates.[19]

God is not merely 'personal', since that anthropomorphic concept is wholly restricted to our cognised world. Then God would be like us. Neither is God 'impersonal', since that reductionist concept is even more restricted, stripping the concept God of some aspects of our cognised world. Then God would be less than us. God is 'transpersonal' openness, incorporating and cancelling consciousness and other features that constitute us, in our anthropic little niche in the universe. God is the affirmation of the anthropic universe, and simultaneously and dialectically the transcendent negation permeating and surrounding it. (S)He/*not*–(S)He is/is-*not*. Borrowing Mahayana terminology, form-and-emptiness, form-emptiness, is God.[20]

Teleology?

From the very limited human vantage point there is not sufficient basis for a belief that the whole evolutionary process had/has a preordained direction and purpose, specifically that it was aimed at the production of humans who were meant to have dominion over the earth and its life. This is something different from the innocuous fact that we as humans cannot but look at the world in terms of ourselves. Yet this vantage point does not exclude the possibility that we as humans may distinguish certain trends in the evolutionary process of the world.

Darwin eschewed the word 'evolution' because of the notion of progress inherent in its vernacular meaning, preferring the more neutral term 'descent with modification'.[21] 'Evolution' became current mainly as a result of the propagation of Herbert Spencer. According to the classical Darwinian view organic change led merely to increasing adaptation between organisms and their environment. Darwin accepted the notion of progress in a qualified sense only, as increasing specialisation in the adaptive struggle. Yet he realised that specialisation could become a death-trap in certain circumstances, and that less specialised forms of life could in fact have better chances of survival. In any event progress was not the hidden motive or driving force of evolution, only a fortuitous by-product. In our day Stephen Jay Gould insists that evolution is not a ladder of unilinear progress. Its shoots grow in many directions.

The religious worldview of the new *'Homo religiosus africanus'* suggested here discards the ideas of linear progression and of humanity as the culmination of such a process. Broad discernible patterns and trends that came into being are the *results* of the ongoing process – but there are no empirical grounds to postulate that those patterns had all along been the *aim*, unwaveringly fixed in advance. Things turned out the way they did because of the myriad ways in which factors interacted. They could have turned out differently. There was room, lots of it, for contingency. Each successful result in the process of change and adaptation may be, from a human point of view, higher (that is closer to us) or lower. But then, that is only one limited perspective and there is no reason to project it onto reality as a whole. In this respect Darwin's nonteleological view is closer to the open, pluralistic view adopted in these essays than the teleological view of Lamarckism.

Sometime this particular process will have run its course and be exhausted, science speculates. Time, as the measurement of change of this universe, will eventually, perhaps a hundred thousand million years from now, run out. What will happen after the end? What happened before the beginning? Can it be known at all? Can such a macrocosmology, synthesising a theory of the evolution of species with relativity theory and quantum physics, be constructed at all? At least we can say that if it is speculatively probable that this universe will end, it is certain that humanity as we know it will end, either by literally reaching a dead end genetically, or through some catastrophe, or by changing into something different from its present form, the process of adaptation renewing itself. *Homo sapiens* as we know ourselves will pass away, as other species preceding it and contemporaneous with it have done, and life will go on. And even if biological life as we know it were to end, the process of being will go on.

Anthropocentrism?

The world process seems to be marked by increasing complexity and, concomitantly, by increasingly explicit awareness. Which is where humanity comes into the picture. As it turned out in the course of events, birds and mammals, and eventually humanity (after a most inconspicuous start) took over the centre stage, just as dinosaurs had done 230 million years before. Had dinosaurs been able to argue, the same logic that has led some members of the very recent species *Homo sapiens* to believe that it is the telos of the world process could have led them to the conclusion that they were the aim and apex of all life, and that the world had been planned and made as a stage for their activities. Although *Homo* cannot claim to be the culmination of the world process, this does not alter the fact that this species occupies a unique position in that process. Nor does it contradict the weak anthropic principle that nature's parameters are indeed extremely finely attuned to allow for the improbable possibility of the existence of observers such as humans in its scheme of things.[22] In this creature an extraordinary awareness of its own poignantly ambivalent existence emerged. It surely exists, both as individual beings and as a species, and yet it is only a spark of the great fire, as the German mystic Jacob Böhme (1575–1624) saw.

The implication of the discovery that beings lose their absoluteness need not be a nihilism which levels all things in dead meaninglessness. In fact, that conclusion is simply a hangover of absolutism and fundamentalism. In the centreless vastness of time and space hinted at by evolution, individual expressions of life take on great significance. Any place or form, any time and any thing, however small and insignificant at one level, could be a window into the great Depth. It *is* important. It becomes a 'Thou', in Buber's sense. In a worldview of radical relativity individual sparks of meaning take on great importance. They are nodes in the flashing network of the world. That is why southern Africa may be a religiously charged locality. And also why humans are invested with great dignity. At one level a human is pitiably insignificant. At another level it is a flash from the depth.

Humanity essentially *co*-evolved with the myriad other forms of life. Indeed, at this very moment it *is* co-evolving with all of them simultaneously in the vastly complex, conditionalist system of the world, constitutively girded by formlessness. The greatness of this creature is that it can be the eye of the world, the seer, the visionary in which the world could come to self-awareness, as happened in the case of the great mystics, artists and scientists of humanity; the healer contributing to the wholeness of the world. Its tragedy has been that it became the exploiter of the world, a cancer in its body. At best, humanity is a flash of insight, but this cosmic moment of a mere two to four million years could pass. Instead of proud owner and lord, humanity may define itself as the mirror, witness and caretaker of the world.

Biological evolutionism as such did not give rise to any one particular system of ethics, philosophy or ideology. In fact, over the last century and a half a variety of ethical and worldviews were married to it.[23] In nineteenth-century England it emerged in a society characterised by a highly competitive outlook. The idea of a hierarchy of races was there long before Darwin and is really quite un-Darwinian, since Darwin did not see evolution as linear, but as a branching process in which no particular being sat at the top of the tree. It was not Darwin, but Herbert Spencer (biologically, a Lamarckian) who elevated the notion of struggle for existence in a world of limited means to a general social ethical rule, coining the term 'survival of the fittest' to legitimise a laissez-faire economic theory and practice. He turned Darwinian evolutionism into a hedonistic way of life in which every individual, cleverly adapting to the mores of a particular society, looks after his or her own interests. Darwin's own position is not unambiguous. The German Ernst Haeckel (1834–1919), combining Darwin and Lamarck in his biological theory,[24] replaced Spencer's individualism with a strong centralist political philosophy and added a potent flavour of nationalism. The noted biological

Darwinist T H Huxley (1825–1895), again, became a strong critic of the ruthless ethic of competition: the world is indeed ruthless, but he saw no reason to turn competition into the supreme rule of behaviour. On the contrary, Huxley became actively involved in programmes of social reform, believing that human beings, by some quirk of evolution, can instil meaning in a universe that they may understand to be meaningless. In practice, this converged with the broad Lamarckian ethos which favoured a cooperative rather than a competitive social morality. In the twentieth century the debate continued. Quite early in the century the social sciences, broadly speaking,turned away from evolutionism, rejecting the idea that human cultures can be ranked, and accepting that every society should be understood on its own terms. Yet biology continued to spill over into human sociology and psychology. Widely read authors such as Konrad Lorenz,[25] Desmond Morris[26] and Robert Ardrey[27] respectively described humans as innately aggressive, descendants of a 'killer ape', dominated by the genetically hereditary 'territorial imperative'. In a different vein sociobiology also insists on the extraordinary strength of the genetic foundations of human behaviour, including traits such as altruism, sexual behaviour and religion.[28]

Linked with evolutionism, the religious imperative referred to earlier demands a return by humanity to nature; assuming, in view of its unique position in the world, full responsibility for it; foreseeing with its remarkable intelligence possible future developments without claiming to know the Aim of it all; acting to ensure the best possible future for all forms of life. Evolution is not something of the past. It is taking place now. Now is the creative moment, retaining what came before, and anticipating what may follow. To an awesome degree the future evolution of all life on this planet is, quite literally, in our hands. The technology which started with the creature that Tobias and others so aptly named *'Homo habilis'* – 'handyman' – has become a threat to all life. In our time creative religion, as the shedding of obsolete modes of adaptation and the creation of optimally fitting ones, means that humanity steps down from the throne of domination over nature and becomes a member species of the others, response-able to all that surrounds it. We cannot go back to the time of *H habilis* when we had only sticks and stones at our disposal. We are now responsible for the earth. Particularly for us in South Africa, who are looking forward to a new beginning, the call to a new religiosity, with a new mysticism and a new morality, is clear. The *new Homo religiosus africanus*, unlike Cain, will be the keeper not only of its human brothers and sisters but of all forms of life.

Such a shift in our awareness would have a wide range of very practical moral implications. For example, the enormous gap between our perception of 'human rights' and the rights of animals would be closed. If humans and chimpanzees share 99 per cent of their genes, they should not be treated as if they existed in two utterly different worlds. Albert Schweitzer's adage about respect for all life takes on new urgency.

When Darwin challenged the human being's position at the apex of creation, few, even within the evolutionist camp, were prepared to follow him. That was not his mistake, however. It was that in his reaction against supernaturalism he lost sight of the extraordinary ability, unequalled in nature, of this creature to be aware of the deeper dimensions of reality. It is said that Robert Broom knelt before the first fossil specimen of *Australopithecus africanus* when he entered Raymond Dart's office at the University of the Witwatersrand to look at it. We in South Africa at the present time have occasion to establish a link with our human, protohuman and prehuman ancestors of Africa. Yet, knowing that human nature is unfinished, we may also look to the future, striving to attain greater inclusiveness of understanding and sympathy, and more finely attuned sentiments than have so far been achieved by humanity, both in dealing with its own intraspecies pluralisms, and with the world at large. Such a future lies within our own minds and hands. We may be reminded that Julian Huxley, while disclaiming any pregiven purpose in the evolutionary process, did find reason to speak of a direction detectable in the past and of progress: 'True human progress consists in increases in aesthetic, intellectual, and spiritual experience and satisfaction.'[29] The future of human evolution may well lie in a widening and deepening of the religious dimension of experience and in working out the implications of discoveries at those new levels.

Evil

The most serious problem for all religious thought is the obvious presence of suffering and evil in the world. Somehow ideas such as that carnivores actually diminish suffering, or that nature is in a state of beautiful balance, are hard to accept. It is the old problem of theodicy. Ideas similar to theodicy also occur in nontheistic contexts, for example when the nineteenth-century 'balance of nature' view reappears in modern ecological garb, claiming that deep down everything is fine the way it is – perhaps even divinely fine. The implication of the approach sketched here is to dispense with any theodicy, that is any view that would justify suffering and evil as a good thing in disguise. This applies not only to any 'realised' theodicy (claiming that things are fine right now), but to a futuristic eschatological theodicy as well (claiming that the world is most certainly on its way to a predetermined perfect balance).

What is the locus of evil? Is it the inside or the outside of the fabric of conditionality? Is it inherent in order, or in dis-order? The submission made here is that it occurs in both, but is not essentially tied to either.

Let us look at the human, moral level first. On that level evil is the frustration of the open process, the disturbance of the dialectic between the two movements. This cuts both ways. It is an absolutising of either side of the threshold. On the one hand it is the absolute affirmation of existing (integral) things, expressed in attitudes and actions of attachment to and desire for them. It absolutises what the process of the world has produced. It is idolatry. By the same token it is a denial or repression of transcendence in its various manifestations. For example, it is the rejection and hatred of the Other (other human being, group, possibility). Conversely, evil is the absolute affirmation of dis-order, the denial of all and any structure. The good exists in the narrow crack between the two. It is the affirmation of the given (compassion, love), simultaneously seeing it as nonabsolute. It is appreciating the *concrete* as *relative*, the real as open, in tenuous balance.

Let us now look at the transhuman, the natural level in general. Here we have to start by acknowledging that we as humans cannot help but project our human perspective on things, and that this no doubt distorts them. We can never escape that. There is no extrahuman standpoint available to us. Our experience is inevitably anthropomorphic. So to make-believe that we can transport ourselves to a position from which we would see that a pack of wild dogs tearing the flesh from living antelope is not cruel is not realistic. It is cruel. But is it evil? I would say no, reserving 'evil' for a quality of human behaviour only. But cruel it is (admittedly in our human perspective), a distortion of the community of beings.

A state of peace may be hoped for, and strong effort may be made to realise that dream deeply dormant in the world (we humans believe), but it cannot be stated as an attainable certainty. Religion cannot guarantee such certainty, although it does awaken us to the ideal of perfect integration of all things, when even the bad will serve the good. That is the last horizon, all-integrating and all-transcending at once. Yet – there is no last, conclusive horizon. Dis-order seems to be given with order. Can faith accept that with equanimity? Nondualistic religions (for example Hinduism) do that, knowing that somehow evil is linked to good in the dance of the world. The evil in the texture of the world provokes us to create good here and now. In its own unintended way the Darwinian view of evolution, by denying that there is a discoverable predetermined goal and pattern of development, cleared space for human freedom, as nineteenth-century pragmatists such as Charles Peirce and William James saw.[30]

Not only humans suffer. Animals do too. But only humans can be morally evil. From the point of view of what may broadly be called conditionalist mysticism, the true 'identity' of individual things appears as their 'nonidentity', their being nonfixable moments of a great multifarious process. Their efforts to secure their individuality go against the grain of the world process, and this is what constitutes and causes suffering and evil. Buddhism stated this insight in the form of the basic noble truths that there is human suffering (*dukkha*) in the world, and that *desire* (to have and to be) is its root cause. Jesus stated it in his invitation to live as the birds of the air and the lilies of the field do. Eckhart stated the same when he upheld *Abgeschiedenheit* (asideness) as the human attitude corresponding most closely to the reality of reality.

This sheds light on the Darwinian view. If evolution is understood in terms of a struggle for survival and the selection of those individuals with the best chances of survival (as Darwinism does), it follows that frustration of the desire to survive would be and would cause suffering. Anyone whose survival is threatened suffers. The difference between other forms of life and human life is that whereas the other forms simply react to the possible termination of their lives with unreflecting instinct, humans invest their struggle for survival with cosmic, metaphysical meaning. They award themselves eternal meaning. The greater the loss, the greater the suffering. This line of argument leads us to realise that the problem of evil lies essentially at the level of *human attitudes* to events. Let us apply this idea to our death. Death is not evil. As our decomposition (disintegration), it is not the opposite of life (of this composite being) but its necessary implicate. There is no life without death. Death is the crossing of the threshold into the great potentiality, into the womb of the world. What is 'bad' is the clinging to life.

Happiness and liberation from suffering would follow from abandoning the notion of the eternal security of one's individual identity. It does not call for grand metaphysical systems but for a change of heart and a change of behaviour: not threatening the insecure hold on life of any weak creature (today even the most powerful inhabitants of the elements – whales, rhinoceros, elephant and the martial eagle – are vulnerable), and letting go of the claim to absolute identity. Instead of the craving to survive eternally, either as single or as collective entities, the powerful will to exist joyfully in the flux, celebrating the opportunity to be part of the wide fellowship of being, becomes the driving force of life. The large-souled human capable of that will also know the suffering of the world. That attitude does not arise from callow sentimentality, but from the nature of reality itself. Life may in fact still be a struggle – not to survive, but to realise the conditional nature of things and to exist in compassion with all.

At this stage, as South African society approaches the twenty-first century, two powerful worldview blocs hold sway: fundamentalist and neo-orthodox religion on the one hand, and materialist/nihilist/scientistic pseudo-religion on the other. Yet the signs of a third religious force, deeply distrusted by both sides but nevertheless promising a new spiritual vision and the moral energy to lead into the future, are certainly there. It may be a renewal of the deepest intentions of religion, a discovery of the religious intent of science, and an effort to heal the rift between the two.

Religious history and faith

Integration of the West with the rest of humanity and of humanity with the process of nature, and realisation of the vastness of the evolutionary timescale renders much of traditional history of religions and theology questionable. Even in the former field of study, which has done much to promote the vision of a universal history of religion, the remnants of Euro-/West-/Christianity-centred ideologies are hard to eradicate. These ideologies entail more than the inevitability of proceeding from where one is situated at a given time, and more than placing one's total faith in a particular religion. There is nothing wrong with those attitudes. But the ideologies in question amount to positioning oneself at the top of a pyramid, looking down on the 'others' on the lower rungs of development.

Homoversal time invites us to view *all* religious history as salvation history (*Heilsgeschichte*). In the long perspective of evolution it becomes apparent that there is no foothold for assertions by any religion (naturally of unique, if not absolute, subjective importance to its adherents) to be 'absolute' – that is, to be essentially perfect, received straight from heaven and therefore superior to all others (if related and comparable to them at all), unconditioned by the forces of nature and society, and hence entitled to the role of universal overseer. Nor does the process of evolution give reason to believe that any particular religion has been the goal of religious history all along. From the depths of this process all religions appear as relative responses by specific individuals and cultures, formulated in specific circumstances, to the ultimate questions of human existence. Certainly some were better than others, but they are all of a kind – all enmeshed in the one process of human presence on earth.

This is not the occasion to examine the implications of what has been said so far for the self-understanding of the dominant religion in South Africa, Christianity. Yet let me use the key of the dialectic of integration and transcendence once again. I do not believe it is possible first to establish, once and for all, the identity of Christianity in abstraction from other historical faiths, and only *then*, extraneously, establish relations with these faiths. On the contrary, I believe that the identity of Christianity can only be approached if it is seen as essentially interrelated with other religions in the vast field in which humans search for ultimate meaning, as a clustering on a wide-ranging, changing continuum. Again, realisation of this conditionalist field would not preclude putting one's entire trust in a particular concrete religious perspective of the world. Yet it is quite true that the kind of religious faith presented here is not to be equated with the absoluteness of doctrinal beliefs claimed by dogmatists. Rather, it is immersion into the flow of the world, seeking no firm hold. It is faith without an object.

In conclusion, the implication of the whole argument of these essays thus far is obviously that evolution itself should not be treated as a dogma, a restrictive focus on things, claiming to mirror 'the' 'objective' reality. As has become clear, there is no such complete view, and none is possible. As for evolution, there are many competing evolutionary models. They are all relative perspectives, originating in the inextricable involvement of the multitude of forces making up the world and the dynamic network of interactions making up human society and culture. The world and the human psyche are one. Such large perspectives are therefore not passive mirrors, but neither are they arbitrary projections foisted on reality. They move with the times. In our cultural epoch, evolution (at the level of science, and extended to the level of religion) offers the kind of inclusive view that would integrate human experience of the world. There is no denying that its function is the same as that of the ancient origin myths of all cultures. In its many variants it integrates experience, explaining the way things are against the backdrop of ultimate mystery, just as the ancient myths did. It explains the relationship between the sexes, the nature of human aggression and altruism, the significance of human technology, the relationship between humans and animals, the nature of human culture, and so on. That is what myths have always been about. They are not timeless.

ENDNOTES

1 M Eliade, *Patterns in comparative religion*, New York: Meridian, 1974 (1958), p 382. No one articulated this nostalgia as clearly as Laurens van der Post in his various books on the Bushmen, for example *The lost world of the Kalahari*, Harmondsworth: Penguin, 1962; *The heart of the hunter*, Harmondsworth: Penguin, 1965.
2 Cf J Fabian, *Time and the other: how anthropology makes its object*, New York: Columbia University Press, 1983 for a critique of 'allochronicity' (that is the pushing back, or temporal distancing of some societies from the anthropological present as though they belong in another time) as a method of domination.
3 P J Bowler, *Evolution: the history of an idea*, Los Angeles: University of California Press, 1984; and *The non-Darwinian revolution: reinterpreting a historical myth*, London: Johns Hopkins University Press, 1988.
4 Cf R Dawkins, *The blind watchmaker*, Harlow: Longman Scientific & Technical, 1986, pp 287ff.
5 The most important fields of discussion and research seem to be the following (cf Mellars & Stringer, *The human revolution: behavioural and biological perspectives on the origins of modern humans*. Edinburgh: University Press, 1989): To what extent was the transition from archaic to modern populations the result of a dramatic process of population dispersal and replacement, and to what extent was it the result of a gradual process of demographic and biological development in each region? And if major population dispersals were involved, what kind of mechanisms operated in these? What models can be advanced to account for the *origins* of both the biological and the behavioural changes in human evolution; for the *varying patterns of change* documented in the various regions inhabited by early humans;

for the possible *relationships* between various spheres of behaviour, for example subsistence patterns, technology, social organisation, demography; or for the relation between changes in behavioural patterns and biological features? To what extent are behavioural changes associated with radical shifts in the innate mental *capacities* of the human brain? These may be broken down into a host of smaller questions. Wider issues in evolutionary research range from the debate between gradualists and punctuationists (Dawkins, *The blind watchmaker* ..., pp 223ff) to the debate on taxonomy raised by cladism (ibid, pp 276ff).

6 S A Kauffman, *Origins of order: self-organization and selection in evolution*, Oxford: Oxford University Press, 1993. He summarised his thesis in The sciences of complexity and 'origins of order', in J Brockman (ed), *Creativity*, New York: Touchstone, 1993, pp 75–107.

7 Cf J S Oosthuizen, *Van Plotinus tot Teilhard de Chardin: 'n studie oor die metamorfose van die Westerse werklikheidsbeeld*, Amsterdam: Rodopi, 1974.

8 After nearly 70 years the holistic metaphysic of the South African philosopher J C Smuts remains a fascinating attempt at dealing with much the same problem as the one examined in these essays, and in a comparable way. However, his wholes were systems of equilibrium (*Holism and evolution*, London: Macmillan, 1927 [1926]), passim, for example pp 132ff, 352ff), slowly but surely developing towards the achievement of the good, fundamentally unchallenged and unthreatened by the forces of breakdown.

9 T Tulku, *Time, space and knowledge: a new vision of reality*, Emeryville, Cal: Dharma, 1977.

10 Confining ourselves, as we are doing here, to glosses on human evolution, the temporal structure of human experience of the world lies beyond our scope. Naturally that is an important part of any religious metaphysic, and there are some very interesting models of it, from Westerners such as Heidegger, Whitehead and Teilhard de Chardin to Buddhist schools and figures such as Nagarjuna, Hua-Yen, Dogen and Masao Abe.

11 Cf Bowler, *Evolution* ...

12 Ibid, pp 155ff.

13 Cf Dawkins, *The blind watchmaker* ..., pp 276ff.

14 G Richards, *Human evolution: an introduction for the behavioural sciences*, London & New York: Routledge & Kegan Paul, 1987.

15 Obviously this applies not only to early human evolution, but to the development of human culture generally. With respect to the Later Stone Age in the northern Cape, for example, A J B Humphreys & A I Thackeray wrote (*Ghaap and Gariep: Later Stone Age studies in the northern Cape*, Cape Town: South African Archaeological Society Monograph Series No 2, 1983, p 292): 'Lithic artefacts do not merely reflect an exploitation pattern, but a multi-faceted tradition of learnt behaviour that changes through time for a host of reasons, ranging from the introduction of new inventions, local inventions, changes in the subsistence base (which could be culturally decided rather than necessarily environmentally controlled), to the whims of fashion. It is probably an impossible task for the archaeologist to isolate the degree to which all these possibilities contributed to cultural change and development ...'

16 Darwinism, which towards the end of the nineteenth century was at times over-

shadowed by other 'non-Darwinian' forms of evolutionary thought, triumphed only when it was synthesised with the Mendelian revolution in heredity theory in the 1930s. The relationship between Darwinism and 'non-Darwinian' evolutionary thought has been described by Bowler (*The non-Darwinian revolution* ...), who demands that more attention be paid to the role of those other forms in the ultimate triumph of evolutionary thought. The synthetic theory, which by the 1960s had acquired the status of biological orthodoxy, has only been challenged to some extent in recent decades by new ideas such as Niles Eldredge and Stephen Gould's theory of 'punctuated equilibrium'. The synthetic theory of evolution is sometimes referred to as 'neo-Darwinism'. This is misleading, because this particular paradigm has roots in Mendelism as much as in Darwinism, and its version of natural selection differs significantly from that of Darwinism (cf V Grant, *The evolutionary process: a critical review of evolutionary theory*, New York: Columbia University Press, 1985, pp 15ff).

17 J Huxley, *Evolution: the modern synthesis*, London: Allen & Unwin, 1974 (1942).

18 The following argument against panentheism given by Polkinghorne (*Science and creation: the search for understanding*, Boston: Shambhala, 1989, p 53) is not convincing: 'Panentheism's defect is its denial of the true otherness of the world from God, which is part of our experience.' How can we experience true otherness, taken seriously? Either it is true otherness, *or* it is part of our experience.

19 Postulating a plurality of universes, be it synchronically or diachronically related to this one, is not necessary. For such speculation, see G Ellis, *Before the beginning: cosmology explained*, London, New York: Boyars/Bowerdean, 1993, pp 67ff.

20 For brilliant discussions of the concept of God in the interface between Buddhism, Judaism and Christianity, see Masao Abe and his discussion partners Thomas Altizer, Eugene Borowitz, John Cobb, Catherine Keller, Jürgen Moltmann, Schubert Ogden and David Tracy in J B Cobb & C Ives (eds), *The emptying God: a Buddhist-Jewish-Christian conversation*, Maryknoll, NY: Orbis, 1991.

21 S J Gould, *Ever since Darwin: reflections in natural history*, New York: Norton, 1977, pp 33ff.

22 Cf J D Barrow & F J Tipler, *The anthropic cosmological principle*, Oxford: Clarendon, 1986; also the excellent book by Ellis, *Before the beginning* ..., pp 89ff. The one cited here is the weak anthropic principle (WAP). The strong anthropic principle (SAP) claims that intelligent life must exist in the universe for a model of the universe to make sense.

23 Bowler, *Evolution* ...

24 His monist philosophy with an evolutionary basis was spelt out in the lecture *Der Monismus als Band zwischen Religion und Wissenschaft: Glaubensbekenntnis eines Naturforschers*, Bonn: Strauss, 1893.

25 K Lorenz, *On aggression*, London: Methuen, 1974.

26 D Morris, *The naked ape: a zoologist's study of the human animal*, London: Cape, 1967.

27 R Ardrey, *The territorial imperative: a personal inquiry into the animal origins of property and nations*, London: Collins, 1969.

28 E O Wilson, *On human nature*, Cambridge, Mass: Harvard University Press.

29 Huxley, *Evolution* ..., p 575.

30 Cf P Wiener, *Evolution and the founders of pragmatism*, Gloucester, Mass: Smith, 1969.

IV

ABORIGINAL KALEIDOSCOPE

12 The haunting absence/presence

The aboriginal hunter-gatherers of South Africa have turned out to be a nemesis, haunting – by their very absence – Euro-Christian society.

The term 'aboriginal' (*ab origine* – deriving not merely from the past but from a creative origin) can be perverted in (at least) two ways. First, it can carry a normative meaning, implying that we could and should return to that origin. That is, of course, impossible. A return to a hunting-gathering existence can only take place in flights of romantic escapist fantasy. Second, it can function as a means of pushing living people – 'the aborigines' – into oblivion, forgetting them, disregarding them.

In what sense, then, may we speak legitimately of their *aboriginal presence*? *Presence* is a spatiotemporal concept. It means being *here now*, in the present. The use of this word attacks the idea that the hunter-gatherers 'were', 'then', 'there', in 'another' Africa at 'another' time. Such a use of time is a strategy of dominant Western anthropology (and culture generally) to keep them at arm's length. In this chapter I shall explore some of the modes of their *presence*, their being *with us now*. Let me say at once that this involves at least four dimensions:

- If humans were hunter-gatherers for 99 per cent of their history since their emergence in the evolutionary process, we can assume that some of the deeply ingrained features of our common psychological makeup will reflect that. In saying this we are not speaking on a transcendental level, but on the level of empirical 'homoversals'.

- Many hunter-gatherers are still alive (but not well) in southern Africa. They, the *now* living, must be taken seriously as our fellow human beings, deserving respect and future support in their far from satisfactory conditions. They are not, and should not be treated as 'the past'.

- Even those hunter-gatherers who have died over the last three and a half centuries under the onslaught of modern colonialism had an ongoing *Wirkungsgeschichte*, an effective history. Gadamer[1] coined his term to capture the impact of the past on the present within *one* cultural tradition. The task of South African religious thought today is to investigate the dynamics of such a process in a historically concrete intercultural, interreligious perspective.

- How were (are) they present in the minds of those who saw them, thought about them or had dealings with them? What sort of mental pictures exist of them?

Religious re-visioning

In making some observations of a religious nature (religious in the sense explained in chapter 4) about the strangely elusive presence of the hunter-gatherers in South African reality, I shall take into account the state of archaeological and historical scholarship, which is impressive indeed. As a matter of fact, hundreds of researchers from many universities all over the world are actively investigating them, adding to an already enormous research output in recent decades.[2] They are one of the most thoroughly researched peoples on earth.

The basic problem of religion – how to cope with the coming into being and perishing of things – operates at various levels and in various timeframes – those of microcosmic events measured in microseconds, of macrocosmic processes stretching over aeons, of the twenty- or eighty-year lifespans of human beings, and of the histories of human societies. It is this latter timeframe that interests us.

Historically, these aborigines arose in or came to this quarter of Africa in the very distant past, lived here for tens of millennia, and now their ancient lifestyle is disappearing before our eyes. Since their first encounter with other (invariably more powerful) groups they found themselves in the position of outcasts. It is only in this century that they have been accorded some measure of dignity as the aboriginal inhabitants of southern Africa. I shall argue that this reorientation should be extended to the sphere of religion. It is time for the adoption of a completely new religiohistorical perspective on the hunter-gatherers, one that would challenge and topple Euro-Christian-centric religious discourse as conducted in this country.

One cannot consider the story of these aborigines without experiencing a feeling of deep loss. How does one account for their lot? Was it inevitable, impersonal, tragic fate? Or were some people guilty of gross injustice? And if so, does it not cast a dark shadow over the values of the past that permitted or even legitimised the woeful lack of understanding of the 'primitives', and the acts that followed? May we be witnessing the disintegration and collapse not only of the classical hunter-gatherer culture and religion, but also of the dominant Western-Christian cultural and religious epoch in this part of the world? And could the downward spirals of both cultures be somehow intertwined in a macabre dance of death? Does the winner in this unequal duel of cultures and religions turn out to be a loser too, the hero a villain – perhaps because it did not act true to its own deepest logic and to the law of true religion? From a religious point of view, we must return to this history and reflect on its proportions and implications. Admittedly, this goes beyond the brief of the academic disciplines of history, anthropology or even religious studies. These academic pursuits do not deal with problems of fate or guilt. Religion does.

Here, in Part IV, the strategy of enquiry developed in Part II will be actualised concretely, that is, it will be grounded in the phenomenon of the hunter-gatherers. In addition to the 'facts', we will try to enter into their world phenomenologically, at the same time engaging in a vigorously reflexive self-understanding of 'us' (by which I mean primarily white South Africans), considering the problem of how 'we' 'moderns' relate to 'them', the 'primitives'. This will proceed to a critique of existing Western Christianity in the perspective of conditionalist religion. It is hoped that this perspective, which was sketched in chapter 4, will deepen through contact with hunter-gatherer religion. In short, the core of Part IV will be a *religious re-visioning* of the place of the hunter-gatherers in South African history, integrating them with a new understanding of South African religious history as a whole.

To adapt the language of phenomenological science of religion, this chapter will largely (not solely) be an exercise in transindividual, collective, national *epoche*, but not as an attempt (foredoomed!) to block out, 'neutralise', suppress, ignore or deny our collective preformative categories. That would simply lead to their entrenchment. On the contrary, what I intend is a reflexive clarification of our own cultural and religious presuppositions – more than that, a critique of those presuppositions. This will lead to a change in their role and status, their structure and content – to a change *in ourselves*.

The human ocean

Our point of departure is that looking at the aboriginal hunter-gatherers 'religiously' does not mean looking at them *sub specie aeternitatis*, that is, under the aspect of some eternally stable order. Rather, we should look at them under the aspect of radical historical contingency.

Neither does it mean looking at them in terms of a *teleological* view of history, either Christian or secular. To the former, their way of life would appear as doomed heathenism, to be eclipsed by the final crowning glory of Christianity. To the second, they would appear as primitives, to be edged out by triumphant technological civilisation. We are searching for another way to relate to them.

Picking up an old metaphor, I want to compare the history of the hunter-gatherers and, in fact, South African religious history as a whole, to the ocean, whose ever-moving waters are not pushed or pulled by any single force, and do not flow in one straight bed from a beginning to an end. It is influenced by a host of factors: differences in salinity in its own composition; contours of coastlines and continental shelves; the depth of the ocean floor and the shapes of underwater plateaus, terraces and ridges; unexpected cascades of dislodged material down continental slopes; the rotation of the earth; the interplay of the gravitational forces of earth, moon and sun; volcanic action on its floor and winds on its surface; polar and equatorial temperatures – all of these, and more, adding up to a vast system of forces resulting in an enormously complex system of movements: the one ocean differentiating in many currents, some moving at its surface and some in its depth, meandering erratically but not chaotically, breaking up and throwing off eddies, but eventually turning back in their circuits; waters welling up vertically from the depth and waters submerged by other streams; deep currents circulating in opposite directions to surface currents; currents dividing, converging and colliding; the circuit of evaporation and rain. No wonder that the alluring depth and the frightening force, the constancy and the caprice, the flowing formlessness and the inexorable regularity of this source of all life has always been a symbol of the nature of the universe and of human consciousness. In the mythologies of all those who sailed it or stood on its shores to observe the play of the rolling waves, the sea evokes the rhythm of forms of life emerging and reintegrating with the whole.[3]

The many and vast cultural and religious differences between the hunter-gatherers, the early white colonists and us contemporary, diverse South Africans, must be acknowledged; also the determining effects of natural and social environment and language on people's ways of thinking. Yet I assume a certain underlying continuity of human consciousness, on the basis of the biological history and constitution of humankind. Henry Rosemont coined the useful concept 'homoversal' (as opposed to the abstract notion of 'universal') to signify what is common to all human beings, physiologically and mentally constituted as they are.[4] Rosemont applies his principle of 'homoversalism' to aesthetics and morals. It may be extended, I suggest, to the domain of religion as well. This is not a new idea, and has been worked out by Mircea Eliade. The great exponent of this kind of approach to religion in our century was certainly Jung, who discovered for the West the deep layer of a collective unconscious, common to all people and containing the psychically inherited ancestral archetypes which are to be found in the myths and legends of all peoples and all times.[5]

What we need is a philosophy that enables us to move from the mere acknowledgment of cultural diversity (*plurality*) to the positive negotiation of plurality in an inclusive religious hermeneutic (*pluralism*). This would yield three gains:

- ☐ It would *relativise* (de-absolutise, force open) closed religious sociocultural blocs. *Ours* is only one of many (very many), different (very different) sociosymbolic systems. The relativising need not end up in relativism – by which I mean the view that linguistic, cultural or religious communities exist incommunicado alongside one another.

- ☐ It would lead to vigorous intercultural, interreligious *communication/dialogue/translation/influence*, a frontier traffic finding and giving real access to those *other* symbolic systems.

☐ It would lead to the cautious exploration of *panhuman continuities* – not as timeless, fixed absolutes, abstracted from the concrete sociohistorical conjunctures in which humans always exist but, taking these conjunctures into account, as patterns of being in the world, common to and changing with the human genus itself.

Instead of using an explanatory scheme consisting of the ideas of a grand design, a predetermined goal, linear development leading to that goal, and a single basic force driving the whole process (a process culminating in the triumph of for example Christianity, or of Marxism-Leninism), we may see the South African processes of consciousness as somehow analogous to the movements of the ocean. Human culture and religion flow in many and diverse streams, and although they may never seem to meet and may flow at various depths and in opposite directions, they all form part of the one ocean of creative human consciousness, sharing the same essential features, interrelated parts of one dynamic whole. In contemporary Western religion elements very similar to those found in 'primitive' religions may well up from the creative psychic depth. And as the present oceans are not eternally permanent, but had a beginning, and a changing and still unfinished history interacting with the formation of the continents and other factors, so the collective human consciousness had a beginning, a changing history through hundreds of thousands of years, and has a future. New, unprecedented events occur in human culture. The metaphor of the sea should not be pushed to the extreme of postulating a closed, merely repetitive historical circuit. It should emphasise the ideas of multiconditional movement and unity in change. Cataclysmic changes may take place, slowly or suddenly. At present we are witnessing such a change – after all, Europe is in the process of meeting Asia and Africa on an unprecedented scale, and that in our part of the world. The panhuman consciousness is moved by a wide variety of factors, both intrinsic (for example the mutually provocative and enriching flow of ideas between cultures and religions) and extrinsic (for example economic forces), in an open system of interdependence.

In the strictly empirical perspective adopted in this study, there is neither ground nor need to postulate the existence and workings of a separate Being completely transcending (that is existing somewhere outside) the limits and possibilities of human consciousness, intervening from the outside into the natural processes. In the conditionalist view, 'God' may more convincingly be understood as the Depth of precisely this autonomous complex process.[6]

This view does not amount to determinism. Unexpected new events occur as the constellations of mutually conditioning factors keep adjusting. The process of evolution continues.

The individual human person and individual human groups respond to their contexts either by secluding themselves in supposed separateness, or by allowing themselves to be integrated with those wider contexts of the human ocean.

Progress in religious feeling is the realisation (clear understanding and expression) of this homoversal solidarity. Regress in religious feeling is losing sight of it, persisting in an imagined separateness. This study itself is nothing but an effort to adjust adequately to the shifting, interrelated, infinitely expanding configurations of conditions which impinge on 'me', 'now' 'here', and on which 'I' – JSK, this particular, contingent, shifting human being trying to make sense of his historical heritage and social situation – impinge.

If I were to speak of the 'meaning' of this historical process, it would consist in grasping the present opportunity to try to appreciate and express the one multifaceted human community, nesting in the universe. It is a matter not of passive contemplation, but of active exertion. We have to try to make the human community happen – without any guarantee that we will succeed.

Looking back at South African history, we can clearly discern the driving forces of greed, suspicion and fear, combined with mutual isolation and lack of understanding, emanating from the expansionist desire for land and power. However, our history also harbours the opposite force, the deeply human need to reach out, forge new contacts and establish wider human networks of community. Is it possible in our time to deabsolutise the limited identities of the past, and to achieve a larger integration on a higher plane than before? The early colonists, the frontierspeople, the hunter-gatherers and the missionaries responded according to their lights within their more limited horizons; today we are invited (or compelled) to come to terms with a wider, inclusive homoverse. Is it at all possible?

It is time for a new religious image of the hunter-gatherers (and with it, a new religious image of ourselves) to emerge, a religious reconstruction of the past, telling the story of how the various cultural and religious streams in this country express a common panhuman mentality, how they converge and how they hang together in their significant but relative uniquenesses -- even in their conflicts. In the past, whites and blacks made the hunter-gatherers what they have become, as the hunter-gatherers made blacks and whites what they have become. Today, whites, blacks and hunter-gatherers are interpenetrating, whether they want to or not. From the future, open possibilities beckon the present generation to reinterpret the past creatively and to realise new forms of mutuality, coexistence, solidarity, communion and compassion.

In understanding the 'togetherness' of hunter-gatherers, European Christianity and all the other religious orientations in southern Africa, cognisance should be taken of both a depth-psychological aspect (the unity of humankind in differences) and a diffusionist aspect (the spread of ideas, customs, etc, through time).

To do justice to *them* in their uniqueness, relativising the West, is obviously difficult, for my understanding can only result from a complex process of interpretation in *Western* categories, via the Western disciplines of archaeology, anthropology and historiography. The very effort to make the 'pristine' hunter-gatherers emerge from the shadows is a *Western* effort. Contrary to our best intentions, *we* indeed allow them to emerge, with us structuring the terms and the manner of their emergence, subtly controlling them, even creating them according to our own needs. This is probably what lay behind the centuries-old European obsession with the 'primitives'; they were mental pictures, projections with a therapeutic value, helping European culture to work through its own problems. What lies behind the efforts of modern Westerners to resurrect the dead who died as a result of their meeting with this civilisation? Still the same arrogance, only in a new form? Ironically, in our effort to meet them, still keeping them at arm's length, talking and allowing them to talk on *our* terms? On the other hand, is it not also true that the 'essence' and 'identity' of 'the Bushmen' (as of 'the West' and 'the East') only emerges in communion with the others? The one can only be 'defined' with reference to the other. 'They' are not without 'us', as 'we' are not without 'them'. We are mirrors to each other. We may be (in fact are!) very dissimilar. But that very dissimilarity, the discovery of 'my' and 'your' uniqueness, implies a togetherness, albeit in contrasts. Without 'them' or 'you', 'we' would not be us. Yet the movement between 'me' and 'you', or 'us' and 'them', is no mere circle. It is a spiral, with the possibility of increasing 'self'-knowledge and 'other'-knowledge. The open process, the dialectic between moving beyond my culture (meeting another culture) and discovering myself, each in the other, is another expression of the theme of transcendence and integration. As we moderns, vaguely dissatisfied with ourselves, grope for the 'primitive' hunter-gatherers, we discover aspects of our hidden selves, which enables us to move beyond our present state. Who we are will always be tied up with these predecessors of ours.

There are therefore no essential (in the sense of timeless) hunter-gatherers, nor an essential West. In this country these streams (and Africa, and the East) flowed alongside one another and mingled, each changing in the process. Each can only be understood as part of that whole, and as part of one another.

In South African religious thought, the kind of approach proposed here has not been explored. The dominant scheme has been that of dark paganism, followed by Christianity that came with the Dutch colonists, or by 'real' Christianity that came with the missionaries.

Fluid (non)identity

The existing population of hunter-gatherers in southern Africa is one of the last remnants following a life-style which, until 10 000 years ago, was the only one known to humankind. To be sure, they are not in the process of dying out as a biological entity in southern Africa, as was widely believed earlier in the century. In Botswana and Namibia they are even reasonably well established numerically.[7] Those traditionally indigenous to South Africa itself have disappeared completely: the last survivor of a small band living near Lake Chrissie in the Eastern Transvaal,[8] an old man, was murdered in 1988. In the aftermath of the Angolan war a small number of semi-traditional people have been brought to Kaggakamma near Ceres in the Cape Province, and a few thousand ex-soldiers and their families to Douglas near Kimberley, but the fate of both groups is desperately uncertain. The second settlement was disbanded in 1993. Throughout southern Africa survival exclusively in the traditional manner is probably coming to an inevitable end.[9] Their traditional hunting grounds have been depleted of game and turned into farming units by governments and private owners, or turned into game reserves. Everywhere they have been reduced to a state of extreme poverty, in spite of efforts by governments such as those of Botswana and Namibia to improve their lot.

The 'Bushmen' ('San') elude every effort to be trapped into a definite identity for several reasons: over the last three centuries they have increasingly become marginalised, existing loosely on the fringes of more powerful groups in various southern African states; their traditional hunting-gathering way of life has been constantly eroded until very little of it remains; and they lead a shifting existence on the periphery of the powerful, slipping in and out of geographical, economical and political concentrations of power.

But that is not all. Prior to these specifically modern developments, for millennia they merged with the flow of human mobility throughout Africa. During that entire time cultural forms and contents were continuously exchanged across cultural boundaries in complex processes. Genetically mixed populations often arose. The concept 'hunter-gatherer' (or 'San', or 'Bushman'), rigidly distinguished from other entities, is an abstraction. That seems to be agreed by anthropologists. One has the feeling of entering a stream of human movement without definite contours. The partitions separating human groups are dramatically less fixed than conventional white South African wisdom would have it.

In a sense they are a series of changing pictures in the minds of their successive despisers. We peer into a kaleidoscope of tumbling mirrors and reflections, with Khoikhoi herders, black farmers, Dutch colonists, travellers and missionaries, modern anthropologists and historians, fiction writers and government officials imposing names, characters and identities on them, varying from scornful to sentimental. Their temporal presence has been dated relative to events which are important in the history of their conquerors: the birth of Jesus Christ, and the coming of the first colonists to the Cape; their spatial presence has been marked relative to the boundaries drawn by stronger forces: provinces, states, game reserves. We have no Bushman-centric perspective of their position in the scheme of things, only a few almost pathetic protestations by themselves that they were the original inhabitants of the land, that they deserve a place in the sun, and that they have a valuable contribution to make.[10]

In religious studies (as has been happening in anthropology and history) an appreciation of the uniqueness of the South African hunter-gatherers and a fascination with the intrinsic value of their particular form of existence is fitting. But this unique particularity should not be construed as some self-identical entity, enduring through time. To give them their due and to understand their uniqueness is to see them as interacting with their total context, consisting of other groups and nature. It is to the first of these two modes of relationship that we are seeking an entry in this chapter, by defining them as essentially relational – not only internally (various groups relating among themselves), but also externally (relating to non-hunter-gatherers). They mirror not only the various southern African non-hunter-gatherers ('Khoikhoi', blacks, whites), but in fact the whole of humanity, past and present. They derive their uniqueness from the whole of humanity, and they contribute to that whole, in a relationship of difference-in-unity, unity-in-difference.

The way Afrikaners, or whites generally, or blacks, are today is the result of acting on the Bushmen and being acted upon by them over some centuries, sharing and competing for the same environment. The way the Bushmen are today is the result of that same process of mutual implication, conditioning, constitution and interpenetration. And all those others with whom they interacted were just as manifold internally, all interacting internally and externally. No more than the Bushmen may the 'Afrikaner', the 'Venda' or any other group be hypostasised. Complex processes of linguistic borrowing and lending, biological gene flow, technological carry-over, cultural adoption, copying and resistance made us all what we are. 'We' reflect 'them' as 'they' reflect 'us', as we both, relatively separate and together, mirror humanity and humanity mirrors our common history. We are each what we are in and through the other, as our relative histories were not enacted temporally parallel, but together. We have been travelling together for a long time now. And now they are present in white 'Christian' society in this country (even if that society may not acknowledge or realise it), just as white 'Christian' society is present in their psyche. To discover something of this strange co-presence is what these essays are about.

All of this leaves us with the quandary of finding a name for 'them'. Even taking into account the provisos against a simplistic fixation of their identity, we cannot avoid some sort of definition or identification of whom we are dealing with here, acknowledging the semi-arbitrary nature of any name.

Various names were in fact attached to this ancient substratum of southern African humanity by various groups interacting with them. Remarkably, they did not have a generic name for themselves over against others, only for various specific groups. The reason is simply that for thousands of years, until 2 500 years ago, there were no others. Each one of the names given to them by others has a long history. The herders ('Khoikhoi') used the blanket term of contempt 'San' to refer to all lowly, despised people regardless of ethnic origin. This name also included destitute white colonists and black agriculturalists. The Bantu-speaking Iron Age farmers called them by various names such as 'Basarwa' (in Tswana), all derived from a common root perhaps meaning something like 'people of the wilderness'.[11] The Dutch immigrants into South Africa called them by a variety of names, of which 'Bosjesmannen' ('Bushmen') became current. Initially also used in a nonethnic sense for all marginal, indigent people, it came to be applied from the 1770s specifically to inland hunter-gatherers believed to be of a distinct ethnic origin. Under the influence of contemporary American anthropologists it has become widely customary to revive the term 'San'.[12]

In the end none of these terms is satisfactory. The term 'Bushman' may have the advantage that it gives a fairly good indication of their life-style, living in and off the veld. But the problem is that for centuries this term had derogatory overtones in South Africa, just like the word 'Hottentot', which was used for the herders encountered by the early Dutch colonists at the Cape. To the seventeenth-century Calvinist Dutch immigrants both names, 'Bushman' and 'Hottentot', had connotations of uncivilised barbarism. They have retained those connotations up to the present time, and have not been purged. In addition, the term 'Bushman' has sexist overtones. Efforts have been made to remedy this weakness by speaking of 'Bushpeople',[13] 'Bushwoman', 'Bushbaby', and so on. In origin, the word 'San' is every bit as discriminatory as 'Bushman'. Elphick speaks of 'aboriginal hunters'.[14] An attractive adaptation of his term is 'aboriginal hunter-gatherers', or (slightly less cumbersome) 'hunter-gatherers', or simply 'aborigines'. The people we are looking at were the aboriginal hunter-gatherers of southern Africa, regardless of their linguistic or physical characteristics.

ENDNOTES

1 H-G Gadamer, *Wahrheit und Methode: Grundzüge einer philosophischen Hermeneutik*, Tübingen: Mohr (Paul Siebeck), 1972.

2 Cf A Barnard, *Hunters and herders of southern Africa: a comparative ethnography of the Khoisan peoples*, Cambridge: Cambridge University Press, 1992, pp 296ff.

3 Cf M Eliade, *Patterns in comparative religion*, New York: Meridian, 1974 (1958), pp 188–215.

4 H Rosemont, Against relativism, in G J Larson & Eliot Deutsch (eds), *Interpreting across boundaries: new essays in comparative philosophy*, Princeton: Princeton University Press, 1989, pp 36–70.

5 Cf C G Jung, *Psychology and religion: West and East. The Collected Works of C G Jung*, Vol 11, London: Routledge & Kegan Paul, 1958.

6 Cf S Odin, *Process metaphysics and Hua-Yen Buddhism: a critical study of cumulative penetration vs interpenetration*, Albany: State University of New York Press, 1982, pp 159ff for a fascinating effort to assimilate 'God' and the 'deep unconscious'.

7 In 1978 P Tobias (*The Bushmen: San hunters and herders of southern Africa*, Cape Town: Human & Rousseau, 1978, p 13) estimated that there were about 55 000–60 000 'Bushmen' alive: Botswana, about 25 000–30 000; Namibia, 26 000; Angola, 4 000; Zambia, 200; South Africa, 25. For other estimates, and the problems pertaining to estimates of the number of hunter-gatherers, cf R Gordon, Once again: how many Bushmen are there?, in M Biesele, R Gordon & R Lee (eds), *The past and future of !Kung ethnography: critical reflections and symbolic perspectives. Essays in honour of Lorna Marshall*, Hamburg: Helmut Buske Verlag, 1986, pp 53–68. M Biesele (*Shaken roots: the Bushmen of Namibia*, Marshalltown: EDA, 1990) estimating the number of hunter-gatherers in Namibia at 33 000, adds that in Namibia the classification 'Bushman' is simply a wastebasket into which all sorts of people living on the land, who do not fit neatly into any ethnic category, have been dumped. According to Gordon (*The Bushman myth: the making of a Namibian underclass*, Boulder: Westview Press, 1992, p 7) contemporary population estimates for Bushmen in southern Africa range from 30 000 to 87 250. In his article Once again: how many Bushmen ..., Gordon explains the vicissitudes of all efforts to count the hunter-gatherers.

8 In 1955 E F Potgieter, (*The disappearing Bushmen of Lake Chrissie*, Pretoria: Van Schaik, 1955) estimated that there were about 32 Batwa left in this area.

9 By 1978 the number of Bushpeople who had no contact with farms was declining drastically, and the prospect was raised that inevitably 'within another generation or two, the hunter-gatherer lifestyle will have become completely extinct among the San' (Tobias, *The Bushmen ...*, p 15). In that year it was estimated that probably no more than one third of the existing Bushpeople could still be regarded as hunters and gatherers. But by then the description 'hunters and gatherers' already covered various degrees of a lifestyle merging with that of squatting farm dwellers. In 1990, only 11 per cent of the San in Namibia retained residential ties with a fragment of their traditional foraging territory, hunting and gathering, while learning new farming skills (Biesele, *Shaken roots ...*).

10 Biesele, ibid.

11 M G Guenther, 'San' or 'Bushmen'?, Biesele, Gordon & Lee, *The past and future* ..., pp 27–51. For a different etymology and reservations about the usefulness of this term, see Barnard, *Hunters and herders* ..., pp 8–9.

12 In 1971 an interdisciplinary group of scholars in Johannesburg agreed to recommend the terms 'San' (as well as 'Khoikhoi' and 'Negro'/'southern African Negro') for the biological entities in question; 'Bushman', 'Hottentot' and 'Bantu' for the linguistic entities; and 'hunter'/'hunter-gatherer', 'herder' and 'cultivator' for the respective economic entities. This suggestion has not met with general approval. Cf the careful study by Guenther ('San' or 'Bushmen'?) of the problem of naming the hunter-gatherers, and Barnard (*Hunters and herders* ..., pp 7–11) who mentions that, although 'San' is gaining wide acceptance among nonspecialists, several ethnographers who formerly used it have now reverted to 'Bushman'. The latest salvo in this battle may have been fired by E Wilmsen (A myth and its measure, *Current Anthropology*, 1992 33[5], pp 611–614) in a stinging attack on Gordon, *The Bushman myth* ...

13 Guenther, 'San' or 'Bushmen'?, p 37.

14 R Elphick, *Kraal and castle: Khoikhoi and the founding of white South Africa*, New Haven: Yale University Press, 1977.

13 Historical interaction

Early prehistory

At the time when the Portuguese rounded the Cape and Jan van Riebeeck and his settlers arrived there in 1652, launching the modern, colonial history of South Africa, the hunter-gatherers still inhabited the whole of southern Africa, from the central highlands in the north and the arid west down to the fertile southern and eastern coasts. Their territory included modern South Africa, Namibia, Botswana, Lesotho, Swaziland, and parts of Zimbabwe, Mozambique, Zambia and Angola.[1] In fact, archaeological remains indicate that 10 000 to 15 000 years ago people very similar to the contemporary hunter-gatherers may have lived in Central and East Africa – indeed, throughout the eastern half of Africa. Culturally and physically they provide the most direct link with ancient Africa, probably having descended from one of the extinct archaic subspecies of modern humans discussed in chapter 10.

The ancestry of the contemporary hunter-gatherers can possibly be traced to the start of the Late Stone Age, or even the Middle Stone Age. That was the time, roughly 30 000 to 40 000 years ago, when they and the blacks (the Bantu-speaking negroes), with whom they shared the same sub-Saharan genetic stock, may have started to divide. Where in Africa this split occurred is unknown. For this early period the term 'Khoisan', which has become customary since the thirties,[2] is really more appropriate. It denotes the original unity of the 'San' and the 'Khoikhoi' until roughly 2 500 years ago, when the Khoikhoi may have seceded from the common parent population.

The original Khoisan may have gravitated to eastern and southern Africa and the blacks to equatorial Africa, the former staying closer to the presumed ancestral African gene-pool than the latter.[3] During the long period of separation between the Khoisan and the blacks, certain genetic and cultural differences arose between the two populations. Whereas the original Khoisan continued with the old hunting-gathering subsistence pattern, the blacks at some stage adopted an agricultural lifestyle, which led to dramatic population increase. This caused territorial expansion and southward migration, which eventually, roughly from the beginning of the Common Era, led to the gradual dissolution of the geographic and genetic isolation between the two populations. We shall return to this process of convergence below.

The classical hunting-gathering life style

Care must be taken not to project what is known of nineteenth- and twentieth-century hunting-gathering culture onto earlier periods.[4] Yet it would not be far-fetched to assume at least some essential similarities between ancient and recent hunting-gathering ways in southern Africa. Neither is it acceptable to relegate them to a closed world of primitivism, incapable of change and transformation. What can be classified broadly as hunting-gathering culture was never static, but changed continuously as innovations and adaptations to changing conditions were made over millennia. As a matter of fact, preliterate cultures may be even more variable than literate ones with their written canons. As Platvoet says: 'Between the prehistoric and the present preliterate forms of religion, even in one tradition, lie many undocumented histories of change. The present ones are by no means the petrified relics of ''primitive'' primordial times as nineteenth and early twentieth scholars took them to be.'[5] Keeping these provisos in mind, for the purposes of this study it would nevertheless be acceptable to construct an ideal-typical summary of the 'classical' hunting-gathering way of life, making use of existing literature on contemporary societies[6] and realising that such a picture will gloss over many differences between the various groups.

What can be said about the configuration of social and economic factors constituting the hunter-gatherer world? Inskeep[7] gives a picture of the prehistoric hunter-gatherers as masters of the art of living off what nature offered, mostly enjoying 'an adequate (and perhaps often more than adequate) food-supply, well-made clothing, shelter and a pleasing degree of personal adornment', employing effective measures against injury and sickness, living a 'peaceful, industrious, idyllic sort of life' for many thousands of years:

lively, mobile societies dividing their time between work and relaxation. We may imagine the women and younger children moving off in the morning with digging stick and collecting bag, knowing precisely the right direction to take to collect edible roots or fruits, or moving along the rocks to collect shellfish; or the menfolk, stepping lightly in single file, with bow, quiver and arrows, spear and knife, and perhaps a net bag with water containers of ostrich-egg shells, in search of something more substantial. We can imagine the smoke rising from the long-dead hearths and catch the smell of roasting meat.[8] *Among the hubbub of domestic chatter and romping children a man sits shaping a bow or refurbishing an arrow, and if we look carefully we may see deft hands shredding sinew or sewing leather, shaping minute beads and forming them into ornate decorations for wrist, arm, head, waist or leg. One may make a mat, while another twists cord from fibre to make a line for fishing, or twine for snares. If the call comes to dance or to sleep, the work is quietly set aside for another day.*

This picture is admittedly idyllic and overgeneralised.[9] Sahlins's identification of the hunting-gathering mentality with the Zen economic outlook[10] does not, I believe, hold water either – the real hunter-gatherers were and are ordinary people, far more similar to moderns and people of all ages in their desire of enjoyments wherever they may be found than to those who have opted for a life of nondesire. Certainly the 'classical' hunter-gatherers fitted into their natural environment (after all, they had no choice!), making full use of available sources of water, game and veld foods of which they had an intimate knowledge.[11] Utterly dependent on the bounty and scarcity of nature, they were – given their very basic technology – simply not in a position to make any significant changes to their environment. In a simple economic system, life depended on maintaining a delicate balance with nature.[12] A constant level of not too arduous work had to be maintained throughout the year to ensure a relatively stable and comfortable life.[13]

On the whole, the average level of economic satisfaction, given their needs and the opportunities to gratify them, would have been higher than that of modern societies. The impoverishment of the hunter-gatherers after they came into contact with other cultures (first the pastoral, then the agricultural, then the modern) has two aspects: their relatively comfortable traditional way of life was eroded and destroyed in an ongoing process, and they were sucked into a world offering bigger and better goods – but not the means of obtaining those desirable commodities. Both these eventualities were tragic. From the relative comfort of their original world they were dragged into extreme poverty in another world.

Socially,[14] the traditional fragile balance with nature found expression in small, closely knit, informal, egalitarian,[15] classless bands or camps composed of several families, occupying and 'owning' a defined territory.[16] According to Barnard[17] hunter-gatherer territories are only partly 'property' as defined in modern Western legal systems: they have rights of special access to a particular territory, but cannot sell these rights or give them away. One can see why *land* was to become the central issue in the confrontation of their simple communal economy with that of the incoming colonists.

The hunter-gatherer bands maintained loose but meaningful relations with others in a wide network of alliances. In a highly mobile society, accumulated wealth such as surplus food or material possessions would have been a hazard rather than an advantage. Surplus items were things to give away as gifts.[18] Reciprocal giving and borrowing was a feature of these small societies. This custom served not only material needs but, more importantly, emotional needs of bonding, cooperation and easing of social tension. Specifically, sharing of meat and veld vegetables was an important feature of hunter-gatherer camp life.[19] The notion of private property, for example honey which had been found and marked,[20] was not wholly absent, but was completely subordinated to the ethos of sharing. Single persons or single nuclear families, however many goods they might have hoarded, would not have been able to survive. In fact, hoarding of any kind would have jeopardised their survival chances.[21]

The individual was totally enmeshed in the group, as the group was enmeshed in nature. Marshall[22] says of the contemporary !Kung:

> *They must belong; they can live no other way. They are also extremely dependent emotionally on the sense of belonging and on companionship. Separation and loneliness are unendurable to them. I believe their wanting to belong and be near is actually visible in the way families cluster together in an encampment and in the way they sit huddled together, often touching someone, shoulder against shoulder, ankle against ankle. Security and comfort for them lie in their belonging to their group, free from the threat of rejection and hostility.*

This does not make them more saintly than any other group. Certainly there were quarrels and conflicts about various issues.[23] But relative peace and cooperation were necessary for survival. It is against this background that their traditional intense aversion to physical violence must be understood. The survival of the camp depended on the physical availability and ability of every member, and on stable social relations.

In their simple communal economic system a certain division of labour obtained between men and women, the men hunting, the women gathering plant foods. Yet decisions were made consensually, if not unanimously, by men as well as women. It is not for nothing that they are known to be one of the most loquacious peoples on earth.[24] We may probably cautiously extrapolate Lee's conclusions on male-female relations among the !Kung to the classical hunter-gatherers generally: women predominated in some spheres of behaviour and men in others, within an overall relation of give and take. Both genders worked equally hard. 'On balance, the evidence shows a relatively equal role in society for the two sexes, and the !Kung data certainly do not support a view of women in "the state of nature" as oppressed or dominated by men or as subject to sexual exploitation at the hand of males.'[25] In this egalitarian structure children received a generally nonauthoritarian upbringing.[26] Serious social crises were mostly resolved by splitting up a camp. Violence was viewed with the utmost horror and occurred rarely. Divorce was easy.

All these well-attested features add up to a picture of a fairly easy-going, generally happy society, integrating men and women, grandparents and children in a small band surviving in their particular niche in a vast world, surrounded by the veld underneath them, animals and plants around them, and the spacious African sky overhead. It was not a perfect existence. Dangers lurked everywhere, and violent deaths were not uncommon. For the group to survive, infanticide had to be practised under certain conditions. And even when people reached a ripe old age, in the end they would have to be abandoned by the group, protected from sun and animals by a few branches, provided with a small supply of food and water. For the hunter-gatherers, as for all people, life had its fair measure of sorrow and pain, as well as its measure of joy.

Their religion will be analysed in greater detail in chapters 17 to 19. At this stage the point to be noted is that their religion was inseparable from their sociocultural existence as a whole, without any trace of the modern Western distinction between 'sacred' and 'profane'. Neither a materialist nor a spiritualist view of their religion would be adequate. Their symbolic and socioeconomic systems were mutually supportive, constantly revitalising each other. Their religion was an effort to penetrate to the mysterious depths of nature and make contact with its sustaining power. It was a truly ecological religion, under conditions that can never be repeated in the history of humanity. Completely dependent on wild animals and uncultivated plants for a living, they did not and could not manipulate their environment. In fact, it may even be postulated that the very success of this type of pact with nature may be one of the reasons that the indigenous hunter-gatherer culture never developed the skills (such as cultivation of plants and animal husbandry) that came to be associated with 'higher' cultural levels achieved elsewhere in the world. Another reason may have been long-standing isolation and lack of external stimulus. It was a self-sufficient type of culture until disturbed by the influx of new cultural forms from elsewhere.

This was the typical hunter-gatherer lifestyle until this century, although it has been under increasing pressure since about 2 500 BP. That was the time of the first encounter with alternative lifestyles, the first one being the pastoralist Khoikhoi existence. About 300 years later a second encounter took place, with negroid Bantu-speaking, iron-smelting agriculturalists and herders. The third, and by far the most traumatic, was the upheaval caused by European colonisation in the seventeenth century.

The Bushmen did not interact with these three waves successively. The pattern was far more complex. The different epochs overlapped and coincided, naturally leading to stresses and strains. Challenged at its frontiers,[27] the earliest civilisation had to adapt. As time passed, the three other cultures, at times in intense interaction with one another, simultaneously exerted pressure on the traditional hunter-gatherer lifestyle, leading to many new social constellations, especially after the European settlement.

It is clear that the hunting-gathering way must be understood as one motif in the intricate tapestry of South African history, involving many groups, large and small; ancient, recent and newly spawned; interacting with one another in a variety of ways ranging from peaceful coexistence to intense conflict; coming to terms with the natural environment by way of various survival strategies, ranging from the simple gathering and hunting of what nature offered with a minimum of disturbance, to animal husbandry and crop cultivation interfering more drastically with natural cycles, eventually being assimilated to large-scale modern sociopolitical and techno-industrial economic systems.

Successive new waves of immigrants and new cultural contacts completely undermined their unique way of being human. As we, the heirs of Western civilisation, reach the limits of our modern way of being human, we are strangely moved by that past.[28]

The pastoral revolution

Roughly 2 500 years BP a change occurred that had such far-reaching repercussions among the aboriginal people of southern Africa that it may be termed a cultural revolution. This was when the hunter-gatherer culture, which had been the way of life of all humankind for 99 per cent of its existence on earth, started to buckle in this part of the world under the pressures of new cultural forms. These latter were dependent on herding and (somewhat later) agriculture. They had made their appearance in human history, far to the north of the African continent, about 8 000 years earlier.

These new cultures represented entirely novel ways of relating to the natural environment, involving a variety of factors such as technological changes (for example the replacement of stone by iron) and the way in which animals were perceived (domesticated wildstock instead of game). Later, with European immigration into southern Africa, the killing of animals would become part of extensive market economies. Changed ways of relating to nature were in turn linked with novel relations between individuals and social organisation. For example, in the new pastoral culture animals represented wealth in addition to food. With the accumulation of wealth came hierarchical, entrenched power and status. The old system of small, intimate, egalitarian, mobile groups was replaced by new systems consisting of larger, more static groups. In the widest sense, in accordance with our idea of religion as discussed earlier, these changes amounted to different religious orientations, carried by different types of myths, enacted in different types of rituals. To this we shall return.

By about 2 500 years ago herding had reached the northwestern parts of southern Africa. At the time some Khoisan hunters probably adopted cultural features such as herding and pottery, most probably in northern Botswana, first by attaching themselves to an unknown newcomer group of herders from farther north, and then seceding from them.[29] 'It is likely that pastoral Khoekhoe society began with the acquisition of various aspects of culture, by southern African Bushmen, from a people of northern origin.'[30] The cultural change from hunting-gathering to herding among some Khoisan bands led to a certain distinction between those hunter-gatherers who continued the old way of life, and the 'Khoikhoi' ('men of men'), as they called themselves, who took to the new way.[31] It is quite certain that in the western parts of the country people with pottery (baked clay pots), domestic stock and dogs moved fairly rapidly southwards at the time.[32]

No indigenous plants had been domesticated in southern Africa up to then, because of the unsuitability of the existing staple foods for farming purposes. As for indigenous animals, herd animals such as eland were available in sufficient numbers to obviate the need for domestication.[33]

The lifestyles associated with the Khoikhoi and the hunter-gatherers remained interchangeable even in historical times. Their technologies (clothing, ornaments, utensils, etc) did not differ sufficiently to act as indicators of two separate, fixed cultural identities. Obviously a hunter-gatherer way of life demands technological simplicity. Yet they were always more than willing to introduce useful new material items into their lifestyle. The lines between the two lifestyles would have been crossed often and regularly as hunting groups adopted elements of a more sedentary herding existence, or Khoikhoi were reduced to poverty and forced to live off the veld. Even individuals would have switched from herding to hunting-gathering and back again more than once in their lifetimes.[34]

The term 'Khoisan' captures not only the original unity, but also the complex process of gene flow and acculturation that continued between these two populations after some differentiation had already taken place. The Khoikhoi herding culture did not represent a serious threat to the hunting way of life. Probably the two cultures were able to adapt fairly easily, some hunters becoming clients of the herders. In fact, Deacon[35] considers it probable that 'had the European colonists not arrived in the southern Cape when they did, the hunter-gatherers would have been assimilated by herders in all but the most inhospitable environments'.

Renewed contact with blacks

Bantu-speaking Iron Age peoples settled in the Transvaal, Natal and eastern Cape areas during the early centuries of the Common Era, even as early as the third century.[36] Contact with the hunter-gatherers, from whom they had been separated for perhaps 40 000 years, was resumed. In the northern Cape the newcomers do not appear to have settled before approximately 1600 CE, due to the unsuitability of this region for their mixed farming economy.[37]

The patterns of interaction between the aboriginal inhabitants and these new immigrants varied. At times and in some localities relations were strained, the hunter-gatherers being driven out by force.[38] At other times and in other localities peaceful coexistence, in various modes and degrees, was the order of the day, ranging from relations of clientship to full physical and cultural integration through intermarriage.[39] Hunter-gatherers often undertook the shamanic task of rainmaking for their Bantu-speaking patrons in exchange for protection. Certainly trade in iron, glass beads, and so on took place on a significant scale.[40]

An interesting example of one type of interaction, which occurred in the northern Cape and western Orange Free State, has come to light. Morris[41] demonstrated that considerable gene flow took place between the aboriginal inhabitants and Iron Age Tswana populations some centuries ago. From a study in that same region, Humphreys[42] concludes that for a period of roughly 400 years (c 1380–1780) there was intensive interaction of a peculiar type with the Tswana. The inhabitants of certain settlements, who were biologically Khoisan, acquired sheep, goats and cattle as well as iron and copper objects and led a reasonably sedentary life while still maintaining their traditional hunting habits. Thus along the Riet River, pockets of Khoisan were to be found who had adopted certain practices of Iron Age lifestyles and merged these with their own traditions and technologies.[43] Because of the low social esteem in which the earlier inhabitants of these settlements were held by the Tswana, no gene flow from the Tswana to them can be detected. Yet there certainly was a significant gene flow in the opposite direction (from the Khoisan to the Tswana), women from the lower (Khoisan) caste being absorbed as wives into the superior Tswana social structure, where their offspring were brought up as Tswana. The offspring of such Tswana-Khoisan cohabitation would have spoken Tswana, in a Tswana social setting. This type of interaction could account for the high incidence of Khoisan features found among contemporary Sotho.[44] This was, however, only one of several modes of interaction between Khoisan and Iron Age people. Whereas the Tswana language shows very little if any influence of Khoisan languages (which would be manifested as click sounds), the Nguni languages (Zulu and Xhosa[45]) in the southeast do. This may demonstrate the occurrence of strong integrationist patterns.

In any event, the overall effect of the new wave of immigration by Iron Age people, however dramatic it may have been in places, was not nearly as traumatic as that of the subsequent European influx which led to the near annihilation of the aboriginal hunter-gatherers in southern Africa.

The trauma of colonialism

The hunter-gatherers were drawn into the modern period with the discovery of the Cape by the Portuguese. Their ancient way of life was not able to withstand the heavy European influx and its devastating effects after the middle of the seventeenth century. By the second half of the nineteenth century they had been pushed back into isolated pockets of South Africa, such as the mountainous Drakensberg area in the east and the Kalahari in the west.

They were, quite simply, overpowered – physically and culturally. Institutionalised religion (both the official church and the non-conformist missionaries) was solidly implicated in the process of European colonialism, which was one unremitting effort to establish a ubiquitous Euro-Christian presence, decreeing a new order for the indigenous people, remapping the world for them, coercing them into the closed European universe of the time, imposing a massive European hegemony on them. Military overpowerment, socioeconomic encroachment and religious intolerance were aspects of the same process. There was no space for another world. Sociomilitary conquest of the hunter-gatherers succeeded to the point of their near extinction in South Africa, but religious efforts to convert them largely failed. The scope of this chapter does not permit a detailed account of the colonialist-Bushman, Christian-heathen interplay. We will have to make do with a broad outline.

After a friendly first encounter in 1655,[46] sporadic encounters of a less amicable nature took place during the following years and decades, involving fights over land and cattle.[47] Often herders joined forces with whites against hunter-gatherers, or herders joined with hunter-gatherers and raided white farms. This war to the bitter end, involving cruelties and atrocities on both sides, was primarily a result of encroachment on indigenous people's traditional hunting grounds by colonists,[48] secure in the God-given right, unquestioned at the time, of superior civilised man to take possession of land occupied by an inferior people such as the hunter-gatherers. It was a brutal clash between apparently irreconcilable cultures: on the one hand the Euro-Christian settlers to whom wealth equalled land, privately owned – land for the pasturing of sheep, cattle and horses and for the cultivation of crops; on the other hand the hunter-gatherers, threatened with expulsion from their traditional, communally owned, inalienable hunting grounds, resorting to cattle theft, often to murder as a deterrent and a means of retaliation and survival.[49]

The war, often amounting to cold-blooded slaughter of aborigines by whites and people of mixed descent, escalated throughout the eighteenth century, reaching a peak in the 1770s to 1790s, with numerous attacks and reprisals from both sides. Hunters stole livestock and killed whites and herders.[50] By then they had been at the receiving end of a broad cultural assault for roughly a century and a half, emanating from the centre of the colony itself and extending to the frontiers with its white and mixed groups of settlers.[51] In 1777 the Council of Policy in the Cape decided on a policy of virtual extermination. Although instructions to spare women and children and to avoid unnecessary bloodshed were issued,[52] women were often killed together with the men. Orphaned and abandoned children were taken alive and distributed as 'apprentices' among the farmers.[53]

Throughout the early centuries they had either to collaborate and be assimilated (many of them did indeed become part of the 'coloured' population[54]), resist (which they did with remarkable success, especially in the eighteenth century), or flee.[55] All the while physical intermixing and acculturation among hunter-gatherers, Khoikhoi, blacks, escaped slaves and whites continued, bringing about a variety of mixed groups on the frontiers of the colony, such as the Griqua and the Bastards.[56]

Towards the end of the eighteenth century things gradually improved. During governor Macartney's administration (1797–1798 – the first British occupation of the Cape took place in 1795) *veldwachtmeesters* on the northwestern frontier were authorised to collect sheep for distribution among the hunters, with some success.[57]

Especially from the early nineteenth century onwards, strained relations between the aboriginal people and the colonists on the frontiers were interspersed with episodes of remarkably friendly coexistence,[58] albeit in the unquestioned framework of Euro-Christian superiority. In 1805 the first missionary to them, J J Kicherer, reported the enthusiastic cooperation of several white farmers in his efforts to evangelise them.[59] When Colonel Richard Collins toured the northeastern part of the colony in 1808–1809 to inspect the hunter-gatherers, he recommended leniency towards them, since they had ceased to offer serious resistance to the advancing Europeans:

> *Some still hung about in the northern Karoo, others lived as they did for many years thereafter in the arid plains of Great Bushman Land south of the middle Orange, others were moving away northward to be cut down by the Griquas or to find a refuge in the Kalahari desert. There was little slaughter by Europeans after 1810, though as late as 1823 commandos took the field in Tarka and the Sneeuwberg.*[60]

After the back of the resistance had been broken, efforts were made (by Lord Charles Somerset) to regularise the treatment of prisoners and abandoned children by insisting on written contracts. On the northeastern frontier the two remarkable *landdrosts* Stockenström (father and son[61]) followed a firm but benevolent policy, controlling commandos and encouraging the hunters to take to stock-keeping.[62] They earned the respect of their compatriots for these efforts and largely succeeded in pacifying the region. Many hunter-gatherers were absorbed into the farming economy, becoming cattle-herds in the service of Boer farmers,[63] and increasingly abandoned their traditional way of life. This became the trend, still continuing today in the whole southern African region, with hunter-gatherers increasingly attaching themselves to white and black farmers.

After the whites moved into Natal, the spiral process of expropriation of traditional hunting grounds by the colonists, retaliatory cattle raids by the hunters, and reprisals consisting of the killing of adults and capture of children by incensed farmers was reenacted.[64] In 1849 and again in 1859 the

British government established buffer locations of black settlements between the white farmers and the hunter-gatherers higher up in the Drakensberg range, leading to increased conflict between them and blacks, both in Natal and Lesotho, and to a tightening of the net around them. This tilted the balance decisively against them.[65]

The patterns set in other parts of the country were repeated in Natal: resistance and retreat (into the inaccessible and therefore relatively safe high Drakensberg range); acculturation (for example through the introduction of horses, cattle and firearms into the hunting-gathering way of life); absorption into the farming lifestyle by some individuals and families; and – finally – their extermination as a people. They simply did not have time to make the transition to a herding economy, which was their only hope of survival.[66] Such a shift would have involved an enormous change in values, especially in their conception of time and the future.[67] They could not manage the necessary changes, and time ran out for them. The pressures were too sudden and too great. Towards the end of the nineteenth century their resistance was finally broken. In the Drakensberg area (the eastern Orange Free State, northeastern Cape, Lesotho, Natal, the Transkei) the last survivors lingered on until the first decade or so of the twentieth century.[68] In Angola, Zimbabwe and Zambia a few hundred survivors may be identifiable. Only in the western parts of southern Africa, in Botswana and Namibia, did reasonably substantial but dwindling numbers manage to continue their traditional lifestyle.

After 40 000 years, they still linger on in southern Africa – dispossessed, demoralised, degraded and despised as the lowest of the low, threatened by alcoholism and malnutrition, imprisoned in a culture of poverty, the overwhelming majority no longer part of the kind of ecosystem that nurtured their forebears physically, culturally and religiously.

A large-scale return to hunting-gathering is out of the question. Yet it is a time of small new beginnings, of being educated to survive in today's world, consolidating socially and becoming part of the political processes in Namibia[69] and Botswana[70]. What the future holds for them is uncertain. While a minority may be able to pursue their traditional lifestyle for an indefinite period, the vast majority will most certainly, in one way or another, increasingly be absorbed into a farming existence. Their fate in the wake of European expansion is a not to be forgotten tragedy. It would be worsened if they were to lose completely what is left of their tenuous heritage. They need time and support to make the required mental adjustments in their own way. They are not to be treated as living cultural fossils, although they are reminders of our common human past and of the relativity of the modern epoch.[71]

ENDNOTES

1 P Tobias, *The Bushmen: San hunters and herders of Southern Africa*, Cape Town: Human & Rousseau, 1978, p 19.

2 Cf I Schapera, *The Khoisan peoples of South Africa: Bushmen and Hottentots*, London: Routledge & Kegan Paul, 1960 (1930). For the history and meaning of the term 'Khoisan', see A Barnard, *Hunters and herders of Southern Africa: a comparative ethnography of the Khoisan peoples*, Cambridge: Cambridge University Press, 1992, p 7.

3 Tobias, *The Bushmen ...*, p 30.

4 Cf R B Lee, *The !Kung San: men, women and work in a foraging society*, Cambridge: Cambridge University Press, 1979, pp 433ff.

5 J G Platvoet, De eigenheid van godsdiensten van volken zonder schrift, in T Chowdhury, W Claesens & W Logister, *Het kosmisch patroon: het vele en het ene in de godsdiensten*, Tilburg: University Press, 1989, p 22.

6 For a survey of the ethnography of various hunter-gatherer groups, see Barnard, *Hunters and herder ...*, pp 39–155.

7 R R Inskeep, The Bushmen in prehistory, in Tobias, *The Bushmen ...*, pp 55ff.

8 Although Bushmen regard hunting as an exciting and gratifying male activity, this is tempered by a certain restraint, 'hunting only for food and never for sport and trophies, killing only those animals needed for food' (Guenther, *The Nharo Bushmen ...*, p 239).

9 Guenther (ibid) points out that the idealistic portrayal no longer applies to farm-associated Bushmen who suffer from chronic malnutrition and cultural disintegration. G B Silberbauer (*Hunter and habitat in the central Kalahari desert*, Cambridge: Cambridge University Press, 1981, p 52), speaking about the /Gwi of the Ghanzi district in Botswana, mentions a belief that the deities' family 'are all vegetarian (ie they do not kill to eat) and that an abundance of water and plant foods exist in their country' (the upper region of the universe).

10 Cf M Sahlins, *Stone Age economics*, Chicago, New York: Aldine Atherton, 1972, pp 2ff.

11 For the outstanding abilities and achievements of the hunter-gatherers in this area, in some respects comparable to Western scientific methods and vastly superior to Western knowledge, see N B Jones & M J Konner, !Kung knowledge of animal behavior (or: the proper study of mankind is animals), in R B Lee & I de Vore, *Kalahari hunter-gatherers: studies of the !Kung San and their neighbors*, Cambridge, Mass: Harvard University Press, 1976, pp 325–348; H J Heinz, The Bushmen's store

of scientific knowledge, in Tobias, *The Bushmen* ..., pp 148–161; L Liebenberg, *The art of tracking: the origin of science*, Claremont: Philip, 1990.

12 See, eg, the description of the subsistence ecology of the /Gwi in the Central Kalahari by J Tanaka (Subsistence ecology of central Kalahari San, in Lee & De Vore, *Kalahari hunter-gatherers*:::, pp 98–119) and Silberbauer (*Hunter and habitat* ..., pp 191–303), and of the !Kung by R B Lee (*Subsistence ecology of !Kung Bushmen*, University of California, Berkeley, PhD thesis, 1965, and *The !Kung San* ...). According to Lee the !Kung way of life is 'not impoverished or precarious', but in fact 'unexpectedly comfortable and secure' (*Subsistence ecology* ..., p 200). 'Perhaps the most telling evidence of the security of life as hunter-gatherers is its extraordinary persistence. Foraging people have been operating in the Dobe area for thousands of years without any evidence for major discontinuities. Personnel have changed, but the way of life has remained the same. During this long period there has been little evidence for technological change: only in the last 100 years have iron tools replaced those of stone and bone' (Lee, *The !Kung San* ..., p 438).

13 Speaking of the !Kung, Lee (*The !Kung San* ..., p 455) declares that the 'actual amount of time devoted by the San to the food quest is modest, amounting to about 17 hours of subsistence effort per adult per week ... Building a house for a rainy season camp is two day's work; shelters for the dry season camp are thrown up in a morning.' Barnard (*Hunters and herders* ..., p 244) points out that the hunter-gatherers may resemble Sahlins' idea of a prototypical 'original affluent society', not because their needs or wants are few, but because they chose to maximise time rather than wealth. Generally speaking, they do not achieve the level of wealth which they desire – although many 'Bushmen groups have until quite recently lived in a state of relative equality and "original affluence", but the decline of this state began the moment economic interaction with the non-foraging world first took place' (in some cases perhaps two millennia ago).

14 Numerous studies describe the typical hunter-gatherer social structure, for example Silberbauer, *Hunter and habitat* ..., pp 138ff on that of the /Gwi, and Lee, *The !Kung San* ..., on that of the !Kung.

15 Cf Barnard, *Hunters and herders* ..., pp 245ff.

16 Lee, *The !Kung San* ..., p 456.

17 Ibid, pp 241ff.

18 See L Marshall's descriptions of gift-giving as a social institution among the contemporary !Kung in her classic paper on their sharing, talking and giving (Sharing, talking, and giving: relief of social tensions among the !Kung, in Lee & De Vore, *Kalahari hunter-gatherers* ..., pp 349ff).

19 Ibid, pp 355ff.

20 Ibid, p 370.

21 Cf Lee, *The !Kung San* ..., p 455: 'The !Kung do not amass a surplus because they conceive of the environment itself as their storehouse.'

22 Marshall, Sharing, talking, and giving ..., p 350.

23 Ibid, pp 370ff; Lee, The !Kung San ..., pp 370–400; I Eibl-Eibesfeldt, *Zur Frage der Kontinuität der San-Kulturen im südlichen Afrika*, in R Vossen & K Keuthmann (eds), *Contemporary studies on Khoisan*, 2 vols, Hamburg: Helmut Baske Verlag, 1986, pp 215–224.

24 See Marshall's fascinating descriptions (Sharing, talking, and giving ..., pp 351ff) of their talking and conversation, and other social mores.

25 Lee, *The !Kung San ...*, p 454.

26 Cf Eibl-Eibesfeldt, Early socialization in the !Xo Bushmen, in Tobias, *The Bushmen ...*, pp 130–136, and the descriptions of P Draper, M J Konner & M Shostak in Lee & De Vore, *Kalahari hunter-gatherers ...*, pp 199–278 for the remarkable freedom of children – no wonder Western travellers and missionaries were shocked.

27 For this concept, widely used by historians, archaeologists and anthropologists, see A J B Humphreys, A prehistoric frontier in the northern Cape and western Orange Free State: archaeological evidence in interaction and ideological change, *Kronos*, 1988 13, pp 3–13.

28 The anthropologist Lee (*The !Kung San ...*, p 461) reminds us: 'A truly communal life is often dismissed as a utopian ideal, to be endorsed in theory but unattainable in practice. But the evidence for foraging peoples tells us otherwise. A sharing way of life is not only possible but has actually existed in many parts of the world and over long periods of time.' Yet M Konner & M Shostak (Ethnographic romanticism and the idea of human nature: parallels between Samoa and !Kung San, in M Biesele, R Gordon & R Lee [eds], *The past and future of !Kung ethnography: critical reflections and symbolic perspectives. Essays in honour of Lorna Marshall*, Hamburg: Helmut Buske Verlag, 1987, pp 69–76) sound a warning against a romanticised and utopian interpretation of the !Kung.

29 R Elphick, *Kraal and castle: Khoikhoi and the founding of white South Africa*, New Haven: Yale University Press, 1977, pp 11ff. For histories of the Khoikhoi, cf R Elphick & V C Malherbe, Die Khoisan tot 1828, in H Giliomee & R Elphick (eds), *'n Samelewing in wording, 1652–1840,* Kaapstad: Maskew Miller Longman, 1982, pp 1–66, and Barnard, *Hunters and herders ...*. See ibid, pp 29ff for theories to account for their origin.

30 Ibid, p 30.

31 Comparative linguistics has confirmed the common source of Khoikhoi and San languages. Westphal suggested that the source area of the Khoikhoi languages was north-central Botswana. According to Elphick (*Kraal and castle ...*, p 10) 'the evidence from the three fields most pertinent to this question [that is the origins of the Khoikhoi, JSK] – linguistics, cultural anthropology, and physical anthropology – can best be explained by assuming both that Khoikhoi originated as a hunter group in southern Africa and that the Khoikhoi and hunters subsequently interacted at many stages of their history'. There are still differences of opinion about the probable route taken by the Khoikhoi in their migration into Namibia and the Cape. For rival hypotheses, cf A J B Humphreys & A I Thackeray, *Ghaap and Gariep ...*, pp 293ff The Khoikhoi were excellent herdsmen, but practised no agriculture. Fat-tailed sheep and cattle (the antecedents of modern South African breeds) played an important cultural – including ritual – role (cf Schapera, *The Khoisan peoples ...*, pp 357–399 for Khoikhoi religion).

When trying to distinguish the 'San' from the Khoikhoi, three factors have usually been taken into account: physical type (cf R Singer, The biology of the San, in Tobias, *The Bushmen ...*, pp 115–129); language (cf A Traill, The languages of the San, in

Tobias, *The Bushmen* ..., pp 137–147); and general culture, including means of subsistence, social forms and technology. However, none of these in itself clearly distinguishes San from non-San. It would, for example, be incorrect to make a strong physical distinction. Light skin pigmentation, sparse, tightly coiled hair and certain facial features characterised both hunters and herders. The hunters were usually described as of exceptionally short stature. The dwarfing typical of the recent hunter-gatherers may have occurred as a result of selective pressures associated with the hunting lifestyle, lightness of physique giving certain hunting advantages. The diet related to the more frugal subsistence may also have played a role (cf Inskeep, The Bushmen in prehistory, p 35). As far as language is concerned, there are great similarities between certain San languages, such as the Tshu-Kwe languages of central Botswana, and certain Khoikhoi dialects such as Nama and Koranna, just as there are great differences between these same San languages and San languages spoken elsewhere (Elphick, *Kraal and castle* ..., pp 6ff; Inskeep, The Bushmen in prehistory, p 35; H C Bredenkamp, The origin of the Southern African Khoisan communities, in T Cameron, *A new illustrated history of South Africa*, Johannesburg: Southern, 1986, p 28). As for social forms and general culture, differences relate to those between a hunting-gathering and a herding subsistence. For example, the classical hunter-gatherers inhabited very flimsy structures made from a few branches, whereas the Khoikhoi built sturdier, more elaborate homes. At a more fundamental level, they would have differed in that hunters do not share herders' future orientation and their attitude towards domestic animals (cf A B Smith, Competition, conflict and clientship: Khoi and San relationships in the western Cape, *South African Archaeological Society Godwin Series*, 1986 5, pp 36–41).

32 Copper work, glass beads and glass artefacts also started to make their appearance roughly 2 000 years ago. The questions of where this new technology came from and who its southern African Stone Age agents were have not been answered satisfactorily. According to one view, they were perhaps a bow-wave preceding the Iron Age farmers who were moving southwards. In other words, the pottery, tools and animals that they brought with them were probably derived from early Iron Age communities in Central and East Africa (J Deacon, Later Stone Age people and their descendants in southern Africa, in R G Klein, *Southern African prehistory and palaeoenvironments*, Boston: Balkema, 1984, p 277). One problem with this view is that by the time such contact with Iron Age people could have taken place in northern Botswana and southern Angola, pottery was already present on the southern Cape coast. Consequently, Stone Age pottery found in the western parts of southern Africa might have derived not from Iron Age influence (cf Humphreys & Thackeray, *Ghaap and Gariep* ..., p 293), but from Stone Age potters further north in Africa. However, in the eastern parts of South Africa and in Zimbabwe pottery did make its first appearance in an Iron Age context. In any event, this new kind of culture spread very quickly throughout southern Africa, from Angola to the southern Cape coast. Pottery and domestic stock were added to the existing manufacture and use of stone tools.

33 Deacon, Later Stone Age people ..., p 323.

34 Cf S Marks, Khoisan resistance to the Dutch in the seventeenth and eighteenth centuries, *Journal of African History*, 1972 XIII(1), pp 55–80.

35 Deacon, Later Stone Age people ..., p 323.
36 Cf P Maylam, *A history of the African people of South Africa: from the Early Iron Age to the 1970's*, Cape Town, Johannesburg: Philip, 1986; T Maggs, The early history of the black people in Southern Africa, in Cameron, *A new illustrated history ...*, pp 37–43.
37 Humphreys & Thackeray, *Ghaap and Gariep..*, p 296.
38 Ibid, p 297.
39 Cf P Vinnicombe, *People of the Eland*, Pietermaritzburg: University of Natal Press, 1976, pp 10, 23; J B Peires, *The house of Phalo: a history of the Xhosa people in the days of their independence*, Johannesburg: Ravan, 1981, pp 22ff; Maylam, *A history of the African people ...*, pp 7, 14.
40 Peires, *The house of Phalo..*, p 24 summarises the relations between hunter-gatherers and Xhosa as follows: 'The Xhosa were, at times, exceptionally brutal towards the San (abaTwa). There was, however, a peaceful side to the relationship. San were renowned rainmakers and useful trading partners, exchanging ivory for cattle and dagga. Intermarriage was rare, but not unknown. San became tributary to Xhosa chiefs and, according to one report, there were more San than Gona Khoi living among the Gcaleka. At least one Xhosa clan, the isiThathu, was partly San in origin. Conversely, Xhosa sometimes joined San bands.'
41 A G Morris, An osteological analysis of the protohistoric populations of the northern Cape and western Orange Free State, South Africa, University of the Witwatersrand, Johannesburg, unpublished DPhil thesis, 1984.
42 Humphreys, A prehistoric frontier ...
43 Morris, An osteological analysis ..., p 320.
44 Ibid, p 293.
45 Cf Peires, *The house of Phalo ...*, p 24.
46 Cf G M Theal, *Chronicles of Cape commanders*, Cape Town: Richards, 1882, pp 57ff on the expedition into the interior led by Jan Wintervogel in 1655, which first made contact with the hunter-gatherers.
47 The sad tale of Boer-hunter animosity has been told in great detail by historians, for example by Theal (*Chronicles ...*, pp 158, 207, 255ff). Also see his *History of South Africa (1691–1795)*, London: Swan Sonnenschein, 1888, passim) and P J van der Merwe, *Die noordwaartse beweging van die boere voor die Groot Trek (1770–1842)*, Pretoria: Staatsbiblioteek, 1988 (1937). J S Marais (*The Cape Coloured people 1652–1937*, Johannesburg: Witwatersrand University Press, 1968, p 18) quotes the surprise of the traveller Thompson in the 1820s that a *veld commandant*, 'in many other points a meritorious, benevolent and clear-sighted man' seemed unconscious of the abhorrence caused by his involvement in acts which had (according to himself) caused the death of 2 700 Bushmen. For other versions of this protracted, wretched history, see E A Walker, *A history of Southern Africa*, London: Longmans 1959 (1928), pp 96ff, 117f and passim; Marais, *The Cape Coloured people ...*, pp 13–31; J B Wright, *Bushman raiders of the Drakensberg, 1840–1870*, Pietermaritzburg: University of Natal Press, 1971, pp 24ff; T R H Davenport, *South Africa: a modern history*, London: Macmillan, 1991 (1977), p 27f; A R Willcox, The Bushmen in history, in Tobias, *The Bushmen ...*, pp 76–87; Elphick & Malherbe, Die Khoisan ..., pp 24ff. For the Namibian history, see R J Gordon,

The Bushman myth: the making of a Namibian underclass, Boulder: Westview Press, 1992.

48 This has been contradicted by Van der Merwe, *Die noordwaartse beweging ...*, pp 139ff. However, neither Van der Merwe, nor Barrow and Dr Philip (against whom Van der Merwe reacts) question the morality of colonial intrusion into lands traditionally occupied by indigenous peoples.

49 Survival should not be defined in too narrow a sense as meaning just food. Wright, *Bushman raiders ...*, pp 188ff points out that, at least in Natal, raiding had come to be a valued means of providing the hunter-gatherers with valuable commodities for barter. They increasingly adopted goods obtainable only from outside and to some extent turned from being 'sheer predators' to stock-keeping. In addition, raiding the white farmers would have paid off in the form of protection and political alliances with powerful black leaders.

50 Cf Marks, Khoisan resistance ..., for a history of Khoisan resistance to the Dutch in the seventeenth and eighteenth centuries.

51 Over against the view that only the frontiersmen were responsible for the massacre of the hunters, M Legassick (The frontier tradition in South African historiography, in S Marks & A Atmore [eds], *Economy and society in pre-industrial South Africa*, London: Longman, 1990 [1980], pp 61ff) points out that the Dutch East India Company and the frontiersmen were equally responsible for the merciless war against them, and that the Griqua and Bastard frontiersmen of the Orange River valley dealt with these cattle-thieves just as harshly as white frontiersmen did. Cf Marais (*The Cape Coloured people ...*, pp 27ff) for chilling information about such killing sprees by Boer and mixed blood farmers in Bushmanland. Giliomee & Elphick (*'n Samelewing...*, p 568) argue that South African racial discrimination had its origin in the settled southwestern Cape as much as in the remote northern and eastern frontier areas.

52 Van der Merwe, *Die noordwaartse beweging ...*, pp 41ff.

53 Marais, *The Cape Coloured people ...*, p 19.

54 Ibid, p 25.

55 Marks, Khoisan Resistance ..., describes these three options open to the Khoisan.

56 Marais, *The Cape Coloured people ...*

57 Ibid, pp 19ff.

58 Ibid, pp 19ff for these efforts. The younger Stockenström 'was indefatigable in inculcating in his frontiersmen a due sense of the value of human life' (ibid, p 21). Van der Merwe (*Die noordwaartse beweging ...*, pp 66–97, 251–256, 276–278) gives an exhaustive description of efforts to befriend the hunters by various means such as hunting for them, involving people like Floris Visser, J G Louw, commandant Nel and Stockenström. Cf Legassick, The frontier tradition ..., p 62 on the fact that the hunters were not universally treated as enemies, but that at times other forms of relationships developed in which officials as well as frontiersmen were involved.

59 J J Kicherer, *Gedenkschriften van het Nederlandsch Zendeling-Genootchap, ter voortplanting en bevordering van het waare Christendom, bijzonder onder de heidenen, opgericht te Rotterdam den 19 van Wintermaand, des Jaars MDCCXCVII. Deel II*, Rotterdam; Cornel & Van Baalen, 1805, pp 226ff.

60 Walker, *A history ...*, p 148.

61 For short biographical sketches of the two Stockenströms, snr (Anders, 1757–1811) and jnr (Andries, 1792–1864), see the contributions by A H Tromp and A H Duminy respectively in *Suid-Afrikaanse biografiese woordeboek,* Vol I, Kaapstad: Tafelberg, 1976, pp 808–813.

62 Cf Van der Merwe, *Die noordwaartse beweging* ..., pp 252ff; Marais, *The Cape Coloured people* ..., pp 20ff.

63 Walker, *A History* ..., p 148.

64 Cf Wright, *Bushman raiders* ..., and Vinnicombe, *People of the Eland*, pp 9ff.

65 Ibid, pp 51ff.

66 This is the most important finding of Wright (*Bushman raiders* ..., p 191).

67 Cf M Wilson & L Thompson, *A history of South Africa to 1870*, Cape Town, Johannesburg: Philip, 1982, p 72. In the hunting existence, patient planning months and years ahead, as is required in a herding economy, and long-term postponement of enjoyment make no sense. One receives what nature offers now.

68 Wright, *Bushman raiders* ..., p 180.

69 Biesele (*Shaken roots: the Bushmen of Namibia*, Marshalltown: EDA, 1990) and Gordon (*The Bushman myth* ...) describe the situation in the aftermath of apartheid in Namibia.

70 Cf H J Heinz, The Bushmen in a changing world, in Tobias, *The Bushmen* ..., pp 173–178; G B Silberbauer, The future of the Bushmen, in Tobias, *The Bushmen* ..., pp 179–186; J C Hermans, *The Basarwa of Botswana: a case study in development*, MA dissertation, American University, Washington DC, 1982.

71 In the words of Silberbauer (The future of the Bushmen ..., p 185): 'there is much in the expert knowledge, cognition and outlook of the "wild" Bushmen which is of value to the rest of the world in confronting the environmental crisis. The intellectual and spiritual resources contained in these cultures should not be extinguished.'

14 In the eyes of Western beholders

The first century and a half

The process of colonisation was traumatic, not only for the hunter-gatherers but for the European settlers as well. On the one hand, confrontation with people so vastly different would have been a shock. To expect of the settlers *not* to have looked at the early inhabitants and their religion from within their own Western-Christian perspective is not realistic. It was inevitable. The real tragedy is that until the middle of this century the European settlement in South Africa never succeeded in breaking out of that mould, to meet the hunter-gatherers on any footing other than that of superior versus inferior. This underlying ideology, no less tragic because it was perhaps inevitable, triggered a series of actions and behavioural patterns that in certain places and periods led to virtual genocide. The whole course of events, however soberly described, amounts to a serious crisis of conscience, a religious crisis (although even today this may not be apprehended by many): is *that* what Christianity could lead to?

By the end of the eighteenth century woefully negative stereotypes had taken firm root among rank and file settlers – not only of the hunter-gatherers, but of 'non-whites' generally.[1] The hunter-gatherers occupied the lowest rung of the emerging social order, despised not only by whites but by all the other segments of the heterogeneous society. Yet by none were they held in such low esteem as by whites, who generally tended to regard them as virtually subhuman until well into the twentieth century.

Whatever the historical causes of racism in South Africa may have been, the general type of Christian outlook prevalent among the European settlers certainly played a role in the formation of discriminatory, racist attitudes – not in isolation, but conjoined as it was with political, economic and other social factors from the seventeenth century onwards. A comprehensive interpretation of that process, analysing the correlativity of such factors, falls outside our present scope.[2]

As far as institutionalised religion is concerned, until the end of the eighteenth century the established church simply did not have the social power, the theological motivation or the will to challenge the developing system of racial discrimination against slaves and the Khoisan.[3] A brief comparison with events in New England across the Atlantic Ocean shows that there other possibilities were realised, at least by a small minority. It is a religious tragedy, with equally tragic social consequences, that the early white dealings with hunter-gatherers in South Africa show no parallels to approaches such as those of Roger Williams (1603–1682) and William Penn (1644–1718), who founded colonies in New England. In Massachusetts Williams protested strongly against the occupation of the land without acknowledgment of the native Americans. The Puritans, like the Calvinists in South Africa, simply accepted as a matter of divine ordination that they had a right to land that was not fenced or farmed, over which the heathen roamed. When he founded his own new colony of Rhode Island in 1635, Williams bought land from the natives. This policy was motivated by an *in*clusive religious philosophy accommodating people of all shades of religious opinion, Christian as well as heathen.[4] Nearly half a century later, in 1682, William Penn founded the colony of Pennsylvania on the same basis. A Quaker from England, his first concern was freedom of conscience, flowing from the belief in an inner, divine light in every human being. He stood for a bold concept of radical freedom, much more than mere moderation or tolerance. When he came to America, his treatment of the native Americans was a natural extension of this philosophy. Before his departure from England he sent messages to the Indians informing them of his intention to settle only 'with your love and consent'. He undertook to seek a fair treaty and a firm 'league of peace', and charged his commissioners to 'be tender of offending the Indians ...; let them know that you are come to sit down lovingly among them'.[5] It did not inaugurate a lasting golden age, and Penn died a disappointed man. Yet acts such as these shine as beacons for generations to come.

It may be quite futile to speculate what could have happened 'if only ...';

yet one cannot help pondering how differently things might have worked out in South Africa *if*, sometime at the beginning, the seeds of a genuinely inclusive religious philosophy had been sown, and had taken root. That never happened, either at the beginning, or later.

By no stretch of the imagination can the Dutch East India Company's insistence that Van Riebeeck treat the Khoikhoi courteously and not harm them be presented as religiously inspired; its policy was meant to procure cattle and safeguard the interests of the Company. It is not without significance that at the first meeting of the Council of Policy Van Riebeeck prayed that decisions might be taken that would be of the greatest service to the Company, would maintain order, and (if possible) eventually spread the true Reformed teaching among 'these wild brutal people'.[6] Compared with the heterogeneity of the European settlements in America, the religious establishment at the Cape, strictly controlled by the Dutch East India Company,[7] was monolithic. None of the free traditions of the Radical Reformation then flourising in Holland, that haven for nonconformists from many countries and various persuasions, made it to the Cape.

The only religious conviction guiding the minds and actions of the colonists during the first century and a half was the Dutch Reformed faith. Until 1780 the Dutch Reformed Church was the only recognised church. Furthermore, the quality of religious leadership at the Cape was uninspiring. As Du Toit has pointed out, the hold of Calvinism on the early settlers was tenuous:[8] it could not inspire them with the notion of being a chosen people, destined to bring Euro-Christian civilisation to the interior of Africa. During its first century and a half the established church at the Cape did not produce or attract religious intellectuals of remotely the same intellectual calibre and moral courage found in New England during the same period. Before 1799 there were no full-time Dutch Reformed missionaries at the Cape. Slaves and indigenous people were completely outside the religious ambit of local parishioners and officials alike. Early efforts by the 'sick-comforters' Willem Wylant and Pieter van der Stael to convert the heathen met with very limited success, and interest petered out before the end of the seventeenth century. The Huguenots who arrived from France in 1688 widened the general outlook of the local Dutch, but the religious liberty that they represented did not extend to tolerance and respect for the Khoisan religions.

The Moravian Georg Schmidt, who arrived in 1737, was forced to leave again in 1744 because he baptised his own converts among the indigenous people. It was only towards the end of the eighteenth century – with the return of the Moravians (1792), the start of the activities of the London Missionary Society (1799), the work of a new breed of Dutch Reformed ministers such as Helperus Ritzema van Lier and M C Vos, and the formation of the South African Missionary Society in 1799[9] – that missionary activity took off. However closely seventeenth century Reformed doctrine, as understood at the Cape, may have been associated with genuine individual piety, it simply could not nurture any other attitude towards the aborigines than one of religious and social disdain. It might have been softened by common human decency, but it did not have the resources to inspire an attitude of religious and social inclusiveness.

What Marais[10] says about the farmers ('Boers') applies equally to the colonial authorities in both Holland and Cape Town: they 'do not seem to have attempted to come to any sort of accommodation with the Bushmen whose hunting grounds they invaded, killing off their game and depriving them of their *veldkos*'. How could they, if the Cape ministers of their church at the time did not have the intellectual motivation and standing, the social independence and spiritual insight to lead them, even if it meant opposing the farmers as well as the civil authorities in Cape Town? From the very beginning of the settlement in the seventeenth century, through the eighteenth and nineteenth centuries, a deep chasm had grown between Christians (that is Europeans) on the one hand, and slaves and the autochthonous peoples on the other. Baptism as it was seen at the Cape was not a gateway to communion, but a wall of division, protecting European property and other rights.[11] This attitude persisted among the colonists during the entire period of their confrontation with the indigenous people.

More than a century and a half after the arrival of the Dutch settlers and after twenty years of virtual genocide in the late eighteenth century, official gestures of appeasement were made by British rulers and Boer inhabitants in the interior, but by then an ethos of violent intolerance had already become entrenched, and the fate of the hunting-gathering lifestyle had been sealed.

In the long term it was probably a foregone conclusion that this way of life would give way before the new economy. But the violent manner in which it happened – impoverishing the hunter-gatherers materially, stripping them of all human dignity, leaving them no realistic choice to adapt (if they wished) at their own pace – casts a morbid shadow over the religious history of the Dutch settlement and its extensions at the frontiers of the colony. Given the European presupposition of African inferiority, they might have had no real chance to come to terms with the hunter-gatherers on any footing other than that of conqueror and conquered. The ancient European belief in the Great Chain of Being enjoyed strong support in Europe at the end of the eighteenth century: European Man occupied the pinnacle of creation and Africans a much lower rung in the hierarchy of living things.[12] At the Cape, this was translated from abstract ontology into brute practice. The Noble Savage, that other great European construct of the time – designed by Europeans for Europeans, expressing European concerns, an indirect means of criticising European vices[13] – could not have found any echo among the settlers, given the conditions of the time.

Missionary efforts since the beginning of the nineteenth century

Did the missionaries, professionally trained to carry Christianity to non-European people, fare better? Before the arrival of Georg Schmidt in 1737 efforts to convert the Khoisan had been sporadic, badly organised and largely unsuccessful. It was only after the beginning of the nineteenth century that a few systematic attempts were made by the London Missionary Society to spread the faith among the hunter-gatherers living in the outlying areas of the colony. These efforts were short-lived and futile.

The first organised mission to the hunter-gatherers was led by the Dutch-born Johannes Jacobus Kicherer, who sailed for Cape Town in 1798 in the company of his compatriot Dr J T van der Kemp. Shortly after his arrival in 1799 he proceeded some 700 to 800 kilometres northeast of Cape Town to the Zak River. There, at *Blijde Vooruitzicht's Fontein* (or *Blijde Verwacht*), he founded a mission station among the hunter-gatherer Bushmen in 1800 on behalf of the London Missionary Society.[14] This missionary effort followed a recent treaty between the hunter-gatherers and the farmer Floris Visser[15] at a time when the farmers must have been appalled by the brutality of the massive killings of previous decades. The hunter-gatherers apparently saw Visser 'solemnly appeal to Almighty God to witness the transaction'.[16] Impressed by his habit of assembling his family for worship (so Moffat recounts in nineteenth century missionary style), they enquired about 'the Divine character' and asked for a Christian teacher. At Visser's insistence the Zak River mission was launched. Although the hunter-gatherers initially turned up in great numbers,[17] the mission among them soon petered out.[18] At most it served as a thoroughfare to the Namaqua and the black tribes in the interior, but it was abandoned completely in 1806. Kicherer eventually became pastor to the Dutch Reformed Church in Graaff Reinet.

In 1814 the London Missionary Society established a station beyond the Graaff-Reinet frontier, at Tooverberg (or Thornberg), in the vicinity of the present town of Colesberg.[19] It was founded by Erasmus Smit,[20] who arrived from Holland in 1804 and worked with Van der Kemp at Bethelsdorp from about 1809 until he moved to the new mission among the hunter-gatherers. Another station (Hephzibah) was founded in 1816 by William Fangler Corner,[21] who had arrived in Cape Town in 1811. Both missionary efforts met with limited success in domesticating the hunter-gatherers. At Hephzibah, gardens cultivated by the hunter-gatherers themselves, were laid out.[22] But eventually the missionaries were trapped between the hunter-gatherers and the farmers. In 1817 or 1818 both stations were abandoned at the instruction of the Cape colonial government.[23]

The last effort of the London Missionary Society to establish a mission among the hunter-gatherers was made near the confluence of the Orange and Caledon rivers, at Bethulie. Named Bushman Station, it was founded by James Clark and George Augustus Kolbe in 1828. Initially it seemed a promising venture. Under the leadership of Landdrost Stockenström, missionaries and farmers jointly undertook to provide meat for the hunters, hoping that it would stop them from stealing. It also proved abortive very soon. The farmers, complaining that the hunters stole from them and then found refuge at the mission station, did not provide meat.[24] In 1833 it became a mission to the Tswana, run by the Paris Mission Society.[25]

Thus not one of these missionary efforts led to any large-scale or lasting establishment of Christianity. There were a few short-lived conversions by individuals, but no lasting translation of Christianity into the hunter-gatherer cultural setting, comparable to the appropriation of Christianity by the agricultural black peoples during the nineteenth century.[26] Given the assumptions of the middle-class European orthodoxy represented by all the missionary schools of the time, no such process was conceivable. The possibility of tapping resources available in the Christian tradition to tie in with the simple hunter-gatherer lifestyle was not considered. Any challenge from the world of the hunter-gatherers to reinterpret Christianity would have been out of bounds, at a time when Christianity was one aspect of the package deal of modern European colonialist expansion.

Since the middle of the nineteenth century the number of hunter-gatherers has dwindled in South Africa. Such remnants as were absorbed into the Cape 'coloured' people were gradually Christianised, but they lost all distinctive features of the hunter-gatherer existence. Outside South Africa, in Namibia[27] and Botswana,[28] various churches have tried since the last century to bridge the chasm dividing Christianity and aboriginal ways. Such efforts were moderately successful, proportionate to the extent that the hunter-gatherers abandoned their traditional way of life. The entire history of missionary efforts seemed to demonstrate that Christianity and the classical hunting-gathering culture were completely incompatible. This was the view held almost universally by Christians/whites. The migratory existence of the hunter-gatherers, making sustained efforts at teaching almost impossible, was certainly an important factor, although not the only one. There was also the unquestioned underlying assumption of the cultural superiority of the colonising Western countries, the acceptance of the ruler's religion by the colonised[29] and the identification of Christianity with Western culture.

If most nineteenth-century missionaries tended to have a very low opinion of African culture generally,[30] their views of the hunter-gatherers were devoid of any respect whatsoever. A few examples of missionary opinions confirm this. In his accounts Kicherer, the first to bring them the Christian gospel, reported that they had no idea of divinity, that they were utterly disgusting, dirty and lazy, staying in holes in the ground like pigs in a sty, viciously killing even their own children without remorse and abandoning helpless old people.[31]

Robert Moffat (1795–1883), the renowned Christian missionary to the northern Cape, had occasional dealings with the hunter-gatherers. He referred to them[32] as 'the feeblest, poorest, most degraded and despised of all the sable sons of Ham', 'the most abject of our species'. In fact, the failure of Kicherer's mission was a blessing in disguise, because God had 'far more extensive ends to accomplish, than simply a mission to the Bushmen'. While admitting that he once was grateful to a Bushman woman for a meal of ant larvae, and acknowledging that 'they can be kind, and hospitable too; faithful to their charge, grateful for favours, and susceptible to kindness', and that they are the way they are because they have been deprived of their livelihood, he declares that with 'the exception of the Troglodytes, a people said by Pliny to exist in the interior of Northern Africa, no tribe or people are surely more brutish, ignorant, and miserable, than the Bushmen of the interior of South Africa'.

Dr John Philip (1775–1851), outspoken champion of the British imperial ideal and severe critic of the Boers, rejected the wholly negative picture of the hunter-gatherers as a caricature.[33] They were, he found, indeed in a very ignorant and degraded state, but this was a result of their depressed conditions, not of any lack of mental capacity. They were susceptible to kindness, grateful for favours, faithful, and disposed to receive instruction.[34] In support of his argument that they were naturally highly talented people, Philip also quoted the following remarkable words of a hunter, addressed to his fellows at a mission station:

> *Why is it that we are persecuted and oppressed by the Christians? Is it because we live in desert lands, clothe ourselves with skins, and feed on locusts and wild honey?...Was not John the Baptist a Bushman? Did he not dwell in a wilderness? Was he not clothed with a leathern girdle, such as we wear? And did he not feed on locusts and wild honey? Was he not a Bushman?*[35]

Philip did not take up this magnificent challenge to Christian theology to see through its own modern Western cultural accretions and its ideological expression of Western expansionism.

He supported Collins's claim 'that there is not upon the face of the globe a people possessed of better natural abilities, or more susceptible of mental or moral improvement'.[36] The bad state they were in, he claimed, was the result of the land-grabbing of the white colonists who bedevilled the efforts of the missionaries to raise them to the heights of Christian European civilisation. In a sense Philip's views anticipated humane attitudes which only really came to the fore in the twentieth century, notwithstanding his naive belief in the superiority of contemporary British civilisation which, to him, was synonymous with Christianity.[37] He did not in the least question the political and cultural conquest of the African people.[38] Missionaries 'are, by the most unexceptionable means, extending British interests, British influence, and the British empire'.[39] White British missionaries, those champions of Euro-Christianity in the interior of the Cape (understood as 'a polarized human universe of unregenerate natives and degenerate Dutchmen'[40]) were the benevolent donors of British politicoreligious goods; the nomads of the interior could only be grateful recipients. Religiously, they had absolutely nothing of value.

The late nineteenth and twentieth centuries

Historians, the designers of the past, are part of the story they tell and reflect the trends discernible in it. The hunter-gatherers existed in the eyes of their beholders, whose mental pictures of them reproduced in South African historiography are variations on larger, ideologically determined, collective themes.[41] Imperialist historians (whether British or Boer) saw them as inferior obstacles to rightful expansion and domination; liberal colonialist historians saw them as objects of condescending pity; and radical anti-colonialists saw them as handicapped heroes. The first and the second categories held them at arm's length with a mixture of disgust and pity. Only the third, like the anthropologists of recent decades, made efforts to establish some positive rapport with them. A few examples will illustrate the point.

The picture of the hunter-gatherers that the historian G M Theal (1837–1919) presented is typical of the scornful attitude that dominated among Europeans until the twentieth-century. He was completely uncritical in his acceptance of European superiority and supremacy in all fields. African peoples (nomads, Khoikhoi and blacks) were simply background figures resisting the efforts of Europeans to bring civilisation to a dark continent. His description of the nomads, given at the close of the nineteenth-century, reveals an astonishing lack of information and understanding of their culture, based on rank Eurocentric racism: they are not only 'hideous in appearance', but also 'vindictive, passionate and cruel in the extreme', sacrificing human life – even that of their nearest kin – at the slightest provocation; it is difficult, he finds, 'to conceive of human beings in a more degraded condition than that of the Bushmen'; 'all their religious ideas were vague and childish', and 'their paintings are not superior to the drawings on slates of European children eight or nine years of age'.[42] His contempt of every aspect of their life, from their physical appearance to their language, permeates every discussion of them. Even their virtues are despised – their gratitude for acts of kindness is merely similar to that of 'those wild animals that in a state of restraint show attachment to their keepers'.[43] As if this was not enough, he construes their rich mythology as the result of their very low 'reasoning power', on a par with that of 'European children five or six years of age'[44] – imagine actually believing that different species of game can converse with each other, or that the stars were once human beings![45] They do, he concedes, possess a faculty of which Europeans are destitute, namely the ability to 'make their way in a straight line to any place where they had been before' – although many inferior animals, notably the dove, have this faculty, 'so that is not surprising to find the lowest type of man in possession of it'.[46] Their dancing 'was a mere quivering of the body and stamping of the feet'.[47] All the efforts made by early nineteenth-century missionaries to improve their situation were in vain, and all reports of some success by missionaries are merely misleading. They are incapable of any 'high civilisation'.[48]

In 1928 the liberal historian Eric Walker conceals his contempt somewhat better than Theal. He too provides the seemingly obligatory sketch of the hunting-gathering way of life, marginally better informed than that of Theal, commenting that their neighbours 'may be pardoned for doubting that they were quite human'.[49] Far more sympathetic is the picture drawn by J S Marais in 1939. He regrets that no effort was made by the incoming Boers to come to an agreement with them, believing that 'given time and a certain amount of protection, the Bushmen were not incapable of advancing to the pastoral stage of civilisation', as they demonstrated by turning into faithful and efficient herdsmen.[50]

It is, however, only in so-called 'radical'[51] historiography that the earlier inhabitants of the country are rehabilitated and given attention as actors in their own right – if not in the popular conception, then at least in some academic circles.[52] This accent concurs with anthropological reappraisals of the hunter-gatherers over the last few decades.[53] At last they were seen not as subhuman, or as mere passive victims of circumstances beyond their control, but as active participants in the ongoing historical process of South Africa. In the next chapter these approaches will be viewed in a wider religiophilosophical framework.

ENDNOTES

1 Cf Giliomee and Elphick, *'n Samelewing in wording, 1652–1840*, pp 562ff. on the final division, by the end of the eighteenth century, between whites, who regarded themselves as Christian and therefore entitled to civil rights and the nonwhite 'heathen'.

2 Giliomee and Elphick (*'n Samelewing* ..., pp 535ff) discuss four explanations of the origin of South African racism, each emphasising different factors: (a) according to the liberal view, it originated in the Dutch period before 1795, as a result of Calvinism, isolation and conflicts at the frontiers of the colony; (b) the revisionist view, inaugurated by Legassick (The Frontier Tradition ...), emphasises the role of industrial capitalism after 1867; (c) the interpretation midway between (a) and (b), proposed by D van Arkel, G C Quispel and R J Ross, *De wijngaard des Heeren? Een onderzoek naar de wortels van 'de blanke baasskap' in Zuid-Afrika*, Leiden: Nijhoff, 1983, maintains that a rigid racial order did arise in the pre-industrial era – not at the frontiers, however, but as a result of the incorporation of the Cape into the world economy during the first half of the nineteenth century; (d) Elphick and Giliomee's view that racial discrimination was introduced by the Dutch East India Company itself in the seventeenth century – it did not arise on the Cape frontiers, and was not the result of economical factors.

3 Cf Giliomee & Elphick, *'n Samelewing* ..., pp 550ff.

4 Cf Edwin Scott Gaustad, *A religious history of America: new revised edition*, New York: Harper & Row, 1990, pp 65ff.

5 Ibid, pp 91.

6 Z J Lazarus, Die stigting en vroeë jare van die Suid-Afrikaanse sendinggenootskappe 1799–1803, MA dissertation, University of Stellenbosch, 1948, p 8.

7 Cf J Alton Templin, *Ideology on a frontier. The theological foundation of Afrikaner nationalism, 1652–1910*, London: Greenwood Press, 1984, p 63f: in 1642 the decree was issued that 'in prescribed lands no other service of religion shall be allowed, much less taught or propagated, whether privately or public, than the Reformed Christian faith which is taught in the churches of the United Netherlands'.

8 Cf André du Toit, No chosen people: the myth of the Calvinist origins of Afrikaner nationalism and racial ideology, *The American Historical Review*, 1983, 88(4), pp 920–952. He argues that the myth was generated by secondary literature about Afrikaner history, and then appropriated by Afrikaners. For a discussion of the role of Calvinism in the early period of Dutch settlement, also see Giliomee and Elphick, *'n Samelewing* ..., pp 539 ff; Andrew Ross, *John Philip (1775–1851). Missions, race and politics in South Africa*, Aberdeen: University Press, 1986, pp 20–22.

9 Cf Lazarus, *Die stigting* ..., pp 23ff.

10 Marais, *The cape coloured* ..., pp 15.

11 Cf Robert C-H Shell, Religion, civic status and slavery from Dordt to the Trek, unpublished paper, read at Conference on People, Power and Culture: the History of Christianity in South Africa 1792–1992, at the University of the Western Cape (12–15 August 1992).

12 Cf Philip D Curtin, *The image of Africa. British ideas and action, 1780–1850*, Madison: University of Wisconsin Press, 1964, pp 37ff.

13 See ibid, pp 48ff for this idea/ideal, which enjoyed great popularity in the last three decades of the eighteenth century, petering out slowly during the first half of the nineteenth century. In fact, Curtin (ibid, p 480) concludes that not only this particular one, but every 'image of Africa, in short, was largely created in Europe to suit European needs – sometimes material needs, more often intellectual needs. When these needs allowed, it might touch on reality; as it did in the empirical victory of tropical medicine. Otherwise the European *Afrika-anschauung* was part of a European *weltanschauung*, and it was warped as necessary to make it fit into the larger whole.' Also cf Comaroff & Comaroff, *Of Revelation and Revolution. Christianity, Colonialism, and Consciousness in South Africa*, Vol One, Chicago: University Press, 1991, pp 109ff.

14 Cf J Sibree, *A register of missionaries, deputations, etc from 1796 to 1923*, London: London Missionary Society, 1923; D J Richter, *Geschichte der Evangelischen Mission in Afrika*, Gütersloh: C Bertelsmann, 1922, pp 275–6.

15 Robert Moffat, *Missionary labours and scenes in Southern Africa*, London: John Snow, 1842, pp 49ff.

16 Ibid, p 50.

17 Kicherer, *Gedenkschriften ...*, pp 230ff.

18 Cf Moffat, *Missionary labours ...*, pp 52ff.

19 Marais, *The Cape coloured ...*, p 30; Sibree, *A register ...*; Richter, *Geschichte ...*, p 276.

20 Smit (1778–1863) was a somewhat pathetic victim of the times, caught in the political and cultural cross-fire, his loyalties divided between the London Missionary Society, the frontier farmers (in 1836 he joined Gert Maritz in the Great Trek) and the indigenous people whom he tried to serve unsuccessfully as missionary (for a biographical sketch, cf F J du Toit Spies, *Suid-Afrikaanse Biografiese Woordeboek*, Vol I, 1976, pp 760–761).

21 According to Sibree, *A register ...*, he was 'a negro', born in Demerara.

22 John Philip, *Researches in South Africa; illustrating the civil, moral, and religious condition of the natives: including journals of the author's travels in the interior; together with detailed accounts of the progress of the Christian missions, exhibiting the influence of Christianity in promoting civilization*, Vol. II, London: James Duncan, 1828, pp 21, 26ff.

23 John Philip, *Researches ...*, pp 23ff.

24 Van der Merwe, *Die noordwaartse beweging ...*, pp 252ff.

25 Moffat, *Missionary labour ...*, pp 61ff.

26 The process of mission work among the Tswana has been analysed by Comaroff & Comaroff, *Of revelation ....* Also cf Elizabeth Elbourne, Early Khoisan Uses of Mission Christianity, unpublished paper, Conference on People, Power and Culture: the History of Christianity in South Africa 1792–1992, University of the Western Cape, 12–15 August 1992; as well as Leon de Kock, The Literary and the Historical: Missionary Discourse at Lovedale in the Nineteenth Century and the Contestation of Subjectivity, paper read at the same congress.

27 On the efforts of the Dutch Reformed Church, the Lutherans and the Roman

Catholics in that country, cf J H Smit (red), *Die Ned Geref Kerk onder die Boesmans – grepe uit die navorsing van die Departement Sendingwetenskap aan die UOVS*, Bloemfontein: Universiteit van die Oranje-Vrystaat, 1986, pp 16ff; Gordon, *The Bushman myth* ..., pp 143ff, 177–181, 210ff.

28 In 1978 Heinz (The Bushmen in a changing world, pp 173ff) described various mission projects among the hunter-gatherers, all aimed at providing them with the skills necessary for survival in the contemporary world.

29 Cf Willem Saayman, *Christian mission in South Africa, political and ecumenical*, Pretoria: Unisa, 1991.

30 Cf Comaroff and Comaroff, *Of revelation* ...

31 Kicherer, *Gedenkschrifte* ..., pp 226ff.

32 Ibid, pp 50ff.

33 Philip, *Researches* ..., pp 7ff.

34 Ibid pp 9ff, based on a very positive estimation of the character of the nomads by the Dutch Reformed minister A Faure.

35 Ibid, pp 12ff.

36 Ibid, p 14.

37 Ibid, pp 354ff on the 'intimate connexion between Civilization and Christianity'.

38 For a recent evaluation of Philip from the point of view of Christian missions, cf Saayman, *Christian mission* ..., pp 38–42.

39 Philip, *Researches* ..., pp ix-x.

40 Comaroff and Comaroff, *Of revelation* ..., p 95.

41 Ken Smith, *The changing past Trends in South African historical writing*, Johannesburg: Southern, 1988 describes the ideological and wider philosopical frameworks of some South African historians.

42 Theal, *History of South Africa* ..., pp 191–5.

43 Theal, *The beginning of South African history*, London: T Fisher Unwin, 1902, p 14.

44 Ibid, pp 15ff.

45 Ibid, p 15.

46 Ibid, p 17.

47 Ibid, p 18.

48 Ibid, pp 18ff.

49 Walker, *A history* ..., p 33.

50 Marais, *The Cape coloured* ..., pp 22ff.

51 Cf Smith, *The changing past* ..., pp 155–228.

52 Among such efforts a fine example is the article by Marks, Khoisan resistance ..., dealing with their resistance to the Dutch in the seventeenth and eighteenth centuries.

53 Gordon, *The Bushman myth* ..., p 216ff gives a recent overview of this change. Matthias G Guenther's article summarises the change tersely: From 'Brutal Savages' to 'Harmless People', *Paideuma*, 1980, 26, pp 123–140.

15 From sociohistoric to religious correlativity

The understanding of the hunter-gatherers proposed here is a concretisation, in the sociohistorical sphere, of various factors, including the author's research and experience of South African realities, the researches of many other people, and a certain theoretical orientation. It is (we trust) a fruitful confluence of these and other factors, not the mere application or projection of an extraneous philosophy onto the data. Neither is it a virgin birth, an interpretation springing from the data. These factors have grown together for the short duration of this book. In turn, each one of them happens to be a confluence itself. The 'meaning' of this chapter, its possible 'truth', is largely a function of these 'meetings' – a negotiated settlement for the time being – between a number of perspectives, including those of students, specialists and general readers. Indeed, there can be no 'settle-ment' in the sense of a fixed, established constant, at all. It lives in its passing away.

Concurrences

The author is a moving locus on a moving sociohistorical field, with a long historical preamble (partly remembered, partly carried unconsciously) and an anticipated future. In every direction the author is surrounded by and embedded in expanding configurations of social relations, each with historical dimensions. And of course the past has not really been left behind at all. It is present now, as it is in the anticipated future. This locus, as well as the grid of which it is a component, is continually changing.

There really is no fixed entity Christianity or Buddhism. Not only are they historically highly multifarious religious complexes, but they 'are' what millions of people (receiving, appropriating and adapting these living organic traditions, and being absorbed into them) have taken them to be. So 'Christianity' and 'Buddhism' in these essays are what the author understands them to be, at the same time being moulded by them and interacting with the understanding of adherents and specialists in the field. Likewise, there is no point in establishing 'Whiteheadianism'. Such a fixation would fly in the face of the multitude of impulses, not perfectly harmonised, coming from the vigorous school of reflection inspired by Whitehead – whose thinking in turn was a series of syntheses of several Western traditions, many facets of his contemporary world and his own biographical experiences; and who (in his own terminology) *is* today, in the mode of 'objective immortality', still functioning. Again (as with the 'Bushmen') a curiously fluid (non)identity, with no fixed boundaries between past, present and future, 'self' and 'others'.

So the understanding of the hunter-gatherers in these chapters is a flickering shaft of cognition, momentarily illuminating ... what? And for whom? Let us first consider for whom. Other people (readers) obviously, singular and plural, each of whom may similarly be broken down into a variety of constitutive factors, each factor involved in ever-widening circles of reciprocally structured connections in which a multiplicity of factors interact simultaneously.

All individuals and societies are devoid of self-sufficient existence. They are interdependent. This does not deny the plurality of social actors, whether individual or collective, as centres of initiative and force, nor does it reduce them all to some undifferentiated entity such as 'humanity'. The 'inter-' distinguishes and differentiates, as well as binds and integrates. It constitutes the uniqueness, the realness, of every specific, concrete human source of action (individual or collective), and creates space for the differences between the plurality of actors. It relativises each by relating it to others. They are conditioned, each by the other, in an ever-widening network of connections. The penetration and intensity of the historical mutuality and interdependence between modern, colonialist Westerners who have made South Africa their home and aboriginal hunter-gatherers are such that it may well be explained (in Hua-yen terminology) as a mutual interpenetration – to the extent that by misunderstanding and harming the hunter-gatherers the moderns were in effect misunderstanding and harming themselves, and that a peaceful accommodation with the hunter-gatherers would have been to the everlasting benefit of those moderns who settled here. The hunter-gatherers are present in the moderns, reminding them of their lost origins, relativising the historical route their culture and religion have taken, forcing their Christian institutions to reflect on their loss of the spirit of the one whom they regard as their founder.

As far as the 'what' of the cognition is concerned, it has become clear that there too we have a pluralistic, kaleidoscopic range of factors. Neither 'the hunter-gatherers' nor 'the whites' nor 'the blacks' should be reified as if they were solid blocs. We cannot avoid using such generalised words, but they are simply shorthand enabling us to communicate somehow. What is more, 'the hunter-gatherers' are not really 'out there'. In a sense, they are present in 'us' moderns, as they were present in their contemporaries in the eighteenth century. There is no such thing as a 'neutral' understanding of them as an 'object' by a completely separate 'subject' or 'subjects'. It is conceivable that in some minds – for example that of Laurens van der Post – the hunter-gatherers could acquire almost mythical status. For they provoke and challenge our complacency about the unquestioned nature of 'Western civilisation', 'Christianity', 'modernity', 'technology', and so forth. In a sense, in spite of having vanished, they are ubiquitous, at least in southern Africa. 'The West', 'Africa' and 'the East' really are interpenetrating complexes. The point is not to deny the existence/reality of such entities, but to see them as the crossing of roads.

What has been said implies that any claim to a totalising interpretation of history is unjustified. All we have is a flickering glimpse of a changeable conjuncture. 'I' may look at the whole of South African history integrally ('religiously'). Even when 'I' look at one aspect of the world (for example the hunter-gatherers), I involuntarily interpret it as an element of a larger pattern, perhaps even of the overall context of my idea of 'the whole' – from where I hover *within* it.

Multiple reciprocal causality

This understanding – moving away from substance to relation, from self-sufficiency to interdependence, from separation to integration, and from identity to differentiation – therefore takes leave of monocausal (one-cause), unidirectional (one-way) explanations of sociohistorical processes. Such an understanding precludes all efforts to stage simple plays with a small cast and a simple plot. None of the actors – not the hunter-gatherers, the Khoikhoi, the blacks, the political administrators, the Boers or the missionaries (consider the multiple identity of Erasmus Smit!) – was a closed entity. Simultaneously and over a long time, internally in each individual group and externally among all of them, a whole gamut of interactions took place, from persuasion to coercion, from protest to withdrawal to submission, and so on. A 'religious' understanding, trying to fathom the complex processes of human integration and dis-integration, would not differ essentially from sociological and cultural-anthropological efforts to unravel the webs of factors knotted in individual events. There is no gap between sociological explanations and religious explanations. A religious explanation is simply a radically conditionalist explanation, following the threads in the webs of correlationality where they lead, as far as possible.

In religious talk, as traditionally conducted in South Africa, God is seen as directing historical events from *outside* those events; or, if he acts from *within* the system of the world, he does so as a distinctly separate Person, an individual writ large. Insofar as historical events have a 'divine' dimension, they point to God, whose finger, hand or footsteps are discernible in the world, or who acts from above and outside. Either that, or rank 'atheism': that is the understanding. According to such arguments, God acted (or acts) particularly and decisively in selected historical events, such as leading Israel from bondage in Egypt; guiding Western Europeans (the Dutch, the Huguenots, the British, the trekboers, the church or the missionaries) to the southernmost tip of Africa and into the interior to civilise and christianise the barbaric heathen; or black resistance to apartheid. The 'religious' talk developed in these essays rejects the view of two realities; of supernatural, ahistorical or absolute entities; of an identifiable first cause, whether inside or outside the context of the empirical world; and of one particular group or organisation with exclusive claims to Truth. Instead, it provides a religiophilosophical underpinning for multifactorial explanations, in terms of reciprocally connected circuits of contingency.

This view does not exclude that certain events, seen as intertwined knots of many strands, are particularly rich in meaning involving the whole of the human race; particularly decisive in their sociohistorical impact; particularly replete with seeds encapsulating the past and anticipating the future – even uniquely so. But such evaluations, however legitimate, are made from the points of view of individuals and groups, small or large (even major cultural and religious communities spanning millennia). To claim that any such evaluation is absolute, as if emerging from a vantage point outside the network of empirical reality, is preposterous. Even if there were such an absolute, humans would only know it in its sociohistorical correlativity. For all practical purposes, it 'is' in no other mode than a sociohistorically conditioned one.

The depth of this contingent world itself – and not some foundation underlying it, grounding that universal interdependence – is 'the divine', or 'God'. Neither the concept 'transcendence' nor 'immanence' is appropriate here, since both imply separateness of being – whether located outside or residing inside the correlative world, or both. In respect of 'God', even Whitehead did not articulate the philosophy of radical contingency consistently. In a sense, to him God remained outside the interdependence of all actual entities in the world.

The concrete South African experience of passing from one sociohistorical epoch to another, an experience fraught with anxiety and possibilities, invites the discovery of the lightness of human existence-in-the-world, a religion of radical 'self-less' reciprocity.[1]

We humans cannot position ourselves outside the field of sociohistorical correlativity. Does this mean that the world is dissolved into human culture? No. In a sense, whatever is is a 'pluriverse': many worlds constituted, known and inhabited by the many individuals and groups. But we may accept that all those relatively idiosyncratic views presuppose a 'homoverse', a pluralistically constituted yet common human world, one with certain characteristics seen by humanity as a genus. Humanity (the common human world) is joined with nature. We humans may constitute the world; but we did not create it. Long before we appeared on the scene, nature was there – as we, *as humans*, know. It seems that we cannot have the one without the other. Neither 'naturalism' nor 'culturalism' is adequate. The world both 'is' and 'is not' apart from us humans, as we humans both 'are' and 'are not' apart from nonhuman nature. Culture and nature cannot be unscrambled, but they cannot be identified either. It does have the implication of (in one sense!) de-anthropo-centring the world. Again: uniqueness-in-solidarity, identity-as-relationality. We are enmeshed in a greater, more than human world of interacting forces, as thinking reeds. We need a synthesis of cosmology and humanism.

Time for change

We live in a time of changes; more than that, in a time of change. These two senses do not coincide. The plural indicates that many things change: familiar institutions are replaced by unfamiliar ones, previously 'independent' states in South Africa disappear, and so on. The singular is far more profound and shattering in its impact, indicating that we are discovering change as such, change as the all-pervading texture of reality itself. In the first case, one can live with many and even dramatic changes, but they can – perhaps – still be treated as exceptions in an overall stable order. In the second case one loses the very notion of a stable metaphysical order; change and time are no longer bearable against the backdrop of something else, namely unchanging eternity. If one wants to speak of 'eternity' at all, one would have to discover it in change and time as such – that is, *in* the experience of radical contingency, finitude, impermanence, not *outside* it. The present epoch in our history forces us to relinquish all notions of a fixed eternity that is somehow outside time. It is 'time for change'.

At least some aspects of such a new attitude seem to be clearly discernible in the perspective that we have adhered to throughout. It would mean learning to immerse ourselves completely in the present moment of change, not yearning for an eternity outside it, or hankering after a past; accepting into ourselves, into this present moment of change, the cumulative process of the past; realising that this present moment is creative, not merely neutral time, but truly a *kairos* filled with possibilities. It is shaped by the past, but it also shapes and reshapes the past by reinterpreting it: by constantly fitting and refitting 'past' events as factors into present, new, changing constellations of meaning. In that sense, the hunter-gatherers are with us in the now. Similarly, events that have passed away (such as the acts of genocide) will be present in the future too. And obviously the present moment is filled with creative possibilities for the future.

The process of history too may be understood in terms of the spiral of 'transcendence' and 'integration': projecting into the unknown future, and returning to the past, absorbing it into the movement into the future. These are two aspects of the same dynamic process. The future is not a mere repeat of the past. Our experience of change and history cannot be merely *cyclical* like the experience of the returning seasons; we cannot become hunter-gatherers again. But neither is the past merely behind us and done with. The notion of *linear* progress like an arrow in flight, against the backdrop of an eternal order, in an onward march towards Westernisation or predetermined Christianisation, has lost its meaning; we have to return to the hunter-gatherers, and from there take off again. So in the spiral of our religious history, it is time for a reintegration with 'primal' religion, for an enriching re-link with the past, precisely in order to move forward beyond the present. It is not a matter of turning around and merely *looking* back from a distance, but – in a sense – of *going* back. Of course it would be nonsensical to even try to forget ourselves, or to leave the present moment. The concrete moment of historical remembrance is really 'con-crete': a 'grown-together'-ness, a 'mutual inter-penetration', a 'co-presence' of hunter-gatherers and moderns, of past and present – but without denying the distance between these. Not repeat, but return (in a sense) – with a view to the future.

Now is the time to *make* a change. The present is the birth of a new set of conditions, not discontinuous with what preceded it, but certainly not static; capable of either closure or opening up further to more inclusive solidarity between human groups and between humans and nonhuman beings. Immersion into the now, into this present set of conditionalist relationships, implies more than keeping up with the ever-changing scene. It implies vigorous commitment to a morality of mutuality, an ethos of actively seeking ever-widening sets of relationships. Adapting Albert Schweitzer's 'reverence for life', one may speak of an all-pervasive reverence for all beings as assemblages.

Beyond religious absolutism

This approach to the hunter-gatherers criticises the ideological alliance of power and piety, Euro-Christian expansionism masquerading as the gospel of Jesus Christ. It is indeed time that we discover the implications of religious pluralism. Far more than vapid tolerance, it would involve rigorous *comparison*, mutual *criticism*, *confrontation* and reciprocal *correction*, culminating in *positive participation*.[2] The latter is possible on the basis of the epistemology and ontology explored here. The inherent logic of Christianity – that of emptying, poverty and the rejection of human idolatry – does not tally with efforts to exempt this particular sociohistoric entity from the rule of universal interdependence. Each religious complex is unique – a unique manifestation of the homoversal religious need. True Christianity is present in the hunter-gatherer way, and vice versa – in their differences. No set of religious symbols is absolute. They emerge and submerge in the endless interplay between humans, and between humans and the world of nature. For some, the symbols of Father and King (or Mother and Queen) express the depth of the world; for others – as we shall see in following chapters – it may be perceived through animal symbolism.

It is easy to criticise ordinary people of one, two and three centuries ago for acting in ways that were legitimised by their religion at the time. Yet the failure of the dominant Euro-Christian culture to integrate with the hunter-gatherer outlook in a common human bond remains a tragedy.

Correlativity and African religious thought

As we have said from the beginning, these essays do not pass through black African religious thought. Yet it is clear that interesting possibilities of convergence open up between that thought, a process philosophy approach, a Christianty reinterpreted along such lines, and Eastern philosophies (notably Taoism). Such explorations cannot be undertaken here. We can only present a few pointers to African analogues.

The African theologian Gabriel Setiloane challenges the missionary identification of the Sotho-Tswana concept of God (Modimo) as 'a' Being. Instead, he finds the essence of (at least) the Sotho-Tswana idea of divinity to be panentheistic.[3] Modimo is 'Participation Vitale' – 'energy that is ever active, initiating action, and maintaining interaction'. Critical of conventional Western Christian thought, he suggests alliances with contemporary science, for example physics and evolutionary biology. African religion is the instinct for relations in every sphere of life. Modimo is the supreme expression of that belief. Which prompts another purely speculative but fascinating 'if ...' question: how would black African intellectuals generally have articulated the African view of God *if* the contact made with an extraneous missionary religion had been with pantheist/panentheist/metatheist Buddhism? For one can speculate that the presentations, by both missionaries and Africans, of the traditional African views as at least fairly similar to monotheism, were efforts to accommodate to a dominant religiocultural power.[4]

The ideas put forward by Setiloane are not idiosyncratic. Both in African philosophy and theology there have been serious attempts to spell out the implications of the African 'root' experience. Instead of giving a résumé of the various views and entering critically into the intricacies of the debates,[5] some ideas of K C Anyanwu may be cited as a sample of one trend in African philsophy: the African's 'basic assumption about nature', he says, is that 'life-force permeates the whole universe and that matter and spirit are an inseparable reality. Behind the natural things and intimately co-existing with them is the non-material power. This life-force ... has existed from the beginning of the world ... is active ... is impersonal and non-conscious yet constitutes the individuality of every living-force or individual[6] ... Since everything is in everything else and conditioned by everything else, there are no static or permanent positions in the universe. There is no firm hold anywhere. The universe of life-force is one of transformation and transmutation ... No clear and definite opposites exist in the African unitary world because everything is one; each in each; all through everybody else'.[7]

The challenge to 'white' South African religious thought is to realise the essential reciprocity between the West and Africa[8] – and, I add with great emphasis, Asia. Only in dialogue – discovering, respecting and appreciating the 'other'-ness and distinctiveness of the other – will the possibility of an open-ended pluralism arise, in mutuality, beyond domination of any kind: not a shouting match, or parallel monologues, but a polyphonic chorus. Strange that such creative experiments have been undertaken in South African painting, sculpture, music – but not in religious academia and ecclesia.

Religious interhistory: a new South African religious historiography

What would a historiography of South African religions intent on *comprehending* (in both senses: *including* all religions, and *understanding* them in their togetherness) entail, according to the stance taken here? The main implications have already been outlined in earlier chapters, and need not be dwelt on here.

Such a historical perspective of South African religion(s) would include *all* religions in south(ern) Africa. This is not as self-evident as it may sound. Among the general public, there is certainly a noticeable need to know about the 'others' who have been pushed from the field of consciousness for so long. As for research, there have been a large number of specialist studies in various disciplines dealing with specific religions in this country, such as various African traditional religions, Christianity, Islam and Hinduism. These cover most of the field, and the number is steadily growing, so much so that it would be unfair to refer to specific authors and titles.[9]

But even an impressive body of specialist studies of the various religions does not add up to a comprehensive history of south(ern) African religion(s). Equally, if not more, important is the question of how these manifold religions should be related. How may the partial perceptions of various specialisms be integrated to form a coherent, inclusive understanding? After all, history is more than a jumble of facts from the past. Some things are selected as important; others are not. The evaluation of something as important presupposes an interpretation. Needed, therefore, is a theoretical framework, comprehensive and encompassing, capable of interpreting the entire religious heritage of South Africa, from the earliest forms up to the present – an integrating view of that religious complex. Obviously such a 'regional theory' would depend upon and may also contribute to wider, more general theorising about religion. The overwhelming majority of the papers read at the annual congresses of the Association for the Study of Religion (southern Africa) are valuable descriptions of aspects of specific religions as they manifest themselves in South Africa, but few acknowledge the need to view them as interwoven with a larger pattern of religions. A fine synoptic volume on the religions of South Africa appeared recently: David Chidester's *Religions of South Africa.*[10] Yet an enormous amount of work remains to be done. It is significant, for example, that the hunter-gatherers do not really feature in Chidester's book.

Obviously, a comprehensive history of religions would work 'from below'. That is, it would interpret the ongoing stream of religious history from a human point of view as the history of human actors. It would not base itself on any supernaturally revealed standpoint, and it would not seek for signs of any superhuman agents operating in the developments. It would be a human and social science like any other. For instance, while it would certainly see the seventeenth century as extremely important in the religious history of this country, it would not attribute those events to a special act of divine providence. As a matter of fact, in an inclusive framework the events of the seventeenth century would appear ambivalent in the extreme.

The intellectual right to look at all religions in the perspective of one religion – for example that of Islam, Judaism or Christianity – is not to be denied. That procedure would yield a variety of different theologies. This is not the place to discuss the merits or demerits of such interpretations of 'other' religions or the criteria that may be applied. Suffice it to say that writers of such histories have to take special care to avoid religious apartheid, which looms threateningly large in theological theories. The kind of religious history we are talking about here would not operate from within any particular religion. Rather, it would explore the spaces between and around the various religions, working according to general scholarly rules, inspired by and culminating in a philosophy of religion rather than a specific theology. Certainly it would not interpret religious history apologetically, vindicating any one religion.

Religious history is not to be viewed in disjunction from the natural (ecological) and the social (economic, political) developments of this part of the world. In a historical perspective, the interface between religion and society has received considerable attention. Over the last few decades an enormous anti-apartheid theological literature has developed, some of it of a very high quality. A weakness of virtually all the theological critiques of apartheid has been the failure of their theoretical (theological) framework to permit an extension of this critique to religious apartheid. Mostly the social and political critiques were launched from theologically conservative foundations, ranging from near-fundamentalism or even fundamentalism to varieties of middle-orthodoxy (Reformed, Roman Catholic, Lutheran, etc, sometimes with an admixture of Marxian social analysis) – but without overhauling those doctrinal presuppositions. Yet precisely that – an opening up to what lies beyond religious apartheid, beyond its present narrow religious parochialism and ethnocentricity – should characterise the new chapter in South African theological development.

The approach needed for an inclusive history of religions would show no trace of religious or cultural triumphalism. Religion in South Africa did not start in the seventeenth century. One of the motives for the present study was the hypothetical question: what might have happened *if* Christianity had been introduced into South Africa completely divorced from colonialism; if it had been presented from the beginning as organically related to the indigenous religions of Africa? How much religious schizophrenia has Africa suffered as a result of the colonial attitude? It is interesting to note that

Western Buddhists today find themselves in a somewhat similar position vis-à-vis Eastern culture to that of African Christians vis-à-vis European culture. To what extent does acceptance of a foreign religion entail accepting the culture in whose garb it arrives? For example, Buddhists ask themselves whether Buddhism is to be presented and accepted as a total package from the East, or whether it may be seen as an articulation of impulses within Western culture and religion. A critical difference between these two situations is the following: Christianity was brought to Africa as part of European colonialism; Buddhism entered Europe over the last century and a half in the wake of that same European colonialism. This has led to completely different patterns of reception. In stead of triumphalism, an inclusive religious historiography would embrace all as expressions of the same search. To adapt Terence, the maxim should be: I am a religious human being; I do not regard anything religious as foreign to me.

Certainly a comprehensive history will not confine itself to a naive description of how harmonious the relationships between the religions supposedly were. Such a picture would be patently untrue. A realistic history of religions will acknowledge the reality of conflict,[11] which is, after all, also a form of interaction. Unexplored as the territory of religious interhistory may be, it unfolds as a highly ambivalent tale, shot through with jarring conflict as well as peaceful acceptance, understanding as well as misunderstanding, continuity as well as blatant impositions. It is the story of some of the earliest humans on earth, their search for meaning evolving into the religions of hunter-gatherer societies; of Khoikhoi herders and Bantu-speaking agriculturalist-herders; of the arrival of the great expansionist missioneering religion of Christianity and the minority religion of Islam in the seventeenth-century, and of the great Indian religions of Hinduism and Buddhism in the nineteenth century; of twentieth-century secularism; and perhaps of a new time of religious understanding and cooperation, a new religious vision, as the twenty-first century approaches.

ENDNOTES

1 For a brilliant statement of this reorientation see R Panikkar, *The silence of God: the answer of the Buddha*, Maryknoll, NY: Orbis, 1989, pp 101ff.

2 Cf A Pieris, *Love meets wisdom: a Christian experience of Buddhism*, Maryknoll, NY: Orbis, 1988, p 17.

3 G M Setiloane, *African theology: an introduction*, Johannesburg: Skotaville, 1986,

p 28. However, in describing it as 'the presence of Divinity in the totality of life' he gives it another turn.

4 Setiloane, *African theology ...*, p 39 suggests as much.

5 For a survey, see the contributions in G Floistad, *Contemporary philosophy: a new survey*. Vol 5. *African philosophy*, Dordrecht: Nijhoff, 1987.

6 E A Ruch & K C Anyanwu, *African philosophy: an introduction to the main philosophical trends in contemporary Africa*, Rome: Catholic Book Agency, 1981, pp 89ff.

7 Ibid, p 93.

8 Of this need an acute awareness is to be found in Attie van Niekerk, *Sáám in Afrika*, Cape Town: Tafelberg, 1992.

9 Since this chapter entails a critical reappraisal of the historical role of Christianity in South Africa, a brief reference to the historiography of Christianity is appropriate.

Methodological and theoretical trends in general historical writing on South Africa have been analysed by K Smith in his *The changing past: trends in South African historical writing*, Johannesburg: Southern, 1988. The most widely accepted general models, starting with the earliest *colonialist* (that is essentially white-centred) perspective, proceeding to *liberal* (that is nonracial, integrative) historiography, and eventually to *Marxist* (that is class-centred, anticapitalist) and *black* interpretations were applied to the history of Christianity as well.

Examples of the first view, not making a radical break with the colonial era, are C P Groves, *The planting of Christianity in Africa,* Vols I-IV, London: Lutterworth, 1948–1958, and P B van der Watt, *Die Nederduitse Gereformeerde Kerk 1652–1975,* 2 vols, Pretoria: NG Kerk-Uitgewers, 1976– . A broadly liberal paradigm, highly critical of traditional church attitudes but drawing its critical tools from mainline theology rather than from the (neo-)Marxist arsenal, is presented in works such as J W de Gruchy, *The church struggle in South Africa*, Cape Town: Philip, 1979, and C Villa-Vicencio, *Trapped in apartheid: a socio-theological history of the English-speaking churches*, Maryknoll, NY: Orbis, 1988. An example of a critical approach firmly based on Marxist premisses is D Taylor's book (published under the pseudonym Nosipho Majeke), *The role of the missionaries in conquest*, sl, sa, which interprets Christian mission in Marxist terms as part of the capitalist exploitation of blacks. J Cochrane, *Servants of power: the role of English-speaking churches in South Africa 1903–1930. Towards a critical theology via an historical analysis of the Anglican and Methodist Churches*, Johannesburg: Ravan, 1987, operates within a similar paradigm. The black historical view of the presence of Christianity in South Africa is strongly articulated in various works, including J C Adonis, *Die afgebreekte skeidsmuur weer opgebou: die verstrengeling van die sendingbeleid van die Nederduitse Gereformeerde Kerk in Suid-Afrika met die praktyk en die ideologie van apartheid in historiese perspektief*, Amsterdam: Rodopi, 1982. There is a dearth of explicit methodological self-reflection in South African historiography on Christianity. One exception is C Landman, *Europe's role in a South African methodology: a sideline and female perspective*, Frankfurt am Main: Lang, 1992. The cutting edge of current South African historiography on Christianity may be represented in various papers presented at the Conference on People, Power and Culture: the History of Christianity in South Africa, 1792–1992, held at the University of the Western Cape, 12–15 August 1992, and in J W Hofmeyr & G J Pillay, *A history of Christianity in South Africa,* Vol 1, Pretoria: HAUM, 1994. However, none of the papers presented at the University of the Western Cape recognised the need to integrate a historiography of Christianity with a history of South African religions generally. Hofmeyr & Pillay made a start in that direction.

10 D Chidester, *Religions of South Africa*, London, New York: Routledge, 1992.

11 This approach is applied effectively by D Chidester, Religious studies as political practice, *Journal of Theology for Southern Africa*, 1987 58, pp 4–17; Stealing the sacred symbols: biblical interpretation in the People's Temple and the Unification Church, *Religion*, 1988 18, pp 137–162; *Religions of South Africa* ...

16 Excursion into Christian theology

Over the last few decades South African Christian theology has increasingly absorbed sociological and other styles of 'contextual hermeneutics', for example in the application of sociological models to the study of the first Christian community, in the development of sociopolitical models (political theology, black theology, feminist theology), and in reflections on the indigenisation of the Christian faith in non-Western societies.[1] So let us take the concept of 'context', as used by theologians, as our point of entry into the debate. The crucial question is whether or not, and how (if at all), such sociological models are integrated with the 'god-talk' of those disciplines (which is what the word 'theo-logy' means, after all). What is needed is some *necessary* connection between *sociological* (anthropological, historical, communication-theoretical, etc) explanations and *religious* explanations; a clarification of the religious (in this case theological) reasons *why* such models are applicable to theology. Are there any *intrinsic* links between 'contextual' talk on the level of human society (be it the first Christian community or contemporary South Africa) and 'god-talk' (God, the trinity, Christology, the church as the body of Christ, etc)? Unless such an integration is demonstrated (that is unless it is clear why and how their sociological analyses are part and parcel of the 'god-talk'), theology may be suspected of merely indulging in fashionable diversions, or of trying to escape from the difficulties of radical religious talk today.

By way of example I analyse five recent books by South African theologians in terms of our problem. Over the years four of them (David Bosch,[2] Albert Nolan,[3] Willem Saayman[4] and Charles Villa-Vicencio[5]) have taken courageous stands against apartheid, and all four adhere to mainline Western Christianity. To what extent do they offer an alternative to the kind of religious thinking that inspired the total disregard of hunter-gatherer religion? The fifth book (by Itumeleng Mosala[6]) articulates a rigorously critical black worker class approach to theology.

Bosch turns his critical attention to what he calls 'the intertwinement of colonialism and mission' in the modern era,[7] its 'compromise with and complicity in imperialism and colonial expansion'.[8] He insists (rightly) that there has always been a persistent critical minority (referring among others to J I van der Kemp and John Philip), but concedes that they never doubted the legitimacy of colonialism. What is more, 'this relationship is but an integral part of the much wider and much more serious project of the advance of western technological civilization'.[9] But in the end a conservative Barthian theology carries the day. The lines are drawn. The church, the gospel, the biblical text and God have, so to speak, one foot in the world and one elsewhere. Of the church it is said that it 'is both a theological and sociological entity'.[10] It looks at itself through two pairs of eyes: those of the world, and those of the believers,[11] but what exactly constitutes the difference is left unclear. The problem is not so much that the church is credited with a 'divine' dimension,[12] but that the *nature* of that dimension is not explained by Bosch. Mission is rooted in the nature of God as *missio Dei*,[13] but the nature of God and his postulated relationship with the world seems to be accepted as self-explanatory. Here, when Bosch deals with what he terms the 'deepest source of mission', his rhetoric is reminiscent of a sermon: 'Mission is, primarily and ultimately, the work of the Triune God, Creator, Redeemer, and Sanctifier, for the sake of the world, a ministry in which the church is privileged to participate ... Mission has its origin in the heart of God. God is a fountain of sending love. This is the deepest source of mission. It is impossible to penetrate deeper still; there is mission because God loves people'[14]. Bosch relies or falls back on a hierarchical view of reality. Below is the world, somehow shot through with 'contextuality'; above it is the divine, supracontextual dimension – in which the church partly shares.

Referring to Schleiermacher, Bultmann and Ricoeur,[15] Bosch makes some attempt to come to terms with the 'essentially contextual nature of the faith' and tentatively criticises the notion of 'suprahistorical and supracultural' ideas and principles,[16] but in the end these attempts remain hesitant and ambiguous. His ideal of a 'creative tension' is not fulfilled. Instead of rigorously pursuing the dialectic between adaptation to, and criticism of given cultural contexts, penetrating to a third position beyond those of (mere captivity in a given 'context') and (trying to leap into a supracontextual realm), he settles for an ambiguous middle position: both-and, not only-but also. Somehow the church has an escape route from the sociohistorical correlativity of its successive historically conditioned epochs. As for theology, 'We therefore – along with affirming the essentially contextual nature of all theology – also have to affirm the universal and context-transcending dimensions of theology.'[17] Between 'text' and 'context' an 'ongoing debate' is advocated,[18] implying that somehow 'text' exists separately from 'context'. The gospel is *norma normans,* 'a universal guide ... to apply as criterion in evaluating the context'.[19] Bosch does not accept into the core of his argument that the gospel itself is as contextually, sociohistorically conditioned as any other cultural phenomenon. According to him, God acts in history as the arena of his activity, and 'God's *vestigia,* God's footprints in the world'[20] must and can be identified, however difficult that may be. But the dilemma is not solved. To pick up the tracking metaphor(a hunter-gatherer theme of great fascination!): unless you already know the eland as part of your world, you cannot identify marks in the sand as *his* spoor. Either marks in the sand are meaningless and nonreferential patches of hollows and scratches, or the maker of those signs is part and parcel of your known world.

Bosch tries to keep the dangerous notion of 'context' within safe bounds. There is a realm outside it, to which we have access. This is the opposite of what I am saying. The church simply cannot choose whether or not to 'enter into the context in which it happens to find itself',[21] as Bosch suggests. Instead of trying to escape from 'context', we must explore the depths of our *wholly* 'contextual' experience. Far from belonging to a different order from the churning ocean on which we have to find our way, the 'lodestars'[22] of which he speaks are part of this very same order and 'context', of the vortices of the one and only universe (homoverse) known to us.

Bosch is representative of a whole generation of white South African theologians, Afrikaans- and English-speaking, who have resisted apartheid – but on the firm foundation of an essentially neo-orthodox Western position. Sociopolitical apartheid was attacked – but from the firm launching pad of Christian apartheid from the world, in which God, the gospel, the church and the biblical text somehow retain supracontextual status. In that sense, theirs was (is) an essentialist, fundamentalist theology. Bosch's book, mirroring the world of theological scholarship, does not succeed in exploding the threat of *closed* contextualism – without trying to escape from the web of conditionality. What is needed is not escape, but deeper penetration into that web. One must conclude that he does not offer the kind of radical critique of Christian missions that would open up a new approach to the culture of hunter-gatherers, or any other culture or religion.

Nolan makes a spirited effort to 'contextualise' the Christian teaching. He attacks the gospel that justified and legitimised colonialism, imperialism and European superiority, a gospel construed by its bearers as a timeless, abstract entity. In fact, he argues, the content of that gospel is completely time-bound, varying from age to age and from place to place, although its formal shape (good news of liberation from every form of sin) remains the same through time. The content of liberation ('God's will') arises from very specific historical circumstances. It is not carried into contextual situations, but can be discerned in them. Therefore religious thought and speech must start from the immediate sociopolitical context. God's will and action will become apparent from that. 'We discover the word of God, we discover what God is doing and saying today, in the signs of our times.'[23] God is in the situation.

Nolan's readiness to start from the present 'context' represents a stride forward. The problem is that he does not 'contextualise' his own religious beliefs, vocabulary and rhetoric, or the original Judaeo-Christian tradition. It turns out that one's experience of God's revelation *now* 'is formed, guaranteed and normatively shaped by the message of Jesus to his contemporaries and by all that is revealed about God in the Bible'[24] – which is not subjected to 'contextualist' critique. He looks at the present South African 'context' – and what emerges with unquestioned self-evidence? A God, individualised and anthropomorphised in unquestioned traditional Judaeo-Christian terms, who 'acts throughout history',[25] who 'became flesh in Jesus and who moves people like a powerful Spirit',[26] a 'crucified God',[27] who 'disapproves', 'condemns' and 'punishes'.[28] The possibility of any other view of the world is not considered. Totally unaware of any problem, Nolan states: 'God is angry, God is absolutely furious, about what is being done to people in South Africa today. I say that without any hesitation.'[29] 'God is exceptionally busy laying the foundations for a new future.'[30] And so forth.

Nolan's readers are impressed by the sincerity of his commitment, the pathos of his resistance against apartheid, and the moving and motivating force that his words must have for those who share his fundamental beliefs. But in the end, fields of forces are reduced monocausally and unidirectionally to a singular noun ('God'), known exactly and described by Nolan in unquestioned traditional Western terms. He does not radicalise 'contextuality' and is not sufficiently aware of the radical historicity of the biblical content, nor of the provisional, relative nature of his own perspective. This approach does not differ essentially from mainline (trapped in religious apartheid) Christianity's relentless intolerance of non-Christian worldviews. It turns out to be a Christian world, internally undifferentiated, and with no windows opening on other worlds. Of course there is a difference between a sermon and theology or philosophy – but is it really possible in South Africa today to preach to a wide audience, made up of pluralistic elements, without a deep awareness of cultural and religious correlativity? I am suggesting that such an awareness would not be contrary to the inherent logic of the phenomenon of Christianity, but would follow from it. The inherent logic of Christianity is that of religion as such: uniqueness can only be celebrated in positive relation.

In spite of his criticism of the complicity of Christian mission with colonialism in South Africa, *Saayman* fails to consider three important questions implied by his critique. First, the limits or edges of the concept 'Christian' are not explored. This is important, for 'Christianity' cannot be so easily extricated from the 'colonialist' package, as if Christianity were a self-evident entity, only entering into extraneous relationships with colonialism (or with any other sociohistorical constellation). Christianity as a sociohistorical force is itself a series of syncretic mixtures, both internally and with wider contexts. Once one admits that Christianity in South Africa is a particular historical syndrome, one has to concede that 'Christianity' has always been, is and will always be a syndrome of various sociohistorical factors, certainly including its Jewish background and impulses originating from Jesus of Nazareth, but also a host of others. Second, and related to the first question, is that Saayman isolates the Christian church from the wide networks of multireligious, syncretic traffic, not only historically, but also as far as its present ecumenical character is concerned. Given his theme (conversion from one religion to another), this is startling. Starting from the admission that the concept *ecumenical* originally refers to 'the whole inhabited earth',[31] he proceeds to restrict it to the unity of Christian believers. Since he begins by unravelling the 'contextuality' of Christianity as manifested in

South African mission, one would expect an investigation of the intricate interrelationships between Christianity and other religions: what are the characteristics of concrete Christianity? To what extent is it part of a larger field of discourse, and essentially involved with other religions in South Africa, particularly African religions (to remain within this region)? Thirdly, and arising from the first two points, Saayman does not explore the reasons and causes, the real *dynamics* of the Christianisation of the black Christian pioneers in South Africa. The bridge and transition from traditional religion to Christianity are not analysed or explained. Their Christianity remains strangely abstract, unmediated, unrelated to their sociocultural backgrounds. Although Saayman affirms at the beginning of his book that its content will of necessity be 'contextual',[32] he does not consistently observe the implications of this claim.

Villa-Vicencio goes considerably further than the first three theologians in developing a consistent model of 'contextual' theology. His proposed methodology[33] requires that theology must be contextually grounded, that is, it must emerge from and relate to the actual, prevailing social situation which it seeks to address. More than that, it must situate itself in an interdisciplinary and interfaith context, involving itself with other academic perspectives and religious perspectives other than that of Christianity. Such a theology, he continues, must be open-ended, 'not securely defined or nailed down for the security of generations to come'.[34] What is more, it must be participatory and democratic, inviting the insight, stories and instinctive solutions of all, particularly those who in the past have been excluded from the dominant structures and dominant ideas. In brief, it is 'contextually responsible' and, at the same time, 'socially transcendent in the sense of challenging society to reach forward'.[35] There are no universal principles.[36] A 'contextual ethic' is one that is formed in the interplay of 'the Christian heritage' and the 'prevailing social context'.[37] Risking itself, it advances into the future without the luxury of certainty.

Two interesting interrelated questions arise here. First, what is the theological or philosophical *reason* for the necessity of contextual theological ethics? Why be a *contextual* theological ethicist? And second, to what extent does Villa-Vicencio understand the Christian heritage itself, which interacts with the prevailing social context, as an entity outside 'contextuality' or, alternatively, as itself permeated by 'contextuality'? Why (and in what sense) be a *Christian* theologian?

Villa-Vicencio is partially successful in avoiding the trap of Christian absolutism by defining Christian theology as an attempt to understand the human situation in terms of and through the historically given symbols of the Judaeo-Christian tradition.[38] Along these lines, a contemporary Christian interpretation would be an extension and critical application of a particular historically given set of symbols, for example that of the return of the Hebrew people to Israel after their exile in Babylon. He admits that the Judaeo-Christian tradition is complex, and that it contains many conflicting elements and internal contradictions, although certain key elements, notably liberation from captivity in any form, are present in the Bible stories.[39] When he deals with the concept 'God', it is done in the context of the biblical tradition. Moving critically between the Bible and contemporary experience, 'who and where God is' can be understood.[40]

Regarding the first of the two questions raised above, I do not see that the notion of 'contextuality' is supported by an appropriate matrix of 'god-talk' ideas. No religious reason for it is given. The concept 'theos' ('God') in the 'theo'-logy of reconstruction is not subjected to critical investigation, hence it functions implicitly as a basis for a relatively solid 'reconstruction' in the liberal tradition. As for the second question, Villa-Vicencio does not pursue the 'contextuality' of the Christian gospel as a historical tradition to the point where it becomes apparent that it too emerged from a wide field of religious movements in late antiquity, and what is more, that it is not only appropriated by present-day people in terms of present-day conditions, but is also constituted by them in terms of those conditions. Undoubtedly an approach such as his may generate considerable power – as long as the continuity with biblical tradition is not disturbed. But what if it is disturbed? What if such traditional symbols lose their meaning, as is apparently happening to increasing numbers of white and black South Africans? What if such symbols are disturbed in their self-evident matter-of-course-ness when confronted, challenged, shocked by a true meeting with *other* religious traditions and non-Christian philosophies? What if the theologian were asked: 'But *why* – and *in what sense* – this particular tradition? How does it relate to, and fit into, the networks of religious pluralism?' At that point innocence would turn into isolationist complacency or uncertainty, unless a deeper reason (equally or better equipped to generate sociopolitical courage) than the mere historical factuality of a religious tradition is found. It strikes one that when Villa-Vicencio deals with the interfaith ingredient of contextual theology, no sense of problem is evident. Christians and others will be 'driven to rediscover the essentials of their own faith, leaving aside the many accretions which have been imposed on their faith as a result of it being used as a tool of conquest and imperial domination'.[41] Clearly, the different religions will remain quite distinct, each content with its own essentials. Apparently Villa-Vicencio believes that Christianity can be put to a different use from being a tool of conquest and domination, without undertaking a radical reflection on its 'essentials'. Villa-Vicencio's programme of 're-construction' cuts short, and thus cancels, the radical and requisite 'de-construction' (not necessarily in a Derridean sense) of theology and Christianity. It is not sufficiently *theologia negativa*.

Mosala roundly criticises Christianity from a specifically black working-class position. From the vantage point of those who have been oppressed by Euro-Christian colonialism, he is keenly critical of any notion of a pure – that is ahistorical Christianity that would remain after being disentangled from the historical configuration of European colonialism. Not only is people's reading of the Bible framed by their history and culture; the Bible itself, in its own internal constitution, is similarly framed. Consistently he points out that each of the entities 'gospel', 'biblical message', 'text', 'Bible', 'Jesus' and 'God'[42] is a multifarious, sociohistorically encoded construct. For example: 'the texts of the Bible ... are products of complex and problematical histories and societies.'[43] Highly critical of a programme of 'contextualisation' in the sense of a mere application of a timeless message – a 'white theology in black clothes'[44] – he refutes any form of suprahistorical universalising conceptualisation, whether of 'the Word of God' or of 'the human'.[45] Consistent with that, he argues vigorously that the very methods (from historical criticism to those of the social sciences) for biblical study are sociohistorically and ideologically implicated, notably in European middle-class settings.[46] The implication of this discovery is the absolute necessity to postulate and articulate the black working-class setting for a critical reading of the biblical texts, which he then illustrates, utilising Micah and Luke. It comes as no surprise that Mosala is keenly critical of neo-orthodox theology with its unquestioned postulate of ahistoric essentials such as 'the Word of God'.[47] In terms of my own perspective, it is clear that Mosala, more than any of the theologians mentioned previously, is keenly aware of sociohistorical correlativity.

My critical question is whether he pursues that line of thought as consistently as he may want to. The critique can be fleshed out in a number of ways.

For one thing, Mosala does not differentiate all his concepts in sociohistorical terms as thoroughly as he does concepts relating to the history of Christianity. For example, in terms of Mosala's logic, it is not consistent to present 'the 'African' as a 'concrete particularizing concept' over against 'the ''human''.'[48] Where is 'the African' to be found? True, he does point out that black theologians are differentially inserted into history and culture, and represent differentiated sets of cultural, ideological and political perspectives,[49] including those of the broad black working class and poor peasant culture.[50] But the question remains: do these two concepts not operate in a totalising, substantialising manner? They are not subjected to the same keen scrutiny as the concepts mentioned earlier. Certainly not all concepts can be investigated equally thoroughly in a given argument; one must proceed from somewhere. Yet it seems that Mosala's razor is simply not used here. This point is not without relevance. For is his own book a black working-class product? Certainly not. It applies and hones arrays of arguments developed in European-North American scholarship. Of course it may be said that his argument is developed *for the sake of* the black working class masses, but it has obviously not been developed *by* them. In precisely what sense can it be called a black working-class hermeneutic? The latter point is what the book is about. What we have here is obviously a complex process of intercultural, interclass mediation and transfer of meaning. But these lines of ambivalent interdependence are not reflexively analysed. Mosala's message, obviously inspired by *his perception* of the black working-class situation, would equally obviously have to be *appropriated* by that class. In other words, neither his own (at least seemingly ambivalent) 'position' nor that of the black working class, vis-à-vis one another and in their manifold correlativity in other directions, is analysed.

A related point is that Mosala argues that the reading of the Bible should and would be structured from the side of the black working class, but the possible input from the side of the Bible is not clarified. He does argue that it will be a reciprocal process, a 'link-up',[51] and refers to 'kin struggles' and a 'source of inspiration',[52] of 'mutual interrogation between text and situation',[53] but it seems that he activates only one line of communication – that leading from the present situation of the readers to the Bible (appropriating it, engaging it, using it as a weapon,[54] etc) – but not the one that might lead from the Bible. For example, in what sense would Luke interrogate the present black working-class situation? Exactly what does *it* 'say' to the black working class? The 'dialectic'[55] of mutual interrogation is not developed. I can appreciate that Mosala's interpretation of John 19:25–27[56] will be a source of inspiration to the poor, but the question remains: is there any sense in which a biblical text would expect or may bring about *changes*? In view of the importance of Mosala's hermeneutic contribution, this weakens his sociohistorical correlativity. The background to my critical question is the story of the hunter-gatherers. Suppose for one moment that early nineteenth-century missionaries had been able to see through their own ideological blindness, exactly *why* and *how* would they have brought the texts of the Bible to South Africa? Would the Christian gospel have been a basic confirmation of hunter-gatherer existence? I am not saying that Mosala has overshot his mark and has become too 'relativistic'; rather, that he did not take his concrete analysis of sociohistorical relationships[57] far enough, and did not analyse in sufficient depth the dynamics, the reciprocal nature of the interaction between the contents of the Bible and its non-Western recipients.

My third question is whether Mosala, as a black theologian, would extrapolate his sociocritical analysis of relationships to a critique of traditional Christian 'god-talk'. This would open up new avenues for a dialogue between Christianity and African religion – one that avoids the trap of 'primitivism' in any form, as he formulates this danger.[58] Mosala does not take his 'contextual' argument far enough. Only by arguing in terms of a metaphysic of correlationality will it be possible to develop criteria for a critique of a universalising, ideological religion.

ENDNOTES

1 For overviews of these developments in Christian theology, see D J Bosch, *Transforming mission: paradigm shifts in theology of mission*, Maryknoll, NY: Orbis, 1991, pp 420ff, and J E Botha, Contextualization: locating threads in the labyrinth, *Scriptura*, 1991, S9, pp 29–46.
2 Bosch, *Transforming missions ...*
3 A Nolan, *God in South Africa: the challenge of the gospel*, Cape Town, Johannesburg: Philip, 1988.
4 W Saayman, *Christian mission in South Africa, political and ecumenical*, Pretoria: Unisa, 1991.
5 C Villa-Vicencio, *A theology of reconstruction: nation-building and human rights*, Cape Town, Johannesburg: Philip, 1992.
6 I J Mosala, *Biblical hermeneutics and Black Theology in South Africa*, Grand Rapids, Mich: Eerdmans, 1989.

7 Bosch, *Transforming mission* ..., p 292.
8 Ibid, p 310.
9 Ibid, p 312.
10 Ibid, p 389.
11 Ibid, p 389.
12 Ibid, p 389.
13 Ibid, pp 389ff.
14 Ibid, p 392.
15 Ibid, pp 422ff.
16 Ibid, p 421.
17 Ibid, p 427.
18 Ibid, p 427.
19 Ibid, p 430.
20 Ibid, pp 428ff.
21 Ibid, p 191.
22 Ibid, p 430.
23 Nolan, *God in South Africa* ..., p 27.
24 Ibid, p 25.
25 Ibid, p 16.
26 Ibid, p 18.
27 Ibid, p 67.
28 Ibid, p 32.
29 Ibid, p 105.
30 Ibid, p 180.
31 Saayman, *Christian mission* ..., p 10.
32 Ibid, pp x, 22.
33 Villa-Vicencio, *A theology of reconstruction* ..., pp 274ff.
34 Ibid, p 278.
35 Ibid, p 280.
36 Ibid, p 283.
37 Ibid, p 283.
38 Ibid, p 23.
39 Ibid, p 24.
40 Ibid, p 26.
41 Ibid, p 277.
42 Mosala, *Biblical hermeneutics* ..., pp 27ff, 37, etc.
43 Ibid, p 20.
44 Ibid, p 22.
45 Ibid, pp 14ff, 21, 24, etc.
46 Ibid, pp 43ff.
47 Ibid, p 17, etc.
48 Ibid, p 24.
49 Ibid, pp 190ff.
50 Ibid, pp 26, 192, etc.
51 Ibid, p 153.

52 Ibid, p 188.
53 Ibid, p 193.
54 Ibid, p 187.
55 Ibid, p 152.
56 Ibid, pp 187ff.
57 Ibid, pp 4ff.
58 Ibid, p 72.

17 The inner veld

We now come to the religion of the early South African hunter-gatherers themselves.

The main focus of the exploration of their religion attempted in the remaining chapters will be the human depth experiences. These are referred to variously as *mysticism*, *meditation*, *contemplation*, *altered states of consciousness*, *transpersonal experience*, *trance*, *spirituality*, *transformation of consciousness* and the like. For our present purposes they are regarded roughly as synonyms. All of them refer to the need or drive evident in all known human societies to go beyond everyday cognition so as to achieve a higher, deeper, purer or truer vision of the world and human society, and one's own place in it all. In that vision both the knower of this new knowledge and the known world are recreated. The glimpses of ultimate peace shimmering in everyday existence are expanded.

Such experiences hover on the threshold between incommunicable privacy and a socially shared cosmology; they are highly ambivalent, and are mediated and expressed by bridging symbols and equivocal *myths* (to be discussed in chapter 18). As threshold experiences, crossing the line from everyday to heightened 'mystical' awareness, they are stimulated in *ritual* settings (to be discussed in chapter 19). They are prepared and remembered in *art* (to be discussed in chapter 20), and are fed back transformatively into the 'ordinary' life of the seer (shaman, prophet, visionary) and the community of which he or she is a saving member. It is the same world as before, but not quite. I will treat belief (myth), ritual and art as three relatively distinct modes of experience, albeit inseparable and mutually implied. None comes first.

These themes occur, I suggest, in primal Bushman religion as much as in the classical 'world religions', and the same themes seek expression on the frontiers of new religiosity. But this has to be demonstrated in the face of the differences which set Bushman religion apart.

The Bushman style of transforming consciousness must be seen against the background of similar efforts worldwide. Their dance and art, aimed at emancipation from habitual, compulsive responses to the world, are comparable to the mediums and procedures used in other religious complexes. These procedures may take various forms, such as sound and music, or silence; bodily movement and gestures, or immobility; thoughts and mental images, or deliberate avoidance of these; the cultivation of emotions, or the practice of affectional neutrality.

The interpretation that follows will observe the following model of mystical consciousness. (Perhaps a mandala rather than a model – a religious pattern rather than a 'scientific' one.)

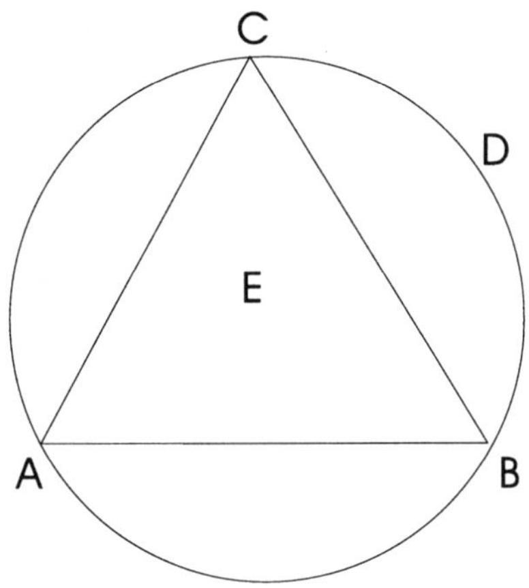

A the social dimension of all such experience

B the rootedness of all human experience, through the evolutionary process, in the realm of prehuman, prepersonal dimensions of existence

C the individual, personal dimension

The fields of A, B and C overlap, and function in the overall context of

D the matrix of the universe, consisting of the multitude of interacting biological, environmental, climatic and other factors influencing human existence. This is the *situation* ('site') of religion. The intuitive postulate of such a context extends to a religiophilosophical – even 'religious' – intuition of the 'whole' as a 'womb': not a totality, but the never-ending moment by moment emergence of events from and their return to

E the centre-point or *origo*: the eternally creative 'now'–'here'. The individual person, societies, the various historical religions express different modes of participation in this 'origin' (by which I do not mean a beginning, diachronically).

This then is the complementary fourfold focus on Bushman religion: its unique sociohistorical setting (A); its sharing in the panhuman modes of religious depth experiences, arising from the biopsychic constitution of the human species (B); its uniquely personal, creative quality (C); and its authentic echo of reality itself (D–E), resonating in its infinite relationality. Whereas A to C are sociological, biological and psychological in nature, D–E is religious. I cannot hope to present the true interpretation of their religion. There is no such interpretation. At most it is a personal perspective (C), conditioned by my own sociocultural preconditions (A), and sharing in the panhuman (B).

The model accommodates the most important emphases in *religious mystical traditions*.[1] Such traditions have developed various modes or procedures for the achievement of mystical transformation by individuals. For example, the mode of *conforming* attaches great importance to social norms (A), the mode of *expression* sets store by descent into the prepersonal (B) and the uniquely individual (C), and the mode of *negation* (in its rigorous forms) approaches silence (E).[2] We shall return to these below.

The model also accommodates some important *theoretical approaches* to mystical experience. In this chapter such approaches, correlating with various dimensions of the model, will be brought to bear on experiences of spiritual transformation. By using them in a complementary way the distortions of ahistorical, physiological, sociological (culturalist) and spiritualist abstractions can be avoided. The perspectives are:

A an emphasis on the conditioning, structuring and controlling role of society and its ideas (focusing on the same area which, in mystical experience, correlates with the mode of conforming)

B an emphasis on the neurophysiological and neuropsychological constitution of the human mind

C the phenomenological description of personal mystical experience

These three overlap and are circumscribed by

D the overall conditionalist perspective, correlating with

E a being drawn by the idea of the empty, ever-renewing centre of the world. Whereas A to C operates on the level of 'science', D–E operates in a 'religious' framework.

A Sociocultural structuring

The mystical mode of *conformity* strives to achieve a transformation of consciousness by emphasising the faithful handing down and reception of social symbols. Shamans/contemplatives place themselves under the discipline of those pregiven patterns, striving to interiorise or assimilate them.[3] In religious traditions, this may foster traditionalism rather than personal spontaneity. Obviously religious tradition has its own legitimacy, making possible individual faith. But it is constantly threatened by the pitfalls of coercion, stagnation and formalism. Such cultural symbols may be visual (for example icons), verbal (for example mantras or prayers), acoustic (for example drums and bells), and physical (for example breathing and dancing).

A vital test of the validity of the interpretation of Bushman religion attempted here is whether it is properly grounded in the sociocultural setting of the Bushmen. This setting has been thoroughly researched by anthropologists. It is neither possible nor necessary to review this vast field of scholarship here.

The main point is that religion is always socially concretised. No mystic/shaman ever started from scratch or operated in a social vacuum. Spirituality flows in sociohistorical continua, however important the innovative role of creative individuals may be. Any persuasive interpretation must therefore distinguish Bushman society and culture (including religion) from other societies, cultures and religions. The distinctive qualities of their cultural complex must be taken into account, not forced into generalised moulds.

However evocative the identification of his people with John the Baptist by the Bushman preacher (mentioned in chapter 14) may have been, he only referred to some striking but rather superficial similarities in lifestyle. As we shall see, at the level of religious symbolism much more profound parallels can be established. These will have to be explained. But first the differences in sociocultural settings, conditioning (preprogramming and limiting) the religious symbolism, must be recognised. Similarly, ideas (or ideals) of Buddhist Bushmen or San Zen, however appealing such romanticising conflations may be, are vapid. For the past 2 000 years and more a Eurasian traffic of ideas from China through India to Spain and back has been well attested. This would explain features of religious thought common to, say, Zoroastrianism, Judaism, Christianity and Buddhism. One such socially shared feature is the idea of a future saviour (Saoshyant, Messiah, Maitreya) found in those religions. Such ideas have a demonstrably common social pool.[4] As far as 'Asia' and 'Europe' are concerned, a reasonably continuous network of communication and dissemination of ideas can be assumed for that period. But for the past 40 000 years and more no comparable channels of communication can be assumed to have existed between the Bushmen and Europe, or between the Bushmen and Asia. No significant diffusion of ideas could have taken place. These populations drifted apart for tens of millennia, developing very dissimilar social, conceptual and linguistic structures.

The stark *differences* between these societies, and the very significant role played by social factors (including language and cosmologies) in moulding religious experience, must first of all be acknowledged. The startling discovery that Euro–Christian postmoderns and hunter-gatherer Bushmen may meet with a shock of mutual recognition will be short-circuited if the real differences in the sociocultural complexes, which to a large degree determine the experiences of transcendence, are disregarded. Experiences of transcendence are framed in concrete historical, sociocultural and religious settings, making them possible but also limiting them.

At what stage (before, during or after 'mystical' experiences) and to what extent society plays its structuring role are problems that have received some attention over the past decades. Stace[5] makes a strong but simplistic distinction between pure mystical *experience* and the *interpretation* of such experience, believing that the experience of mystics in all ages and places is essentially the same. Only the interpretations differ, mainly for reasons of communicating the raw experiences. Katz and others, on the other hand, come out strongly in favour of the sociolinguistic contextuality and therefore the plurality of religious experiences: language creates the contours of experience. The world is shaped and produced by our theories and interpretations.[6]

I will follow the approach that due recognition must be given to the role of socially and linguistically conditioned ideas which not only determine the transformation of consciousness throughout the process, but also cast that experience in interpretive moulds afterwards.[7] After all, the English word 'consciousness' literally means 'knowing together'. But in the concrete act of interpretation this intracultural accent must somehow be unified with a view that makes sharing and translation of meaning between different cultural and linguistic groups understandable. We must assume some form of panhuman connectedness between hunter-gather Bushmen and modern Westerners. Otherwise, how do we account for the measure of understanding of meaning which we assume to occur? Human societies, however unconnected historically, are not necessarily mutually incommunicado. But the two perspectives must converge not through shrinking the web of contextuality in any way, but through expanding it to cover *more* than historical links and sociolinguistic conventions, and to cover the human species in its *entirety*. The 'Sea of Meanings' (Cupitt[8]) is deeper than the cultural flow of words and concepts. Although Cupitt's thinking is open to the dimension of metaphysical emptiness, I believe that he unjustifiably bypasses the transcultural, collective dimension. Certainly, there are no 'absolute' truths. All experience is moulded by cultural repertoires. But these various stocks of religious traditions themselves drift in wider contexts.

In interpreting Bushman religion, it must be approached as an internally coherent unit of sociocultural dynamics. Complementarily, the particular and unique historical context of the Bushmen will be viewed as reciprocally and inextricably linked in a nexus which *also* involves the underlying panhuman homoversal structures and functions of consciousness,[9] as well as the all-inclusive context of infinite conditionality. A *coincidentia oppositorum* of historical religions may be postulated, not underplaying the starkness of the differences, and not confusing 'coincidence' with 'identification'.

B Biopsychic genesis

No matter how high the human mind may soar above the limitations of everyday convention, it never becomes disembodied. On the contrary, I assume that progress in religious sensibilities includes at least in some degree the ability to return to the realm of prerational responses to the operational world out there – a descent into and a rediscovery of the forgotten realm of primordial images and experiences that sprout from the biopsychic constitution of the mind, phylogenetically rooted in the prehuman layers of life and nonlife. This does not amount to an animalisation of the person. It may be here, at the subrational levels of consciousness, that we find equivalences underlying Bushman religion, Buddhism and the emerging ecological religion.

The religious mode of *expression* descends into the realm of homoversal symbols underlying cultural modifications. Shamans/contemplatives not merely strive to leave behind all socially predetermined expectations, but are guided by the promptings from the depths of their own – and humanity's – nature. Receptivity to their own spontaneity[10] and acceptance of all that exists are cultivated. Here lie the origins of the visionary experiences and inspired utterances of the shaman, of spirit possession and similarly ecstatic phenomena. The soul, separating from the body, travels to other places and levels of life and is possessed by other spirits, animal or divine. These are the sort of experiences which in Zen may be dismissed as *makyo* – simply hallucinations of devils, wild animals and so on, and not worth paying attention to. Shamanism as a type of mysticism, whether in Siberia, Tibet or Africa, whether in primal or in postmodern cultural settings, embodies the mode of descent and expression.

On a theoretical level, as far as the Bushmen are concerned, since 1988 Lewis-Williams and Dowson[11] have developed a neuropsychological model of human optic perception during altered states of consciousness. At this stage we need only note the basic premises of their argument. They proceed from the proposition that the human nervous system is structured so that it has a potential for producing universal entoptic phenomena. This means that during certain altered states of consciousness (produced in a variety of ways ranging from the use of electric stimulation to rhythmic movement) the visual system generates a range of luminously coloured, moving percepts that are independent of light from an external source. These visual phenomena take certain geometric forms such as grids, dots and spirals. These percepts (*entoptic phenomena*) derive from the human nervous system and occur universally. They are liable to be perceived by 'all people who enter certain altered states of consciousness, no matter what their cultural background'.[12] Entoptics are distinguished from more complex *hallucinations*,[13] which do not originate from the actual *structure* of the optic system. Hallucinations include iconic visions such as animals, and are largely *culturally* controlled. In altered states of consciousness the brain of the person having the special experiences (entoptics) attempts to match them against a culturally learned store of experience, as it does with ordinary sense impressions during normal states of consciousness. They are 'recognised' in terms of known concepts, such as animals, and so forth. This means that the geometric forms and iconic imagery tend to blend as the visionaries (shamans) try to make sense of the entoptic raw material. This raw material may be slightly or vastly overlaid with iconic elaboration. In the final stage of such altered states of consciousness the visionaries no longer merely witness but participate in a hallucinatory world made up of spontaneous iconic elements.

This hypothesis implies a structural model of human consciousness, in that it acknowledges a level of panhuman, neurologically mediated experience prior to differential cultural channelling of such experience. The limitations of the model at this stage of its development seem to me to be the following:

- It focuses on visual experiences only, and does not integrate these with other dimensions of altered states of consciousness, opening up into a more comprehensive theory of such states.

- Although the avenue to a link-up between their model and theorising about religion in a broader sense is certainly kept open by maintaining that Bushman art is essentially shamanist art, such a wider framework is not provided.

An impressive move towards such a widened perspective has been made by the biogenetic structuralist school.[14] Their point of departure is that the world of our experience is largely a construct of our nervous system, and that the cognised world and all 'things' in it are manufactured in the mind. The reality of the 'world out there' (the 'operational environment') is not denied – but that 'world' is an undifferentiated energy field. All human experience has a neurognostic structure – that is, the experience of the world 'out there' is mediated and initially organised by the neural network which has emerged phylogenetically in the process of evolution. Biogenetic structuralism introduces the elements of adaptation to the environment as well as change over time, through the process of evolution. The nervous system constructs models for processing information about the world. This neurognostic structure of consciousness accounts for the universal attributes of mind, usually unconscious in activity, that have been discovered in cross-cultural studies.

The most basic layer of the cognised environment consists of tiny momentary sensory events (mental particles) called 'dots'.[15] All cognised phenomena are composites, produced by networks of neural cells, and consist of swarms of dots appearing and disappearing within the sensorium (the nervous system of the perceiver). They contribute to and are organised into more enduring events such as forms, patches of colour and textures, as well as images and percepts.[16]

Configurations of experience occur in distinct phases, for example feeling excited and feeling tired, dreaming and being awake. There is a universal human drive to explore phases of consciousness other than those manifested in normal, everyday waking life. This is the universal shamanic principle. Phases of consciousness are divided by definite thresholds or doorways, called 'warps',[17] crossing which is often, in cases of drastic transformation of consciousness, a matter of great difficulty needing the assistance of ritual. Not all cultures attach the same value to such radical transformations of consciousness. For example, modern North Americans tend toward monophasic consciousness, regarding only the waking phase as valid ('normal'), and denigrating (for example) dreams to the level of pathology. However, as ethnography demonstrates, people in most societies operate in a cosmos composed of multiple realities and display a *polyphasic consciousness*.[18] Individuals as well as societies may in fact be ranged on a continuum, from monophasic to polyphasic.[19]

By means of various techniques such as dancing, fasting, and so on (all amplified by ritual), all religious systems in the world utilise symbols to activate the crossing into alternative states of consciousnesss. Extraneous symbols such as animals, water or gender (masculinity and femininity) can penetrate to neural networks that are suppressed or latent in normal waking consciousness. These include phylogenetically old limbic and brain stem models (the palaeomammalian and reptilian complexes of the brain). In alternative states of consciousness the extraneous symbols employed in various religions activate the universal symbols (in Jungian terms, the archetypes), which are invariantly present cross-culturally. These most basic neurognostic patterns include (for example) ascent to the sky or descent to the underworld, dismemberment[20] and bright lights.[21] We live in a world of symbols which are structurally (neurologically) generated, yet in interaction with the surrounding milieu. The system that generates experience processes only symbolic material: everything entering or registered by the sensory apparatus of the person (including the 'dots') is transformed immediately to adapt to symbolic elements in the person's own neural structure.[22]

Through various techniques the shaman can descend lower into the structural field to levels where images and nonhuman forms materialise; to still deeper layers yielding even more primitive and less articulated imaginary and geometric figures; until right at the base of the structural field the archetypes are encountered.[23] The arising of universal symbols is often associated with feelings of bliss, ecstasy and intuitive insight. An eruption of this previously unconscious material may result in profound alteration of personality, understanding and behaviour.[24] The ego, and the world as previously known, may be shattered.

> *As one experientially converges toward the vortex of the internal structuring process, individual and cultural variations vanish to reveal a profound, common structure. This structure, embedded neurognostically in the human brain, is experienced by shamans everywhere in their realization of the interrelatedness of all things, of energy flow, and of the existence of a nonprofane world outside the bounds of conditioned normal perceptions.*[25]

Culturally generated cosmologies determine the interpretation of individual experiences, which is a post hoc activity.[26] These are elements in a wider, complex cycle of meaning, in which there is negative and positive feedback between the socially defined cosmology, the expression of that cosmology through cognised symbols, the experience of transformed consciousness, and the interpretation of such experience within the framework of the cosmology.[27]

This approach of transpersonal neurophysiology-cum-anthropology integrates the socio- and biogenetic aspects of mystical experience (A and B of our model). It also ties in with the broad Jungian and phenomenological approach to depth experiences, and it links up with a philosophy of radical relationality.

C The depth of the person

Here the focus is not on social pressures or on biological drives, but on the *subjectivity* of the *individual* human being, who through introspection discovers the inner world of experience. Yet, as the mandala of religious experience shows, this individual subjectivity cannot for a moment be isolated from the other factors involved. While it is true that individual personal experience is largely preformed by society and nature, it is equally true that society and nature are experienced in personal terms. While it is true that the human person is constituted by being part and expression of the conditionalist world (as I shall point out again below), it is equally true that the human being can express that transpersonal depth only in human-like, person-like pictures. Social forces, natural forces, ideas, 'dead' things, the intuition of the depth are all personified.[28] The dark might of crime and guilt, cruelty and revenge, operative in society take on a life of their own in spite of good people's best intentions. A bureaucratic system gone berserk becomes a monster breathing in the dark its stinking breath of repression, killing or being killed (apartheid). Cars and hurricanes receive human names. Justice is blindfolded, democracy fair. Instinctual drives become personae in the human drama. The religious consciousness hovers between knowing that any naming of the Depth is anthropomorphic and therefore skewed, and knowing that without such naming no conscious relationship with it is possible. Myths simultaneously distort and reveal reality. They intimate ultimacy but only in human garb. It is lived by telling stories of princely Manjusri, loving Father, merciful Allah, dancing Shiva, wild Dionysus, crafty /Kaggen.

I did not have access to the individual subjectivity of Bushman people. Neither am I aware of any well-developed study in this regard,[29] notwithstanding the empathic quality of much of the anthropological work done with various Bushmen groups. Through such research the interior landscape of Bushman persons can be approximated to a certain extent. Understanding is not a matter of everything or nothing. The point I am making is that the relative autonomy and even primacy of the individual Bushman shaman must be upheld, even if only 'in principle' (because his/her inner experiences cannot be described here).

The Jungian line of investigation does not concern itself directly with the social (A) or psychophysical (B) bases of alternative states of consciousness. Neither does it go into (D-E), the religious/metaphysical dimensions of these experiences as such. Jung's concepts of the collective unconscious and archetypes[30] certainly have a strong biological implication. However, their major focus is the interior quality of those experiences.[31] He operates on the continuum B to C. In the perspective of the Jungian archaeology of the mind the shaman/contemplative intuits the archetypal domain within the individual human being, also collectively present in humankind and phylogenetically inherited from our earliest ancestors. It is an exploration of the primordial levels of consciousness, of the domain of archetypal patterns around which all experience is organised. This archetypal material surfaces transculturally in institutionalised religious symbolism, spontaneously in individual dreams and fantasies, in therapy and in meditation. Fear is overcome in the shaman/contemplative's *descensus ad inferos*, into those depths of one's being where one confronts the outwardly projected hidden aspects of one's psyche, the forces within. One cannot deny the enormously suggestive force of the elaborate Jungian constructions of the mind, balanced between scientific explanation and mythological evocation.

Jung's theorem of the collective unconscious was anticipated by the Buddhist Yogacara school[32] with its concept of the *ālaya-vijñāna* ('storehouse-consciousness'), which accounts for the fact that all people of all times perceive things in largely similar ways. The *ālaya*, the humanly primordial, generic and collective mode of consciousness functioning prior to defiled ego-consciousness, stores all karmically transmitted experiences as 'seeds'. These potent residues sprout when they are awakened ('perfumed') by outside stimuli in an ongoing reciprocity between consciousness and phenomena.

The general Jungian line of interpretation permits a distinction between cultural symbols and precultural basic symbolic motifs. Extrapolating Jungian themes, the former may be seen as manifestations of the latter, derived from them. An image of the Buddha is a cultural symbol. The circle, square and triangle are elementary, essential forms, as red, blue and yellow are elementary, essential colours.[33] In mystical experience the elementary symbols, the fundamental metaphors, are not seen as arbitrary creations of individuals or cultures, but as emanating from the isomorphic structures of reality, consciousness and the human body. All experience proceeds from them and returns to them. However, the emphasis on the social dimension of symbolic expression remains vital. Unless this link is maintained, the interpretation of such expressions can become quite arbitrary and fanciful. This is certainly the great temptation for a Jungian approach.

Staying with some great primordial visual symbols, since they will interest us a great deal when we come to Bushman religion: however different and wide-ranging they may seem, they mostly express a set of associations closely related to the notions of centring, ordering and integrating. Here we return to the theme of chapter 4. For example, a cross (with its lines meeting at its centre) and a circle both have a centre as source, end or point of balance. Related to these are the associations of harmony, regularity and coherence, conciliation of opposites or unity in multiplicity, expressed by symbols such as the Taoist yin-yang and the symmetric star of David. Similarly, the sacred syllable OM, beginning with the mouth open and ending with the mouth closed, also represents universal reconciliation of opposites.

At the same time objects of contemplation more often than not have associations of radiation and emanation, even dispersal and emptying (death). For example, plant symbols express emanation in the form of growth. The seed must die to give life. At the centre of the lotus flower and the circle is emptiness. The lines of the cross meet in the vanishing nothingness of a mathematical point. Fire implies notions of perishing and death.

Some themes of focus combine and integrate the two emphases. For example, the sun as symbol of contemplation potently expresses the twin ideas of circular centrality and radiation. Likewise the heart stands for both centre and circulation. The circle contrasts and combines centre and periphery, nothingness and eternity, the one and the many. The cross is a good example of the interlocking of cultural (particular) and precultural (homoversal) meanings. In Christianity it is suffused with a set of socially constructed theological meanings derived specifically from the life and death of Jesus Christ. But the cross also derives its powerful symbolic meaning from the primordial level, where it combines the ideas of return to the centre, radical emptying and all-pervading extension.

Dwelling on such symbols is not merely a fixing of attention on some external object or sound, but disinterested identification with it, causing the contemplative to centre on the core of selfhood – there to discover selflessness as relatedness to all. Identity is found in the abandonment of identity, true 'self' (as nonself) in the abandonment of 'ego' and 'self'.

The individual mystic is completely dependent on social repertoires and homoversal religious themes. Yet through these there is individual originality and creativity – that is, being open and transparent to the origin. The person searches beyond itself, reflects the original light and is, in this derivative sense, original. In this perspective, the person is not a self-sufficient being, but a focus of the world and on the world; a significant centre of activity and interest; a point (an intersection without magnitude) of origin and convergence of interactivity; an appearance defined in the reflection of mirrors – and, paradoxically, self-consciously *aware* of all of this.

D–E Conditionalist negation

On the level of effecting transformation of consciousness, the mystical mode of *negation* emphasises withdrawal from external perceptions and socially established images, rituals and ideas. To mention one example, Buddhist *vipassana* meditation, cultivating 'bare attention', simply observes without embracing or pushing away, without clinging or hatred, whatever presents itself to consciousness from without or within, as it comes and goes.[34] Closely related to this is *shikantaza* ('just sitting') in Soto Zen.

Although they may be analytically distinguished and may be seen by their practitioners as sharply contrasting, the three mystical modes mentioned earlier (*conformity, expression* and *negation*) are different ways of descent into the depth, not wholly different journeys. They merge.

A neat separation between the structuring role of society and the eruptions from the depths of the collective soul is not necessary or possible. Concentration on culturally preformed symbols does not differ essentially from expression of precultural homoversal symbols, since the standardised forms and symbols on which contemplatives concentrate have, after all, originated from the soul. Conversely, surrender to ecstatic spontaneity is not a plunge into chaos, but is the discovery and expression of a structure common to *homo sapiens*. Mystic abandonment to the uncharted dimensions of one's own nature is really an exploration of the panhuman potentiality for the creation of symbols and patterns, wider than the range captured in any particular religiocultural system.

Neither is the negative way the opposite of concentration. Absorption in a single preformed object of contemplation necessitates the elimination of everything else that may distract attention.

Likewise, to develop the receptivity necessary for surrender to what emerges requires active effort to eliminate the intrusion of preformed contents of consciousness. Conversely, the practitioner of detached *vipassanā* meditation finds that the attitude of radical nonattachment allows unexpected guests from the depths of consciousness to cross the threshold of explicit awareness. The line between negative attitude (for example choiceless, detached awareness in *vipassanā*) and being open to what occurs within is thin indeed – 'detached' implying the element of 'negativity' and 'awareness' the element of openness to experience.

In the model proposed here, radical negation (the space of emptying) is the essential moment in the ongoing spiral from the 'old' to the 'new', from conventionalised forms threatened with petrification, to creative expressions of the human search for meaning, constantly rising up in the soul – themselves inevitably taking on new form and new content, which will have to be negated in due course. Mystical systems, like all systems of meaning, seem to have a built-in tendency to become closed. The more that happens, the more prestructured, stereotyped symbolisms are imposed on individuals, blocking and paralysing the inherent, spontaneous workings of their religious imagination.

I now wish to turn to the more than theoretical – indeed the religious (in the sense described in chapter 3 and 4) – context for interpreting Bushman spirituality: ultimate conditionality and the empty centre.

As said in earlier chapters, the idea of conditionality has never been made the centre of philosophy and religion so radically as in Buddhism. There, ideas such as those of self and collective unconscious are subverted at base. As a psychiatrist, Jung understandably refused to move outside the limits of psychology as a discipline, not wanting to religionise psychology or psychologise the divine. But his theory is limited, and he does not escape from hypostasising the 'unconscious'. Whereas he affirms (or at least does not question) the notion of self, consisting of the 'ego' (the known consciousness) and the unknown unconscious (both in a personal and collective sense), early Buddhism teaches that the 'self' is merely an unenduring, functional composite of matter, sensation, perception, emotional and volitional factors, and consciousness, all of which co-originate interdependently. This nonsubstantial node is the true 'self'. Through meditation a breakthrough to this bottomless realisation, where nothing is realised, is achieved. *Vipassana* meditation is awareness of what transpires within, indeed deeply within; but more than that, it is the discovery that the 'within' is empty, and that self and world are a nondual, evanescent flux.[35] The bottom falls out. The person is pluralised and relativised. Jung did not develop similarly radical metaphysical ideas.[36] For him the collective unconscious as a psychological category was the end of the road as far as the search into the depths of the soul and its contents was concerned.

The 'un-' in 'unconscious' has a derogatory meaning. What is required is a term such as 'trans-' or 'meta-conscious', to describe the opening of consciousness to infinity, to origin itself. The word 'trance' as it is mostly used is equally inapposite. It has taken on the meaning of a sleep-like un-/half-conscious state of unresponsiveness. In fact, the word derives from 'transire' (to go across or beyond), just as 'ecstasy' originally refers to a state of being 'outside' oneself. Trance and ecstasy, when used here, actually refer to states of superresponsiveness: the individual 'transpersonally'[37] decentralising the self, responding to a deeper and wider integration of things.

Buddhism pushes through the level of the 'un-'conscious', beyond subject-object duality as such. For example, in the Pali suttas the second of the *arūpāyatana* (immaterial spheres of meditation) is that of boundless consciousness (*viññāṇañcāyatana*[38]). Consciousness without limitation, but consciousness all the same, and seemingly deeper than the Jungian collective unconscious from where the psychic archetypes erupt in full force. An even deeper sphere is that of *ākiñcaññāyatana*[39] (the sphere of 'no-thingness'), which seems to point to a final transcendence of any form of subject-object distinction. The latter is achieved in the experiential dimension of 'neither-perception-nor-nonperception' (*nevasaññānāsaññāyatana*[40]). This is the cessation of consciousness. Cessation of the subject-object division is probably also what Yogacara aimed at.

Whereas Indian Buddhism, both in its early phase and in Yogacara philosophy, rested mainly with the nonexperience of nonconsciousness on the psychological level, it was left to Chinese, Korean and Japanese Buddhism to articulate the cosmological implications of the intuition of emptiness. This was done, most impressively, in Hua-yen philosophy[41] by interpreting emptiness as radical relationality: the world is the nonfixable interplay of the simultaneous mutual mirroring of all events in all other events, past, present and future. The interpenetrative biunity of humanity and the world, of consciousness and reality, is light and open. The phenomena of the universe are transparent, not to some monumental noumenon outside it, but to its own quality of mutual interpenetration. Never was this view expressed more profoundly than by Dogen (1200–1253). To him all concrete phenomena are symbols of (for example nondualistically shot through with) the symbolised (that is absolute emptiness), without any hiatus between symbol and symbolised. They *are* emptiness.[42] In this sense, dreams, illusions and pictures are also pregnant with symbolic value,[43] in that they too concretise absolute emptiness immediately. Myths and symbols do not point to or express something other than themselves. They simply are part and parcel of reality – the absolute now of radical impermanence.

Bushman religion will be viewed, in all its human frailty, as transparent to and reflecting an original light glowing through this fragmented world, of which it is both a part and an expression. I am offering an unashamedly 'religious' appreciation of their form of cosmic orientation – an appreciation differing vastly from traditional Christian contempt, liberal Christian condescension and the romanticising it has been subjected to in the past. Adapting the Christian idiom of Augustine, I understand their religion as *memoria Dei*[44] – remembrance of God; in Quaker terminology, as reflection of 'the Inward Light', of 'That of God in everyone'. It is Original Memory, Mandalic Imagination of the Depth.

ENDNOTES

1 As H F de Wit, *Contemplative psychology*, Pittsburg, Pa: Duquesne University Press, 1991, points out, the various contemplative traditions to be found in practically all religions contain, at least implicitly, highly developed psychological insight into the structure of the contemplative life. 'Contemplative psychology', as he calls it, is not a Western academic-style 'third-person psychology' *about* contemplative experience (the legitimacy of which he does not reject), but a study from inside

such a contemplative tradition. Staal's criticism of psychology (having done with philology, history and phenomenology of religion) is cutting: the right kind of psychologist's first action may in fact be to contemplate (F Staal, *Exploring mysticism*, Harmondsworth: Penguin, 1975, p 186).

2 These modes have been described by C Naranjo & R E Ornstein, *On the psychology of meditation*, London: Allen & Unwin, 1972.

3 Cf ibid, p 129.

4 Cf G A van den Heever, Die motief van die wêreldbrand. Zoroastrisme, formatiewe Judaïsme en vroeë Christendom: patrone van interaksie, Unpublished MA dissertation, University of South Africa, Pretoria, 1993.

5 W T Stace, *Mysticism and philosopy*, London: Macmillan, 1961.

6 D Cupitt, *The time being*, London: SCM, 1992, p 38: 'I don't see the world raw; it has to be culturally cooked in order to be seen.'

7 See P G Moore, Problems in the analysis of mystical experience with special reference to the work of R C Zaehner, W T Stace and M Laski, University of Lancaster, PhD thesis, 1977, for a discussion of the complex relationship between ideas and mystical experience. Mystics may proceed from individual beliefs and collective doctrines as intellectual conditions, but experiences may confirm, modify or undermine ideas. Ideas could function retrospectively as interpretations, or accompany the actual experiences.

8 Cupitt, *The time being* ..., p 66.

9 W Dupré, *Religion in primitive cultures: a study in ethophilosophy*, The Hague: Mouton, 1975 seems to make the same point when he states that culture is always concrete and universal at once – 'a concrete culture is a definitive representation of humanity' (p 20). Following a transcendental line he ties this argument to the theoretical postulate of a 'meta-empirical reality' (p 23) – that of a 'proto-culture' (that is 'primitive culture') as the 'all-present beginning that sustains and permeates every cultural action and deed' (p 22). This (he correctly claims) would not consist in a cross-culturally valid doctrinal system, but rather in a universality of function (p 245).

10 Naranjo & Ornstein, *On the psychology* ..., p 129.

11 Cf J D Lewis-Williams & T A Dowson, The signs of all times: entoptic phenomena in Upper Palaeolithic art, *Current Anthropology*, 1988, 29(2), pp 201–245 for their application and consolidation of the neuropsychological experimental work of H Klüver, M J Horowitz and others in a model of the apprehension of entoptic phenomena. As they readily admit, the basic idea has been around for quite a while. See also T A Dowson, *Rock engravings of Southern Africa*, Johannesburg: Witwatersrand University Press, 1992, pp 29ff.

12 Lewis-Williams & Dowson, The signs of all times ..., p 202.

13 Hallucinations are therefore clearly a 'sense-making' interpretive activity. The authors are not entirely consistent in their terminology. Dowson (*Rock Engravings* ..., p 29) shifts the meaning of the term 'hallucination' from the *interpretation* of entoptics to being itself part of the *object* of interpretation – in fact, the inclusive term for all stages of visual experience. He claims that 'hallucinations are the same in structure for all groups of people'.

14 The most recent restatement and further development of their views is to be found in C D Laughlin, J McManus & E G d'Aquili, *Brain, symbol and experience: toward a neurophenomenology of human consciousness*. Boston, Shaftesbury: Shambhala, 1990.

15 Ibid, pp 108ff. Other terms for these mental particles are 'epoches', 'waves', 'frames', 'monads', 'actual entity' and 'actual occasion' (derived from Whitehead). Although not mentioned by the authors, the Buddhist Abhidharma concept of 'dharma' (the multiple, momentary, ultimate constituents of the phenomenal world) affords an interesting comparative angle (see for example E Conze, *Buddhist thought in India: three phases of Buddhist philosophy*, London: Allen & Unwin, 1983, pp 96ff). It seems that 'dots' refer to an even more elementary level of experience than 'dharmas' (which may include definite images).

16 Laughlin et al, *Brain, symbol and experience* ..., p 111.

17 Ibid, pp 142ff.

18 Ibid, p 155.

19 Ibid, pp 292ff.

20 Ibid, p 272.

21 Ibid, p 205.

22 Ibid, pp 245ff; 246: 'To a large extent, then, what the ego experiences is itself, its own organizing, symbolizing activities.'

23 Ibid, p 263. Closer to normal consciousness, the archetypes are experienced in more familiar terms as animals and human-like figures. The greatest cultural variation is found near the surface where 'the cultural definitions having greater formative influence ...' (ibid p 275).

24 Ibid, p 197.

25 Ibid, p 275.

26 Ibid, p 326.

27 Ibid, p 214.

28 As expounded by J Hillman, *Re-visioning psychology*, New York: Harper & Row, 1975, who makes a case for the rehabilitation of imaginative personification of the world, rectifying the modern split of 'I' (and 'God') (the only capitalised words left in English) over against a dead world of objects.

29 T A Dowson (Revelations of religious reality: the individual in San rock art, *World Archaeology*, 1988, 20[1], pp 116–128) and J D Lewis-Williams (*Images of power: understanding Bushman rock art*, Johannesburg: Southern, 1989, p 32) refer to the idiosyncratic element in Bushman art.

30 C G Jung, The symbolic life, in *The collected works of C G Jung,* Vol 18, 1977, London: Routledge & Kegan Paul. In his last statement on these (*Man and his symbols*, London: Pan, 1964, pp 57–8), Jung refers to the 'immensely old psyche', product of evolutionary history. In the 'biological, prehistoric, and unconscious development of the mind in archaic man, whose psyche was still close to that of the animal' is contained the 'instinctive trend' of the archetypes, 'as marked as the impulse of birds to build nests, or ants to form organized colonies'. They reproduce themselves 'in any time or in any part of the world – even where transmission by direct descent or "cross fertilization" through migration must be ruled out'. On the

other hand Jung also gave a distinctly religious connotation to the archetypes – they have a *numinous* quality, possessing a certain autonomy and specific transformative energy because of the *numen* stored in them; experience of them 'seizes and possesses the whole personality, and is naturally productive of faith' (C G Jung, Symbols of transformation: an analysis of the prelude to a case of schizophrenia, in *Collected works,* Vol 5 ..., 1956, p 232).

31 Psychological experience is 'the only immediate experience we can have and the sine qua non of the subjective reality of the world' (Jung, Symbols of transformation ..., pp 231ff).

32 The central message of this school (5th century CE) has been variously interpreted, from Absolute Idealism (A K Chatterjee, *The Yogacara idealism*, Delhi: Motilal Banarsidass, 1975) to realistic pluralism (T A Kochumuttom, *A Buddhist doctrine of experience,* Delhi: Motilal Banarsidass, 1982). Comparable points may also be established between the Jungian concept and the Hindu Yoga concept of *vasanas* (impersonal, collective tendencies inherent in the structure of the human organism). See P Faber & G S Saayman, On the relation of the doctrines of yoga to Jung's psychology, in R K Papadopoulos & G S Saayman, *Jung in modern perspective*, Craighall: Donker, 1984, pp 165–181.

33 Lama Anagarika Govinda, *Creatieve meditatie en multidimensioneel bewustzijn*, Deventer: Ankh-Hermes, 1987, pp 204ff.

34 Cf Nyanaponika, *The heart of Buddhist meditation*, London: Rider, 1983.

35 Views very similar to the ones expounded here have been set forward by Felicity Edwards – cf her Vipassana meditation and transcultural consciousness, *Journal for the study of religion* 1988 1/2, pp 37–51; and Cutting through contending ideologies: the new paradigm and the new commandment, in J Mouton, A G van Aarde & W S Vorster (eds), *Paradigms and progress in theology*, Pretoria: Human Sciences Research Council, 1988, pp 239–251.

36 But from a Jungian point of departure, Hillman (*Re-visioning psychology* ..., pp 165ff) does move in such a direction with his notion of a 'polytheistic psychology'. For a critique of Jung's hypostasisation of the self from a Buddhist perspective, see M Abe, The self in Jung and Zen, in D J Meckel & R L Moore, *Self and liberation: the Jung/Buddhism dialogue*, New York: Paulist Press, 1992, pp 128–140. However, he admits that Buddhism (Zen) may learn from Jungian psychology about the origination of unconscious mental fabrications. Jung saw Buddhist meditation as a surrender to the collective unconscious, an introverted journey into self-absorption.

37 To borrow a term from K Wilber, *Up from Eden: a transpersonal view of human evolution*, Boston: Shambhala, 1986.

38 This has been dealt with comprehensively but scholastically in the fifth century CE by Buddhaghosa in his *The path of purification (Visuddhimagga)*, translated from the Pali by Bhikkhu Nyanamoli, Kandy: Buddhist Publication Society, 1979, pp 360ff.

39 Ibid, pp 362ff.

40 Ibid, pp 364ff.

41 Cf F H Cook, *Hua-yen Buddhism: the Jewel Net of Indra*, University Park, London: Pennsylvania State University Press, 1977; Garma C C Chang, *The Buddhist teaching*

of totality: the philosophy of Hwa Yen Buddhism, University Park, London: Pennsylvania State University Press, 1977. Also see S Odin's daring and challenging (if somewhat overplayed) effort to integrate the Whiteheadian concept of the bipolar God, Jungian depth-pschology and Hua-yen Buddhism: *Process metaphysics and Hua-yen Buddhism: a critical study of cumulative penetration vs interpenetration*, Albany: State University of New York Press, 1982.

42 Cf H-J Kim, *Dogen Kigen: mystical realist*, Tuczon: University of Arizona Press, 1987, pp 81ff.

43 See ibid, p 90, where Kim points out how Dogen differs from traditional Buddhism in this respect.

44 J Hillman, *The myth of analysis*, Evanston, Ill: Northwestern University Press, 1972, pp 168ff suggested a link-up between the 'collective unconscious' and the *memoria Dei*: 'Part of the soul is continually remembering in mythopoetic speech, continually seeing, feeling, and hearing *sub specie aeternitatis*' (p 177).

18 A fluid, ambiguous world

Bushman beliefs relate to Bushman ritual (dance) and art as the shell of a tortoise relates to the rest of its body: it encapsulates, structures and shields the softer, more vital parts; and it is itself part of the body: it grows, is vulnerable and ages.

Even within the very small timeframe of the twentieth century Bushman beliefs vary considerably from epoch to epoch,[1] from group to group, and even from individual to individual.[2] Therefore, any picture of a pan-Bushman set of general beliefs[3] is at best an ideal-typical construction, based on general family resemblances among various groups. The anthropological accounts cover only the nineteenth and twentieth centuries, but the general picture may apply to the earlier periods as well.

Drawing on anthropological case studies, I shall review the Bushman belief system cursorily, interpreting it in terms of the theoretical perspective developed in previous chapters. That means looking at their belief system as part of an overall Bushman endeavour to respond adequately and creatively to the sets of conditions impinging on them.[4] Like a child's toy top, a religion spins around its own axis, dancing on its tip as it maintains its balance while responding to uneven patches on the ground. Sooner or later its momentum spends itself, or it bumps into obstacles that cut short its dance. I therefore look at Bushman religion as their response (strictly speaking, their plurality of responses) partly perpetuating itself as it consolidates, creates order and structures reality; partly risking and adapting itself as it disintegrates, de-stabilises order and de-structures reality – depending on specific historical contexts.

One important aspect of the contextual interaction of Bushman religion is its syncretic accommodation to the worldviews of other groups, specifically various forms of traditional black religion and Christianity, with which it had extensive contacts over a long time via various white and black groups.[5]

Like all religions, Bushman religion is dynamic and syncretic, changing with time. It is not easy to determine to what extent such outside influences have affected the formation of the various forms of Bushman religion that have come down to us. Yet that such a process of interaction with other groups in South Africa has taken place over several centuries in some cases and over millennia in others must be borne in mind throughout.

In what follows, the core of traditional Bushman 'beliefs' will be reconstructed, but not in the sense of a set of definitive views; by 'core' I simply understand a fairly dense, central cluster of ideas shared by many groups.

For this overview of the framework of the Bushman cosmos I follow Silberbauer's account of the G/wi of central Botswana,[6] on the assumption that his findings may be extended to Bushpeople generally. The problem with such efforts is that they award a degree of systematic coherence to a religion vastly exceeding the reality experienced by its adherents.[7] More than that, I differ from his view that the religious beliefs of a people 'represent their most comprehensive ideas of order'.[8] I believe that the rendering of a pan-Bushman integrated cosmos must be countered dialectically by an account of the contrasting force of dis-integration. Dis-ordering is not merely hovering on the outer fringes of the ordered Bushman cosmos/world-orientation as a threat, but is necessarily, inextricably and creatively intertwined with it, as its duet partner, its alter ego. The one evokes the other, challenging and needing it at the same time. Not so much 'to be' *or* 'not to be', but to 'be' *and* to 'dissolve' – that is the question in understanding Bushman religion. To that aspect we turn in the second part of this chapter.

The cosmos ...

In delineating the Bushman cosmos, I begin with the basic coordinates of *space* and *time*, and thereafter deal with the powers that fill the world and the relationships obtaining between them.

□ *Space* is three-tiered, consisting of *earth* (the arena of human life and interaction with the other forms of life), and the peripheral and unknown realms of *sky* (*heaven*) and *underworld*. The earth (which includes the space between the ground and the heavenly bodies) has finite but unknown boundaries. Direction is expressed with reference to specific, known localities in their geographical frame, and distance is measured by the time it takes to walk it. The heavenly bodies (sun, moon and stars) are situated just above the highest clouds.

- *Time* is measured in days, months and the seasons which make up a year. Past years are remembered in terms of elapsed winters. Bushpeople are principally present oriented, with little interest in the past and a distant future.

- Bushman religion accepts the existence of a *creator deity*, variously named, and married. Ultimately the Bushperson refers all events, both comprehensible and incomprehensible, to the deity, who is the source of power, although rather remote. This concept was not evolved under Christian influence.

- There is also a *second, lesser divinity*, of cunning and erratic disposition but with far less power and knowledge than the creator.

- Bushpeople do not identify closely with or venerate their *ancestors* as the southern African blacks do, and are not bound by the past.

- *Humans* are complementarily involved with but not hierarchically favoured above other life forms. On the basis of their common humanity, all Bushpeople are related to each other (from close family and clan to mistrusted or feared strangers) and to all life forms in ever-widening concentric circles. A high value is placed on harmonious social relationships and on the virtues of friendliness, generosity, calm, and so forth. The enormous cognitive distance between traditional Christianity and traditional hunter-gatherer religion emerges clearly in Silberbauer's[9] statement:

  > *... (although) the G/wi cognitive map stratifies life-forms in concentric rings that are nearer or farther from man, there is not a matching stratification of authority over life-forms nor of rights to resources in the environment. All N!adima's creatures have equal rights to existence. Each species, with its own characteristics, has a*

place in N!adima's world. Some prey upon others and some have to struggle harder to survive, but none is thought to be uniquely favored by N!adima and to have been set above others by him ...

- ☐ Unlike animals, humans have life after death in the form of *spirits*, which inhabit the underworld or the sky.

- ☐ All beings are dynamically interrelated in a *matrix of interdependence*, a network of causality. 'The structure of causal explanation is not linear, with each event being ascribed to a single cause, which, in turn, is the effect of a chain of one-to-one relationships. There is a web of causation. Factors combine in multiple causation and the strands merge where different events have in common one or more causal factors'[10] – thus Silberbauer points out the similarities with general systems theory.[11] For example, the seasons consist of aggregations of factors (the availability of food and water, wind, etc).[12] Weather is a 'unified whole',[13] a system composed of various constituent elements (including the will of the deities), and can thus be predicted fairly accurately (given the limited range of phenomena accessible to Bushpeople). Occurrences such as disease are mostly seen as the results of patterns involving several combined factors. The relative remoteness of the creator does not mean that the universe is understood as a closed, completely self-regulatory, inanimate system. The universe is constituted by animate, personalised actors and forces. The sense of natural causality motivates a pragmatic, empirical, realistic orientation to nature, with no fear of intimidation or haunting,[14] and allowing for practical, rational measures. Although prayers and entreaties to the deities occur, recourse to magic is not typical.

- ☐ *Animals* (of which the Bushpeople display an astounding empirical knowledge) must, as the property of the creator, be respected. But they may be killed in self-defence or for food. The relationship between humans and animals varies from competition and predation to a measure of cooperation. Mammals feature far more prominently than other species and are closer to humans. Birds, reptiles and other forms (all classified in taxonomies) are much less important.

- ☐ *Plants* are distinguished from animals by their absence of mobility and volition. However, like animals, they are (as the property of the deity) conserved and protected against wanton destruction and exploitation. Food plants are regarded with more emotional neutrality than meat.

The above presentation, while correct, is one-sided. In categories steeped in Western systems theory, Silberbauer explains the Bushman cosmology:

> *The world, then, is seen as a gigantic version of a self-regulating life-support system in which component subsystems, themselves self-regulating within certain limits of tolerance, interact to correct perturbations ... There is constant interaction and motion, local and temporary changes occur, but the overall character and identity of the system continues unchanged – N!adima's universe as he created it.*[15]

This version of their religion will now be counterbalanced by a closer look at its 'chaotic' aspect, dialectically contrasting this with the stabilising aspect.

... is polymorphous and oscillating

The theoretical perspective developed in chapters 2 to 4 is supported by Guenther's comparison of Bushman religion in the two different contexts of village farming (the 'modern' context) and hunting-gathering (the 'traditional' context).[16] In the process of upheaval of the 'old' (hunting-gathering context), he says, their traditional way of life and the related cultural patterns (cooperation, the sharing ethos, general social wellbeing) disintegrated and the Ghanzi Bushmen tumbled into states of physical, social and existential maladjustment (disease, drunkenness, fighting, spouse beating, etc). In the old, proven, accepted, stable yet relaxed order[17] stress was generally low, and religious expressions were conceptually loose, fragmented, amorphous, 'ludic'. In the new social and environmental disorder and the high levels of stress it engendered, beliefs tended to become standardised and highly structured as the Bushmen struggled to find a meaningful orientation.

My argument is that if an easy-going order has been achieved, the urge for cosmic orientation ('religion') relaxes into 'amorphous', 'fragmented', 'ludic', 'surrealistic', 'disengaged', 'unclear', 'inchoate'[18] modes of being, feeling and thinking. To the extent that an order becomes rigid and closed, the religious urge to 'transcend' counters the threat of absolutism antistructurally. But when the threat of chaos is deadly serious, the 'religious' urge would express itself as the counterbalancing search for 'integration'. I suggest that this accounts for the 'antistructural' nature of traditional Bushman religion.

The dual need to explode order *and* tame the chaos results in the strangely liminal ambiguity that I have called the locus of 'religion': between safety and threat, security and challenge, domestication and wildness; both, and neither in isolation from the other. The relation between the religion of the gathering-hunting and the farm Bushmen with their different but complementary emphases is parallelled by the roles of Taoism and Confucianism in classical China. Traditional Bushman religion and classical Taoism indeed seem to be kindred, both skipping and floating lightly through the world.

Virtually all the field reports refer to the widely divergent, sometimes conflicting views found even among members of the same group. To the traditional Bushmen themselves this is not an embarrassment. They are not in need of a neat doctrinal system. Ambiguity is no threat.

The ambiguity becomes manifest in Bushman concept(s) of the *deity* itself.[19] It is more than a mere divergence of views: what is at stake here is the *nature of knowledge* and the *manner of relating* to the deity. Among the traditional Ghanzi Bushmen investigated by Guenther, for example, the deity (generally known as N!eri[20]) is the creator, the sky god, good and helpful but remote. To the !Xo the deity (Gu/e) is not remote but all around them in close, even intimate contact that permits discourse with him. He may be addressed on a personal plane at any time.[21] Concerning the !Kung in the sixties, Marshall reported (undoubtedly in overgeneralised terms) that they 'believe' in two gods, a greater creator god (Gao!na) and a lesser one (//Gauwa). Both have wives (created by the great god) and children, are attended by the spirits of the dead, and live in the sky – the great god in the east, the lesser one in the west.[22]

What about the shadowy figure of the *second deity*?[23] Is he identical with the creator, or perhaps his son or jealous rival? And what is his nature? Is he a visible (and quite abominable looking) person, or a spirit, or something else? Is he one or many? Is he associated with the sky (albeit with a lower region than the creator), or with the earth, or with both? And how is he related to these domains: is he somehow one with earth (or sky), or does he merely live and move *in* and *between* them? Is he good or evil? He may be all of these! In fact, all the 'ors' inserted in the questions above are misplaced. The point is precisely that he need not be one *or* the other, this *or* that. All the field reports indicate that the Bushmen are well aware of the limitations of their knowledge. But ambiguity (which is what I wish to highlight) should not be confused with ignorance or uncertainty. The important point is that in the relatively balanced setting of traditional Bushman culture there is no need to make hard and fast divisions between good and evil, deity and humans, deity and hero-trickster, divinity and nature.[24] I suggest that in their inconsistent and teasingly contradictory accounts and stories about //Gauwa and Gao!na, the !Kung (to confine ourselves to that single group for now) maintain that good as well as evil, creation as well as destruction[25] are divine works, somehow cohering in the ruptured nature of things – but not fixable in a stable synthesis. Yet ultimately good prevails over evil. That is why any ordinary shaman can see the 'the lesser god' //Gauwa during the healing dance, and rush at him, striking him and hurling insults at him.

The trickster-deity changes appearance and form at will (animal, human or plant[26]) and plays pranks in which the normal order of things is turned upside down. The question vexing Western scholars – whether /Kaggen is insect *or* god – may turn out to be a pseudo-problem after all: ambiguously, he can be both.[27] At night around the fire the trickster can be the subject of bawdy jokes[28] as well as an object of fear ('awe'). Totally unconventional, he transgresses even the strictest taboos such as those on incest and cannibalism.[29] He is hero and antihero rolled into one: shuttling and shoving to and fro across the divides of everyday life by changing himself into various forms, changing people into animals, bringing them back from death to life, and so on; at the same time he is 'subject to passions, hungers, sins, stupidities, failures, frustrations and humiliations' – only on a larger scale and more grotesquely than humans,[30] as Marshall puts it.

The polarities of good and evil, divine and human, animal and human, life and death flow, separate, merge and are held together in their differences in the religious imagination.[31] That is why good and evil are distinct but not separated: the two principles (gods) may be at cross-purposes, but they may also talk things over and agree.[32] The opposing centrifugal and centripetal forces of life remain in tension, and are never stabilised in a stasis, allowing for shifts of emphasis as the situation requires.

Marshall's description of the character of Gao!na vividly illustrates the !Kung's cognitive ambiguity – and her own bewilderment. Although the great god and the trickster share the same name, we are told, the 'two beings' 'could hardly be more different', and the people imagine them as 'different'. Yet by 'some sense of logical necessity', thinking 'that somehow in the rightness of things these two beings must be one', the !Kung identify the two in a 'forced and superficial verbal resolution'.[33] Marshall realises that 'current needs' may have led the !Kung to upgrade Gao!na's role as powerful creator, controller of all things (even of death, which was not the case in earlier religion[34]), and deeply interested in humans.[35] Yet she does not offer any explanation for the change.[36] According to the argument developed above, this emphasis on Gao!na as the guarantor of order (drawing even death into this orbit) would counterbalance the threat of a complete breakdown of the old traditions and of all stability, entailed by the !Kung's drift into the 'modern' epoch on the outskirts of farms. The unstructured, polymorphous abandon of the old religion was curtailed as new conditions posed new threats. Despite the accuracy of her fieldwork Marshall misses this point when she finds the consistency of their logic suspect.

Schmidt's[37] treatment of the extremely multivalent and polymorphous /Xam supernatural being /Kaggen reveals the same bias.[38] She describes /Kaggen as simultaneously a stupid, evil trickster and the fearsome lord of the animals; manifestation and function of the supreme god; source of evil and helper of people. It becomes apparent that modern Westerners do not easily rid themselves of the dissociative, rationalist logic of 'identity' (either-or thinking) when she imposes an *un*ambiguous *dis*continuity between deity and insect: the insect shares the deity's name but is not 'identical'[39] with him.

The Bushmen represent a mode of thought[40] which is prior to the philosophical monisms of India; the monotheistic, substantialised dualities of God and Evil, God and (hu-)Man, God and World of western Asia; as well as the polytheistically[41] differentiated pantheons of the Indo-Europeans to which contemporary critics of 'modern' Europe usually turn. Bushman thought engages in a nonanalytical involvement with the world around them. In Eurasia this kind of approach was overtaken roughly three and a half to two and a half millennia ago by analytical, reflexive-systematic modes of thought. At that time iron technology appeared, writing was simplified and its application extended among an elite, first in the Middle East, then in India, China and Greece.[42] Even the orally transmitted myths of Greece have come down to us in much more formalised (that is 'constructed' as well as 'fixed') format than the Bushman stories. In an exuberance of individual spontaneity, the traditional Bushman stories grow and adapt as life proceeds on its course. There is no canon of Bushman lore, no authoritative stock available for 'application' or 'reinterpretation', no store of standardised stories,[43] no elite of specialist bards.[44] Certainly there are recurring themes, but they are constantly recreated around the camp fire. Theirs was an essentially oral culture, without an 'original' text – and hence without absolute truth;[45] constantly remade as the many small egalitarian bands of extremely loquacious people, men and women alike, shared their ongoing life in the world: existing on the fluid edge where order and chaos meet.

An implication of what has been said above is that it is not sufficient to rehabilitate the traditional Bushman mode of thinking by defining it as 'mythical' reason, distinguishing it from the 'demythologising' mode manifested in modern culture – at least not if we accept the view that a 'myth' makes present some primordial realities, or that it recounts a primordial event, thus guaranteeing the meaning of life, portraying a saving power and providing a paradigm for action;[46] or that it is an authoritative, final and unquestionable narrative, legitimating and illuminating some underlying structure, and referring to eternity and necessity.[47] Bushman stories simply do not have those 'awesome', serious qualities.[48] Shallow superficiality, or nonprofound profundity? In terms of Eliade's[49] rather heavy concept of myth, the Bushman narratives certainly pertain to a *coincidentia oppositorum*, but this is not situated in a seriously 'sacred' *illud tempus* that existed (or will come to pass) sometime,[50] as opposed to a 'profane' now. If one takes the word 'myth' in that serious sense (and it seems to be the most generally held scholarly view), Bushman thought is fascinatingly 'demythologising'. When reading the stories of traditional Bushmen one is immediately struck by their light-hearted, gambolling quality. They do not have 'myths' in the heavy sense of the word.[51] Their traditional thought, situated in a veld environment, seems to be pre-'mythical', and not in a temporal sense. Their stories express a very direct, immediate experience of the world. The dimension of a very distant, creative past is certainly there,[52] but it is not *re-presented* now – not in the sense of a qualitatively very different order of being made present again, or copied, or repeated, or returned to. At most it is an aetiological fringe to the present. There is no awesome Past or Future, no inexorable cyclic view of Time, no antithetic 'sacred' and 'profane', no ontological dichotomy. Eliade's theory does not allow for that possibility.[53] In transcending the differences between human and divine, profane and sacred, now and that hallowed time (*illud tempus*), Bushman religious intuition in fact comes very close to that of some mystical sages from classical Indian and Chinese religions[54] – and in a shockingly jocular vein, debunking the seriousness of existence. There is just life in all its moments, sometimes sad and sometimes happy, and being part of it, not setting oneself up outside it. The happy science that Nietzsche strove so hard to achieve they just lived, seemingly without effort.

A dilemma of the interpretation that I am presenting in this chapter is that, like even the most sympathetic anthropological accounts or poetic renderings of their stories, it *stands outside* the charmed circle of the Bushman participatory mode, their involvement with things, through which boundaries dissolve and all share in all. Far from *us* 'interpreting' their 'primitive' stories by recasting them in other (our) terms, *they* are a step ahead. Far from Christianity (in its highly institutionalised and theologised forms) being self-evidently superior to this outlook as has always been taken for granted, it is challenged to its very solid (*precisely those very solid*) foundations. Traditional Bushman religion wafts almost imperceptibly, like a light breeze over a sun-baked landscape; minimally institutionalised, decentralised, diffuse. But what an unsettling, transformative agent it is turning out to be!

Instead of being easily relegated to a superseded primitive stage of human mental development, it is coevally claiming a position as worthy partner in intercultural dialogue. For example, I suggest that, on a metaphysical level, Taoism and the Buddhist Hua-yen intuition of the mutual interpenetration of a *plural*-istically conceived *uni*-verse articulates well with the style of Bushman religion. This book explores the extent to which this most ancient religion of southern Africa may – posthumously, it tragically seems – contribute transformatively to the spiritual quality of our existence in our shaking contemporary world. These essays are about how they remind us of almost forgotten dimensions of religion that can still be retrieved from the mystical and mythical experiences of our tradition.

The epistemology of ambiguity is coupled with an ontology of fluidity. The fluid world is not, need not, and cannot be pigeon-holed. To modern Europeans the almost incomprehensible connection of seemingly contradictory characteristics was the real cause for the unclear picture of Khoisan religion.[55] Therefore, even if (some, perhaps even most of) the present !Kung 'believe' (Marshall[56]) that the great god created the lesser god, the status of such a 'belief' would differ vastly from that of a dogma, analytically and intellectually espoused. The differences of opinion between various

Bushman groups are not equivalent to those between, for instance, rival Christian groups.

Their speech about God does not pretend to correspond with his nature. It is expressive, not realistic, whether uncritical or critical. To some !Kung he has black hair, a long beard and hair on his chest, wears white pants, a shirt and a hat as he rides majestically across the earth and the sky on his horse, a gun in his hand which he fires every so often. He lives in a double-storeyed stone house with a roof of shining corrugated iron, where he feasts on a superabundance of honey, locusts, fat flies and butterflies.[57] This image is every bit as anthropomorphic as all god-talk inevitably is. But, more specifically, it operates completely unselfconsciously in the narrow cracks between old and new, between identity and the dissolution of identity, Bushman and European, might and vulnerability, like a flower sprouting from a cleft in a rock. It explores those ruptures, and at the same time seeks to establish some new connection. God appears in the contrasts, emphasising and harmonising them.[58]

Their 'theology', 'demonology' and 'cosmology' are not expressed in rigorously analytical, conceptualised, precise dogma, but in stories. The actors are animals, the absolute distinction between humans and animals is blurred. This is more than a mere personification in which human qualities are attributed to animals. These animals have nonanimal attributes: they speak, are married and have kinsmen, and they override the ontological difference between animals, humans and heavenly bodies. Among the /Xam, the stars Alpha and Beta Centauri were once humans and, at the same time, lions; all the stars[59] and the sun were once people; the most incongruous (to Western eyes) animals are mated: mantis's wife is dassie, his sister blue crane, his daughter porcupine, his grandson ichneumon.[60] Among the G/wi the offspring of the great deity N!adima include nonhuman creatures.[61] Thus the ontological boundaries are overstepped and diluted in an all-inclusive reticulation of beings.

The acute observation of animal behaviour for which the Bushmen are renowned is linked to a cosmology of interdependence and fluid identity of the various kinds of beings; boundaries are deliberately and humorously broken down, or playfully leaped across, and positions are reversed.[62] Among the nineteenth century !Xam, baboons were not only presented as speaking the Bushman language, as Dia!kwain told Bleek and Lloyd in the

1870s, but they (like the quagga) 'were once people at the time when we who are people were not here'.[63] In embodiments other than their usual bodies, shamans turn into jackals, birds or lions to see whether their dependants are safe.[64] At death the shaman's heart becomes a star.[65] Nature is a network of uncanny communication between humans and animals, even deceit barely masking understanding.[66] Types and degrees of knowledge, action and influence that in the modern Western worldview would be rejected as impossible or side-lined as supernatural, fall within the bounds of the normal, if at times the extraordinary.

Between the hunted in the throes of death and the hunter exists a sympathetic bond,[67] in the sense of simultaneous reciprocal sensation: the eland is not simply shot and its death awaited as a matter of course as the poison works through the body. The hunter limps along and simulates in other ways a dying eland, thereby influencing the wounded animal to die.[68] Springbok know when people are about to die.[69] Dividing lines between humans and natural forces blur as the wind cries its sympathetic foreknowledge of death and warns people of impending disaster.[70] At times the modern interpreter is bound to be confused by the ease with which seemingly insurmountable ontological barriers are crossed. In Dia!kwain's stories of the water bull, realism blends with surrealism, fact with poetry (in modern Western categories) as the shamans, in a transformed but completely natural state of consciousness, open to the deep potency of the world, drag the water bull from the water, kill it, cut it up and scatter its meat, thereby causing the rain to fall.[71] This is neither arbitrary and fanciful analogy, nor naive confusion of reality with hallucination. It articulates an intensely dynamic cosmos, simultaneously pluralistic, multidimensional and harmonious, accessible on a variety of levels (waking state, trance, dream). In this polymorphous world of the Bushmen dreams are windows, stories are doors and trance states are avenues to deeper and more potent levels of reality than are accessible to ordinary awareness.[72] This enables the shaman to move around at night on extracorporeal travels,[73] and to heal his people.

The Bushmen were not naive. To them, life and death depended on meticulous observation and logical inference.[74] But their shrewd, down-to-earth matter-of-factness operated in a multivalent world. Surrounded by animals, partly living off animals, in a cognitive framework that allowed for the transformation of human into animal and vice versa, the Bushmen experienced at least some animals as symbols of transcendence par excellence.

In this framework the eland, for example, could become an extraordinarily potent metaphor and symbol of divine power experienced by Bushman dancers in a state of trance.[75]

As said, it is not just a matter of a multiplicity of Bushman views on the various issues discussed above.[76] The attributes of 'amorphousness, fragmentation and fluidity'[77] displayed are important. But whereas Guenther sees their beliefs as 'isolated' from the practical economic and social reality[78] of traditional veld Bushmen, I see them as essentially related to this reality. They fulfil the important function of overriding restrictions and loosening the system, keeping the ordered, fairly comfortable life of the veld Bushmen open. That is why the qualities and agents of the 'other' world are associated with the ludic qualities of 'amusement, imaginativeness and enchantment'.[79] In their stories, abounding with scatological and sexual overtones and jokes, the matter-of-fact, prosaic, common-sense 'facts' of everyday life (of which they are perfectly aware!) are often surrealistically de-absolutised.[80] The relatively secure veld life of traditional Bushmen *needs* this. *And* it can *afford* it. Veld Bushmen, ensconced in the world, joke and laugh. Faced with the total collapse of the traditional order and the disjointedness of everyday life as experienced by impoverished farm Bushmen, this would not happen. In that situation, the *intuition of the horizon* (which may be a definition of religion) would become primarily the source of order, as is indeed the case among the farm Bushmen. But it must be stressed that the relativising goes hand in hand with the ordering, nonidentity with identity.

Barnard to some extent confirms the theoretical approach adopted above. He is correct in stating that Guenther underestimates the structural uniformity of Khoisan religions. But he defines fluidity as strictly secondary to structure,[81] whereas I see them as essentially equal, co-originating and mutually conditioning partners in the same process. There is always the horizon, encircling the here and now. Felt intuitively (mystically), approximated symbolically, enacted ritually and expressed mythically, the dreams of distant realms seek a balance between safety and freedom, which is peace.

To account for Bushman epistemology, we do not need hypotheses such as that of a 'primitive mentality' supposedly representing an earlier stage in human biopsychological evolution. Their way of thinking is an epochal phenomenon, tied to the hunting-gathering stone-wielding conditions of an earlier, never to be repeated period of human history. But who knows what is in store for humanity – now that its 'modern' ways of thinking are clearly exposed to being correlationally tied to the peculiar sociocultural, technological syndrome of recent centuries, one which is in the throes of an epochal transition to something new? In earlier epochs, humanity's ways of cosmic orientation had been similarly related to the concomitance of iron smelting, crop cultivation, animal husbandry and the settlement of larger conglomerations of people. We are in fact witnessing a need to discover and experiment (or play) with other modes of relating to divinity than those formulated in theology and dogma. The Bushmen remind us of such possibilities. How the wheel has turned ...

Let us pause for a while to ponder this remarkable revolution of the wheel of religious history. Of course we are not witnessing a mere return to the past. In fact, the sociocultural conditions obtaining in traditional Bushman society and those in contemporary South African society are poles apart. But there can be no doubt that the tone and mode of religious sentiment in the most 'primitive' and the most 'advanced' types of society converge in some respects: in both, beliefs tend to be vague, variable, selective, pragmatic, tolerant and adaptable.[82] Far from being a curio from a distant, 'primitive' past, Bushman religion is a challenging dialogue partner across the centuries, and makes a unique contribution to a conditionalist religious philosophy, a truly South African spirituality that encompasses the whole of South African history. Such a religious philosophy and spirituality would avoid the twin pitfalls of a simplistic *philosophia/religio perennis*, and of sheer discontinuity between then and now.

Certainly the religion of the Bushmen may not be extrapolated to become a model of 'original', 'primal' or 'proto'-religion of humankind. Bushman religion, like the religions of other hunter-gatherer societies known from the recent past, stands not at the *beginning* but at the *end* of a development of many millennia. And the differences between the various hunter-gatherer religions are very real, in spite of certain common features linking ancient America with ancient Europe, Australia and Africa. Yet they speak to us. Compelled to respond to overwhelmingly difficult conditions impinging on their traditional lifestyle, the hunter-gatherers remind us of the openness of being.

ENDNOTES

1 Cf M G Guenther, Bushman religion and the (non)sense of anthropological theory of religion, *Sociologus*, 1979, 29(2), pp 102–132 on the differences between 'traditional' and 'modern' beliefs in mid-twentieth century Botswana. These two epochs conflict and interact in the same chronological era.

2 H J Heinz, Elements of !ko Bushmen religious belief, *Anthropos*, 1975, 70(1/2), pp 17–41. M Guenther, *The Nharo Bushmen of Botswana: tradition and change*, Hamburg: Helmut Buske Verlag, 1986, p 216 accounts for this as the result of the absence of religious specialists in Bushman society, the lack of any formal religious education for children, and the mobility and isolation of groups.

3 That such an attempt need not be arbitrary is claimed by A Barnard, *Hunters and herders of Southern Africa: a comparative ethnography of the Khoisan peoples*, Cambridge: Cambridge University Press, 1992, pp 251ff. See also J D Lewis-Williams & J H N Loubser, Deceptive appearances: a critique of Southern African rock art studies, *Advances in world archaeology,* Vol 5, Academic Press, 1986, p 265.

4 Their technology (technologies) would be another set of creative-adaptive responses. What I have in mind may be fairly similar to Parkington's use of the concepts 'time' and 'place' with reference to stone tool manufacture – 'time' referring to the continuous tradition, and 'place' (which is much more than mere locality) to 'the set of opportunities', the nexus of circumstances, eliciting specific activities (J Parkington, Time and place: some observations on spatial and temporal patterning in the Later Stone Age sequence in Southern Africa, *South African Archaeological Bulletin*, 1980, 35, pp 73–83).

5 Cf L Marshall, !Kung Bushman religious beliefs, *Africa*, 1962, XXXII(3), p 221; Heinz, Elements of !ko Bushmen ..., pp 33ff; Guenther, Bushman religion and the (non)sense ..., p 110.

6 G B Silberbauer, *Hunter and habitat in the central Kalahari desert*, Cambridge: Cambridge University Press, 1981, pp 51–137.

7 Cf J G Platvoet, De eigenheid van godsdiensten van volken zonder schrift, in T Chowdhury, W Claesens & W Logister (reds), *Het kosmisch patroon: het vele en het ene in de godsdiensten*, Tilburg: Tilburg University Press, 1989, p 34, for the *etic* descriptions of the worldviews of all preliterate cultures, leading to synthetic pictures, far more systematic, coherent and clear than was possible in the minds of those people themselves. For a general but useful synoptic description of the characteristics of 'the community religions of small preliterate societies' (whose beliefs tend to be 'vague, varied, adoptive and adaptable'), cf Platvoet, The place of African Traditional Religions among the religions of mankind, sl, sa.

8 Silberbauer, *Hunter and habitat* ..., p 51, following Clifford Geertz.

9 Ibid, p 52.

10 Ibid, p 116.

11 Ibid, p 116.

12 Ibid, p 100.

13 Ibid, pp 100–101 on the 'interrelationship of meteorological phenomena'.

14 Heinz, Elements of !ko Bushmen ..., p 34.

15 Silberbauer, *Hunter and habitat* ..., pp 120ff.

16 Guenther, Bushman religion and the (non)sense ...,; *The Nharo Bushmen* ...

17 As Heinz (Elements of !ko Bushmen ..., p 37), concurring with Guenther, points out: 'Religious beliefs, including food taboos, are particularly subject to personal interpretation because a !ko is just not uniformly exposed to the strict interpretation of a closed community.'

18 Guenther (Bushman religion and the [non]sense ..., p 119) regards the explanation of this as 'probably the greatest theoretical challenge in the field of Bushman studies'.

19 Guenther (Bushman religion and the (non)sense ..., p 106) contrasts the ambiguity of the traditional Ghanzi Bushmen concept of God with the much more clear-cut theology of the farm Bushmen. Heinz (Elements of !ko Bushmen ..., p 22), whilst distinguishing the deity *Gu/e* from the created, subservient 'second force' */oa* among the !Xo, significantly adds in a footnote: 'But perhaps *Gu/e* and */oa* are one and the same without a clear distinction. During various discussions I gained the impression that the !ko recognize that there are forces of good and evil. Though they tend to equate *Gu/e* with the former and */oa* with the latter, this distinction is not always apparent or clear ... the !ko seem to waver in making a clear distinction. Their uncertainty appears to arise also from the recognition that to do either, that is good or evil, requires power or strength which in the final analysis, they attribute only to the creator.'

This shows that the Bushmen grappled with the problem of theodicy (if a good God, then whence evil?), just like the philosopically more sophisticated religions of the world. The Bushmen side with the more pantheistically inclined religions of (e g) India (Hinduism, Jainism, Buddhism), rather than with the dualistically inclined religions of the Near East (Zoroastrianism, Judaism, Christianity, Islam), where God and Evil are metaphysically opposed to one another. For an account of the multivalence of Khoisan concepts of the divinity, see Barnard (*Hunters and herders* ..., pp 251–264). He also refers to the 1930 classic of Schapera (*The Khoisan peoples of South Africa: Bushmen and Hottentots*, London: Routledge & Kegan Paul, 1960 [1930], p 396): 'The beliefs regarding //Gaua ... are not crystallized into clear-cut conceptions, but are vague, inconsistent, and ambiguous.'

20 Given the complexities and differences in orthography, and because this is not a specialised study of the Bushmen, diacritical marks will be kept to a minimum.

21 Heinz, Elements of !ko Bushmen ..., p 36.

22 Marshall, !Kung Bushman ..., p 223. For an account of recent !Kung creation beliefs, see p 234.

23 Called //Gauwa by the Nharo Bushmen of Ghanzi, /oa by the !Xo.

24 This ambivalence also applies to heavenly bodies and other natural phenomena. In her careful formulations Marshall (Kung Bushman ...) allows for a range of possibilities regarding the divine character or otherwise of heavenly bodies, and of rain among the many Bushmen groups.

25 Ibid, pp 238ff. Biesele (Religion and folklore of !Kung Hunter Gatherers, 2 vols, thesis presented to the Department of Anthropology, Harvard University, 1975, Vol I, p 164) summarises that the 'Lesser God ... is generally thought of as the destroyer.'

Among the G/wi of central Botswana, says Silberbauer (*Hunter and habitat* ..., pp 55ff), the relationship between N!adima (the creator) and G//amama (the second, polymorphous divine being, intent on harming humans) is 'unclear', but generally they 'were considered to be separate and distinct and were not seen as differing aspects of the one entity', although this idea is entertained by some scholars. He does not indicate whether there are any differences between the hunter-gatherer and farm-squatting G/wi.

26 Referring to the !Kung in the 1950s, Marshall (!Kung Bushman ..., pp 228ff) reports a similar multivalence in respect of the trickster Gao!na.

27 According to Barnard, *Hunters and herders* ..., pp 84–85.

28 The !Kung 'howl and roll on the ground with laughter at his (that is Gao!na's) humiliations' (Marshall, !Kung Bushman ..., p 228).

29 Thus Gao!na among the !Kung (Marshall, !Kung Bushman ..., pp 228ff; cf S Schmidt, Die Mantis religiosa in den Glaubensvorstellungen der Khoesan-Völker, *Zeitschrift für Ethnologie*, 1973, 98(1), p 119). Whereas Prometheus stole fire from heaven for the benefit of humankind, Gao!na only 'wanted fire for himself because he liked cooked food and gave the fire to man rather as an afterthought' (Marshall, !Kung Bushman ..., p 228). Cf J David (*Interweaving symbols of individuation in African and European fairy tales: a Jungian perspective*, Cape Town: Kaggen Press, 1991, pp 63–72) on the trickster archetype with its total lack of conventionality, breaking all possible rules, in whom 'the primal, daemonic energies of the world pulse, as they do not in the merely good and law-abiding'.

30 Marshall, !Kung Bushman ..., p 229.

31 Biesele's framework for understanding the Bushman tales (Biesele, *Folklore and ritual* ..., pp 149–175, 280, etc) is structuralist, positing binary oppositions which are harmonised. But it seems to me that this limited degree of 'unity in diversity' (p 280) is effectively belied by her own fieldwork. Another point: for obvious reasons she restricts herself to the role of an anthropologist in the Western academic tradition, refusing to be drawn into a fusion of horizons (Gadamer) that would dramatically challenge Western cultural assumptions. It is precisely this kind of '*coincidentia oppositorum*' that I am exploring here.

32 Marshall, !Kung Bushman ..., p 245.

33 Ibid, p 228.

34 Ibid, p 234.

35 Ibid, p 244.

36 'I am sure that current emotional needs and the imaginations of the people who are now living have continued to be at work upon the image, interpreting it, recreating it, and bringing it to its present form' (ibid, p 233).

37 Schmidt, Die Mantis religiosa ...

38 Of course, I should acknowledge the potential implications of my own use of the words 'supernatural' and 'being' in this sentence. Both derive from a particularly Western cognitive frame, and are not directly transferable to the Bushman context.

39 Schmidt, Die Mantis religiosa ..., p 124. Bushman logic sheds a most interesting light on Christian logic in its efforts to articulate the nature of divinity (the trinity), the relationship between divinity and the humanity of Jesus (christology), and the

relationship between the body and blood of Christ and the elements of holy communion. Concepts such as *homoousios, homoiousios, monophysitism, modalism, theotokos, filioque* and *an-/enhypostasis* all attest to this long struggle.

40 Not to be confused with a different type of 'logic' in which the principle of non-contradiction or consistency is supposedly not recognised. No such assumption is called for.

41 Biesele, Religion and folklore ..., p 162 comments on the difficulty of determining whether Bushmen believe in one god or in many gods.

42 For a detailed sociohistorical and religiohistorical scheme, cf Platvoet, De wraak van de 'primitieven': godsdienstgeschiedenis van Neanderthaler tot New Age, *Nederlands Theologisch Tijdschrift*, 1993, 47(3), pp 227–243.

43 The G/wi, says Silberbauer (*Hunter and habitat.*, pp 57ff), do not have a strong sense of tradition, 'and tradition is not petrified and perpetuated by its elevation to sacredness.' Platvoet (De eigenheid van godsdiensten ..., pp 27ff) points out that preliterate societies and religions without formal education and a culture of reflective, systematic thought cannot have a strong historical sense either. With due appreciation of the intentions and execution of S Watson's *Return of the moon: versions from the /Xam*, Cape Town: Carrefour Press, 1991, there is an unintended irony in the way some Bushman stories told to Bleek are turned into a collection of written poems – thus making them a literary monument.

44 Biesele, Folklore and ritual..., Vol I, pp 96ff.

45 See M Detienne's linking of these two (*The creation of mythology*, Chicago: University of Chicago Press, 1986). Among preliterate cultures there is no orthodoxy, no missionary drive to convince others of the rightness of a particular set of ideas, no heretic-hunting (Platvoet, De eigenheid van godsdiensten ..., pp 34ff).

46 Thus J Degenaar, Imagination and myth, in M Clasquin, J D Ferreira-Ross, D Marais & R Sadowsky (eds), *Myth and interdisciplinary studies*, Pretoria: Unisa, 1992, p 21.

47 Following C Seerveld, 'Mythologising philosophy' as historiographic category, in Clasquin et al, *Myth and interdisciplinary studies* ..., pp 28–48.

48 This emerges from both nineteenth- and twentieth-century anthropological accounts. Cf D F Bleek, Customs and beliefs of the /Xam Bushmen, Part I: Baboons, *Bantu Studies*, 1931, 5, pp 167–179; Part II (the Lion), Part III (Game animals), Part IV (Omens, wind-making, clouds), *Bantu Studies*, 6, 1932, pp 47–63, 233–249, 321–342); Part V (Rain), Part VI (Rainmaking), *Bantu Studies*, 1933, 7, pp 297–312, 375–392); Part VII (Sorcerers), *Bantu Studies*, 1935, 9, pp 1–47); Part VIII (More about sorcerers and charms), *Bantu Studies*, 1936, 10, pp 163–199). Also Biesele, *Folklore and ritual* ... For example, most of the stories featuring the trickster god 'are bawdy and scatological, and are cause for great hilarity among the !Kung' (Biesele, *Folklore and Ritual* ..., Vol I, p 114, containing some samples of these stories).

49 M Eliade, *Patterns in comparative religion*, New York: Meridian, 1974, pp 410–436. Strangely, in describing the radically integrating character of the *coincidentia oppositorum*, Eliade nevertheless retains a basic dichotomising tendency which characterises and skews his view of religion: the *coincidentia oppositorum* (which is 'one of the most primitive ways of expressing the paradox of divine reality'), 'in which all contraries are reconciled (or rather, transcended) constitutes what is, in

fact, the most basic definition of divinity, and *shows how utterly different it is from humanity ...'* (ibid, p 419, my italics). This 'awesome' difference does not characterise the Bushman view.

50 Biesele (*Folklore and ritual ...*, pp 81ff) makes the telling point that the !Kung have no stories of either a 'Golden Age' or a future apocalypse, or of journeys to another world. The loci of the tales are simply the camp and the bush. Likewise '/Xam narratives tend not to be set in an ancient or other-wordly time' (Barnard, *Hunters and herders ...*, p 82).

51 This is confirmed in respect of at least the !Kung by Biesele (*Folklore and ritual ...*, p 101) when she says that there is no 'formal distinction between 'sacred' stories and 'profane' stories. No sort of story is considered to be 'more true' than another. I tried in vain to find verbal equivalents for 'stories which are considered true' and 'stories which are considered false', or for 'myths' versus 'folktales', or for other distinctions'.

52 Biesele (ibid, p 99) establishes that 'it is hard to tell an ordinary narrative of a recent, actual event from a narrative of the olden times (though there do exist specific distinguishing features)'. Accordingly, though 'there is keen enthusiasm over the performance of stories, their contents themselves are looked upon with scorn. The stories are heard with anything but awed reverence. Instead, amused indignation greets the outrageous or bumbling adventures of the long-ago people' (ibid, p 100).

53 As Platvoet, De eigenheid ..., p 31 points out with reference to preliterate peoples generally, the *etic* conceptual pairs of sacred-profane, natural-supernatural, church-world, etc, being derived mainly from the Christian world, do not apply. Not only is there a minimum of institutional differentiation and stratification within the group, but the net of complex kinship is extended to *include* the spirits. In various ways they are part of society.

54 This, of course, does *not* imply that the enormous differences between the socioreligious contexts of the Bushmen and the other complexes may be overlooked.

55 As Schmidt (Die Mantis religiosa ..., p 123) pointed out.

56 Marshall, !Kung Bushman ..., p 223.

57 Ibid, p 236.

58 Consistent with the ambivalent character of God, only the greatest and bravest shamans can see him in the flesh; mostly he appears to anyone, but only in dreams, and 'helps all his people' (ibid, pp 237ff).

59 This is denied in respect of present-day G/wi by Silberbauer, *Hunter and habitat ...*, p 109. One certainly gets the impression that the now extinct southern /Xam Bushmen had livelier imaginations and stronger artistic inclinations than the inhabitants of the northern parts of Southern Africa.

60 D F Bleek, Bushman folklore, *Africa*, 1929, 2, pp 302–313. The 'border line between the powers of nature and animals is vague, that between animals and man more so. In all their fables and myths animals are said to have been men ...' (p 309).

61 Silberbauer, *Hunter and habitat ...*, p 53.

62 Expressed by Guenther (*The Nharo Bushmen ...*, p 238) as follows: 'Unlike the western world view, in which man is depicted as a being unique on earth, qualitatively

distinct from and superior to the animals, it is the Nharo view that men and animals are kindred beings. This notion is embedded within the central creation myth of Nharo culture, the myth of double creation, which states that the people of today were the animals of the past and the animals of today were the dawntime people. Animals carry within themselves humanness, men animalness ...'

63 Bleek, Customs and beliefs ..., Part I, p 175. In fact, according to the /Xam all living creatures were once people (Bleek, Special speech of animals and moon used by the /Xam Bushmen, *Bantu Studies*, 1936, 10, p 165).

64 Bleek, Customs and beliefs ..., Part VII, pp 15ff, 43ff; ibid, Part VIII, pp 131ff. In the latter story a shaman relates killing a Boer farmer's ox when in his lion's body, and being shot by the farmer.

65 Bleek, Customs and beliefs ..., Part VII, p 24.

66 For example, Bleek (ibid, Part II, pp 47ff) recorded instances of the /Xam understanding of the communication between people and lions: the lion puts his tail into his mouth when he wants to sound like a human; the crow and the owl warn people against the lion; flies tell the lion when people speak ill of him, so his name is not mentioned by children.

67 Biesele (*Folklore and ritual* ..., Vol I, pp 160ff) speaks of ritually expressed 'sympathetic identification' with the prey.

68 Bleek, Customs and beliefs ..., Part III, pp 233ff.

69 Ibid, pp 242ff.

70 Ibid, Part IV, pp 330ff.

71 Ibid, Part VI, pp 375ff.

72 Bleek records the touching story of Dia!kwain's dream, reflecting the clashes between hunter and farmer in the nineteenth-century northern Cape. Dreaming of a sheep theft, whereafter the irate farmer beat his father to death, Dia!kwain knew in advance that his father would die. In fact, it turned out, his father had died of an old back ailment (Customs and beliefs ..., Part IV, pp 326ff).

73 Ibid, Part VII, pp 24, 26.

74 Heinz (Elements of !ko Bushmen ..., p 34): he is 'very much a realist, pragmatist and protoscientist, if we restrict this to imply that he is capable of minute observations and correct deductions from his observations', and of 'certain predictions regarding developments that will take place in the future'.

75 As has been explained in detail by Lewis-Williams & Loubser, Deceptive appearances ... Cf Dowson (Revelations of religious reality ..., pp 122–125) on the 'ambiguous eland'.

76 As with the deities, the notions of the *soul, spirits of the dead* and the *afterlife* vary immensely (cf Marshall, !Kung Bushman ..., pp 238ff; Guenther, Bushman religion and the (non)sense ..., pp 110ff; Heinz, Elements of !ko ...). According to one view found among the Ghanzi Bushmen by Guenther, the dead just dissolve; according to others, they become ghosts. The !Xo believe in an afterlife, the spirits of good people going to Gu/e, those of bad people to /oa – (Heinz, ibid, p 24). The Nyae Nyae !Kung believe that when people die, *gauwasi* (transformed spirits of the dead) fetch their spirits, hearts and blood and carry these (via the dwelling of the lesser god in the western sky) to the dwelling of Gao!na in the eastern sky, where he

transmutes them into *gauwasi* (cf Marshall, !Kung Bushman ..., pp 242ff). All people, whether good or bad, go to this same place. Among the Nyae Nyae !Kung the *gauwasi* serve Gao!na and //Gauwa, and people fear them and pray to them to invoke their mercy or sympathy (Marshall, ibid, p 241). They may interfere with people's lives and kill them by various means such as causing them to fall from trees or allowing animals to gore or maul them to death. Basically malicious and waiting for a chance to inflict harm, they are nevertheless not wholly evil. People fear them, but they can be driven away (Marshall, ibid, p 244).

The discontinuities between this life and the afterlife contain continuities: *gauwasi* are not merely spirits but have bodies and can eat food. They grow older but are rejuvenated by Gao!na and have everlasting life. They may have spouses but do not beget children (ibid, p 243). To get a wife, a *gauwa* may kill an attractive living woman. They have their own implements and in this respect they need nothing from living people. According to one !Xo view, souls of people who lived before are reborn in babies (Heinz, Elements of !ko ..., p 24).

77 Guenther, Bushman religion ..., p 110.

78 Ibid, p 110.

79 Ibid, p 111.

80 Ibid, p 109.

81 '... fluidity in belief supplements such frameworks and allows them to persist' (Barnard, *Hunters and herders* ..., p 262). Yet his admission that the 'fluidity of religious belief and religious discourse ... is sometimes difficult to define in purely structural terms' (p 263) amounts to an acknowledgment of the inadequacy of the structural paradigm.

82 Cf Platvoet, De wraak van de 'primitieven' ..., p 243.

19 Dancing in between

No great number of rituals has been reported of any Bushman society, past or present. Furthermore, as the Bushmen drift into modern society, all rituals except the healing dance (and perhaps funeral rites[1]) seem to be on the decline.

Despite many variations, the healing dance is fairly uniform in its general character and is by far the most important ritual among all groups. It is the focus and centre of their religious life. It has been described and filmed often enough, and with great empathy, by anthropologists.[2] It is to this ritual, as practised by the traditional !Kung of about thirty years ago, that I now turn.

Here we take a ritual to be a set of rhythmic, repetitive actions in which a number of individuals take part in a coordinated manner and with religious intent. The difficult question (and a vital one from the point of view of this study) is exactly what is 'religious' intent? In what sense is it 'religious'?

Before explaining in detail how I understand that, we need to observe the dance in our mind's eye, with some excellent anthropological field accounts to guide us. After this brief, ideal-typical description of a !Kung healing dance, we shall consider its 'religious' implications.

But first, let me posit some general points of departure and some prompting questions. If I call the dance a 'religious' act, I mean that in and through the dance the Bushman group strives to achieve an optimal and very profound connectedness with the vast world surrounding them and the forces that impinge on their lives. This implies both curbing the threats of chaos and challenging certain limits. They step right over the line – which is not an absolute line to begin with. The dance is essentially a liminal event,[3] taking place 'in between'.

We shall be interested not only in the internal coherence of the dance as a complex, but specifically in how it relates to the cognitive pattern of the !Kung (discussed in chapter 18). How does it depend on and promote, express and reinforce a particular way of looking at the world? How does the ritual relate to altered states of consciousness[4] that occur among the !Kung when they dance? Furthermore, could one establish some sort of relation with different forms of altered states of consciousness, found in other religions? Here we shall take care not to digress into abstract comparative schemes, but will stick concretely to one other religious complex (Buddhism).

Throughout, I work on the assumption that the Bushman healing dance is culturally conditioned to a very large degree. It is stereotyped but uniquely Bushman, and it would require an act of interpretive violence that will bring its own retribution to level the differences between that ritual and, say, Buddhist ritual. Futhermore, I shall bear it in mind that the dances are subject to innovations introduced by inspired individuals and are experienced differently by individual dancers, as anthropological reports show. But in the end I shall assume that at a profound level what transpires at those dances are true homoversal events, like language and marriage, and that the dance expresses a homoversal religious meaning.

Dancing ...

The following is an ideal-typical description of the basic choreography of a !Kung healing dance.[5] It usually takes place at night, at full moon, and often lasts all night long. The !Kung may dance to celebrate, but the main purpose is to drive away evil and cure sickness.

In a circle around a fire which is kept burning all night the women sit, clapping and singing. In a wider circle around them, closer to the darkness surrounding the firelight, the men dance, occasionally joined by a woman, sometimes by a number of women. Sometimes people sit around smaller fires. Steadily, hour after hour, the dancers wear a furrow into the ground as they dance their meticulously executed short steps, bodies erect. The only musical instruments are rattles they may be wearing around their legs. An occasional dancer may carry a walking stick. Above the staccato rhythm of clapping hands, stamping feet and rattles, the medicine songs, named after the powerful forces of rain, sun, giraffe, eland, honey, buffalo and mamba, are sung.

After several dances power (*n/um*) is activated in some of the dancers. This power, heated by the fire, the clapping of the women and the dancing, starts to boil in the pit of the stomach and moves up the spinal columns of the dancers into their heads. They start to shake violently, stagger and fall down. Entering into another dimension of consciousness (*!kia*), a few men begin to cure their people. They touch the sick with their hands and draw the sickness into themselves. Then, howling, they throw it out into the darkness where the trickster deity and the spirits of the dead are lurking, waiting to carry the spirits of the sick away. The shamans pick up coals, rub these into their hair, hurl burning sticks at the spirits and storm out into the darkness to confront them. Their spirits leave their bodies through the head in order to fight with god and the spirits, pleading with them, cajoling and forcing them to take back the evils they have brought. Then the shaman may fall into a state of deep unconsciousness and utter exhaustion, resembling death. Other dancers work him over to restore him and his spirit returns.

... in between

Marshall[6] refers to the motif of the circle throughout the ritual:

> *... the women's circle, the circle that the dancing men imprint in the sand, the circle of firelight, and the circles around the little fires. One is strongly aware also, in that flat, desert land, of the circle of the horizon, and, as one sits through the night, of the circling stars. Humans, earth, and stars appear in like arrangement.*

The circle – symbol of centring integration and of peripheral expansion – points to the ritual situation as a transitional boundary situation. Barriers are crossed and various realms of experience converge. Contrasts between order and dis/trans-order remain, but they lose their character of dualistic opposition. The ritual reflects the cognitive style of Bushman religion, as discussed in chapter 18. In the dance the essential ambiguity, the fluidity between ordinary and extraordinary in Bushman life, becomes manifest on a variety of levels. Centripetal and centrifugal movements operate simultaneously all the time.

In the traditional dance the divisions within a camp, resulting in fear and hostility, are overcome. The dance does not require or permit any esotericism. There are no priests or gurus. The dance and the power engendered by it are equally accessible to all, men and women alike. As the people support one another for the sake of the group, so the power flows through the whole community. The camp is reintegrated.[7] According to Lee[8] the Bushmen seek benevolent power *within* the social body, and project the blame for malevolence *outside* it, onto the deity and the spirits of the dead, thus uniting the living in a common front against hostile external forces. The holistic unity of the camp is suspended between inner conflict and outer conflict. The inner conflict must be overcome, and the outer conflict serves the inner peace, but is also relativised.

The aim of the dance is to heal, which is described by Katz[9] as 'a process of transition toward meaning, balance, wholeness, and connectedness, both within individuals and between individuals and their environments'. It ranges across an all-inclusive spectrum, from physical to emotional to social and cosmological.[10] Whereas illness is a manifestation of some imbalance within the individual and the group in the total context of the surrounding field of forces, healing represents the achievement of some balance. But balance is not the same as standstill. People still die, in spite of dancing and curing. Death remains alien, and the Bushmen do not forget that. Even those who were good people during their lifetimes still become hostile spirits, even under the hands of the shamans. Yet death itself is incorporated in an expanded horizon, in a larger relationship of the community with the gods and the spirits. The limits remain, but they are pushed back a little.

The Bushmen may not exactly be dancing paradisially on Nietzsche's slippery ice; but on the limits between life and death, sickness and health, human community and spirits, they dance through the night. The normal boundaries between people and the spirits of the dead, bent on taking away the spirits of the living, are crossed. Overcoming fear of death, the healers confront the deity and his messengers face to face as they enter the realm of death itself. Ordinary behaviour is reversed as boldness replaces caution.[11]

In traditional Bushman society, the dance is a moment of unequalled intensity in which they seek to expand the ambit of health and life in the face of sickness and death – but without assuming a dichotomy between sacred and profane in the Western sense.[12] The dances do not represent a separate realm of life, and the dancers themselves are not removed from the context of daily living. Especially early in the dance, before the mortal battle with the spirits and the exhaustion set in, there is a lot of banter and fun. The limit of their power, beyond which lies greater power over which they have no control, does not disappear, nor is it entrenched. It is permeable and it is perforated by powerful dancers.

The *n/um* that has been put into the medicine songs, medicine plants and the bodies of the dancers[13] by the great god, is highly ambivalent. It is both beneficial and dangerous.[14] Marshall compares it to electricity, 'powerful and invisible, capable of beneficent effects, but highly dangerous if too strong'.[15] To this divine healing power the healers and their community become connected.

The !Kung dance is a hyperkinetic or 'hyperergotropic'[16] physical activity during which the body is exerted to the utmost. There is no dualistic division between body and spirit/soul. The cosmic *n/um*, activated in the spinal column of the body, is 'spiritual energy'.[17] For the Bushmen there is no route to profound spiritual experience of transcendent realms other than via the body. The intense state of *!kia* is a peak experience, significantly altering and enhancing the healer's normal capacities of consciousness.[18] He may see inside people and into far distances,[19] and undertake terrifying extracorporeal journeys to the home of the deity to save people. It is an experience of transcendence, not merely more intense, but penetrating to deeper levels of perception and knowledge.[20] It is a crossing of boundaries. Yet, says Katz, the boundaries between ordinary awareness and *!kia* (like those between various levels of depth experience) are permeable, not definite. Operating on a primarily intuitive level, *!kia* demands from the healer 'an openness to the unfamiliar', and is closely related to vivid fantasy life.[21] The pursuit of *n/um* and *!kia* leads to psychological and spiritual growth, even to a transformation of personality and change of lifestyle.[22] Clearly the experiences attained during the dance by some dancers are profoundly 'religious' in the sense that they transcend the boundaries of everyday life.

The decline of traditional society has disturbed this harmonious interplay of stark contrasts. As some farm Bushman groups are pushed into marginalised positions over against their stronger black and white masters, the line between the realms of their power and their powerlessness becomes impermeable. Their religion and ritual dance become more institutionalised relative to other areas of life, and become the primary rallying centre of resistance. Firm lines are drawn as they distinguish themselves from the oppressive others. Guenther[23] emphasises this internally integrative role of the dance with reference to suppression from outside by other peoples, even to the extent of establishing a separate Bushman 'identity' over against whites and blacks. Yet it seems that at this point the price of achieving this fixed identity is the weakening of inner coherence. A fixed identity is established at the cost of the old easy inner flow of relationships. Various distinctions unknown in traditional society become pronounced. Boundaries between male and female become more rigid and hierarchical than before. Even in the dance a power struggle beomes evident as some dancers set themselves up as professional healers distinct from the rest of the camp, dancing for payment.[24] The easy-going interplay of *this* and *that* is replaced by rigid divisions.

Bushman religion is a unique manifestation of the perennial spiritual search of humanity. Obviously phenomena must not be abstracted from their contexts, and their relative positions in those contexts must be taken into consideration. But when all provisos against simplistic and superficial comparisons have been taken into account,[25] convergences even with seemingly unrelated phenomena such as Buddhist meditation can be pointed out.

The phenomena are not so fundamentally different in type and quality as to preclude relating them in one framework of understanding. The healing dance is as much a spiritual technique as the Buddhist *ānāpānasati* (mindfulness of inbreathing and outbreathing). Both are rituals in that they are repetitive, rhythmic activities of the body, one as physically strenuous as the other is light, but both effecting altered states of consciousness. Even if non-tantric Buddhist meditation may have attained its contemplative levels in conscious opposition to 'hyperergotropic' techniques, the states of altered consciousness remain of a kind.[26] The *jhānas* (deep states of absorption) of Theravada Buddhism, comparable to the !Kung experience of *!kia*, mark a deepening of concentration. And comparable to the release of power (*n/um*) in the dance and the breakthrough of the apparently fixed moulds of ordinary perception, the early Buddhists also accommodated the six higher powers (*abhiññā*): like the Bushman dancer, the Buddhist yogin attaining those powers may have the sensation of diving into the earth and rising up again as if through water, of floating through the air like a winged bird, or of hearing 'sounds both heavenly and human, far and near'.[27] Taking into account the cultural differences, we may see in both the actualisation of primordial patterns of transcending-integrating, transformed consciousness or 'mature contemplation'.[28] We could go further and relate the Bushman experience of *n/um* boiling up the spine with the *kundalini* experiences of Indian yogins, and understand both 'religiously' as the transcendence of the ordinary and the reintegration of life on a higher plane of awareness. The point of my argument is not to present an interesting array of one-to-one correspondences between Bushman religion and some other so-called 'classic' 'world religions', but to draw attention to the possibility of seeing them as aspects of the same gestalt of spiritual experience.

While on this topic, an aside on South African Buddhism is too tempting to resist. It is tantalising to speculate that had early Buddhists come to Bushman Africa, they might have achieved the same kind of syncretic accommodation between the philosophically 'raw' indigenous culture and Yogacara and Madhyamika thought as they did in Tibet. Comtemporary South African Buddhism sets itself the task of adopting and internalising Tibetan or Chinese/Japanese syncretisms of the message of nonsubstantiality with other local cultures where the Buddhist message has spread – but does not as yet explore the possibility of forging an African synthesis. This is a normal stage, one also experienced by Africans adopting a religion (Christianity) from another very different sociocultural setting. The classic Buddhist teaching proceeded from a very specific Indian context of roughly two thousand years ago. Over the centuries, it adopted cultural traits of various non-Indian contexts and was absorbed into them in a process of mutual give and take. In South Africa, at present, that teaching is being negotiated on the border where influences between (various forms of!) East, West, and Africa interact. Yet in South Africa Buddhism is very much Euro-American centred. A process of local syncretism has not yet started to take shape consciously, as it may be doing in Euro-America.

A merging of the two religiocultural horizons of Christianity and Bushman, once (in South African theology) considered irreconcilably different, is feasible, even necessary – for the sake of the Christian gospel. But up to now there has been no attempt to undertake the task of absorbing this part of the African religious heritage into South African Christian reflection. It may lure Christianity into a truly ecological frame of thought. Still referring to this religion, which has yet to atone for its contempt for this oldest religion in South Africa: the same open-ended encounter with an evasive mystery occurring so profoundly in a Greek Orthodox celebration of the eucharist or the silence of a Quaker meeting, can be discovered in Bushman religion. Like forms of Hindu, Buddhist, Christian, Jewish, Islamic or Baha'i mysticism, it culminates in an experience of all-inclusive community of being.

ENDNOTES

1 Overgeneralising to some extent, it may be said that both individual *prayer* and some *divination* occur as they did in the past. Apparently neither *marriages* nor *births* were occasions for ritual celebration in traditional Bushman culture. Among some Bushmen, for example farm Nharo and the !Xo, *funeral* rites seem to be receiving more attention (cf A Barnard, *Hunters and herders of Southern Africa: a comparative ethnography of the Khoisan peoples*, Cambridge: Cambridge University Press, 1992, p 72). Both male and female *initiation* are reported to be declining as well (M Guenther, *The Nharo Bushmen of Botswana: tradition and change*, Hamburg: Helmut Buske Verlag, 1986, pp 274ff on the Nharo, and Barnard, *Hunters and herders ...*, pp 59ff, 71, 112ff, and 154 on the !Kung, !Xo, G/wi and Nharo respectively).

2 By, amongst others, L Marshall (!Kung Bushman religious beliefs, *Africa*, 1962, XXXII[3]), R B Lee (The sociology of !Kung Bushman trance performances, in R Prince (ed), *Trance and possession states*, Canada: R M Bucke Memorial Society, 1968, pp 35–53) and R Katz (*Boiling energy: community healing among the Kalahari !Kung*, Cambridge, Mass: Harvard University Press, 1982), on whose detailed accounts of !Kung dances I have drawn. For the Nharo, see M Guenther (The San trance dance: ritual and revitalization among the farm Bushmen of the Ghanzi district, Republic of Botswana, *Journal of the South West African Scientific Society*, 1976, 30, pp 45–53) and (*The Nharo Bushmen ...*, pp 253ff). In several publications Lewis-Williams, cross-fertilising nineteenth-century ethnography of the southern /Xam (Wilhelm Bleek) and the ethnography of the northern Kalahari dwellers, has drawn attention to the healing dance as a central theme in nineteenth-century and earlier southern Bushman paintings, thus establishing the religious significance of most of the rock art (cf The economic and social context of Southern African rock art, *Current Anthropology*, 1982, 23(4), pp 429–449; Paintings of power: ethnography and rock art in Southern Africa, in Biesele et al, *The Past and Future of !Kung Ethnography ...*, pp 231–273; and [co-authored with Thomas Dowson], *Images of Power: understanding Bushman rock art*, Johannesburg: Southern, 1989).

3 Cf V Turner's antistructural concept of 'liminality' (*The ritual process: structure and anti-structure*, Ithaca, NY: Cornell University Press, 1989 [1969], pp 94ff).

4 It should be remembered that 'in almost 90 per cent of societies around the world for which there are available data on the subject, some sort of altered states of consciousness manifest themselves in one way or another as a part of ritual behavior.

This indicates not only that ritual behavior is universal among human societies but that some form of dissociative state is associated with cultic rituals in nearly all societies' (E G d'Aquili & C D Laughlin, The biopsychological determinants of religious ritual behavior, *Zygon*, 1975, 10(1), p 32).

5 I here follow mainly the descriptions of L Marshall (The medicine dance of the !Kung Bushmen, *Africa*, 1969, 39[4], pp 347–381), Lee (The sociology of !Kung Bushman ..., pp 35–53) and Katz (*Boiling energy* ...).

6 Marshall, The medicine dance ..., p 357; cf Lee, The sociology of !Kung Bushmen ..., p 37 for the tight symbolic organisation of the dancing circle.

7 Marshall, The medicine dance ..., pp 379ff.

8 Lee, The sociology of !Kung Bushmen ..., p 51.

9 Katz, *Boiling energy* ..., p 3.

10 Ibid, pp 53ff.

11 Marshall, The medicine dance ..., p 350. The Bushman 'trance' is clearly of a non-possession type (cf E Bourguignon, World distribution and patterns of possession states, in Prince, *Trance and possession states*, pp 3–36). Barnard (*Hunters and herders* ..., p 153) refers to one case of involuntary spirit possession among the Nharo, 'the only one recorded among any Khoisan group' – who was, however, saved by a man entering a voluntary state of spirit possession.

12 Katz, *Boiling energy* ..., p 52: 'What Westerners might call the 'sacred' and the 'profane' merge playfully and dramatically at the dance.'

13 And a variety of other concrete things such as the sun, rain, bees, honey, blood, etc (Marshall, The medicine dance ..., p 351).

14 Katz, *Boiling energy* ..., p 93.

15 Marshall, The medicine dance ..., p 351.

16 Cf C D Laughlin, J McManus & E G d'Aquili, *Brain, symbol and experience: toward a neurophenomenolgy of human consciousness*, Boston: Shambhala, 1990, pp 319ff. The sustained and intense concentration on physical activity such as racing, dancing, etc, leads to 'a sense of access to an endless source of energy' (p 300).

17 Katz, *Boiling energy* ..., p 9.

18 Katz, *Boiling energy* ..., pp 42ff. The blind Kau Dwa tells Katz (p 216): 'Right now, during the day, I don't see people. But at a dance, when people sing and clap, I see everybody. When the women sing, I can see everything, even if there's a snake crawling through the bush out in the dark.'

19 Lee, The sociology of !Kung Bushmen ..., p 45.

20 Katz, *Boiling energy* ..., pp 93ff.

21 Ibid, p 236.

22 Ibid, pp 239ff.

23 Guenther, The San trance dance ..., pp 49ff. The dance affirms a positive ethnic self-image, gives ethnic identity, and crystallises a strategy for action against oppression.

24 Guenther, The trance dancer as an agent of social change among the farm Bushmen of the Ghanzi district, *Botswana Notes and Records*, 1975, 7; Katz, *Boiling energy* ..., pp 178ff, 250ff.

25 Cf O Petterson & H Åkerberg, *Interpreting religious phenomena: studies with reference*

to the phenomenology of religion, New York: Humanities Press, 1981: (a) comparing without regard for different contexts, (b) comparing data so different in type and quality that they are incomparable, and (c) treating historically related phenomena as if they were historically unrelated.

26 Cf A Wayman, The religious meaning of possesssion states, in Prince, *Trance and possession states*, pp 167–179.

27 *Dīgha Nikāya 34, (Dasuttara Sutta)*, in T W Rhys Davids (ed), *Sacred books of the Buddhists*, Vol 4, London: Pali Text Society, p 257.

28 Cf Laughlin, McManus & D'Aquili, *Brain, symbol and experience ...*, pp 296ff.

20 Bushman mandala

Southern African rock art displays enormous diversity and variability in age, place and content.[1] After all, we are dealing with a timespan of roughly 25 000 years, and a geographical area the size of Europe. Conscious of this, I wish to draw attention to the recurring motif of the circle/spiral in Bushman engravings, interpreting it as expressive of Bushman religion, albeit not only of Bushman religion. These figures express and evoke associations of beauty, truth and open-ended inclusiveness for us who live on the edge of Western-Christian power. In short, it is a powerful religious symbol in the sense explained in chapter 4; clearly perceptible, it mingles with our vague background feelings of the coherence of things. The perspective I am presenting makes no claim to correspond with an objectively present Bushman world; also I make no attempt to escape from the spiral of understanding, shuttling between my own presuppositions and the world of the Bushmen.

It is now widely accepted[2] that the paintings found in mountainous areas of southern Africa and the engravings found on its central plateau represent a body of religious art second to none in the world. The artistic quality of this body of art and the wealth and subtlety of its themes are such that in previous decades many (sometimes blinded by prejudice) could not bring themselves to accept that the art had been created by Bushmen. Today there is no serious doubt that they were indeed the creators of these thousands of masterpieces.[3]

The engravings have received considerably less attention than the paintings from anthropologists and connoisseurs and theorists of Bushman art. As in the paintings, we find exquisite renderings of human and animal figures, but in the engravings the frequency of abstract, geometric designs is higher.[4] They consist of a variety of figures, such as lines, grids, zigzags, and dots. Circles and spirals of various shapes are also numerous.

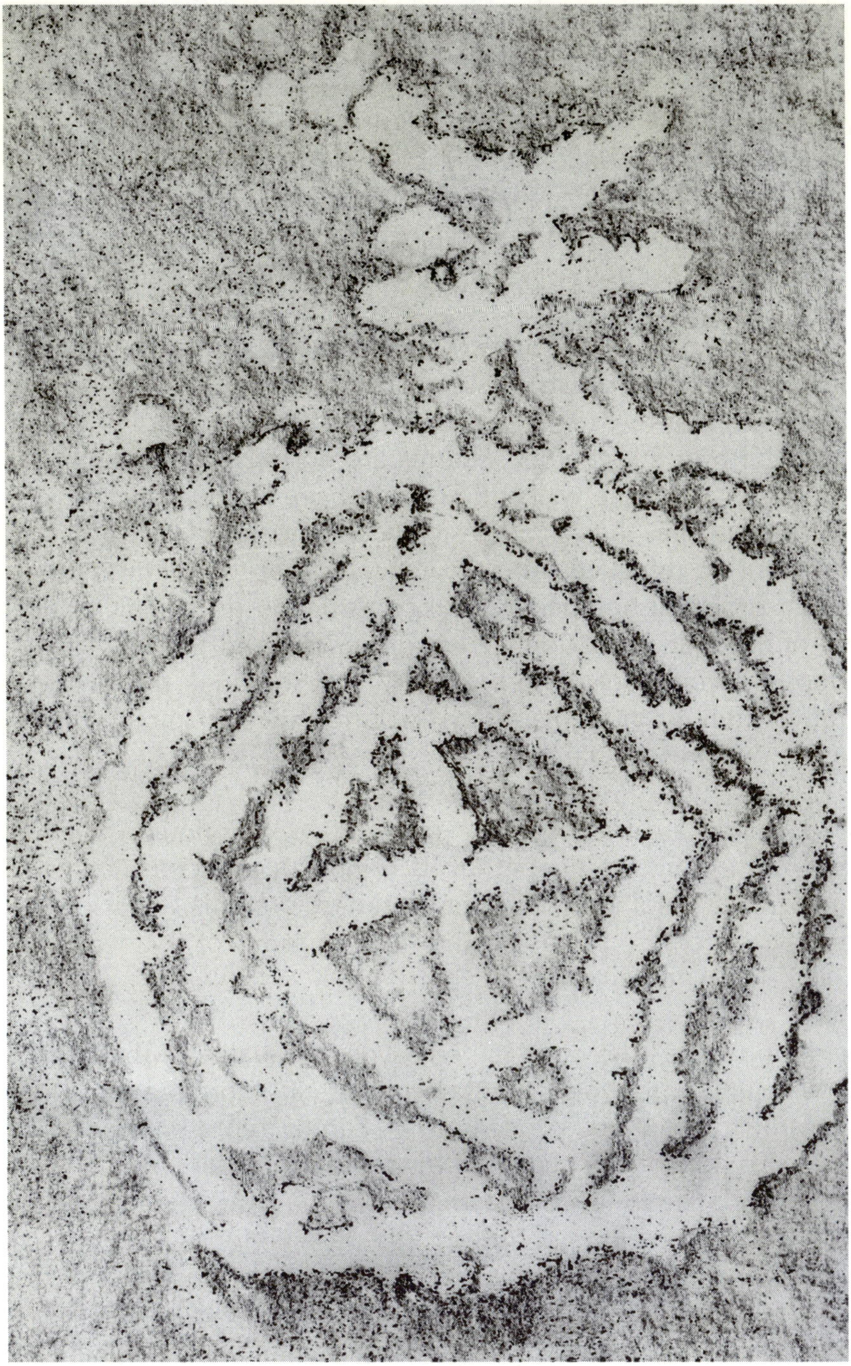

Pp 327, 329, 330, 331 and 333: Rubbings of geometric art. Herbert district.

As can be seen at Driekopseiland, circles occur in various forms: simple circles; circles containing crosses, emanating rays; concentric cicles; or open-ended spirals.[5] These may be interpreted, I suggest, as mandalas. A Sanskrit word meaning 'circle' or 'disk', mandala in tantric Buddhism refers to a mystic cosmogram (symbolic map) of the outside world and the inner world of the meditator. In a wider religious application, it may be used as a visual symbol expressing the search for perfection and transcendence, both within oneself (the microcosm) and in the universe (the macrocosm).[6]

It is not possible, or (in this context) necessary, to 'prove' that this is what the individual Bushman artists consciously intended. We no longer have access to the minds of the artists, and the exact social and cultural settings which gave birth to the geometric forms are no longer accessible. We cannot ask them. At the time when they could have been asked, no Westerner did. Yet I suggest that the religious significance of the circles and spirals can to some extent be retrieved from a *convergence* of the following two resources: a probabilistic, ideal-typical construction of Bushman religion on the basis of the available evidence;[7] and the idea and theory of religion that was proposed throughout these essays. A third resource, that is a detailed comparative study of the religious symbolism of circles/spirals worldwide, falls outside our present scope.

Circles and spirals are homoversal expressions of a profound religious intuition.[8] They arise from the deeper levels of human consciousness, which is a storehouse of powerful symbols. These primary symbols I consider to be mediated by, concretised in and interpreted in terms of sociocultural as well as personal, idiosyncratic forms.

The spiral emphasises the open-ended, dynamic quality of the circle. The Chinese *yin-yang* symbol does the same. One can look into the spiral, or rather be drawn into it and proceed to its centre (representative of empty, pure potentiality) along a concentric inward path or perhaps via the tortuous passages of a labyrinth. Or, starting from the heart, one can move outwards towards the receding periphery, the probing loose end, bursting with novelty. The first movement is that of integration; the second that of transcendence, representing the cutting edge of the spherical expansion ad infinitum. A spiral is a flat, two-dimensional presentation of a sphere, resting in itself, yet full of potential. In Bushman engraving it is a primary symbol, expressing and inspiring certain basic experiences of world-orientation as

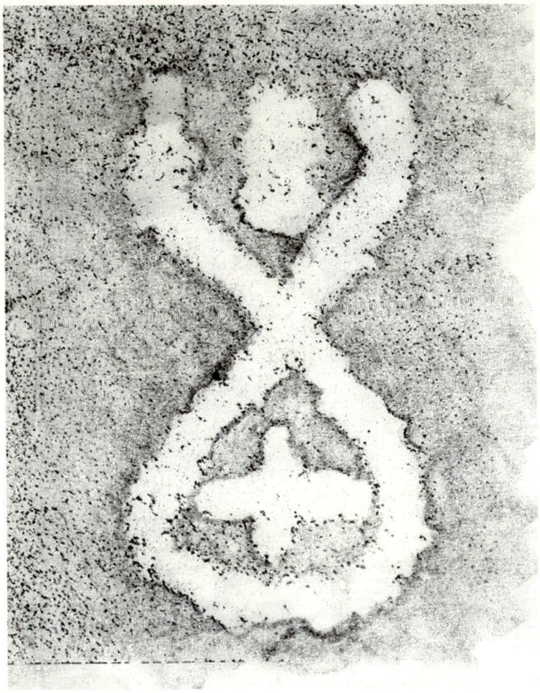

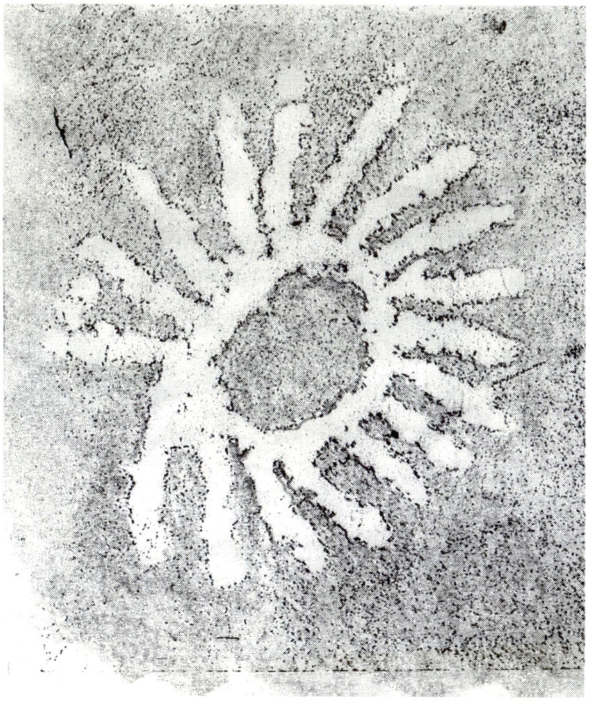

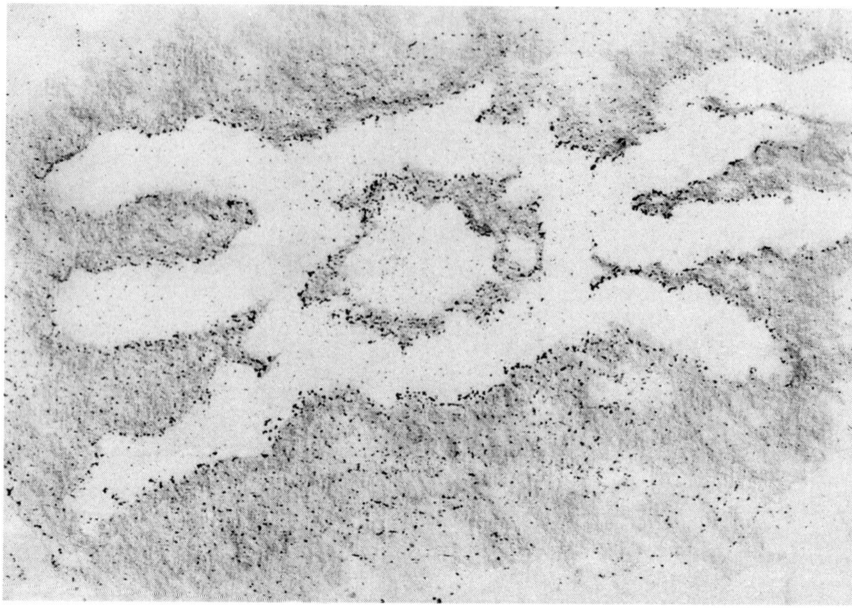

these have come to light in the previous chapters. It reflects the delicate balance of Bushman religion dancing in a fluid, ambiguous world, the complementary contrast between the safety of order and the threat/attraction of chaos, centring and expansion, harmonising and transformation.

The circular engravings may also encapsulate and inspire the fluid coherence of the individual dancing shaman, the wider Bushman community, and the expanding realms of animals, spirits, gods and heavenly bodies. The crosses inside many of the circles suggest the same coordination of all that is. On the basis of the historical evidence, one may think that what in our contemporary culture can only be a mandala as dream was closer to the picturing of an experienced reality in traditional Bushman religion. Viewed from within our own shattered world, the Bushman mandalas appear almost as if *ex illo tempore*, from a mystical past.

The question underlying the chapters of this book is this: in spite of the shattering of the Bushman world and other worlds, could it yet be possible to enter into a new phase of religious history, constructing a new mandala, a new inclusive consciousness, a new sense of the interdependence of all things – without the tyranny of closure? I believe it is possible. That is the religious dream.

ENDNOTES

1 See, amongst others, D Morris, Engraved in place and time: a review of variability in the rock art of the northern Cape and Karoo, *South African Archaeological Bulletin*, 1988, 43, pp 109–121.

2 Thanks to the work of P Vinnicombe, Myth, motive and selection in southern African rock art, *Africa*, 1972, 42(3), pp 192–204; *People of the Eland*, Pietermaritzburg: University of Natal Press, 1976, pp 347–354); J D Lewis-Williams, Science and rock art, *South African Archaeological Society, Goodwin Series*, 1983, 4, pp 3–13; Cognitive and optical illusions in San rock art research, *Current Anthropology*, 1986, 27(2), pp 171–178; A dream of eland: an unexplored component of San shamanism and rock art, *World Archaeology*, 1987, 19(2), pp 165–177; Art as a window to other worlds, *Suid-Afrikaanse Tydskrif vir Wetenskap*, 1987, 83, p 245; Beyond style and portrait: a comparison of Tanzanian and Southern African rock art, in R Vossen & K Keuthmann (eds), *Contemporary studies on Khoisan*, 2 vols, Hamburg: Helmut Buske Verlag, pp 93–139; Paintings of power: ethnography and rock art in Southern Africa, in M Biesele, R Gordon & R Lee (eds), *The past and future of !Kung ethnography: critical reflections and symbolic perspectives. Essays in honour of Lorna Marshall*, Hamburg: Helmut Buske Verlag, pp 231–273; *The world of man and the world of spirit: an interpretation of the Linton rock painting*, Cape Town: South African Museum, 1988; Southern Africa's place in the archaeology of human understanding, *Suid-Afrikaanse Tydskrif vir Wetenskap*, 1989, 85, pp 47–52; *Discovering Southern African rock art*, Johannesburg: Philip, 1990); T Dowson, Revelations of religious reality: the individual in San rock art, *World Archaeology*, 1988, 20(1), pp 116–128; *The state of the art: advances in world rock art research*, Johannesburg: Rock Art Research Unit, 1989; Dots and dashes: cracking the entoptic code in Bushman rock paintings, *South African Archaeological Society, Goodwin series*, 1989, 6, pp 84–94; *Rock engravings of Southern Africa*, Johannesburg: Witwatersrand University Press, 1992; T Dowson & A L Holliday, Zigzags and eland: an interpretation of an idiosyncratic combination, *South African Archaeological Bulletin*, 1989, 44, pp 46–48; J Parkington, Interpreting paintings without a commentary: meaning and motive, content and composition in the rock art of the western Cape, South Africa, *Antiquity*, 1989, 63, pp 13–26; R Yates, J Parkington & T Manhire, *Pictures from the past: a history of the interpretation of rock paintings and engravings of Southern Africa*, Pietermaritzburg: Centaur, 1990; and others.

3 Cf G J Fock, *Felsbilder in Südafrika,* Teil I, Köln, Wien: Böhlau Verlag, 1984, pp 25–29 for the engravings; J D Lewis-Williams & T Dowson, *Images of power: understanding Bushman rock art*, Johannesburg: Southern, 1989, pp 4ff for the paintings.

4 At Driekopseiland in the Riet River, for example, nearly 90 per cent of the engravings consist of geometric designs. According to Fock, *Felsbilder ...*, Teil III, pp 76–77 these could have been produced between 2 500 and 2 200 BP, and after 1 300 BP.

5 See Fock, *Felsbilder ...*, and Thomas A Dowson, *Rock engravings of southern Africa.* Johannesburg: Witwatersrand University Press, 1992 for numerous copies of these forms.

6 Samples of the vast literature on mandalas are J & M Argüelles, *Mandala*, Boulder,

London: Shambhala, 1972; J Purce, *The mystic spiral: journey of the soul*, London: Thames & Hudson, 1974; and C G Jung, The symbolic life, in *The collected works of C G Jung*, Vol 18, London: Routledge & Kegan Paul, 1977.

7 Which makes it unlikely, for example, that the artists associated the circles with a sun cult, as was the case in ancient Europe (cf M Green, *The sun-gods of ancient Europe*, London: Batsford, 1991).

8 In this view, they are more than hallucinations triggered by stimulation of the neural system, inherently devoid of meaning, and elaborated post hoc into shapes familiar to those who 'see' them ('entoptics') – a position approached by Dowson, *Rock engravings* ...

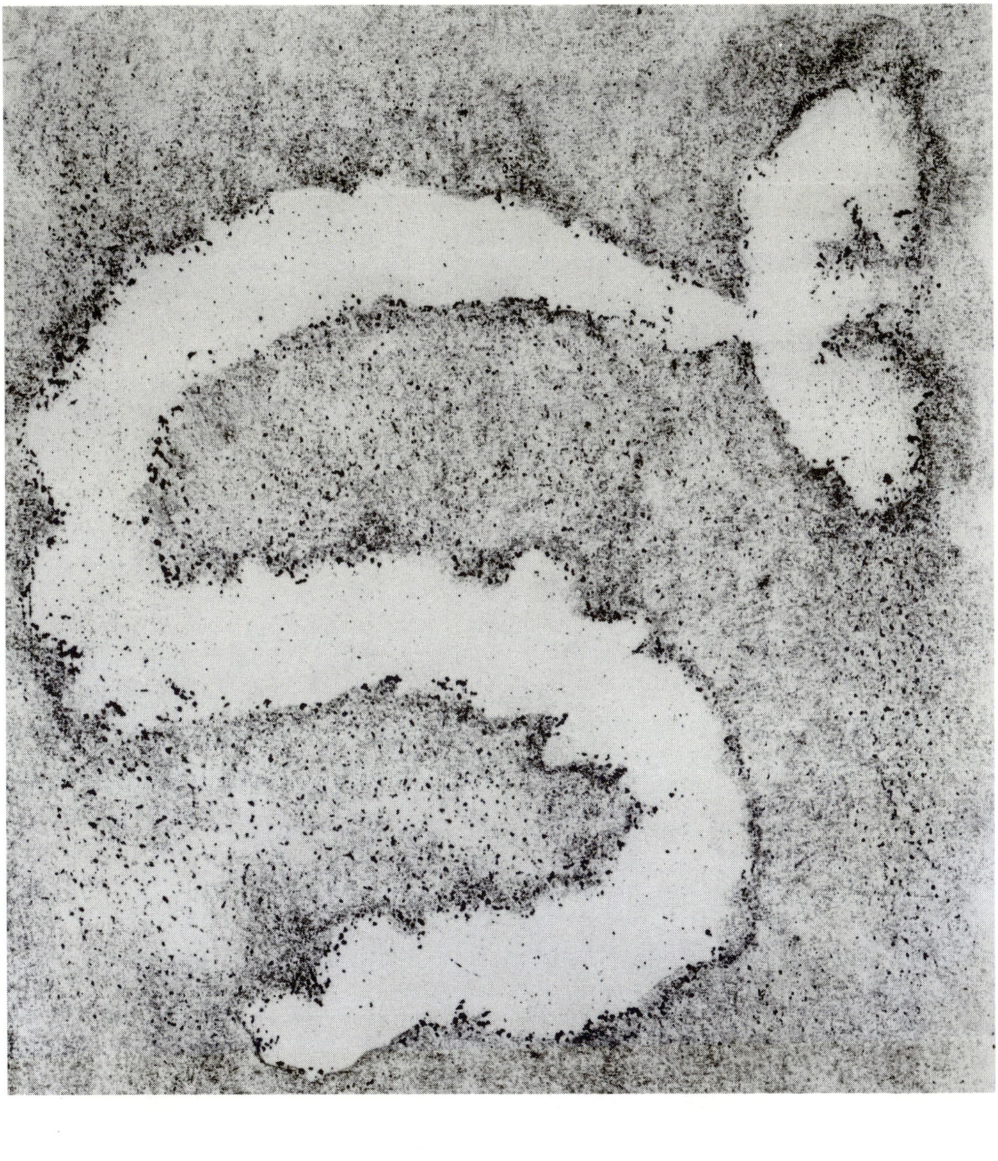

BIBLIOGRAPHY

Abe, Masao. *Zen and Western thought*. London: Macmillan, 1985.

Abe, Masao. The self in Jung and Zen, in Meckel and Moore, 1992, pp 128–140.

Achinstein, P. Function statements. *Philosophy of Science*, 44, 1977, pp 341–367.

Adonis, J C. *Die afgebreekte skeidsmuur weer opgebou. Die verstrengeling van die sendingbeleid van die Nederduitse Gereformeerde Kerk in Suid-Afrika met die praktyk en die ideologie van apartheid in historiese perspektief*, Amsterdam: Rodopi, 1982.

Albert, Hans. *Traktat über kritische Vernunft*, Tübingen: J C B Mohr (Paul Siebeck), 1968.

Alexander, John. Early frontiers in southern Africa, in Hall, M et al (eds), 1984, pp 12–23.

Alexander, Richard D. Evolution of the human psyche, in Mellars & Stringer, 1989, pp 455–513.

Allen, D. *Structure and creativity in religion. Hermeneutics in Mircea Eliade's phenomenology and new directions*, The Hague: Mouton, 1978.

Ardrey, Robert. *The territorial imperative: a personal inquiry into the animal origins of property and nations.* London: Collins, 1969.

Argüelles, Jos and Miriam. *Mandala*. Boulder and London: Shambhala, 1972.

Ayer, A J. *Language, truth and language*. Harmondsworth: Penguin, (1936) 1971.

Badiner, Allan Hunt (ed). *Dharma Gaia: a harvest of essays in Buddhism and ecology*, Berkeley: Parallax, 1990.

Baird, R D. *Category formation and the history of religions*, The Hague: Mouton, 1971.

Baird, R D. *Methodological issues in religious studies,* Chicago: New Horizons Press, 1974.

Banton, Michael (ed). *Anthropological approaches to the study of religion*, London: Tavistock, 1966.

Barnard, Alan. *Hunters and herders of Southern Africa: a comparative ethnography of the Khoisan peoples*. Cambridge: Cambridge University Press, 1992.

Barnes, Linda M. *Religion and folklore amongst the Basarwa in Letlhakane, Botswana*. Gaborone: Government Printer, 1980.

Barrow, John D and Frank J Tipler. *The anthropic principle*, Oxford: Clarendon Press, 1986.

Bartley, W W. *The retreat to commitment*, New York: Chatto & Windus, 1964.

Battiss, Walter W. *The amazing Bushman*. Pretoria: Red Fawn Press, 1939.

Battiss, Walter W. The aesthetic value of our rock art, in Schoonraad, 1971, pp 42–43.
Beaumont, Peter and David Morris. *Guide to archaeological sites in the Northern Cape*. Kimberley: McGregor Museum, 1990.
Beaumont, Peter and John C. Vogel. Patterns in the age and context of rock art in the northern Cape. *South African Archaeological Bulletin* 44, 1989, pp 73–81.
Beaumont, Peter B, Hertha de Villiers and John C. Vogel. Modern man in sub-Saharan Africa prior to 49 000 Years BP: a review and evaluation with particular reference to Border Cave; *SA Journal of Science*, 74, 1978, pp 409–419.
Beaumont, Peter. The time-depth of aesthetic and symbolic behaviour in southern Africa. *Southern African Association of Archaeologists*, Biennial Conference, University of Cape Town, Book of Abstracts, 1–4 July 1992.
Bendall, D S. *Evolution from molecules to men*. Cambridge: University Press, 1983.
Berger, P L and Thomas Luckmann. *The social construction of reality. A treatise in the sociology of religion*, Harmondsworth: Penguin, 1966.
Berger, P L. *The sacred canopy: elements of a sociological theory of religion*. New York: Anchor, 1969.
Berger, P L. *A rumour of angels: modern society and the rediscovery of the supernatural*. Harmondsworth: Penguin, 1969.
Bettis, J (ed). *The phenomenology of religion*, London: SCM, 1969.
Biesele, M A. *Folklore and ritual of !Kung Hunter gatherers*. Thesis presented to the Department of Anthropology, Harvard University, 2 vols, 1975.
Biesele, Megan. Religion and folklore, in Tobias, 1978b, pp 162–172.
Biesele, Megan (ed). *The past and future of !Kung entnography*. Hamburg: Helmut Buske Verlag, 1987.
Biesele, Megan, Robert Gordon and Richard Lee (eds). *The past and future of !Kung ethnography. Critical reflections and symbolic perspectives. Essays in honour of Lorna Marshall*. Hamburg: Helmut Buske Verlag, 1987.
Biesele, Megan. *Shaken Roots. The Bushmen of Namibia*. Marshalltown: EDA Publications, 1990.
Binford, L R and C K Ho. Taphonomy at a distance: Zhoukoudian – the cave home of Beijing man? *Current Anthropology*, 26(4), 1985, pp 413–442.
Bleek, D F (ed). *The mantis and his friends. Bushman folklore*. Cape Town: Maskew Miller, 1923.
Bleek, D F. *The Naron. A Bushman tribe of the central Kalahari*. Cambridge: University Press, 1928.
Bleek, D F. Bushman folklore. *Africa*, 2, 1929, pp 302–313.
Bleek, D F. Customs and beliefs of the /Xam Bushmen, Part I: Baboons. *Bantu Studies*, 5, 1931, pp 167–179.
Bleek, D F. Customs and beliefs of the /Xam Bushmen, Part II: The lion. Part III: Game animals. Part IV: omens, wind-making, clouds. *Bantu Studies*, 6, 1932, pp 47–63, 233–249, 321–342.
Bleek, D F. Beliefs and customs of the /Xam Bushmen. Part V: The rain. Part VI: Rainmaking. *Bantu Studies*, 7, 1933, pp 297–312, 375–392.
Bleek, D F. Beliefs and customs of the /Xam Bushmen. Part VII. Sorcerers. *Bantu Studies*, 9, 1935, pp 1–47.

Bleek, D F. Beliefs and customs of the /Xam Bushmen. Part VIII. More about sorcerers and charms. *Bantu Studies*, 10, 1936, pp 131–162.
Bleek, D F. Special speech of animals and moon used by the /Xam Bushmen. *Bantu Studies*, 10, 1936, pp 163–199.
Bleek, W H I and L C Lloyd. *Specimens of Bushmen folklore*. Cape Town: C Struik, 1968.
Bodhi, Bhikkhu, *The great discourse on causation. The Mahanidana Sutta and its commentarial exegesis*, Kandy: Buddhist Publication Society, 1984.
Bohm, David, *Wholeness and the implicate order*, London: Routledge & Kegan Paul, 1980.
Bosch, David J. *Transforming mission. Paradigm shifts in theology of mission*. New York: Orbis Books, 1991.
Botha, J Eugene. Contextualization: locating threads in the labyrinth, *Scriptura*, S9, 1992, pp 1–18.
Bourdillon, Michael. Anthropological approaches to the study of African religions. Unpublished paper, Regional Conference on the Study of Religions in Africa, University of Zimbabwe, 15–19 September 1992.
Bourguignon, Erika. World distribution and patterns of possession states, in Raymond Prince, 1968, pp 3–36.
Bowler, Peter J. *Evolution. The history of an idea*. Los Angeles: University of California Press, 1984.
Bowler, Peter J. *Theories of human evolution. A century of debate 1866 – 1964*. Oxford: Basil Blackwell, 1986.
Bowler, Peter J. *The non-Darwinian revolution. Reinterpreting a historical myth*. London: Johns Hopkins University Press, 1988.
Brain, C K. Some principles in the interpretation of bone accumulations associated with man, in G L Isaac and E R McCown (eds). *Human origins: Louis Leakey and the East African evidence*. Menlo Park, California: W A Benjamin Inc, 1976, pp 97–116.
Brain, C K and A Sillen. Evidence from Swartkrans Cave for the earliest use of fire, *Nature*, 336, 1988, pp 464–6.
Bräuer, Günter. *The evolution of modern humans: a comparison of the African and non-African evidence*, in Mellars & Stringer, 1989, pp 123–156.
Bredenkamp, H C. The origin of the southern African Khoisan communities, in Cameron, 1986, pp 28–30.
Brockman, John (ed). *Creativity*. New York: Touchstone, 1993.
Brümmer, Vincent (ed). *Interpreting the universe as creation*. Kampen: Kok Pharos, 1991.
Buddhaghosa. *The Path of Purification (Visuddhimagga)*. Translated from the Pali by bhikkhu Ñanamoli. *Kandy, Sri Lanka: Buddhist Publication Society, 1979.*
Burkert, Walter. Greek religion, archaic and classical. Oxford: Blackwell, 1985.
Cameron, Trewhella. *A new illustrated history of South Africa*. Johannesburg: Southern Book, 1986.
Campbell, C. Images of war: a problem in San rock art research. *World Archaeology*, 18(2), 1986, pp 255–268.
Campbell, Colin. Art in crisis: contact period rock art in the South-Eastern mountains of

South Africa. Unpublished MA dissertation, University of the Witwatersrand, 1987.
Carter, Robert (ed). *God, the self and nothingness. Reflections Eastern and Western*. New York: Paragon, 1990.
Chang, Garma C C. *The Buddhist teaching of totality: the philosophy of Hwa Yen Buddhism*. London: Pennsylvania State University Press, 1977.
Chatterjee, A K. *The Yogacara Idealism*. Delhi: Motilal Banarsidass, 1975.
Chidester, David. Religious studies as political practice. *Journal of Theology for Southern Africa*, 58, 1987, pp 4–17.
Chidester, David. Stealing the sacred symbols: biblical interpretation in the People's Temple and the Unification Church, *Religion*, 18, 1988, pp 137–162.
Chidester, David. *Religions of South Africa*. London: Routledge, 1992.
Chowdhury, T, W Claesens & W Logister (eds). *Het kosmisch patroon: het vele en het ene in die godsdiensten*. Tilburg: University Press, 1989.
Clark, J Desmond. Leaving no stone unturned: archaeological advances and behavioural adoptation, in Tobias 1985(a), pp 65–88.
Clasquin, M, J D Ferreira-Ross, D Marais, R Sadowsky (eds). *Myth and interdisciplinary studies*. Pretoria: University of South Africa, 1992.
Cobb, John B. *Beyond dialogue: toward a mutual transformation of Christianity and Buddhism*. Philadelphia: Fortress Press, 1982.
Cobb, John B and Christopher Ives. *The emptying God. A Buddhist-Jewish-Christian conversation*. Maryknoll, New York: Orbis, 1991.
Cockrane, James. *Servants of power, The role of English-speaking churches in South Africa 1903–1930. Towards a critical theology via an historical analysis of the Anglican and Methodist Churches*. Johannesburg: Ravan Press, 1987.
Comaroff, Jean and Comaroff John. *Of revelation and revolution. Christianity, colonialism, and consciousness in South Africa*. Vol One. Chicago: The University of Chicago Press, 1991.
Conze, Edward. *Buddhist thought in India. Three phases of Buddhist philosophy*. London: George Allen & Unwin, (1962) 1983.
Cook, Francis H. *Hua-yen Buddhism: the Jewel Net of Indra*. London: Pennsylvania, 1977.
Cook, Francis H. The dialogue between Hua-Yen and process thought. *Eastern Buddhist*, 17, 1984, pp 12–29.
Cook, Frances H. The Jewel Net of Indra, in J Baird Callicott and Roger T Ames. *Nature in Asian traditions of thought: essays in environmental philosophy*, New York: State University Press, 1989, pp 213–229.
Coward, Harold. *Pluralism: challenge to world religions*. New York: Orbis, 1985.
Coward, Harold. *Derrida and Indian philosophy*, New York: State University of New York Press, 1990.
Crosby, Donald A. *Interpretive theories of religion*, The Hague: Mouton, 1981.
Cox, James. Methodological considerations relevant to the truth of African traditional religions: a phenomenological perspective. Unpublished paper, Regional Conference on the Study of Religions in Africa, University of Zimbabwe, 15–19 September 1992.
Cumpsty, John S. *Religion as belonging: a general theory of religion*. New York: University Press of America, 1991.

Cupitt, Don. *The time being*. London: SCM Press, 1992.
Curtin, Philip D. *The image of Africa. British ideas and action, 1780–1850*. Madison: University of Wisconsin Press, 1964.
d'Aquili, Eugene G, Charles D Laughlin Jr and John McManus. *The spectrum of ritual. A biogenetic structural analysis.* New York: Columbia University Press, 1979.
d'Aquili, Eugene G and Charles Laughlin Jr. The biopsychological determinants of religious ritual behavior. *Zygon*, 10(1), 1975, pp 32–58.
Daniélou, Alian. *Gods of love and ecstacy. The traditions of Shiva and Dionysus*. Rochester, Vermont: Inner Traditions, 1992.
Darwin, C. *The descent of man, and selection in relation to sex.* London: William Pickering, (1871) 1989.
Davenport, T R H. *South Africa. A modern history*. London: Macmillan, (1977) 1991.
David, Julian. *Interweaving symbols of individuation in African and European fairy tales. A Jungian perspective.* Cape Town: Kaggen Press, 1991.
Dawkins, Richard. *The blind watchmaker*. Harlow: Longman Scientific & Technical, 1986.
Day, Michael H. Hominid locomotion – from Taung to the Laetoli footprints, in Tobias 1985(a), pp 115–127.
Deacon, H J. Late Pleistocene palaeoecology and archaeology in the Southern Cape, South Africa, in Paul Mellars & Chris Stringer (eds), 1989, pp 547–563.
Deacon, Janette. Later Stone Age people and their descendants in Southern Africa, in Klein, Richard (ed), 1984, pp 221–328.
Deacon, Janette 1986. 'My place is the Bitterpits': the home territory of Bleek and Lloyd's /Xam San informants. *African Studies*, 45(2), 1986, pp 135–155.
Deacon, Janette. The power of a place in understanding southern San rock engravings. *World Archaeology*, 20(1), 1988, pp 129–140.
De Kock, Leon. The literary and the historical: missionary discourse at Lovedale in the nineteenth century and the contestation of subjectivity. Unpublished paper, read at Conference on People, Power and Culture: the History of Christianity in South Africa 1792–1992, at the University of Western Cape, 12–15 August 1992.
Degenaar, Johan. Imagination and myth, in Clasquin et al (eds), 1992, pp 3–27.
De Gruchy, John. *The church struggle in South Africa*. Cape Town: David Philip, 1979.
Denwood, Philip and Alexander Piatigorski (eds). *Buddhist studies ancient and modern*. London: Curzon Press, 1983.
Detienne, Marcel. *The creation of mythology.* Chicago: University of Chicago Press, 1986.
De Wit, Han F. *Contemplative psychology.* Pittsburgh, Pennsylvania: Duquesne University Press, 1991.
Dourley, John P. *Jung and Paul Tillich: the psyche as sacrament*. Toronto: Inner City Books, 1981.
Dowson, Thomas A. *The state of the art. Advances in world rock art research*. Johannesburg: Rock Art Research Unit, 1988.
Dowson, Thomas A. Dots and dashes: cracking the entoptic code in Bushman rock paintings. *South African Archaeological Society Goodwin Series*, 6, 1989, pp 84–94.
Dowson, Thomas A and Anne L Holliday. Zigzags and eland: an intepretation of an

idiosyncratic combination. *South African Archaeological Bulletin*, 44, 1989, pp 46–48.
Dowson, Thomas A. Revelations of religious reality: the individual in San rock art, in *World Archaeology*, 20(1), 1988, pp 116–128.
Dowson, Thomas A. *Rock engravings of Southern Africa*. Johannesburg: Witwatersrand University Press, 1992.
Du Bruyn, J. Missionaries in South African historical writing. Unpublished paper read at Conference on People, Power and Culture: the History of Christianity in South Africa 1792–1992, at the University of Western Cape, 12–15 August 1992.
Du Bruyn J T. *Die aanvangsjare van die Christelike sending onder die Tlaping, 1800–1825*. Pretoria: Die Staatsdrukker, 1989.
Du Plessis, J. *A history of Christian missions in South Africa*. London: Longmans, Green and Co, 1911.
Dupré, Wilhelm. *Religion in primitive cultures. A study in ethnophilosophy.* The Hague: Mouton, 1975.
Duminy, A H. *Suid-Afrikaanse Biografiese Woordeboek*. vol I, 1976, pp 809–813.
Dunne, John. *The way of all the earth. An encounter with Eastern religions.* London: Sheldon Press, 1973.
Durkheim, Emile. *The elementary forms of the religious life*. London: Allen & Unwin, 1957.
Du Toit, André. No chosen people: the myth of the Calvinist origins of Afrikaner nationalism and racial ideology. *The American Historical Review*, 88(4), 1983, pp 920–952.
Edwards, Felicity. Vipassana meditation and transcultural consciousness; *Journal for the study of religion* 1(2), 1988, pp 37–51.
Edwards, Felicity. Cutting through contending ideologies: the new paradigm and the new commandment, in J Mouton, A G van Aarde & W S Vorster, *Paradigms and progress in theology*. Pretoria: Human Sciences Research Council, 1988, pp 239 – 251.
Eibl-Eibesfeldt, Irenus. *Zur Frage der Kontinuïtät der San-Kulturen im südlichen Afrika*, in Vossen & Keuthman, Vol 1, 1986, p. 215–224.
Eibl-Eibesfeldt, Irenus. Early socialization in the !Xo Bushmen, in Tobias 1978, pp 130–136.
Elbourne, Elizabeth. Early Khoisan uses of mission Christianity. Unpublished paper, read at Conference on People, Power and Culture: the History of Christianity in South Africa 1792–1992, at the University of Western Cape, 12–15 August 1992.
Eliade, Mircea. *Shamanism. Archaic techniques of ecstacy*. London: Arkana, 1989.
Eliade, Mircea. *Patterns in comparative religion*. New York: Meridian Books, (1958) 1974.
Eliade, Mircea and J M Kitagawa. *The history of religions. Essays in methodology*. Chicago: University of Chicago Press, 1959.
Ellis, George. *Before the beginning. Cosmology explained*. London/New York: Boyars/Bowerdean, 1993.
Ellwood, Robert. *Introducing religion from inside and outside.* Englewood Cliffs: Prentice Hall, 1983.
Elphick, Richard. *Kraal and castle. Khoikhoi and the founding of white South Africa.* New Haven: Yale University Press, 1977.

Elphick, Richard. Writing about Christianity in history: some issues of theory and method. Unpublished paper read at Conference on People, Power and Culture: the History of Christianity in South Africa 1792–1992, at the University of Western Cape, 12–15 August 1992.

Elphick, Richard and V C Malherbe. Die Khoisan tot 1828, in Giliomee and Elphick, 1982, pp 1–66.

Evans-Pritchard, E E. *Theories of primitive religion*. Oxford: Clarendon Press, 1980.

Faber, Phillip and Graham S Saayman. On the relation of the doctrines of Yoga to Jung's psychology, in Papadopoulos and Saayman 1984, pp 165–181.

Fabian, Johannes. *Time and the other. How anthropology makes its object.* New York: Columbia University Press, 1983.

Fernando, Antony and Leonard Swidler. *Buddhism made plain. An introduction for Christians and Jews*. New York: Orbis, 1985.

Fernando, Antony. *Christianity made intelligible (as ONE of the world's religions)*. Eldeniya: Sri Lanka: Inter-Cultural Book Promoters, 1990.

Flew, Antony. Theology and falsification, in Flew, A and A MacIntyre. *New essays in philosophical theology*, London: SCM, 1955.

Floistad, G (ed). *Contemporary philosophy. A new survey.* Vol 5. *African philosophy.* Dordrecht: Martinus Nijhoff Publishers, 1987.

Fock, Gerhard J. *Felsbilder in SüdAfrika. Teil I, II, III.* Köln, Wien: Böhlau Verlag, 1979, 1984, 1986.

Forman, Robert KC. *The problem of pure consciousness.* Oxford: University Press, 1990.

Fourie, J, S C J Joubert & J A Loader. Environmental education – an approach based on the concept of life. *Koedoe*, 33/1, 1990, pp 95–109.

Frankenberry, N. *Religion and radical empiricism*. New York: State University of New York Press, 1987.

Frazer, James George. *The belief in immortality and the worship of the dead*. 3 Vols. London: Macmillan, 1913.

Frazer, James George. *The magic art and the evolution of kings*. 2 Vols. London: Macmillan, (1890) 1932.

Gadamer, Hans-Georg. *Wahrheit und Methode.Grundzüge einer philosophischen Hermeneutik*. Tübingen: J C B Mohr (Paul Siebeck), 1972.

Gaustad, Edwin Scott. *A religious history of America: new revised edition*. New York: Harper and Row, 1990.

Giliomee, Hermann en Richard Elphick (red). *'n Samelewing in wording, 1652–1840*. Kaapstad: Maskew Miller Longman, 1982.

Gordon, Robert. Once again: how many Bushman are there? in Biesele, Gordon and Lee (eds), 1986, pp 53–68.

Gordon, Robert J. *The Bushman myth. The making of a Namibian underclass*. Boulder: Westview Press, 1992.

Gould, Stephen Jay. *Ever since Darwin. Reflections in natural history.* New York: Norton, 1977.

Govinda, Lama Anagarika. *Creative meditation and multi-dimensional consciousness*. London: Allen & Unwin, 1977.

Grant, Verne. *The evolutionary process. A critical review of evolutionary theory.* New York: Columbia University Press, 1985.

Green, Miranda. *The sun-gods of ancient Europe*. London: Batsford, 1991.

Griffin, David Ray and Thomas J J Altizer. *John Cobb's theology in process*. Philadelphia: Westminster Press, 1977.

Griffin, David Ray (ed). *Sacred interconnections. Postmodern spirituality, political economy, and art*. New York: State University of New York Press, 1990.

Groves, C P. *The planting of Christianity in Africa*, Vols I-IV. London: Lutterworth, 1948–1958.

Guenter, Mathias G. The trance dancer as an agent of social change among the farm Bushmen of the Ghanzi district. *Botswana Notes and Records*, 7, 1975, pp 161–166.

Guenther, M G. The San trance dance: ritual and revitalization among the farm Bushmen of the Ghanzi district, Republic of Botswana. *Journal of the South West African Scientific Society*, 30, 1976, pp 45–53.

Guenther, Mathias G. From 'Brutal Savages' to 'Harmless People'. *Paideuma*, 26, 1980, pp 123–140.

Guenther, Mathias. *The Nharo Bushmen of Botswana. Tradition and change.* Hamburg: Helmut Buske Verlag, 1986.

Guenther, Mathias Georg. Bushman religion and the (non)sense of anthropological theory of religion. *Sociologus*, 29(2), 1979, pp 102–132.

Guenther, Matthias. *'San' or 'Bushmen'?*, in Biesele, Gordon & Lee (eds), 1987, pp 27–51.

Habermas, Jürgen. *Zur Logik der Sozialwissenschaften*. Frankfurt: Suhrkamp, 1978.

Habermas, Jürgen. *Technik und Wissenschaft als Ideologie*. Frankfurt: Suhrkamp, 1978.

Habito, Ruben L F. *Total liberation: Zen spirituality and the social dimension*, Maryknoll, New York: Orbis, 1989.

Haeckel, Ernst. *Der Monismus als Band Zwischen Religion und Wissenschaft. Glaubensbekenntnis eines Naturforschers*. Bonn: Strauss, 1893.

Hall, M, G Avery, D M Avery, M L Wilson and A J B Humphreys. Frontiers: South African archaeology today. Cambridge Monographs in *African Archaeology* 10, BAR International Series 207. Oxford: BAR, 1984.

Hall, Martin. Frontiers in Southern African archaeology, in Hall, M et al (eds), 1984, pp 1–10.

Hare, R M. Religion and morals, in Mitchell, Basil, *Faith and logic*, London: Allen & Unwin, 1957.

Harris, Marvin. *The rise of anthropological theory. A history of culture*. London: Routledge & Kegan Paul, 1968.

Hausman, Alice Jane 1980. *Holocene human evolution in Southern Africa: the biocultural development of the Khoisan*. PhD thesis, State University of New York, 1980.

Hawking, Stephen W. *A brief history of time from the big bang to black holes*. London: Bantam, 1988.

Heine, Steven. *Existential and ontological dimensions of time in Heidegger and Dogen*. New York: State University of New York Press, 1985.

Heinz, H J. Elements of !Ko Bushmen religious beliefs. *Anthropos*, 70, 1975, pp 17–41.

Heinz, Hans J. *The Bushmen in a changing world*, in Tobias, 1978, pp 173–178.

Heinz, Hans J. *The Bushmen's store of scientific knowledge*, in Tobias, 1978, pp 148–161.

Hempel, C G. *Philosophy of natural science*. Englewood Cliffs: Prentice-Hall, 1966.

Hermans, Janet Gallagher. *The Basarwa of Botswana: a case study in development*. Washington, DC: The American University, MA dissertation, 1982.

Hick, John and Hasan Askari. *The experience of religious diversity*. Aldershot: Gower, 1985.

Hillman, James. *The myth of analysis*. Evanston, Ill: Northwestern University Press, 1972.

Hillman, James. *Re-visioning psychology*. New York: Harper and Row, 1975.

Hitchcock, John. *The web of the universe: Jung, the 'new' physics and human spirituality*, New York: Paulist Press, 1991.

Hoens, D J, J H Kamstra & D C Mulder. *Inleiding tot de studie van de godsdiensten*. Kampen: Kok, 1985.

Hofmeyr, J W and Gerald J Pillay. *A history of Christianity in South Africa*, Vol 1. Pretoria: HAUM, 1994.

Holdstock, Len 1985. Africa realm of soul. *Odyssey*, 9(2), 1985, pp 16–19.

Hollenback, Jess Byron. *Mysticism: a comparative historical Study*. University of California, Los Angeles, 1988.

Holloway, R L. Human brain evolution: a search for units, models and synthesis. *Canadian Journal of Anthropology*, 3(2), 1983, pp 215–230.

Hospital, Clifford G. *Breakthrough. Insights of the great religious discoverers*. New York: Orbis, 1985.

Howells, William. *Evolution of the genus Homo*. Reading, Massachusetts: Addison-Wesley, 1973.

Humphreys, A J B. A prehistoric frontier in the Northern Cape and western Orange Free State: archaeological evidence in interaction and ideological change. *Kronos*, 13, 1988, pp 3–13.

Humphreys, A J B and Anne I Thackeray. *Ghaap and Gariep. Later Stone Age studies in the northern Cape*. Cape Town: The South Africa Archaeological Society Monograph Series No. 2, 1983.

Husserl, Edmund. *The crisis of European sciences and transcendental phenomenology*. Evanston, Ill: Northwestern University Press, 1970.

Huxley, Julian. *Evolution. The modern synthesis*. London: George Allen & Unwin, (1942) 1974.

Inskeep, Ray R. *The Bushmen in prehistory*, in Tobias 1978(b), pp 33–56.

Isaac, Glynn L. Aspects of human evolution, in Bendall 1983, pp 509–545.

James, William. *The varieties of religious experience*. New York: Modern Library, 1902.

James, William. *Essays in radical empiricism. A pluralistic universe*. Gloucester, Mass: Smith, 1967.

Johanson, D C and M E Edey. *Lucy. The beginnings of humankind*. London: Granada, 1981.

Johanson, Donald and James Shreeve. *Lucy's child. The discovery of a human ancestor*. New York: Morrow, 1989.

Johanson, Donald C. The most primitive Australopithecus, in Tobias 1985(a), pp 203–212.

Jones, Ken. *The social face of Buddhism: an approach to political and social activism*. London: Wisdom, 1989.
Jones, Nicolas Blurton and Melvin J Konner. *!Kung knowledge of animal behaviour (or: the proper study of mankind is animals)*, in Lee and De Vore, 1976, pp 325–348.
Jung, C G. *Symbols of transformation. An analysis of the prelude to a case of schizophrenia*. Collected works, Vol 5. London: Routledge & Kegan Paul, 1956.
Jung, C G. *Psychology and religion: West and East*. Collected Works, Vol 11. London: Routledge & Kegan Paul, 1958.
Jung, C G. *Man and his symbols*. London: Pan Books, 1964.
Jung, C G. *The symbolic life*. Collected Works, Vol 18. London: Routledge & Kegan Paul, 1977.
Kaufmann, Stuart A. *Origins of order. Self-organization and selection in evolution*. Oxford: University Press, 1993.
Kalupahana, David J. *Causality: the central philosophy of Buddhism*. Honolulu: University Press of Hawaii, 1975.
Kaplan, Abraham. *The conduct of inquiry. Methodology for behavioral sciences*. New York: Crowell, 1964.
Katz, Richard. The painful ecstasy of healing. *Psychology Today* 10(7), 1976, pp 81–86.
Katz, Richard. *Boiling energy: community healing among the Kalahari Kung*. Cambridge, Mass and London: Harvard University Press, 1982.
Katz, Steven (ed). *Mysticism and philosophical analysis*. London: Sheldon Press, 1978.
Katz, Steven. *Mysticism and religious traditions*. Oxford: University Press, 1983.
Katz, Steven (ed). *Mysticism and language*. Oxford: University Press, 1992.
Keenan, John P. *The meaning of Christ. A Mahayana theology*. Maryknoll, New York: Orbis, 1989.
Kicherer J J. *Gedenkschriften van het Nederlandch zendeling-genootschap, ter voortplanting en bevordering van het waare Christendom, bijzonder onder de heidenen, opgericht te Rotterdam den 19 van Wintermaand, des Jaars MDCCXCVII. Deel II*. Rotterdam: Cornel en Van Baalen, 1805.
Kim, Hee-Jin. *Dogen Kigen. Mystical realist*. Tucson: University of Arizona Press, 1987.
King, M B and R A Hunt. *Measuring religious dimensions. Studies of congregational involvement*. Dallas: Southern Methodist University, 1972.
Klein, Richard G (ed). *Southern African prehistory and paleoenvironments*. Boston: A A Balkema, 1984.
Klein, Richard G. Biological and behavioural perspectives on modern human origins in Southern Africa, in Mellars and Stringer 1989, pp 529–546.
Klostermaier, Klaus K and Larry W Hurtado (eds). *Religous studies: issues, prospects and proposals*. Atlanta, Georgia: Scholars Press, 1991.
Kochumuttom, T A. *A Buddhist doctrine of experience*. Delhi: Motilal Babarsidass, 1982.
Kourie, C E T. *Elizabeth Catez of the trinity, 1880–1906: An interpretation of her mysticism*. DTh thesis, University of South Africa, Pretoria, 1990.
Krüger, J S. *Studying religion. A methodological introduction to science of religion*. Pretoria: Unisa, 1982.
Lanczkowski, G. *Selbstverständnis und Wesen der Religionswissenschaft*. Darmstadt: Wissenschaftliche Buchgesellschaft, 1974.

Landman, Christina. *Europe's role in a South African methodology. A sideline and female perspective.* Frankfurt am Main: Peter Lang, 1992.

Larson, Gerald James and Eliot Deutsch (eds). *Interpreting across boundaries. New essays in comparative philosophy.* Princeton: University Press, 1989.

Laughlin, Charles D, John McManus & Eugene G d'Aquili. *Brain, symbol & experience. Toward a neurophenomenology of human consciousness*. Boston: Shambhala, 1990.

Lazarus, Z J. Die stigting en vroeë jare van die Suid-Afrikaanse sendinggenootskappe 1799–1803. Universiteit van Stellenbosch: MA-verhandeling, 1948.

Leakey, L S B, P V Tobias & J R Napier. A new species of the genus *Homo* from Olduvai Gorge. *Nature*, 202, 1964, pp 7–9.

Leclerc, Ivor. *Whitehead's philosophy between rationalism and empiricism*. Leuven: Center for Metaphysics and Philosophy of God, 1984.

Lee, R B. *Subsistence ecology of !Kung Bushmen*. Ph D thesis, University of California, Berkeley, 1965.

Lee, R B. *Subsistence ecology of !Kung Bushmen.* Doctor's Thesis in Anthropology, University of California, Berkeley, 1966.

Lee, Richard B. *The sociology of !Kung Bushman trance performances,* in Raymond Prince, 1968, pp 35–53.

Lee, R B. *The !Kung San. Men, women, and work in a foraging society*. Cambridge: University Press, 1979.

Lee, Richard B and Irven De Vore. *Man the hunter*. Chicago: Aldine, 1968.

Lee, Richard B and Irven De Vore. *Kalahari hunter-gatherers. Studies of the !Kung San and their neighbors*. Cambridge, Massachusetts: Harvard University Press, 1976.

Legassick, Martin. The frontier tradition in South African historiography, in Marks and Atmore, 1990, pp 44–59.

Lévi-Strauss, Claude. *The savage mind*. London: Weidenfeld & Nicolson, 1966.

Lévi-Strauss, Claude. *The raw and the cooked*. London: J Cape, 1968.

Lewis-Williams, J D. *The world of man and the world of spirit: an interpretation of the Linton rock painting.* Cape Town: South African Museum, 1988.

Lewis-Williams, J D. Southern Africa's place in the archaeology of human understanding. *Suid-Afrikaanse Tydskrif vir Wetenskap,* 85, 1989(a), pp 47–52.

Lewis-Williams, J D and Thomas Dowson. *Images of power. Understanding Bushman rock art.* Johannesburg: Southern, 1989.

Lewis-Williams, J D. The economic and social context of Southern San rock art. *Current Anthropology*, 23(4), 1982, pp 429–449.

Lewis-Williams, J D 1983. Science and rock art. *South African archaeological Society*. Goodwin Series 4, 1983, pp 3–13.

Lewis-Williams, J D. Cognitive and optical illusions in San rock art research. *Current Anthropology*, 27(2), 1986, pp 171–178.

Lewis-Williams, J D. A dream of eland: an unexplored component of San shamanism and rock art. *World Archaeology*, 19(2), 1987(a), pp 165–177.

Lewis-Williams, J D. Art as a window to other worlds. *Suid-Afrikaanse Tydskrif vir Wetenskap*, 83, 1987(b), pp 245.

Lewis-Williams, J D. Beyond style and portrait: a comparison of Tanzanian and Southern African rock art, in Vossen, Rainer & Klaus Keuthmann (eds), 1987(c), pp 93–139.

Lewis-Williams, J D. *Paintings of power: ethnography and rock art in Southern Africa*, in Biesele et al, 1987(d), pp 231–273.
Lewis-Williams, J D. *Discovering Southern African rock art*. Johannesburg: David Philip, 1990.
Lewis-Williams, J D and J H N Loubser. Deceptive appearances: a critique of Southern African rock art studies. *Advances in World Archaeology*, 5, 1986, pp 253–289.
Lewis-Williams, J D and T A Dowson. The signs of all times. Entoptic phenomena in upper Palaeolithic art. *Current Anthropology*, 29(2), 1988, pp 201–245.
Liebenberg, Louis. *The art of tracking. The origin of science*. Claremont: David Philip, 1990.
Loy, D. *Nonduality: a study in comparative philosophy*. New Haven: Yale University Press, 1988.
Lorenz, Konrad. *On aggression*. London: Methuen, 1974.
Luckmann, Thomas. *The invisible religion. The problem of religion in modern society*. New York: Macmillan, 1967.
Luckmann, Thomas. Religion in der modernen Gesellschaft, in J. Wössner (Hg). *Religion in Umbruch: soziologische Beiträge zur Situation von Religion und Kirche in der Gegenwärtigen Gesellschaft*, Stuttgart: Enke Verlag, 1972.
Ludwig, Arnold M. Altered states of consciousness, in R Prince, 1968, pp 69–95.
Luhmann, N. *Funktion der Religion*. Frankfurt am Main: Suhrkamp, 1977.
Machalek, R. Definitional strategies in the study of religion. *Journal for the Scientific Study of Religion*, 16, 1977, pp 395–401.
Macmillan, W M. *Bantu, Boer and Briton. The Making of the South African native problem*. Oxford: Clarendon Press, (1928) 1963.
Macy, Joanna. *Mutual causality in Buddhism and general systems theory. The Dharma of natural systems*. New York: State University Press, 1991.
Maggs, T. The early history of the Black people in southern Africa, in Cameron, 1986, pp 37–43.
Majeke, Nosipho. *The role of the missionaries in conquest*. sl, sa.
Malinowski, B. *Magic, science and religion and other essays*. London: Souvenir Press, 1974.
Manhire, Tony, John Parkington and Royden Yates. Nets and fully recurved bows rock paintings and hunting methods in the Western Cape, South Africa. *World Archaeology* 17(2), 1985, pp 161–174.
Marais, J S. *The Cape coloured people 1652–1937*. Johannesburg: Witwatersrand University Press, (1939) 1968.
Marks, Shula. Khoisan resistance to the Dutch in the seventeeth and eighteenth centuries. *Journal of African History*, XIII (1), 1972, pp 55–80.
Marks, Shula and Anthony Atmore (eds). *Economy and society in pre-industrial South Africa*. London: Longman, (1980) 1990.
Marshack, Alexander. Early hominid symbol and evolution of the human capacity, in Mellars, 1990, pp 457–498.
Marshall, Lorna. !Kung Bushman Religious Beliefs. *Africa*, XXXII(3), 1962, 221–251.
Marshall, Lorna. The medicine dance of the !Kung Bushmen. *Africa* 39(4), 1969, pp 347–381.

Marshall, Lorna. Sharing, talking, and giving: relief of social tensions among the !Kung, in Lee and De Vore 1976, pp 349–371.

Mason, Revil. *Prehistory of the Transvaal. A record of human activity.* Johannesburg: Witwatersrand University Press, 1969.

Maylam, Paul. *A history of the African people of South Africa: from the Early Iron Age to the 1970's*. Cape Town & Johannesburg: David Philips, 1986.

Meckel, Daniel J and Robert L Moore. *Self and liberation. The Jung/Buddhism Dialogue*. New York: Paulist Press, 1992.

Mellars, Paul (ed). *The emergence of modern humans. An archaeological perspective*. Edinburgh: University Press, 1990.

Mellars, Paul and Chris Stringer (eds). *The human revolution. Behavioural and biological perspectives on the origins of modern humans.* Edinburgh: University Press, 1989.

Minnema, L. *Bespiegelingen aan het venster. Anthropologische bouwstenen voor een vergelijkend-godsdienswetenschappelijke verheldering van interreligieuze dialoog. Naar aanleiding van K Nishitani's boeddhistische en K Rahner's christelijke godsdienswijsbegeerte*. Kampen: Mondiss, 1990.

Moffat, Robert. *Missionary labours and scenes in Southern Africa*. London: John Snow, 1842.

Mol, Hans. *Identity and the sacred. A sketch for a new social-scientific theory of religion*. Oxford: Blackwell, 1976.

Moon, Ralph H and Stephen Randall. *Dimensions of thought. Current explorations in time, space, and knowledge*, vol I. Berkeley, California: Dharma Publishing, 1980.

Moore, P G 1977. *Problems in the analysis of mystical experience with special reference to the work of R C Zaehner, W T Stace & M Laski*. PhD thesis, University of Lancaster, 1977.

Morris, Alan Gregory. An osteological analysis of the protohistoric populations of the northern Cape and western Orange Free State, South Africa. DPhil thesis, submitted at the University of the Witwatersrand, Johannesburg, 1984.

Morris, David. Engraved in place and time: a review of variability in the rock art of the Northern Cape and Karoo. *South African Archaeological Bulletin*, 43, 1988, pp 109–121.

Morris, Desmond. *The naked ape: a zoologist's study of the human animal.* London: Jonathan Cape, 1967.

Mosala, Itumeleng J. *Biblical hermeneutics and black theology in South Africa.* Grand Rapids, Michigan: Eerdmans, 1989.

Mynarek, Hubertus. *Ökologische Religion. Ein neues Verständnis der Natur*. München: Goldmann Verlag, 1986.

Naranjo, Clandio and Robert E Ornstein. *On the psychology of meditation*. London: George Allen & Unwin, 1972.

Niebuhr, H Richard. *The responsible self. An essay in Christian moral philosophy.* New York: Harper & Row, 1963.

Nolan, Albert. *God in South Africa: The challenge of the gospel*. Cape Town and Johannesburg: David Philip, 1988.

Nyanaponika, Thera. *The heart of Buddhist meditation.* London: Rider, 1983.

Odin, Steve. *Process metaphysics and Hua-Yen Buddhism. A critical study of cumulative penetration vs interpenetration.* Albany: State University of New York Press, 1982.

Oosthuizen, J S. *Van Plotinus tot Teilhard de Chardin. 'n Studie oor die metamorfose van die Westerse werklikheidsbeeld.* Amsterdam: Rodopi, 1974.
Orpen J M. A glimpse into the mythology of the Maluti Bushmen. *The Cape Monthly Magazine*, 9, 1874, pp 1–13.
Otto, Rudolph. *The idea of the holy. An inquiry into the non-rational factor in the idea of the divine and its relation to the rational*. London: Oxford University Press, (1917) 1950.
Otto, Rudolph. *Mysticism East and West: a comparative analysis of the nature of mysticism*, New York: Meridian (1932) 1957.
Pager, Harald. *Ndedema*. Portland, Oregon: International Scholarly Book Services, 1972.
Paley, William. *Natural theology: or, evidences of the existence and attributes of the deity collected from the appearances of nature.* London: R Fauldner, 1802.
Panikkar, Raimundo. *The silence of God. The answer of the Buddha.* New York: Orbis, 1989.
Pannenberg, Wolfhart. *Theology and the philosophy of science*, London: Darton, Longman & Todd, 1976.
Papadopoulos, Renos K and Graham S Saayman. *Jung in modern perspective*. Cape Town: Donker, 1984.
Parkington, John. Time and place: some observations on spatial and temporal patterning in the Later Stone Age sequence in Southern Africa, *South African Archaeological Bulletin*, 35, 1980, pp 73–83.
Parkington, John. Interpeting paintings without a commentary: meaning and motive, content and composition in the rock art of the Western Cape, South Africa. *Antiquity*, 63, 1989, pp 13–26.
Parsons, Talcott. *The structure of social action*. New York: Free Press, 1968.
Parsons, Talcot. *The social system*. London: Routledge & Kegan Paul, 1970.
Peires, J B. *The house of Phalo. A history of the Xhosa people in the days of their independence.* Johannesburg: Ravan Press, 1981.
Penner, H H. The poverty of functionalism. *History of Religions*, 2, 1971, pp 91–97.
Petterson, O and H Åkerberg. *Interpreting religious phenomena. Studies with reference to the phenomenology of religion*. New York: Humanities Press, 1981.
Philip, John. *Researches in South Africa; illustrating the civil, moral, and religous condition of the native tribes: including journals of the author's travels in the interior; together with detailed accounts of the progress of the Christian missions, exhibiting the influence of Christianity in promoting civilization.* Vol II. London: James Duncan, 1828.
Phillips, D Z. *Faith and philosophical enquiry*. London: Routledge, 1970.
Phillips, D Z. *Faith after foundationalism*. London: Routledge, 1988.
Pieris, Aloysius. *Love meets wisdom. A Christian experience of Buddhism*. New York: Orbis Books, 1988.
Pilbeam, David. *The ascent of man. An introduction to human evolution.* New York: Macmillan, 1972.
Pilbeam, David. Patterns of Hominoid Evolution, in Eric Delson. *Ancestors: the hard evidence.* New York: Liss, 1985.

Platvoet, J G. Verschuivingen in een West-Afrikaanse godsdienst: hekserij, bekentenissen en de opkomst van de 'beul'-goden in de godsdienst van de Ashanti. *Bijdragen, Tijdschrift voor Filosofie en Theologie*, 34(3), 1973, pp 15–30.
Platvoet, J G. De eigenheid van godsdiensten van volken zonder schrift, in Chowdhury T, W Claesens & W Logister (ed). *Het kosmisch patroon: Het vele en het ene in de godsdiensten*. Tilburg: University Press, 1989, pp 21–48.
Platvoet, J G. De wraak van de 'primitieven': godsdientgeschiedenis van Neanderhaler tot New Age. *Nederlands Theologisch Tijdschrift*, 47(3), 1993, pp 227–243.
Platvoet, J G. The definers defined: traditions in the definition of religion. *Method and Theory in the Study of Religion*, 2(2), 1990, pp 180–212.
Platvoet, J G. Normative and non-normative positions in the study of religions. Unpublished lecture, 1991.
Platvoet, J G. Programmatic statements from Africa 1982–1992. *Numen*, 40, 1993, pp 322–342.
Plessner, H. *Die Stufen des Organischen und der Mensch. Einleitung in die philosophischen Anthropologie*. Berlin: de Gruyter, 1928.
Polkinghorne, John. *Science and creation: the search for understanding*. Boston: Shambhala, 1989.
Popper, Karl. *Objective knowledge. An evolutionary approach*. Oxford: Clarendon Press, 1972.
Popper, Karl. *The open society and its enemies*. London: Routledge & Kegan Paul, 1973.
Popper, Karl. *Conjectures and refutations. The growth of scientific knowledge*. London: Routledge & Kegan Paul, 1974.
Potgieter, E F. *The disappearing Bushmen of Lake Chrissie*. Pretoria: Van Schaik, 1955.
Preuss, J S. *Explaining religion: criticism and theory from Bodin to Freud*. New Haven: Yale University Press, 1987.
Prince, Raymond (ed). *Trance and possession states*. Canada: R M Bucke Memorial Society, 1968.
Prigogine, Ilya and Isabelle Stengers. *Order out of chaos. Man's new dialogue with nature*. London: Heinemann, 1984.
Prinsloo, E D. Logic and culture. *South African Journal of Philosophy*, 8(2), 1989, pp 94–99.
Prozesky, Martin. Is there a place in religious studies for the criticism and reformulation of religion? *Religion in South Africa* 6(1), 1985, pp 71–81.
Prozesky, Martin. *A new guide to the debate about God*. Pietermaritzburg: University of Natal Press, 1989.
Purce, Jill. *The mystic spiral. Journey of the soul*. London: Thames and Hudson, 1974.
Pye, M and R Morgan (eds). *The cardinal meaning: essays in comparative hermeneutics: Buddhism and Christianity*. The Hague: Mouton, 1973.
Pye, Michael. Religious studies in Europe: structures and desiderata, in Klostermaier, Klaus K and Larry W Hurtado, 1991.
Radcliffe-Brown, A R. *Structure and function in primitive societies. Essays and addresses*. London: Cohen & West, 1952.
Rhys-Davids, T W (ed). *Sacred books of the East*, Vol IV, London: Pali Text Society, 1969.

Richards, Graham. *Human evolution. An introduction for the behavioural sciences*. London & New York: Routledge & Kegan Paul, 1987.
Richter, D Julius. *Geschichte der evangelischen Mission in Afrika*. Gütersloh: C Bertelsmann, 1922.
Ricoeur, Paul. *The symbolism of evil*. Boston: Beacon Press, 1969.
Rightmire, G P. The fossil evidence for hominid evolution in Southern Africa, in Klein, Richard (ed), 1984, pp 147–168.
Rightmire, G Philip. Middle Stone Age humans from Eastern and Southern Africa, in Paul Mellars & Chris Stringer (eds), 1989, pp 109–122.
Rorty, Richard. *Philosophy and the mirror of nature*. Oxford: Blackwell, 1980.
Rorty, Richard. *Consequences of pragmatism*. Brighton, Essex: Harvester Press, 1982.
Rosemont, Henry Jr. Against Relativism, in Larson and Deutsch 1989, pp 36–70.
Ross, Andrew. *John Philip (1775–1851). Missions, race and politics in South Africa*. Aberdeen: University Press, 1986.
Roth, John and Frederick Sontag (eds). *The defence of God*. New York: Paragon, 1985.
Rouhani, Shahin. *Molecular genetics and the pattern of human evolution: plausible and implausible models*, in Mellars & Stringer, 1989, pp 47–61.
Ruch E A and K C Anyanwu. *African philosophy. An introduction to the main philosophical trends in contemporary Africa*. Rome: Catholic Book Agency, 1981.
Rudner, Jalmar and Ione. *The Hunter and his art*. Cape Town: Struik, 1970.
Russell, Robert John, William R Stoeger and George V Coyne (eds). *Physics, philosophy and theology: a common quest for understanding*. Vatican City State: Vatican Observatory, 1988.
Saayman, Willem. *Christian mission in South Africa, political and ecumenical*. Pretoria: Unisa, 1991.
Sahlins, Marshall. *Stone Age economics*. Chicago & New York: Aldine Atherton, 1972.
Schapera, I. *The Khoisan peoples of South Africa. Bushmen and Hottentots*. London: Routledge & Kegan Paul, (1930) 1960.
Scharfstein, Ben-Ami et al. *Philosophy East/philosophy West. A critical comparison of Indian, Chinese, Islamic, and European philosophy*. Oxford: Blackwell, 1987.
Sharpe, Eric J. *Comparative religion: a history*. London: Duckworth, 1975.
Schmidt, Sigrid. Die Mantis religiosa in den Glaubensvorstellungen der Khoesan-Völker. *Zeitschrift für Ethnologie*, 98(1), 1973, pp 102–127.
Schmidt, Sigrid. The rain bull of the South African Bushmen *African Studies*, 38, 1979, pp 201–224.
Schutz, Alfred. *Collected papers, Vol I. The problem of social reality*. The Hague: Marthinus Nijhoff, 1973.
Seerveld, Calvin. 'Mythologising philosophy' as historiographic category, in Clasquin et al, 1992, pp 28–48.
Setiloane, Gabriel M. *African theology. An introduction*. Johannesburg: Skotaville, 1986.
Shell, Robert C-H. Religion, civic status and slavery from Dordt to the Trek. Unpublished paper, read at Conference on People, Power and Culture: the History of Christianity in South Africa 1792–1992, at the University of Western Cape, 12–15 August 1992.
Shevoroshkin, Vitaly. The mother tongue. How linguists have reconstructed the ancestor of all living languages. *The Sciences*, 30(3), 1990, pp 20–27.

Sibree, James. *A register of missionaries, deputations, etc. from 1796 to 1923*. London: London Missionary Society, 1923.
Sierksma, F. *De religieuse projectie. Een anthropologische en psychologische studie over de projectie-verschijnselen in de godsdiensten*. Delft: W Gaarde, 1957.
Silberbauer, George B. *The future of the Bushmen*, in Tobias, 1978, pp 179–186.
Silberbauer, George B. *Hunter and habitat in the central Kalahari Desert*. Cambridge: University Press, 1981.
Singer, Ronald. *The biology of the San*, in Tobias, 1978(b), pp 115–129.
Smart, Ninian. *The phenomenon of religion*. London: Macmillan, 1973.
Smart, Ninian. *The religious experience of mankind*. New York: Scribner's, 1976.
Smart, Ninian. *Beyond ideology. Religion and the future of Western civilization*. London: Collins, 1981.
Smart, Ninian. *Concept and empathy. Essays in the study of religion*. London: Macmillan, 1986.
Smit, J H (ed). *Die Nederduitse Gereformeerde Kerk onder die Boesmans – grepe uit die navorsing van die Departement Sendingwetenskap aan die UOVS.* Bloemfontein: Universiteit van die Oranje-Vrystaat, 1986.
Smith, Andrew B. Competition, conflict and clientship: Khoi and San relationships in the Western Cape. *South African Archaeological Society Godwin Series*, 5, 1986, pp 36–41.
Smith, Ken. *The changing past. Trends in South African historical writing.* Johannesburg: Southern Book Publishers, 1988.
Smuts, J C. *Holism and evolution*. London: Macmillan, 1927.
Southey, Nicholas. Historians and religion: the treatment of Christianity in South African historiography. Unpublished paper read at Conference on People, Power and Culture: the History of Christianity in South Africa 1792–1992, at the University of Western Cape, 12–15 August 1992.
Spiegelberg, H. *Doing phenomenology. Essays on and in phenomenology*. The Hague: Nijhoff, 1975.
Spies, FJ du Toit. *Suid-Afrikaanse Biografiese Woordeboek* Vol I, 1976, pp 760–761.
Staal, Frits. *Exploring mysticism.* Harmondsworth: Penguin Books, 1975.
Stace, W T. *Mysticism and philosophy*. London: Macmillan, 1961.
Stein, Murray and Robert L Moore. *Jung's challenge to contemporary religion*. Wilmette, Ill: Chiron Press, 1987.
Stern, J T and R L Susman. The locomotor anatomy of Australopithecus Afarensis. *American Journal of Physical Anthropology*, 60, 1983, pp 279–317.
Steyn, Anna Catharina. *Rotsskilderinge op die plaas Kleintheespruit*. MA dissertation, Unisa, 1980.
Stoneking, Mark & Rebecca L Cann. *African origin of human mitochondrial DNA*, in Mellars & Stringer, 1989, pp 17–30.
Stow, George William. *Rock-paintings in South Africa from parts of the Eastern Province and Orange Fee State.* With an introduction and descriptive notes by Dorothea F Bleek. London: Methuen, 1930.
Tanaka, Jiro. *Subsistence ecology of Central Kalahari San*, in Lee and De Vore, 1976, pp 98–119.

Templin, J Alton. *Ideology on a frontier. The theological foundation of Afrikaner nationalism, 1652–1910*. London: Greenwood Press, 1984.
Ter Haar, Gerrie and Jan Platvoet. Bezetenheid en christendom. *Nederl Theol Tijdschrift*, 43(3), 1989, pp 177–190.
Thackeray, A I. Dating the rock art of Southern Africa. *S Afr archaeol Soc Goodwin Ser*, 4, 1983, pp 21–26.
Thackeray, Anne I, J Francis Thackeray, Peter B Beaumont and J C Vogel. Dated rock engravings from Wonderwerk Cave, South Africa. *Science*, 214, 1981, pp 64–67.
Theal, G M. *Chronicles of Cape commanders*. Cape Town: W A Richards, 1882.
Theal, G M. *History of South Africa (1691–1795)*. London: Swan Sonnenschein, 1888.
Theal, G M. *The beginning of South African history*. London: T Fisher Unwin, 1902.
Thelle, Notto R. *Buddhism and Christianity in Japan. From conflict to dialogue, 1854–1899*. Honolulu: University of Hawaii Press, 1987.
Thorpe, S A. *African traditional religions*. Unisa: Pretoria, 1991.
Tillich, Paul. *Symbol und Wirklichkeit*. Göttingen: Vandenhoeck & Ruprecht, 1962.
Tobias, P V. From Linné to Leakey: Six Signposts in Human Evolution. Proceedings of a Nobel Symposium organized by the Royal Swedish Academy of Science and held at Karlskoga, Sweden on 21–27 May 1978. Reprinted in *The Leech*, 60, 1991, pp 16–25.
Tobias, Phillip V (ed). *The Bushmen. San hunters and herders of Southern Africa*. Cape Town: Human & Rousseau, 1978(b).
Tobias, Phillip V. *Dart, Taung and the 'Missing Link'*. Johannesburg: Witwatersrand University Press, 1984.
Tobias, Phillip V (ed). *Hominid evolution. Past, present and future*. New York: Liss, 1985(a).
Tobias, P V. *The dawn of the human family in Africa*, in Cameron, 1986(a), pp 11–19.
Tobias, P V. *The last million years in southern Africa*, in Cameron, 1986(b), pp 20–27.
Tobias, P V. The brain of *Homo habilis*: a new level of organization in cerebral evolution. *The Leech*, 60, 1991, pp 31–48.
Tracy D, and J B Cobb. *Talking about God: doing theology in the context of modern pluralism*. New York: Harper, 1984.
Traill, Anthony. *The languages of the San*, in Tobias 1978(b), pp 137–147.
Tromp, A H. *Suid-Afrikaanse Biografiese Woordeboek* Vol I. 1976, pp 808–809.
Tulku, Tarthang. *Time, space and knowledge. A new vision of reality*. Emeryville, California: Dharma Publishing, 1977.
Turner, Victor. *The ritual process. Structure and anti-structure*. Ithaca, NY: Cornell University Press, (1969) 1989.
Tylor, Edward B. *Primitive culture. Researches into the development of mythology, philosophy, religion, language, art and custom*. New York: Brentano's, (1871) 1924.
Underhill, Evelyn. *Mysticism. A study in the nature and development of man's spiritual consciousness*. New York: Dutton, (1911) 1961.
Van Arkel, D, G C Quispel and R J Ross. *'De Wijngaard des Heeren? Een onderzoek naar de wortels van 'de blanke baasskap' in Zuid-Afrika*. Leiden:Nijhoff, 1983.
Van Baaren, Th P and H J W Drijvers (eds). *Religion, culture and methodology*. The Hague: Mouton, 1973.
Van den Heever, G A. *Die motief van die wêreldbrand. Zoroastrisme, formatiewe*

Judaïsme en vroeë Christendom: patrone van interaksie. MA dissertation, University of South Africa, 1993.
Van der Leeuw, G. *Religion in essence and manifestation*. London: Allen & Unwin, 1964.
Van der Merwe, PJ. *Die noordwaartse beweging van die Boere voor die Groot Trek (1770–1842)*. Pretoria: Die Staatsbiblioteek. (1937) 1988.
Van der Post, Laurens and Jane Taylor. *Testament to the Bushmen*. Harmondsworth: Penguin Books, 1985.
Van der Watt, P B. *Die Nederduitse Gereformeerde Kerk 1652–1975*, (2 vols). Pretoria: NG Kerk Uitgewers, 1976.
Van Niekerk, Attie. *Sáám in Afrika*. Kaapstad: Tafelberg, 1992.
Villa-Vicencio, Charles. *Trapped in apartheid. A socio-theological history of the English-speaking churches*. Maryknoll, New York: Orbis, 1988.
Villa-Vicencio, Charles. *A theology of reconstruction. Nation-building and human rights*. Cape Town: David Philip, 1992.
Vinnicombe, P. Myth, motive and selection in Southern African rock art. *Africa*, 42(3), 1972, pp 192–204.
Vinnicombe, Patricia. *People of the eland*. Pietermaritzburg: University of Natal Press, 1976.
Volman, Thomas P. Early prehistory of Southern Africa, in Klein, Richard (ed), 1984, pp 169–220.
Von Bertalanffy, Ludwig. *General systems theory*. New York: Braziller, 1968.
Vossen, Rainer & Klause Keuthmann (eds). *Contemporary studies on Khoisan, vol I and 2*. Hamburg: Helmut Buske Verlag, 1986.
Vroom, Hendrik. *Religions and the truth. Philosophical reflections and perspectives*. Grand Rapids, Mich: Eerdmans, 1989.
Waardenburg, J. *Reflections on the study of religion*. The Hague: Mouton, 1973.
Wach, J. *Understanding and believing*. Westport, Conn: Greenwood Press, 1975.
Wainscoat, J S et al. Geographic distribution of Alpha- and Beta-globin gene cluster polymorphisms, in Mellars & Stringer, 1989, pp 31–38.
Walker, Eric A. *A history of Southern Africa*. London: Longmans, (1928) 1959.
Washburn, Sherwood L and C S Lancaster. The evolution of hunting, in Lee & DeVore, 1968, pp 293–303.
Watson, Stephen. *Return of the Moon. Versions from the /Xam*. Cape Town: Carrefour, 1991.
Wayman, Alex. The religious meaning of possession states, in R Prince, 1968, pp 167–179.
Weber, Max. *Wirtschaft und Gesellschaft*. Tübingen: J C B Mohr (Paul Siebeck), 1972.
Westerlund, David. *Pluralism and change. A comparative and historical approach to African disease etiologies*. Stockholm: Institute of Comparative Religion, at the University of Stockholm, 1989.
Whaling, F. *Contemporary approaches to the study of religion, 2 vols*. Berlin: De Gruyter, 1983, 1985.
Whitehead, A N. *Religion in the making*. Cambridge: University Press, 1927.
Whitehead, A N. *Symbolism. Its meaning and effect*. Cambridge: University Press, (1927) 1958.

Whitehead, A N. *Nature and life*. Chicago: University Press, 1933.
Whitehead, A N. *Process and reality*. Corrected edition, edited by David Ray Griffin and Donald W Sherburne. New York: The Free Press, (1929) 1979.
Whitehead, A N. *Adventures of ideas*. New York: Free Press, (1933) 1967.
Wiebe, D. *Religion and truth: towards an alternative paradigm for the study of religion*. The Hague: Mouton, 1981.
Wiebe, D. *The irony of theology and the nature of religious thought*. Montreal, Kingston: McGill-Queen's University Press, 1991.
Wiener, Philip. *Evolution and the founders of pragmatism*. Gloucester, Mass: Peter Smith, 1969.
Wilber Ken, Jack Engler and Daniel P Brown. *Transformations of consciousness. Conventional and contemplative perspectives on development*. Boston & London: Shambhala, 1986.
Wilber Ken. *Up from Eden. A transpersonal view of human evolution*. Boston: Shambhala, 1986(a).
Willcox, Alex R. *The Bushman in History*, in Tobias, 1978(b), pp 76–87.
Wilman, M. *The rock-engravings of Griqualand West & Bechuanaland South Africa*. Cape Town: Balkema, 1968.
Wilmsen, Edwin N. Of paintings and painters, in terms of Zu/'hoasi interpretations, in Vossen & Keuthmann, vol 2, 1986, pp 347–372.
Wilmsen, Edwin N. Khoi and San religion, in M Eliade (ed). *The Encyclopedia of religion*, vol. 8. New York: Macmillan, 1987, pp 292–295.
Wilmsen, Edwin N. A Myth and its measure. *Current Anthropology*, 33(5), 1992, pp 611–614.
Wilson, Edward O. *On human nature*. Cambridge, Massachusetts: Harvard University Press, 1978.
Wilson, Monica and Leonard Thompson. *A history of South Africa to 1870*. Cape Town & Johannesburg: David Philip, 1982.
Wisdom, John. *Philosophy and psychoanalysis*. Berkeley: University of California Press, 1969.
Wiltshire, Bruce. *William James and phenomenology*. Bloomington: University of Indiana Press, 1968.
Wolpoff, Milford H. Multiregional evolution: the fossil alternative to Eden, in Mellars & Stringer, 1989, pp 62–108.
Wood, Bernard. Origin and evolution of the genus *homo*. *Nature*, Nature 355, 1992, pp 783–790.
Wright, John B. *Bushman raiders of the Drakensberg 1840–1870*. Pietermartizburg: University of Natal Press, 1971.
Yates, Royden, John Parkington and Tony Manhire. *Pictures from the past. A history of the interpretation of rock paintings and engravings of Southern Africa*. Centaur, 1990.
Zaehner, R C. *Mysticism: sacred and profane*. Oxford: Claredon Press, 1957.
Zijderveld, A A. *De relativiteit van kennis en werkelijkheid. Inleiding tot de kennissociologie*. Meppel: Boom, 1974.
Zubrow, Ezra. The demographic modelling of Neanderthal extinction, in Mellars & Stringer, 1989, pp 212–231.

SUBJECT INDEX

D

E

F

G

H

I

J

K

L

M

N

O

P

Q

R

S

T

U

V

W

X

Y

Z

NAME INDEX

D

E

F

G

H

I

J

K

L

N

O

P

R

W

Z